Challenging Oppression and Confronting Privilege

Challenging Oppression and Confronting Privilege

A Critical Social Work Approach

Second Edition

Bob Mullaly

OXFORD
UNIVERSITY PRESS

OXFORD
UNIVERSITY PRESS

8 Sampson Mews, Suite 204, Don Mills, Ontario M3C 0H5
www.oupcanada.com

Oxford University Press is a department of the University of Oxford.
It furthers the University's objective of excellence in research, scholarship,
and education by publishing worldwide in

Oxford   New York

Auckland   Cape Town   Dar es Salaam   Hong Kong   Karachi
Kuala Lumpur   Madrid   Melbourne   Mexico City   Nairobi
New Delhi   Shanghai   Taipei   Toronto

With offices in

Argentina   Austria   Brazil   Chile   Czech Republic   France   Greece
Guatemala   Hungary   Italy   Japan   Poland   Portugal   Singapore
South Korea   Switzerland   Thailand   Turkey   Ukraine   Vietnam

Oxford is a trade mark of Oxford University Press
in the UK and in certain other countries

Published in Canada by Oxford University Press

Library and Archives Canada Cataloguing in Publication

Mullaly, Robert P
Challenging oppression and confronting privilege : a critical social work
approach / Bob Mullaly. —2nd ed.

First ed. published under title: Challenging oppression.

Includes bibliographical references and index.
ISBN 978-0-19-542970-1

1. Oppression (Psychology). 2. Equality. 3. Social work with minorities.
I. Title.

HM821.M84 2009   305   C2009-904333-5

Cover image: Laurie McGregor

Printed and bound in the United States of America

12 13 14 — 16 15 14

Contents

Acknowledgements

I wish to thank the University of Manitoba for granting me a one-year leave of absence, which provided me with uninterrupted time to carry out the research for this book and to write it.

I am grateful to the Faculty of Social Work students in my 2007 doctoral course on critical social theory at the University of Manitoba, who engaged with me in a dialogue on much of the material in this book and who gave me much valuable feedback. I also wish to thank the three anonymous reviewers who provided helpful comments on the first edition of this book. I hope my revisions do their suggestions justice. I am very grateful to Peter Chambers of Oxford University Press, who worked with me throughout the entire project. He was quick to respond to all my questions and concerns and provided me with helpful advice. I especially want to thank Juliana West, who carried out an exhaustive literature search for me and who engaged me in informed conversations about oppression and privilege. I could not have asked for a better research assistant. I want to pay special tribute to my chocolate Lab, Seamus, and my two Burmese cats, Iris (after Iris Marion Young) and Benny (after Ben Agger), who have been with me since I lived in Australia, and to my Newfoundland cross, Angus, whom I adopted after he was found with his siblings and mother almost frozen to death out in the bush in northern Manitoba. These wonderful animals provided me with love, loyalty, amusement, diversion, and comradeship throughout the lonely journey of writing this book.

Most of all, I want to acknowledge the work and efforts of all the social workers on the front lines and in administrative positions who engage in anti-oppressive social work every day, often in the face of seemingly insurmountable odds and obstacles. I also want to acknowledge the important work of faculty members who teach anti-oppressive material in the classroom and are often ridiculed, trivialized, and marginalized because of it. Finally, I want to thank all the writers who, like me, struggle every day to make sense of the complex world of oppression and privilege and work on developing ways out of it. It is to these groups that I dedicate this book.

in solidarity,

bob mullaly
Fredericton

Preface

Anti-oppressive social work is by now a prominent part of social work theory and practice in Canada, the UK, Australia, and New Zealand and to a lesser extent in the US. In Canada, as a standard of accreditation, every university-based social work program must demonstrate its commitment to social justice and anti-oppressive objectives and principles in its curriculum content, its faculty composition, and its student admissions. Although the term 'anti-oppressive social work' is relatively new, Garrett (2002) reminds us that the ideas and strategies associated with anti-oppressive social work are not new but rather by-products of the struggles throughout civil society from the late 1960s on the part of a variety of social movements. These include a reinvigorated struggle for workers' rights and workplace democracy, the campaigns for women's equality and for gay and lesbian liberation, the fight for racial equality and civil rights, the birth of the disability movement and grey power, the decolonization struggle of First Nations, and the mental health survivors' movement. Accompanying these social movements has been the development of contemporary emancipatory social work theories and practices beginning in the 1970s with the emergence of radical social work. In the 1980s, progressive forms of social work theory and practice expanded beyond radical social work and its major preoccupation with class-based oppression to encompass gender, race, and several other forms of oppression. Then in the early 1990s, anti-oppressive social work began to emerge, with a focus on intersecting bases of oppression—a focus that was absent in the earlier singular approaches to oppression.

I have been involved in teaching and developing progressive forms of social work for the past 17 years. However, because I occupy a number of privileged social positions— that is, I am a white, Anglo-Saxon, bourgeois, heterosexual, non-disabled, Canadian-born, Christian (or assumed to be Christian) male who is not yet old enough to experience ageism—I am frequently asked how I can write about oppression when I do not appear to be a member of an oppressed group. In other words, how credible is my teaching and writing about oppression? What business do I and others like me have in talking about issues with which we have had little direct experience, regardless of our commitment to the cause? Leaving aside any arguments that I have experienced oppression in my lifetime (as has just about everybody), I respond to this question in the following way.

It is true that I cannot fully understand the experience or phenomenology of many forms of oppression, but lived experience is not the only legitimate source of knowledge. To believe otherwise is a form of parochial reasoning. Why would we bother studying or researching any form of social phenomena if experience were the only way of understanding it? None of us can experience everything in the social world, but we can supplement what we know from our own experiences by studying the experiences, research, and writings of others, which I have been doing since I received my PhD in social work 26 years ago. During that time, I have designed and taught courses in structural and anti-oppressive social work and critical social work theory. I have written several articles and books on these subjects. I have been active in a leadership role in a number of social action campaigns and with the trade union movement in New Brunswick, and I have given presentations to a variety of organizations across Canada and Australia.

With respect to my credibility in teaching and writing about oppression, I have found that oftentimes I have more credibility among privileged group members than do members of oppressed groups. I know, for example, from my presentation of feminist issues in my teaching of anti-oppression or structural social work that male students are more likely to take me seriously than they do my female colleagues teaching the same material. My credibility stems from two main sources: (1) my membership in a privileged group, which means that I possess an assumed (and unearned) authoritative status and (2) no perceived self-interest on my part in what I am teaching—in fact, what I teach would seem to run against my own privileged interests. Many members of privileged groups feel defensive when they are presented with material on oppression, especially if they are white or male or heterosexual or non-disabled or middle class. Johnson (2006) contends that this defensive reaction has probably done more than anything else to perpetuate our current paralysis with respect to taking steps to eliminate dominant–subordinate relations in society. As a member of several privileged groups, I know about defensive feelings from my own life. But as a researcher and theorist, I also know that it is possible to understand the world and my place in it in ways that help me to go beyond my defensive feelings and allow me to work for fundamental social change.

To some extent, this book cannot help but have a white, male, straight, non-disabled, middle-class point of view, because this is who I am. Although these characteristics may limit me in some ways, they also, as argued by Johnson (2006), provide me with a bridge from my own experiences to some part of almost every reader's experiences. I cannot know, from my own experiences, for example, what it is like to be female or disabled or gay or of colour or Aboriginal in this society. But I can bring my experience of white privilege to the struggle of white people to deal with white supremacy. Similarly, I can bring my experience as a heterosexual person to the challenges faced by straight persons who want to overcome heterosexism and homophobia. I can bring my experiences as a man to challenge sexism and male privilege. I can bring my experiences as Canadian-born to confront obstacles and discriminatory policies and behaviours directed at refugees and immigrants. I can use my experience with privilege as a non-disabled person to help other non-disabled people support and participate in the disability movement. I can also bring my experiences with privilege as an assumed Christian to help confront and overcome persecution of non-Christian groups. These are some of the areas of oppression and privilege where I have struggled in attempting to lessen or alleviate the effects and hurt that my privileges have caused subordinate groups. And, of course, it is these experiences that I bring to this book. I do not feel either guilty or proud about being white, male, non-disabled, and so on, because I had no say in or control over these characteristics. What matters is what I do with my privilege. As a privileged member of society, I feel a strong moral obligation to study and understand the privileges that have been conferred upon me by society on the basis of the social groups in which I find myself and to engage in political action to try to change the society that confers privilege on a minority and oppression on the majority. For me, the first step in my anti-oppressive scholarship and practice was to admit that I had benefited from privilege. This does not mean that I believe I am a fraud with respect to any success I may have achieved, but it does mean that I have a choice about what I do with my success. Writing a book such as this is one important choice that I have made.

The book begins in Chapter 1 by taking social work to task for not paying enough attention to causal explanations for social problems. The chapter emphasizes the need for sound theory as the basis of good social work practice and presents the theoretical framework used in the book to analyze and explain oppression and to develop anti-oppressive social work practice. Chapter 2 discusses the concept and nature of oppression, including its origins, its causes and sources, its various forms, its dynamics, the social processes and practices that produce and reproduce it, the political functions it performs for dominant groups, and the three levels of society at which it occurs. Oppression at the personal level in both overt and covert forms is discussed in Chapter 3, along with some of the ways that oppressed persons cope with their oppression. Chapter 4 examines several cultural contexts for oppression, including the mass media, entertainment, and advertising, as well as negative stereotypes and dominant discourses. Chapter 5 looks at oppression at the structural or institutional level and shows how oppression at this level is actually a form of violence or social terrorism perpetrated on oppressed persons. The psychology of oppression and the concepts of internalized oppression and domination are examined in Chapter 6, and an attempt is made to explain why oppressed persons will often behave in self-harming ways that contribute to their own oppression. Chapter 7 considers the notion of multiple or interlocking oppressions and presents several models showing the complex interactive nature of oppression. The chapter also discusses the heterogeneity that exists within any oppressed group. Using the material from previous chapters, Chapter 8 articulates an anti-oppressive social work practice at the personal and cultural levels, including oppression at the organizational level. Similarly, Chapter 9 presents an anti-oppressive social work practice at the structural level, along with a number of principles that are prerequisites for or correlates of anti-oppressive social work practice. The final chapter, which is new to this edition, presents an overview of the flip side of oppression—privilege. I believe that privilege is much more difficult to confront than oppression, because it is easier to explore the problems of oppressed groups than it is to explore our own roles in perpetuating oppression. The chapter explores the nature of privilege (its dynamics and invisibility) presents examples of privilege in several areas, discusses how social work has overlooked privilege as a practice issue, and offers ideas on what we can do to deal with privilege.

Chapter 1

Theoretical and Conceptual Considerations

Critical social theory conceives human liberation as the highest form of intellectual activity.

—Ben Agger

The Imperative of Theory

Unfortunately, many of those who work and study in the helping professions too often view theory as esoteric, abstract, idealistic, and something people like me discuss in universities. Practice, on the other hand, is considered common-sense, concrete, and occurring in the real world (i.e., outside the ivory towers of universities). Social work is seen by many as essentially carrying out pragmatic and practical tasks. Theory has little direct relevance and actually may obscure the practical nature of social work. Spontaneity and the personal qualities of the worker are often considered more important than theory. New graduates from social services educational programs and students in field placements are often described by some experienced practitioners as naive, idealistic, and in need of 'seasoning' (i.e., practical experience). These experienced practitioners are sceptical of the theory being taught in educational programs, especially progressive theories, and emphasize instead the value of experience (Barbour 1984).

David Howe (1987) contends that this tendency to elevate theoretical ignorance to a level of professional virtue is wrong for two main reasons: (1) theory is part of everyday life—we all use theory; and (2) theoretical ignorance is not a professional virtue but a convenient excuse for sloppy and dishonest practice. We often use theories in our everyday life without being aware that we are doing so. If we see dark clouds and tell ourselves it is going to rain, we have expressed a theory about the relationship between dark clouds and rain. Without such a theory, we would often get wet if we saw clouds and did not prepare for rain, because we did not deduce that it might rain (Williams and McShane 1988). Just as we often use theory in our personal lives without realizing it, so too do social workers often use theory in their professional lives without realizing it.

Howe (1987) takes to task those 'practical folk' social workers who declare that their practice is not related to theory and demonstrates how all social work practice is related to theory. Everyone (including social workers) sees people and their situations in one way or another. These perceptions are never theory-free because they are based on certain fundamental beliefs and assumptions about people, society, and the relationship between the two. These beliefs and assumptions enable workers to make sense of any situation, and making sense is a theory-saturated activity. And just because a social worker cannot imagine any other way of viewing a situation does not mean that his or her perspective is unrelated to theory. It just means that this one taken-for-granted reality (theory) is the worker's entire world of sense. In other words, social workers who call themselves eclectic, pragmatic, or commonsensical base their practice on personally constructed theory (i.e., based on their own experiences) rather than on a systematic construction of theory.

Personally Constructed Theory

Lesley, a social work student, was placed in a child protection agency as her final placement. Part of her orientation to the agency was to meet with several staff members individually and find out what they did. Dan, an experienced practitioner, told Lesley in a somewhat patronizing manner that she should forget all the theory that the School of Social Work taught her. Dan said that he had been practising for years using only his common sense and his experience and that they had served him well. Lesley asked Dan in a respectful way where his common sense and experiences came from. Dan looked perplexed and asked, 'What do you mean?' Lesley replied, 'I was just wondering whether your common sense and experiences, which you say guide your practice, would be the same as those of people who are not male, white, middle-class, and English-speaking.'

Theory carries out four basic functions: description, explanation, prediction, and control and management of events or changes. Social work is practice-based and pursues all four of these functions: it describes phenomena; it attempts to explain what causes them; it predicts future events, including what will happen if certain interventions occur (or do not occur); and it attempts to control and manage events or changes at all levels of human activity (Reynolds 1971). Howe (1987, 17) asserts that 'If drift and purposelessness are to be avoided, practice needs to be set within a clear framework of explanation, the nature of which leads to a well-articulated practice.'

It is important to remember that theories are not laws. They do not contain ironclad guaranteed explanations of social phenomena, because the human condition and social conditions are too complex to permit the formulation of universal laws. The social sciences do not have any laws (although some economists and members of the business establishment present market forces as economic laws), but they do have some very good theories. Currently, there is much discussion on the nature, dynamics, forms, functions, and causes of oppression, but there is no dominant theory of oppression or dominant approach to anti-oppression. Indeed, an examination of the current literature, along with a look at the curricula of social services educational programs and just listening to practitioners talk about the subject, could lead one to conclude that everyone believes that he or she is writing about or teaching or practising anti-oppressive social work. I am not suggesting that there should be only one theory of oppression or one anti-oppressive approach to practice, but at present anti-oppressive practice seems to be whatever one wants it to be (as happened with the concept of empowerment in the 1980s and 1990s). This unfocused analysis of oppression on the part of social work involves a tacit recognition by most social workers that oppression does indeed exist, but consistent with social work in general, three broad approaches are used to deal with this oppression: (1) helping oppressed persons cope with their oppression; (2) attempting to modify/reform the system so that oppressed persons can better fit into it; and (3) contributing to a total transformation of society. Although the three approaches are not inherently mutually exclusive, most social workers have adopted the first and/or the second approach, while a minority have adopted the third approach.

I agree wholeheartedly with Macey and Moxon (1996), who call for more theoretical and analytical rigour in developing anti-oppressive practice and, conversely, for less attention to theoretical fashion. It is in this spirit that I write this book, which reflects a particular theoretical position (i.e., critical social theory). It is not intended as the only or the definitive treatment of the subject, but its development is meant to be analytical and rigorous.

Social Problems: The Great Paradox of the Helping Professions

The work of the social services sector is to treat, ameliorate, and/or attempt to eliminate the causes and consequences of social problems such as poverty, crime, alienation, homelessness, child abuse/neglect, spousal abuse, runaway adolescents, and so on. However, although there is a long and voluminous social science literature on social problems, there is no agreed-upon definition or explanation of what a social problem is or why it occurs. For example, in their frequently cited book, *The Study of Social Problems*, Rubington and Weinberg (1995) present seven competing sociological perspectives on social problems (outlined below).

In spite of the multiplicity of views, a review of the sociological literature reveals that attempts to define social problems contain several common elements (Fleras 2001; Jamrozik and Nocella 1998). There has to be: (1) a condition that is societal in nature

(2) that affects a significant number of people (3) in ways considered undesirable (4) about which something can be done to rectify the condition. These elements are not self-evident, however, since many questions remain unanswered. Is the condition real or imagined? Does it affect a significant number of people or a number of significant people? Who considers the condition undesirable? What can be done to rectify the condition, and who decides this? Should a social problem imply the primacy of human agency, or should it focus on values and social structures? Should the magnitude of an event or condition be the criterion for calling it a social problem? There are, of course, no standard answers to these or similar questions. Like all social phenomena, social problems are, in whole or in part, social constructs based on subjective, objective, and ideological factors (Berger and Luckmann 1966). As such, social problems will have different definitions, interpretations, and proposed remedies.

Evidence of the contentious and pluralistic nature of social problems lies in Rubington and Weinberg's (1995) presentation of seven current theoretical perspectives on social problems that have been developed over time. They are: (1) the social pathology view; (2) the social disorganization perspective; (3) the value conflict perspective; (4) the deviant behaviour perspective; (5) the labelling perspective; (6) critical theory; and (7) the constructionist perspective. Although a comprehensive explanation of these perspectives on social problems is well beyond the limits of this book, the following presents a brief outline of each of them.

1. The social pathology view originated at the end of the nineteenth century. It attributes social problems to character flaws in the individual experiencing the social problem and uses the medical analogy of a sick or maladjusted person who must be treated. In social work, this approach is often called the medical model (diagnosis of character flaws and a prescription to deal with them) with the goal of 'changing the person.' Although this was the dominant approach to social problems and those experiencing social problems adopted by early social workers, it still remains in various forms today, as illustrated in Table 1.2.

2. The social disorganization perspective developed in the 1920s. It ascribes social problems to the social disorganization that emanates from large changes in people's living and work environments, such as rapid industrialization and urbanization or globalization of the economy. This social disorganization, in turn, causes personal disorganization that is often manifested in alcoholism, family breakdown, domestic violence, and so on. The approach to social problems from this perspective is to provide humanitarian social care to persons disrupted by large changes and to bring equilibrium back to the system by way of minor social reforms. In other words, its purpose is to fine-tune rather than overhaul the system. General systems theory and ecological models are correlates of this perspective.

3. The value conflict perspective developed in the 1930s as a result of the Great Depression. It attributes social problems to competing interests, differential

access to resources, and other social conflicts that arise in a pluralistic society. As in any competition, there are winners and losers. The resolution of social problems from this perspective is to ensure that no group in society is deprived of opportunities and resources and that everyone is subject to the same rules (even though the rules are made by and favour the dominant group).

4. The deviant behaviour perspective became popular in the 1950s and 1960s when law and order seemed to be the dominant social problem. It explains social deviance as the means for many (disadvantaged) people to overcome the structural barriers to achieving culturally propagated and cherished social goals such as the American (or Canadian or Australian) 'dream.' Social deviance, then, is seen as a form of adaptation to structural arrangements that preclude the achievement of social goals and expectations by legitimate and acceptable ways. The strategy to combat social problems from this perspective is to open up the opportunity structures to persons who are disadvantaged by social structures.

5. The labelling perspective developed in the 1950s. It turned attention away from deviant acts or deviant people towards those who had the power to define or label certain conduct or people as deviant. The study of social problems from this perspective focuses on how powerful people (including professionals) can preserve their privileged social positions by authoritatively defining (i.e., labelling) social reality as good/normal or bad/deviant.

6. Critical theory had its origins in the 1930s but became prominent in the 1970s with respect to the study of social problems. It attributes social problems to social structures that favour certain groups in society and oppress others along lines of class, race, gender, and so on. The oppressed or subordinate groups are susceptible to all manner of social problems. The solution is to transform society into one in which social equality replaces dominant–subordinate relationships.

7. The constructionist perspective is an elaboration and extension of the labelling perspective. It is applied to a wide range of social phenomena today, including social problems. However, it does not focus on the social condition that is perceived as a social problem but on the processes through which social phenomena and social problems are constructed and interpreted. Much attention is given both to the social actors who make claims that a particular condition constitutes a social problem and to the effects of such claims. The identification of social problems is therefore a 'claims-making activity' (Fleras 2001; Spector and Kitsuse 1987). By identifying those who make their claims stick, the constructionist perspective enables the identification of some aspects of the power structure in society (Jamrozik and Nocella 1998).

Although postmodernism has not developed a general perspective on social problems, Foucault's analysis of criminology converges with labelling theory and constructionism in that he argues that criminology is a practice or discourse that creates the category of criminality (Anleu 1999). Given postmodernism's rejection of grand theories or generalized explanations, it remains to be seen whether or not it can ever develop a 'general' perspective on social problems. Jamrozik and Nocella (1998) contend that postmodernism has limited value for the study of social problems because the notions of class division and of an overriding structure of inequality are not accepted. Conversely, postmodernists such as Bauman (1998) and Lyman (1995) would argue that the imposition of an interpretation of a social problem might not take into account the subjective awareness of those persons judged to be experiencing social problems. Surely the views and experiences of those negatively affected by social problems would constitute an important element in the study and treatment of social problems.

What perspective of social problems, then, does this book adopt? My approach is not to adopt one particular perspective and then to defend it to the death. Rather, it is to select aspects of different perspectives (mainly conflict and social constructionist informed by postmodern insights) without sacrificing consistency and compatibility. This approach is similar to the one espoused by Fleras (2001, 3):

> Social problems are thought to involve conditions that are socially constructed and contested, yet reflect objective reality; vary over time and place; frequently exhibit a life-cycle from birth to demise to rebirth; are inseparable from the broader context in which they are located; and respond differently to treatment.

Unlike the sociological literature, there is a dearth of discussion or explanation of the nature and causes of social problems in the social work literature. David Gil (2004) makes the point that many social work authors seem to view social problems as a normal feature of society to be dealt with by social policy measures and/or social work practice. He contends that social problems are not normal features of any society but are consequences of societies characterized by hierarchy, inequality, and oppression. It is an unfortunate paradox that the helping professions in general, and social work in particular, which deal with the victims of social problems on a daily basis, tend to accept social ills as an inherently problematic given. Consequently, they fail to provide a general definition of or explanation for social problems. For example, in a recent content analysis study of 14 introductory American social work textbooks[1] published between 1988 and 1997, Wachholz and Mullaly (2000) found no discussion of the concept, nature, or explanation of social problems, although most of the books contained entire chapters on working with people experiencing problems of housing, domestic violence, unemployment, poor health, poverty, racism, and so on. In the absence of any theories or discussions on the nature and causes of social problems, social workers in general, and beginning social work students in particular, will tend to adopt the prevailing lay or agency-based definitions of social problems, which have traditionally been victim-blaming (Rose and Black 1985). This is not to say that social work or other social services areas are totally devoid of any literature or theoretical work that discusses the nature, causes, and effects of social problems. Explanatory accounts of social problems may be found in the social services literature, but only in an exceptional and inconsistent way.

Of the various theories and perspectives that do exist in the social work literature, there are three major competing but unequally held explanations for the existence of social problems in liberal democratic societies such as Canada, Australia, and the United States (Coates 1991; Mullaly 2007). Broadly speaking, they include the personal deficiency explanation, which corresponds to the social pathology view and which was the dominant social work view up to the 1960s and 70s; the liberal-humanist explanation, which corresponds to the social disorganization and deviant behaviour views and which is the dominant social work view today (it includes general systems theory and ecological approaches); and the social conflict (or change) explanations, which correspond to the critical and labelling views and which underpin transformative social work approaches such as feminist social work, structural social work, and anti-oppressive social work. This does not mean that other perspectives are entirely absent, but these three perspectives are currently dominant in the social work literature.

Parking Lots and Social Problems

A few years ago, I was involved in the social policy controversy regarding workfare programs for unemployed social assistance recipients (Mullaly 1995, 1997b; McFarland and Mullaly 1996). It seemed to me that the attitudes towards workfare and unemployed persons corresponded with the above three explanations of social problems. These perspectives were particularly evident in a media panel discussion on workfare in which I participated. One panel member attributed people's unemployment to unemployed persons being irresponsible, shy or fearful of work, and dependent on social assistance and therefore advocated a tough, mandatory, and simple 'work-for-welfare' scheme. A second panel member attributed people's unemployment to lack of education and job skills and advocated a workfare program that would emphasize training and job search counselling. My position was that as long as there were more people looking for and needing work than there were jobs, then workfare would not decrease unemployment or reduce welfare costs. I presented the analogy of a parking lot to make my point. If you have a parking lot that holds 100 cars and 120 cars to be parked there, then the attendants may shift cars in and out of the lot all day, but there will still be 20 cars outside the lot unless it is expanded. I argued that one could blame unemployed people for unemployment or blame unemployment on a lack of skills and education, but until the labour market (like the parking lot) was enlarged enough to accommodate everyone who needed and wanted work, there would always be people left outside of it. And workfare does nothing to make the labour market bigger.

Although classification schemes of any kind tend to be arbitrary to a degree, they can be helpful in making some sense of what Carniol (1979) calls 'the jumble of confusion' taught to social work students in the form of an eclectic knowledge base. How do students make sense of social problems when there are so many competing perspectives but so little discussion or analysis or definition of the nature of social problems in the classroom or in the literature? Since many writers of social work textbooks seem to take societal ills as a given, the only question addressed in the books is how to tackle them. And since there are so many competing answers to this question, the student and/or worker is continuously confronted with the 'jumble of confusion.' The classification scheme used here to make sense of social theory in general and social problems in particular consists of two competing perspectives of society and social problems: the order perspective and the conflict (or change) perspective.[2] Order theories are sometimes called mainstream, conservative, or traditional, while change theories are sometimes called radical, critical, progressive, or conflict. Order theories focus on and support the current social order, while critical/change theories focus on the lack of social justice in a society and lead us to change it.

Order and Conflict/Change Perspectives

Order and change perspectives represent two opposing views on the nature of people, society, and social problems. The former views society as orderly, stable, and unified by shared culture, values, and a consensus on its form and institutions. The latter views society as a continually contested struggle among groups with opposing views and interests. From a change perspective, society is held together not by consensus but by differential control of resources and political power. Individuals or groups who benefit from the maintenance of the status quo employ order models of society and social problems, whereas dissident or subordinate groups, striving to institutionalize new claims on society, favour a conflict or change analysis (e.g., Horton 1966; Reasons and Perdue 1981).

Reasons and Perdue have set forth two sets of logically interrelated and essential assumptions, one underpinning the order view of society and one underpinning the change view. Table 1.1 contains a modified version of both sets of assumptions, which concern: (1) the nature of human existence, (2) the nature of society, (3) the nature of the relationship between the two, and (4) the nature of social problems. It is important to note that the order and change perspectives are not absolute categories requiring that people fall into one or the other. Most people will hold views that belong to both sets of perspectives. For example, progressive social workers can utilize psychodynamic and/or systems theories in their practice. The difference is that the progressive social worker would recognize the limitations of order theories in that they do not adequately deal with structural variables such as class, race, and gender, nor do they adequately deal with power relations or conflict. Order and conflict/change perspectives represent two ideal types or ends of a continuum along which there is fluidity back and forth rather than two discrete categories with impenetrable boundaries between them (i.e., a dualism or binary).

Order Perspective

The order perspective, which currently dominates social thought in Anglo democracies, is associated with Durkheim and Weber and more recently with Talcott Parsons. Parsons is usually regarded as the founder of an explicitly functionalist theory of society (McDaniel and Agger 1984), which is synonymous with a systems analysis (i.e., structural–functional analysis) of society and social problems (Horton 1966).

Society. Any society is comprised of people who are by nature competitive, acquisitive, self-absorbed, individualistic, and therefore predisposed towards disorder. To establish and maintain order, enduring social institutions are created and rules (laws) established so that human interaction can be regulated. In this way, all parts of society can be coordinated so that members of society and society's organizations and institutions all contribute to the support, maintenance, and stability of the social system. The basic assumption is that there is agreement on the values and rules of society so that they, along with the social institutions regulating the system, must be learned, respected, and revered by everyone. 'We learn what is expected of us in the family, at school, in the workplace and through the media' (Howe 1987, 35).

Social problems. If a person does not behave in ways expected of, say, a parent, a wage-earner, or a law-abiding citizen, it is assumed that something went wrong in that person's socialization process. To guard itself against disequilibrium, society will attempt to return the person to normal functioning through its social institutions. If society's official agents, such as teachers, social workers, or police, fail to correct or control the malfunctioning or out-of-step person, then he or she may have to be removed from society and the individual's behaviour neutralized by institutionalization. This removes a threat to social stability and also serves as an example to other would-be non-conformists and deviants.

Because the order view assumes that there is essential agreement among members of society on the nature of the prevailing institutions and dominant ideology, their existence is taken for granted and the existing order legitimated (Reasons and Perdue 1981). And because these institutions and their supporting ideology fend off disequilibrium, discontinuity, and disorder of the system, their preservation becomes a social imperative. The assumption that social institutions are good, necessary, and agreed to, as well as the belief that people are contentious and must be controlled, leads order theorists to conclude that social problems are best described and understood by focusing on lower levels or plateaus of society rather than on the societal or structural level. In other words, order theorists look at three levels of society for describing, analyzing, and explaining social problems: (1) the individual level, (2) the family level, and (3) the subculture level (Reasons and Perdue 1981).

Table 1.1   Assumptions of Order and Conflict Perspectives

	Order	Conflict/Change
Beliefs about human beings	competitive, contentious, individualistic, acquisitive	co-operative, collective, social
Nature of social institutions	must endure and regulate human interactions (political, economic, educational, religious, family) to avoid disorder	dynamic, with no sacred standing; facilitate economic co-operation, sharing, and common interests
Nature of society	consists of interdependent and integrated institutions and a supportive ideological base; viewed as an organism or system with each part contributing to the maintenance of the whole	in a society of structural inequality, the social nature of human existence is denied, with social institutions seen as serving private rather than public interests
Continuity of social institutions	prevail because of agreement (consensus) among society's members	prevail in a society marked by dominant–subordinate relations because of control and coercion
Nature of relationship between people and society	members are expected to conform and adapt to consensus-based social arrangements	acceptance, conformity, and adaptation to a coercive and hierarchical social order is questioned; faulty socialization is more a matter of discriminatory institutions and defective rules that promote the interests of the dominant group
Nature of social problems	socialization will occasionally fail whereby reverence for institutions and respect for rules will not be learned; such occurrence on a large scale is a social problem	institutions, ideology, and social processes and practices must be changed to protect the social nature of human existence and promote the celebration of cultural diversity
Approach to social problems	a) behaviour must be changed through resocialization (rehabilitation, counselling) or neutralized through formal systems of state control (criminal law, prisons, asylums, etc.) b) social reform can only involve minor adjustments that are consistent with the nature of the existing system	behavioural change can only involve minor adjustments consistent with co-operative and collective nature of society; massive commitment to behavioural change is a form of blaming the victim
Social work theories and approaches	psychodynamic, systems, ecological, behavioural, problem-solving, strengths perspective	feminist, radical, structural, anti-racist, narrative therapy, just therapy, anti-oppressive

At the individual level, it is believed that the source of social problems lies within the person himself or herself. This is consistent with the social pathology view of social problems. A person is not conforming to the rules, norms, and expectations of society because of some individual trait. Poverty, mental illness, drug addiction, and criminal activity are blamed on supposed personal defects. As Reasons and Perdue point out, at the individual level social problems are personalized. Poverty and crime, for example, are blamed on some defect of the person, and what emerges is 'a biographical portrait that separates the individual from society' (1981, 8). Individuals are carefully scrutinized (diagnosed, assessed) to discover the explanation for the problem.

Examples of this level of explanation would include Cesare Lombroso's explanation of criminal activity as the result of persons who were physically distinct from non-criminals and Freud's psychoanalytic theory in which intra-psychic phenomena were hypothesized as the determinants of maladjusted behaviour. Much of social work's earlier casework and psychodynamic practices were based on individual explanations for social problems. Sociobiology is a contemporary development of a theory that holds that genetic information explains social behaviour. For example, in 1988 a psychology professor at the University of Western Ontario in Canada created international controversy when he published an article alleging that race was connected to intelligence, sexual restraint, and personality, among other personal characteristics (Rushton 1988).

Most order theorists (and many social workers), because they operate from a systems perspective or employ an ecological model when dealing with social problems, are not satisfied with individual levels of explanations for social problems. From this comes the liberal-humanist concept of social disorganization. This concept is based on the notion that the present liberal–capitalist social order contains some defects that create disorganization and bring harm to some people and that it is the job of social services workers to rectify these defects (i.e., to fix the parts of society not working properly so that society can work better and is able to persist). Systems theory and an ecological approach to social work, however, do not try to change the fundamental (oppressive) nature of the system but deal with individuals and/or environmental influences within the system. The types of environmental influences most frequently dealt with by 'order social workers' are the family and the subculture.

The family as an important social unit has received enormous attention from social workers and others since the early 1960s. Family disorganization has been cited as an explanation for most of the social problems with which social workers deal. The family is routinely analyzed in an attempt to identify its contribution to situations of poverty, juvenile delinquency, mental illness, alcoholism, family violence, poor school performance, and so on. Family therapy was at one time (and still is, by some social workers) viewed as almost a panacea to society's problems, and 'family dysfunction' replaced 'individual pathology' as the popular explanation for social problems (but did not eliminate individualistic explanations). Rather than blaming social problems on some defect of the person, as neo-conservatives would, order theorists and social workers saw the source of problems as lying within the family and attributed these problems to poor parenting, undeveloped communication skills, and the like—in other words, on 'maladaptive' or 'dysfunctional' families. Social problems became family problems.

Explanations for social problems at the subcultural level of society focus on various categories of people who are distinct from the larger majority population by reason of such features as race, ethnicity, sexuality, and class. Subculture theorists believe that these subcultural groups have distinctive values that put them at a disadvantage to or in conflict with the larger or dominant culture (Reasons and Perdue 1981). Social problems are not blamed on a defective individual or a dysfunctional family but are attributed to an inferior culture. Today, many mainstream explanations for social problems tend to blame one's culture (i.e., cultures associated with race, gender, ethnicity, sexuality, class, and so on or any combination of these factors) (Dant 2003; Dominelli 2002; Gil 1998; Nelson and McPherson 2003; van Wormer 2004).

An example of a subcultural theory is the 'culture of poverty,' or what is often termed 'the cycle of poverty theory,' which attempts to explain poverty by assuming that there are common traits among poor people (feelings of inferiority, apathy, dependence, fatalism, little sense of deferred gratification). These traits are said to be passed on to subsequent generations through the process of socialization so that by the time poor children are of school age, they have internalized the basic traits of poverty and are not psychologically prepared to take advantage of the opportunities available to them. Little, if any, thought is given in this theory to the possibility that many of these so-called traits of poor people are actually adaptations and adjustments on the part of the poor to cope with poverty rather than actual causes of poverty.

Another subcultural theory is the 'cultural deprivation theory,' which attempts to explain the situation of Aboriginal peoples and other minority groups. This theory attributes the second-class status of indigenous people and other minority groups to an inferior culture. In other words, Aboriginal culture is inadequate to prepare Aboriginal persons to function properly (successfully) in the larger society. Examples include: Aboriginal parents do not read to their children; they do not take vacations abroad to expand their children's horizons; motivation for school achievement or for work is low; Aboriginals have no concept of the importance of time; welfare and alcoholism are part of this inferior culture. The inevitable conclusion of this subcultural theory is that children of Aboriginal ancestry are culturally deprived. Once so labelled, of course, they are expected to fail in school and often do.

Both of the above subcultural explanations for social problems are part of a larger process of 'blaming the victim.' William Ryan (1976) outlines this process:

1.   Identify the problem.
2.   Study those affected by the problem and discover how they are different from the rest of society.
3.   Define the differences, which are in fact often the effects of injustice and discrimination, as the causes of the social problem.

4. Assign a government bureaucrat to invent a humanitarian action program to correct the differences by changing the people affected by the problem.

Thus, the solution to social problems originating at the subcultural level is to try to untangle, correct, and make up for the deficiencies of these inferior cultures by altering the behaviours of the people themselves. This strategy involves counselling, resocialization, cultural enhancement services, upgrading, rehabilitation, and community education programs. In effect, people are worked on so that they can better fit into the mainstream, into the culture of the majority or dominant group. This process of acculturation or assimilation leaves society's social institutions unchanged. It is considered better to change a minority culture than to change social institutions so that they can accommodate the minority culture.

Social work and the order perspective. Most current social work theories and practices are based on the order perspective. Major activities are personal reform, limited social reform, and advocacy, all of which are carried out in an effort to humanize capitalism, not to change it (Mullaly 1997a). The major theories—psychoanalytic, family therapies, general systems theory, and the ecological approach—all emanate from the order perspective. In the case of psychoanalytic theory, the major task, clearly, is personal reform. In the case of family therapy and general systems theory, the major task is to repair the harm or disruption that has upset the healthy functioning of the family or the equilibrium of the system. The ecological approach aims to find the best fit between the person and the system. In none of these theories or approaches is any thought given to the possibility that the source of the problem lies not within the system but is the system itself. This critical omission is the Achilles heel of conventional, mainstream social work carried out in the order tradition.

This is not to say that progressive social workers would never use general systems theory or the ecological approach. These perspectives are useful in that they provide the social worker with a snapshot of the situation with which they are dealing. They can identify the relevant actors and organizations in an individual's life situation and help to clarify the relationships among them. However, by themselves they only describe situations and do not provide any causal explanations for a problem or situation. Although these approaches may include the person's immediate environment in their examination of a particular situation, they do not deal with larger-order structural phenomena. By emphasizing only those aspects of the social environment considered amenable to social work practice, systems theory and the ecological approach ignore broader structural social forces, and this in effect reinforces social inequality (Gould 1987).

Conflict/Change Perspective

The harmony and consensus extolled in the order perspective as characterizing society are not recognized in the conflict/change perspective. Or if they are, they are seen as the result of an illusion created by the dominant group in society to lead the less powerful into accepting an unequal social order in which the dominant group is the main beneficiary (Howe 1987). The conflict or change perspective is strongly identified with critical theory, which attributes social problems to social structures, processes, and practices that favour certain groups in society and oppress others along lines of class, race, gender, age, and so on. Examples of critical theory (or theories) are feminism, Marxism, political economy, anti-racism, the structural approach, post-colonialism, and anti-oppression.

Society. Conflict theorists accept the view of society as a system of interrelated parts but do not believe that the parts are held together by consensus and shared interests and values. Rather, they see society comprising inherently opposing groups with respect to interests, values, and expectations. These groups compete for resources and power, and those who win exercise their control and power by imposing an ideological world view that holds capitalism as the best of all economic systems (McDaniel and Agger 1984). The ideological climate or hegemony established by the dominant group involves the formulation of laws, the creation of social institutions, and the distribution of ideas that favour the dominant group. This results in structured inequality marked by vast differences in wealth, status, and power, and consequently the social nature of human existence is denied (Reasons and Perdue 1981).

Conflict theorists do not accept the present social order. They want radical change, reasoning that a truly just order can only come about through the radical reorganization of society, not through the extension of social control (Horton 1966). Conflict theorists' vision of society is one in which a new set of social relations is attained, with no one group dominating another (Howe 1987).

Social problems. Conflict theorists do not believe that social problems normally[3] originate within the individual, the family, or the subculture, as do order theorists, but rather 'arise from the exploitive and alienating practices of dominant groups' (Horton 1966, 704). Given the nature of a society marked by inequality and structured along lines of class, gender, race, age, and ability/disability, the explanation for social problems must lie at a higher societal plane than those perceived by order theorists. For conflict theorists, the structural level is where social problems are more realistically described, analyzed, and explained (Reasons and Perdue 1981). This level includes society's institutions and its supportive ideology. At this level a social problem is defined as:

> a condition that involves the social injury of people on a broad scale. The injury may be physical in manifestation (as with disease stemming from a health service geared to income), social-psychological (as with alienation), economic (as with poverty), political (as with the oppression of dissident groups), or intellectual (as with nonexistent or inadequate education). Social problems ensue from institutional defects and are not to be best interpreted or understood through individuals, families, or subcultures. Thus, the social problem as such is not an aberration but rather a normal consequence of the way in which a society is organized [Reasons and Perdue 1981, 12].

Reasons and Perdue point out that the above definition of social problems does not mean that conflict theorists ignore individuals, families, and subcultures as areas for study. The difference is that conflict theorists will always connect these societal planes with the broader structural order of society. In other words, the conflict theorist will always look to public issues (i.e., social institutions and their supportive ideology) as the source of private troubles. And because social problems are rooted in the social order, they cannot be resolved by technical or administrative reforms. They can only be resolved by a massive reorganization or transformation of the social system. In sum, the major postulates of the conflict perspective are:

- Society is the setting within which various struggles occur among different groups whose interests, values, and behaviours conflict with one another.
- The state is an important agent participating in the struggle on the side of the powerful groups.
- Social inequality is a result of coercive institutions that legitimate force, fraud, and inheritance as the major means of obtaining rights and privileges.
- Social inequality is a chief source of conflict.
- The state and the law are instruments of oppression controlled and used by the dominant groups for their own benefit.
- Classes are social groups with distinctive interests that inevitably bring them into conflict with other groups with opposed interests. (Reasons and Perdue 1981, 13–14)

Social work and the conflict perspective. The conflict-oriented social services worker must fight for change at all social, economic, and political levels. A conflict analysis of society reveals who is benefiting from established social arrangements; it shows how domination is maintained; and it suggests what must be done to bring about changes in power and resources. To assist the victims of an oppressive social order, the social worker needs to know who holds the power, whose interests are being served by maintaining the status quo, and what devices are being used to keep things as they are (Howe 1987).

As suggested above, the conflict perspective of social problems does not preclude social intervention at the individual, family, and subcultural levels. The difference between the mainstream and conflict social services worker is that instead of dealing with each of these levels separately, the conflict worker in every case would search for a connection between people's private troubles and the probable structural source of these troubles. Rather than looking to the individual or family or subculture for the source of distress, the conflict worker—with the person or group experiencing the distress—would seek to understand how the larger social order perpetrates and perpetuates problems. Although the conflict practitioner would do many of the same things as the order practitioner, many differences emanate from the different explanations each holds about the nature of society and for social problems. These differences will be highlighted throughout this book.

Whereas the order perspective underpins much of traditional social services work, the conflict perspective underpins progressive forms of social work practice. For example, most feminists subscribe to the view that society is set up and operates in ways that privilege males (the dominant group) over females (the subordinate group). Correspondingly, anti-racist social workers hold that our laws, social institutions, and ideological climate favour white people as the dominant group over people of colour. Similar positions of privilege are enjoyed by dominant groups with respect to class, sexuality, age, ability, and so on. Conversely, the subordinate groups experience social problems in greater number and with more severity than their privileged counterparts. In other words, dominant groups enjoy their privilege at the expense of subordinate groups by way of an oppressive system of social relations and an unjust set of social conditions (Gil 1998).

The fundamental argument underpinning the conflict perspective of society in general, and anti-oppressive social work in particular, is that 'the contemporary social order is characterized by a range of social divisions (class, race, gender, age, disability and so on) that both embody and engender inequality, discrimination, and oppression' (Thompson 1998, 3). In their development of anti-oppressive practice using the law, Dalrymple and Burke support this argument. They point out that we live in a society characterized by difference but that differences are not always regarded positively. 'Differences are used to exclude rather than include. This is because relationships within society are the result of the exercise of power on individual, interpersonal, and institutional levels' (Dalrymple and Burke 1995, 8). From the conflict perspective, then, oppression—not individual deficiency or social disorganization—is the major cause of and explanation for social problems. This, of course, necessitates an anti-oppressive form of social work practice to deal with these problems in any meaningful way. Such a practice requires an understanding of the nature of oppression, its dynamics, the social and political functions it carries out in the interests of the dominant groups, its effects on oppressed persons, and the ways that oppressed people cope with and/or resist their oppression. These are some of the topics discussed in the next chapter.

Critical Social Theory

The conflict perspective is part of a larger body of social theory known as critical social theory (or critical theory). Critical social theory is a macro theory that examines social structures, institutions, policies, practices, and processes with respect to how they treat all groups in society; it contains an explanation for social problems and a political practice to deal with them. One of the foremost writers on critical social theory today, Douglas Kellner, contends that the job of critical theorists is to provide criticisms and alternatives to traditional or mainstream social theory. Critical theory is motivated by an interest in those who are oppressed, is informed by a critique of domination, and is driven by a goal of liberation (Kellner 1989). It is concerned with moving from a society characterized by exploitation, inequality, and oppression to one that is emancipatory and free from domination.

Karl Marx is arguably the founder of critical social theory. His entire intellectual life was devoted to showing how capitalism was both inhuman and unworkable, with the intention of changing it. His ideas and emancipatory intentions with respect to class and capitalism have been extended by such notable theorists as Lukács, Gramsci, the Frankfurt School, and its heir apparent, Jürgen Habermas (see Agger 2006; Jay 1973). This analysis has been further extended into non-class forms of oppression by feminists, critical race theorists, gay and lesbian liberation writers, cultural studies, and post-colonial theorists. One writer defines critical social theory in the following way:

> A critical theory of society is defined as a theory having practical intent. As its name suggests, it is critical of existing social and political institutions and practices, but the criticisms it levels are not intended to show how present society is unjust, only to leave everything as it is. A critical theory of society is understood by its advocates as playing a crucial role in changing society. In this, the link between social theory and political practice is perhaps the defining characteristic of critical theory, for a critical theory without a practical dimension would be bankrupt on its own terms [S. Leonard 1990, 3].

Critical theory, then, is different from most social science theory constructed according to the canons of scientific inquiry. Traditional social theory may describe and explain social processes and practices, but it is quite independent of any attempts at political practice to change the social processes and practices that are exploitative and discriminatory. Its commitment is to the advancement of knowledge by attempting to understand the world as it really is. Conversely, critical theory is committed to changing the world 'in ways that can help "emancipate" those on the margins of society' (Leonard 1990, xiii). Agger (1998, 15) sums it up best when he says that critical social theory 'conceives human liberation as the highest purpose of intellectual activity.'

Stephen Leonard (1990) outlines three undertakings of a critical social theory: (1) it must locate the sources of domination in actual social practices; (2) it must present an alternative vision (or at least an outline) of a life free from such domination; and (3) it must translate these tasks in a form that is intelligible to those who are oppressed in society. Agger (1998) argues that for a theory to be considered a critical theory, it must have (to some degree) the following features:

- It opposes positivism because knowledge is an active construction by scientists and theorists who necessarily make assumptions about the worlds they study and thus are not strictly value-free.
- It attempts to raise consciousness[4] about present domination, exploitation, and oppression and to demonstrate the possibility of a future society free of these phenomena.
- It argues that oppression is structural—that people's everyday lives are affected by politics, economics, culture, discourse, gender, race, and so on.

- It also argues that structures of oppression are reproduced through the internalization of dominant–subordinate relationships, and it attempts to cut through this internalization of oppression by emphasizing the power of agency, both personal and collective, to transform society.
- It avoids determinism and endorses voluntarism by arguing that social change begins in people's everyday lives—in their family roles, workplace, consumer patterns, and so on.
- It rejects economic determinism by conceptualizing a dialectical relationship between structure and agency—structure conditions everyday life, but knowledge of structure can help people change social conditions.
- It holds people responsible for their own liberation and warns against any revolutionary expediency of oppressing others in the name of some future liberation.

To Agger's set of critical theory beliefs, Tim Dant (2003, 163) adds another that emphasizes culture and further clarifies the nature and political intent of critical theory:

- The lives of individual human beings in modern societies are unnecessarily dominated, constrained, and restricted, in terms of both what they can do and what they can think, by the cultural forms through which they must live their lives together as a society.
- These restrictions are not the result of natural or supernatural forces but the product of human history.
- These restrictions may have their origins in the patterns of economic arrangements for collectively meeting material needs that Marx describes as 'capitalism,' but they are sustained, refined, and experienced at the level of culture—that is, as ideas, signs, images, beliefs, rules, injunctions, and so on.
- These restrictions, which constitute a degree of 'unfreedom,' could be undone to liberate individual lives without creating chaos or increasing the restrictions on the lives of other people.
- The way by which these restrictions can best be undone is by collective recognition and rejection of them through cultural means—through refusal to accept what is taken for granted, resisting what is not desired, criticizing and negating received ideas and values that are presented as universal.
- The theoretical strategy of 'critique' exposes the cultural form of constraints and restrictions in a way that can contribute to their recognition and rejection.

Critical social theory is not a singular or unified body of thought. Rather, it is a theory cluster. Several current examples of theory contain enough of the above characteristics to be considered a critical theory—liberation theology, Freire's pedagogy of the oppressed, some forms (i.e., transformative forms) of feminist theory, structural social work theory, and post-colonial theory. Some critical social theories focus on a singular form of oppression, while others adopt an umbrella approach and include all sources and forms of oppression in a single framework. Examples of the former are feminism, which perceives patriarchy as the source of women's oppression; critical race theory, which perceives racism as the cause of oppression of people of colour; and queer theory, which perceives heterosexism as the fundamental cause of homophobia. Theorists in the latter category include cultural studies theorists, who believe that oppression occurs because of a dominant or ruling culture; structural social work theorists, who believe that it is mainly the social structures that oppress by privileging dominant groups over subordinate groups; and anti-oppressive theorists, who believe that all subordinate groups are oppressed on personal, cultural, and institutional levels by visible and invisible structures and by conscious and unconscious means.

My own treatment of oppression and anti-oppression falls unambiguously in the critical social theory cluster. No attempt is made to formulate an overarching (or totalizing) theory of oppression, because one theory cannot possibly account for the many forms and sources of oppression, their dynamics and impacts, their interactions and internalizations, their subjective and objective aspects, and so on. And as Chris Weedon (1997) points out, theory itself is constantly in process. This book focuses on theories and ideas that seem to have explanatory power at this point to help us better understand the oppressive social structures, processes, and practices within which we live and our position within them. In the critical social theory tradition, the political aim of this understanding is to change these structures, processes, and practices.

Critical Social Work Theory

Critical social work theories, perspectives, and approaches fall within the critical social theory camp. They are all critical of existing systems of social arrangements as unjust (and oppressive); they have a vision of a society based on a set of egalitarian values; and they are committed to social work practices to move from the current unjust society to one that is free of dominant–subordinate relations. Table 1.2 presents some selected social work perspectives or approaches indicating those that are order- or consensus-based and those that are conflict- or change-based. Other terms for order- or consensus-based approaches are mainstream, conventional, or traditional, whereas other terms for conflict- or change-based approaches are progressive, critical, or transformative. As described above in the section Order Perspective, the personal change approaches (see Table 1.2) seek to bring about change in the person or in the family as the way to deal with social problems. The person-in-the-environment approach assumes that there is a 'goodness-of-fit' between the individual and society and that the job of social work is to find this fit by changing the person and/or bringing about change in the immediate environment that the individual inhabits. And although change in one's environment may occur, it is usually limited change—for example, removal of a family member or a change in a policy or the establishment of a program to better accommodate the individual's needs. However, in the final analysis, no substantive change has been made to the larger system or structures of society that tend to favour the dominant group at the expense of subordinate groups. Amelioration may have taken place, but fundamental social change has not.

Historically, tension has existed between social workers who subscribe to the order- or consensus-based approaches and those who subscribe to social transformative approaches. The conventional or mainstream group was seen by its social change counterparts as conforming to established institutions, thus reinforcing, supporting, and defending the very system that caused problems for individuals and families in the first place. The progressive or change-based group was seen by its counterpart as idealistic and unrealistic with no workable solutions for social problems, because although the system might not be perfect, mainstream social workers believed it was the best one possible and that it could not be transformed but only fine-tuned to help meet human need.

In contrast to the conventional view, the progressive or critical view does not hold that our present social institutions are capable of adequately meeting human need. Social workers holding this view are quick to point out that in spite of the existence of a social welfare state as well as social work interventions over most of the past century, social problems are not decreasing but on the contrary appear to be worsening. They also point to the growing gap between rich and poor, to the worsening plight of traditionally disadvantaged groups in the face of globalization, to the resurrection of conservatism, and to the social control functions of welfare programs and social work practice as proof that the present set of social arrangements does not work for large numbers of people. Although there has always been a progressive or radical contingent within social work, theirs has been a minority voice. However, the contingent's numbers have been growing over the past three decades, as have their challenges to the conventional view. For example, whereas only a few radical or progressive social work courses were offered in Canadian schools of social work 30 years ago, today the standards of accreditation of the Canadian Association of Schools of Social Work, now called the Canadian Association for Social Work Education (CASWE), require that schools of social work demonstrate their commitment to social justice and anti-oppressive social work in their curricula, admissions, faculty complements, policies, and procedures. Table 1.2 illustrates the breadth and rich diversity of progressive social work approaches, all of which share the goal of social transformation but with different emphases. All are based on and contribute to the larger field of critical social theory.

It is worth noting that general systems theory and the ecological approach, which are still considered core social work theory in many social work programs and by many social work practitioners, are not even theories. A theory by definition has descriptive, explanatory, and predictive capacities. Both of the foregoing approaches are descriptive only and contain no explanatory or predictive capabilities. Neither of them, for example, contains a theoretical explanation for poverty, domestic violence, racism, or any other problem that social work encounters. Nor do they accommodate

Table 1.2   Selected Conventional and Progressive Social Work
Perspectives/Approaches

Conventional (consensus/order-based)		Progressive* (conflict/change-based)
personal change (goal = change the person)	*person-in-environment* (goal = personal change and/or limited social change)	*fundamental social change* (goal = social transformation)
• psychodynamic	• general systems theory	• feminist social work
• behavioural	• ecosystems (ecological)	• Marxist
• client-centred	• life-model	• radical
• psycho-social	• problem-solving strengths	• structural
• clinical	• perspective	• anti-racist
• family therapies		• anti-oppressive
• casework		• critical postmodern
		• post-colonial
Note: Any of the above can be used within a critical or progressive framework, although traditionally this has rarely occurred.		• indigenous (decolonization)
		• narrative therapy
		• just therapy

* Progressive social work today recognizes that fundamental social change cannot occur without fundamental personal change also occurring. Earlier versions of progressive social work tended to emphasize structural changes and psychological preparation to participate in social change activities but gave little or no consideration to the impact of oppressive structures on oppressed groups and how to respond to them in a way that was meaningful.

or explain such social work concerns as conflict within the system, power relations or differentials within the system, cultural variables, or larger oppressive social structures. Their focus on the here-and-now situation and possibilities for intervention contributes to a neglect of history, and social problems are believed to result from a breakdown between individuals and the subsystems (e.g., family, school, welfare office) with which they interact. They operate to maintain the status quo, since the goal is to restore (not transform) the system back to normal functioning. General systems theory and ecological perspectives have been the subject of critique now for more than 30 years, and it is time that social work took that critique seriously. This is not to say that we should abandon these perspectives, since they do have analytical utility in terms of presenting a snapshot in time of a particular system or systems, but it does mean that we should stop considering these perspectives as core social work knowledge in our curricula and practice.

Modernism and Postmodernism

Modernism has been defined as 'a particular view of the possibilities and direction of human social life [that] is rooted in the Enlightenment and grounded in faith in rational thought' (Johnson 2000, 232). A modernist perspective holds that truth and

Not All Theories Are Created Equal—In Spite of What the Instructor Implies

Over the years, I have been struck by the realization of how many (too many) social work educators teach social work theories. The impression sometimes given to students is that there is a large warehouse containing all the social work theories that exist or that there is a smorgasbord of theories from which the student or practitioner can select those that seem most appealing. Indeed, one of the reviewers of an earlier edition of one of my published books on structural social work faulted it because it did not expose students to all the other social work theories they had to learn. (It might have helped if the reviewer had thought about the title of the book.) The suggestion seems to be that all social work theories are basically the same, since they contain the same properties of a theory, were developed to assist social workers in helping people, and are relatively equal in merit. Therefore, the job of the theory instructor is to expose students to as many theories as possible and leave it up to them to make their choices. The decision regarding which theory to use really depends on the social worker's personal preference; after all, social work is social work. Table 1.2 above should dispel the myth that all theories are created equal. For example, some are macro theories that analyze the place of social work in society (whether it supports or challenges the status quo) and contain an explanation for the existence of social problems. Others are micro theories that focus on the relationship and interactions between a social worker and service users and contain no social analysis or social problem explanation. In other words, there are lower-order and higher-order theories (as well as other ways to categorize social work theories; see Mullaly 2007). The conventional social work theories in Table 1.2 are examples of the former, and the progressive theories are examples of the latter. Micro theories of practice can be carried out as part of the larger strategy of the macro theories, but by themselves they have no political mission, which in effect supports the way things are.

knowledge exist as objective reality (as do morality and beauty) that can be discovered, examined, understood, and explained through rational and scientific means and then controlled, used, and exploited for the betterment of the human condition (Howe 1994; Johnson 2000). Postmodernism, a rival perspective to modernist thought, has assumed major attention over the past three decades (Harvey 1989). It proposes that truth, beauty, morality, and social life have no objective reality beyond how we think, talk, and write about them. No social units are fixed entities, and although some representations of social life are more privileged and/or given more legitimacy than others, ultimately no one version of reality is better or truer than another. The debate between these two perspectives strikes at the heart of two basic sets of competing assumptions that underpin the attempts of each to understand the world and our experience of it (Johnson 2000).

For more than a decade and a half now, a substantial literature on postmodernism and post-structuralism has developed in both the humanities and the social sciences.

However, there is still a tendency on the part of some to impose a complete, clear, and time-defined break (i.e., a great divide) between anything written in the period now known as modernity (which includes most critical theory writings) and writings in the era of postmodernity. Such a position is, of course, neither informed nor critical nor scholarly. Although there are major differences and antagonisms between the two, what is often ignored, overlooked, or not known in the first place is that post-modernism and critical social theory share a common intellectual heritage. The postmodern writers Baudrillard, Derrida, Foucault, and Lyotard all wrote within the period of modernity, none rejected leftist causes, and all based their critiques of the Enlightenment on the thinking of Nietzsche and Heidegger. The latter is seen by many as the archetype and trend-setter of postmodernism. Similarly, Nietzsche and Heidegger influenced the Frankfurt School's critique of civilization. Both sets of critiques reject the Cartesian philosophy of identity (with its omission of the Other), the emancipatory myth of teleology, and positivism (Nietzsche declared not only God dead but all impostor gods such as science and philosophy as well).

Homi Bhabha (1994, 4–5) takes to task those people who would use the prefix 'post' in the jargon of our times—postmodernism, post-structuralism, post-colonialism, post-feminism—to indicate sequentially 'after' (e.g., after-feminism) or polarity (e.g., anti-modernism). He contends that these uses of 'post' are profoundly parochial. Bhabha takes up Heidegger's (1971) view that a boundary (such as that inherent in the concept of 'post') is not the point at which something stops but rather the point from which something begins its 'presencing.' For example, Bhabha argues that the broader significance of postmodernism is not that we recognize the fragmentation of the grand narratives of post-Enlightenment rationalism, but that the epistemological limits of such ethnocentric ideas are also the 'enunciative boundaries' at which a range of other dissonant and dissident voices and histories begin—women, people of colour, colonized nations, and so on.

There are many books worth consulting for general overviews and critiques of post-modernism (e.g., Agger 2006; Bauman 1992; Best and Kellner 1991; Harvey 1989; Seidman 1998), and it is not my intention to reproduce these overviews and critiques. It is important to note that postmodernism includes but is not restricted to post-modern social theory (Agger 1998). It also encompasses postmodern architecture, art, and design, as well as postmodern literary and cultural theory. With respect to postmodern social theory, there are a variety of perspectives. At one end of the continuum, postmodernism is a conservative, individualistic, and nihilistic doctrine, which holds that there is no potential for solidarity among oppressed persons or for social change efforts because every person is his or her own moral agent—a position that Ife (1997) calls an 'anything goes brand of politics' and what Geertz (1986) calls 'witless relativism.' At the other end of the postmodern social theory continuum are writers who have taken postmodern analyses and criticisms of modernity on board and are attempting to use them as essential ingredients in a necessary (in my view) revitalization of critical social theory. Examples of such social theorists are Ben Agger, Stanley Aronowitz, Nancy Fraser, David Harvey, Frederic Jameson, Douglas Kellner, and Timothy Luke. Theorists within the social work and social welfare areas include Jim Ife (1997), Peter Leonard (1997), Bob Mullaly (2007), and Bob Pease and Jan Fook (1999). This book and its treatment of oppression/anti-oppression follow this 'critical postmodernist' approach. It is informed mainly by the critical theories of Marxism, the Frankfurt School, transformative forms of feminism, critical race theory, the Birmingham School of Cultural Studies, critical postmodernism, and post-colonialism.

Major Concepts Associated with Oppression/Anti-oppression Framework

Because I am developing a framework of oppression/anti-oppression based on two bodies of social thought (modernist and postmodernist) that are often antagonistic towards one another, it is necessary for me to explicate some of the major concepts that will become part of this framework. These concepts will be used regularly in subsequent chapters of this book.

Structures of Oppression

All societies set up organizations to carry out certain functions necessary for them to maintain themselves. Examples include an economic system to ensure the production, distribution, and consumption of needed (and desired) goods and services; a legal system to protect people's rights and to facilitate peace and order; a welfare system to attend to the plight of economically deprived people; an education system to provide persons with the knowledge and skills required to participate in the labour force; and religious organizations to tend to the spiritual needs of the population. These organizations are called social institutions. With their patterns of organization, their procedural rules of operating, their policies governing the delivery and use of their services, and their social practices, they constitute what are known as social structures. These structures affect everyone in society.

Traditional critical social theory has always emphasized social structures as a major source of oppression. Because they were originally established by and for the most part are still dominated by a particular social group—bourgeois, Christian, heterosexual males of European origin—they primarily reflect and reinforce the assumptions, views, needs, values, culture, and social position of this group. Furthermore, this group enjoys its privilege at the expense of other groups in society—people of colour, the working class, non-Christians, gays, lesbians, and bisexuals, women, and so on. Our social structures are imbued with racism, sexism, patriarchy, and classism in that there is a privileged or dominant group within each one of these social divisions that has more political, social, and usually economic power than the subordinate groups. The dominant relations of men over women, white people over persons of colour, affluent people over poor people, heterosexual over homosexual and bisexual persons, physically able persons over physically and mentally challenged persons 'have been so internalized into the structures of society that they have also become intrinsic to the roles, rules, policies and practices of [social] institutions' (Haney 1989, 37).

This internalized phenomenon is part of an 'invisible structure' of oppression. In addition to visible social institutions, there are also invisible structures of oppression. In fact, these invisible structures are probably more important and effective today than visible structures in promoting conformity to a system that oppresses people on the basis of gender, race, class, sexuality, age, and so on. The major invisible structure is a dominant ideology or a world view, which is discussed below.

Domination is not necessarily a conscious or intentional choice on the part of the dominant group (nor is subordination a conscious choice of subordinate group members), since few people in society would consider themselves oppressors. Freire (1994 [1970]) argues that it is more a matter of the dominant group not seeing or not being aware of any viable alternative social, economic, or political structures that might be antithetical to dominant–subordinate social relations. Members of the dominant group perceive their monopoly on 'having more' not as a privilege that might dehumanize others but as their inalienable right for having taken advantage of the opportunities that exist for everyone (in their view) in society. Those who do not take advantage of opportunities are either lazy or incompetent, and it is only right that they occupy a subordinate position in society. Little thought is given in this perspective to the possibility that access to opportunities and resources is based largely on one's social position or location rather than strictly on merit or effort. Awareness of the oppressive nature and functions of our current social structures is an essential element of anti-oppressive theory and practice.

Structural Determinism and the Autonomous Subject

Is the individual a relatively autonomous moral agent who is able to act on the surrounding world either to maintain or to change it? Or is the individual's sense of self, of identity, and of autonomy a product of dominant structures and their supportive ideologies? In other words, are human subjects the creators or the products of the social structures that surround them? Whereas traditional critical social theory has tended to emphasize the significance of structural determinants in forming subjectivity and constraining individual agency (i.e., structural determinism), postmodernism has tended to focus on the micro-processes of people's lives and the everyday choices they make (i.e., human agency).

To be sure, there are extremists in both the modernist and postmodernist camps. For example, some Marxist theorists (e.g., Althusser) reject the human actor as a significant factor in any social change and see changes as the results of impersonal historical factors—even though Marx himself argued that humans produce change and that all history could be seen as the 'history of class struggle'—that is, as the result of human agency (Leonard 1997). Conversely, some postmodern writers, in my view, overemphasize the role of human agency in social change and thereby reinforce the conservative notion that people are self-directed individuals able to act in societies with relative freedom of choice and will make decisions to maximize their well-being. The danger here is that people who are resource-poor or living on the margins of society will be viewed as irresponsible, deviant, and not worthy of any assistance because they did not make use of their human agency.

The position taken in this book is that an emphasis on one position only is reductionist in that either micro or macro issues are overlooked, ignored, or rejected. Consistent with the approaches of such writers as Peter Leonard (1997) and Neil Thompson (1998), my approach here is that both structural forces and human agency are integral in developing an understanding of oppression and anti-oppressive practices. To adopt one position as the only viable approach is to create a 'false dichotomy' in critical social theory terms, and to see them as 'either-or' oppositionals is to create an 'invalid binary' in postmodern terms. Sibeon (1991, 24) states the case for including both in any understanding of society, human action, and social change:

> To attempt to account for 'structure' in terms of agency is (micro) reductionist . . . equally, to attempt . . . to 'explain' human agency in terms of structure is (macro) reductionist. . . . Social life is not reducible to a single reductionist principle of 'micro' or 'macro' explanation. Neither is it possible to arrive at an 'accommodation' or 'compromise' based on a synthesis of both of these forms of reductionism [cited in Thompson 1998, 48].

Power and Resistance

Related to social structures and human agency are the concepts of power and resistance. Traditional critical social theory tended to view power as a social phenomenon that resided or was concentrated mainly in large structures (e.g., institutions of the state, big business, the church) and was used or abused by powerful individuals and institutions to maintain dominant–subordinate relationships. To counteract or overcome this use of power, critical theorists advocated for large-scale social movements to mobilize and change the power structures (e.g., the civil rights movement, the women's liberation movement, the trade union movement). A corollary to this belief in collective action to bring about social change is that the individual, by himself or herself, has no power and thus has to collectivize to obtain some power. Much of the community organization or development literature is predicated on these assumptions of power.

Postmodern theorists have a different view of power. They do not believe it is ultimately concentrated in large structures; rather, power can be found in different localities, contexts, and social situations. The prison, the school, the hospital, the social worker's office are all examples of places where power is dispersed and built up independent of any systematic strategy of class or gender or ethnicity. What happens at each locality cannot be explained by some overarching meta-theory (Harvey 1989). Foucault saw power not as something that people either did or did not possess but as an aspect of all social relations, a feature of the interactions between individuals, groups, and organizations. It is a fluid phenomenon open to constant influence and change (Thompson 1998). Because power can be either constraining or enabling (Rojek, Peacock, and Collins 1988), an ongoing assessment must be made of who is exercising the power, in whose interests, and who has defined the interests (Healy and Leonard 2000).

Foucault, in his later writings (e.g., 1988), argued that power is always faced with resistance, that every exercise of power is contested, and that resistance itself is an act of countervailing power. This idea has enormous potential for anti-oppressive practice. It challenges the view that individuals or subordinate groups are helpless to do anything about the dominant discursive practices that subjugate and oppress them. Such dominance can be challenged through acts of resistance (i.e., through the use of countervailing power) to undermine the ideas, assumptions, paradigms, and discourses that constitute the dominant discursive practices.

Given the above two competing or contrasting views of power—that it is concentrated within large structures or that it is dispersed and a critical part of every social relationship—which view is most appropriate for an understanding of oppression and for developing strategies to overcome oppression? My position here is that both views have merit and must be considered in developing anti-oppressive social work practice. Both social structures and individuals are able to exercise power. However, it is patently obvious that a social institution is able to exercise more power than an individual and that an individual from the dominant group is, for the most part, able to exercise more political, social, and economic power than a member of a subordinate group. Power may be dispersed throughout society, but it is not dispersed equally. I agree with Baines (2003) who argues that power is possessive as much as it is relational, which means that people can have power as well as exercise it. It also means that in relative terms, some people are more powerful than others, no matter how confident, talented, expressive, or assertive the latter may be. Addressing this point, Fraser (2008) contends that the relational aspect of power can be confronting, especially for those who want to believe that power resides exclusively within the individual and within his or her interpersonal realm. Furthermore, it poses particular difficulties for those who may want to wish the possessive aspects of power away by suggesting that it all comes down to how people exercise power individually. Although the notion of 'acts of resistance' would seem to be a powerful tool for anti-oppressive workers (especially, but not exclusively, in the micro-practice area), one must still be sensitive to the need for collectivization and mobilization as social change strategies. We will return to these issues in the final chapter of the book when an anti-oppressive social work practice is outlined.

Discourse and Language

Traditional critical social theory tended to hold that language simply reflected reality and that knowledge (obtained or given through language) was empowering. The task of progressive social services work from this perspective was to increase one's knowledge of oppression and use this knowledge when working with oppressed groups. However, postmodernism has helped to show us that there is no one universal reality but many realities and that language does not have the properties of absolute truth but is historically, culturally, and socially contextualized and largely reflects the interests and world views of dominant groups (Mullaly 2007). Language is not politically neutral, as evidenced by Howe's (1994, 522) summary of the relationship between power and language:

> Whereas modernity believes that increasing knowledge of the essential and true nature of things produces power, postmodernity reverses the formula, recognizing that the formation of a particular discourse creates contingent centres of power which define areas of knowledge, passing truths and frameworks of explanation and understanding. Those with power can control the language of the discourse and can therefore influence how the world is to be seen and what it will mean. Language promotes some possibilities and excludes others; it constrains what we see and what we do not see.

A concept related to language is discourse. Discourse includes not only language but the rules governing the choice and use of language and how the ideas and language will be framed. A discourse is a framework of thought, meaning, and action (Thompson 1998), which does not reflect knowledge, reality, or truth but creates and maintains them. Knowledge, according to Foucault, is produced by discourse—it is 'the way in which power, language and institutional practices combine at historically specific points to produce particular ways of thinking' (Featherstone and Fawsett 1994, cited in Stainton and Swift 1996, 77). Although there is always more than one discourse at any point in time, there is usually one dominant discourse. The current dominant discourse consists of a set of assumptions about the social world that largely reflects the interests of capitalism, patriarchy, and people of European descent. As Agger (1989) points out, even our textbooks are largely written within this dominant discourse. The knowledge that appears in the social science literature assists in the reproduction of the existing social order through: (1) the incorporation of ideas that support the current socio-political order and (2) the suppression and/or marginalization of scholarship that seeks to challenge or transform it (Agger 1989, 1992; Wachholz and Mullaly 2000).

The concept of discourse is another important tool for understanding oppression and for developing anti-oppressive practices. For example, in our own personal and work lives, we can avoid language and discourses that reflect and reinforce inequality (Thompson 1998). By understanding a dominant discourse, we can deconstruct it and expose any discriminatory or oppressive assumptions, ideas, and beliefs that may underpin it. And we can develop counter-discourses based on the ideals of equality, fairness, and social justice. These ideas and practices will be examined at greater length in Chapter 8.

Ideology

A concept related to discourse is ideology. The meaning of ideology here goes beyond the narrow Marxist view of it as a set of ideas that serve to hide the exploitative and alienating aspects of capitalism. Rather, an ideology is defined here as any consistent set of social, economic, and political assumptions, beliefs, values, and ideals[5] (Mullaly 2007). Ideologies provide frameworks for making sense of the social world; in other words, they provide us with a world view. Our thoughts, actions, and interactions are filtered through one or more ideologies (Thompson 1998). Donald and Hall (1986, ix–x) refer to ideologies as 'frameworks of thought' that 'enable us to make sense of perplexing events and relationships—and, inevitably, impose certain "ways of looking" . . . on those events and relationships which we are struggling to make sense of' (cited in Thompson 1998, 20). Through the process of socialization, dominant ideologies become so ingrained that we consider them as taken-for-granted views or common-sense knowledge. An ideology will determine the nature and causal explanations ascribed to social problems, as well as the solutions to these problems, including the types of social interventions and social work activities to be used (Mullaly 2007). Thompson (1998) defines ideology as the power of ideas that sustains or confronts discrimination, oppression, and inequality. Although there is some overlap between the two, a discourse may be viewed as the linguistic embodiment of an ideology (Foucault notwithstanding).

More than one ideology tends to exist at any one time, but as with the concept of discourse, there is usually one 'dominant' ideology, with the others 'subordinate' to it. A dominant ideology is the one that represents the position and supports the best interests of the dominant group. For example, capitalism as a social and economic system serves the bourgeoisie more than it does the working class. A subordinate or countervailing ideology is not as prominent as the dominant ideology and is usually in opposition to it. Ideologies based on collectivism and equality (e.g., various forms of socialism, anarchism, non–Soviet Union forms of communism) are subordinate to capitalist ideology (based on individualism and inequality), which is found in all Anglo democracies. Because the dominant ideology is so ingrained, both within the dominant group and within many people in the subordinate groups, any other ideology or world view is seldom given credence as containing a workable social or economic system. The existing systems are seen as natural, normal, and inevitable.

Any alternatives are either not recognized or deemed to be mystical, unrealistic, or too problematic to be worth the effort of even considering. Gramsci (1971) refers to the unquestioned dominance of all conformist ideas and beliefs that support the interests of the group promoting them as 'hegemony' (more will be said about this in Chapter 4).

Obviously, ideology is an important component in understanding oppression and developing strategies of anti-oppression. An analysis of the dominant ideology enables us to identify and expose the thought structures that rationalize oppression and, conversely, to promote countervailing ideologies based on social justice and equality. It also helps us to better understand 'internalized oppression,' which is why people often develop loyalty to and defend a social system that discriminates against them. This is not to say that ideological analysis is straightforward today, if it ever was. Critical social theorists have always argued that ideology has been routinized in everyday life through various discourses and practices that suggest the inevitability and rationality of political conformity (Agger 1998). In talking about the dominant group's preferential access to social opportunities, Adam (1978, 10) says, 'The privileged develop ideologies and the coercive means to protect the[ir] hierarchy of access.' Ideology in postmodern capitalism has become even more dispersed into the symbols and discourses of everyday life (a subject to be taken up in Chapter 4). Featherstone (1991) argues that postmodern ideology is so deeply implanted in daily popular culture that it is difficult to differentiate truth from falsehood and reality from illusion, which is required in any program of consciousness-raising. However, Agger argues that the interpretative tools of deconstruction (another postmodern concept) should be invaluable in detecting and debunking oppressive ideologies.

A Politics of Difference and a Politics of Solidarity

Traditional critical theory emphasizes solidarity among oppressed people but does so through various meta-narratives and by assuming the notion of a fixed identity. For example, orthodox Marxism calls for solidarity of the working class against capitalism, and early second-wave feminism called for solidarity among women against sexism and patriarchy. Solidarity among those who have had common experiences of oppression has been the essence of critical social theory's political practice. Solidarity has underpinned all significant social movements. It is the glue that holds alliances and coalitions together and provides them with their strength as measured by the numbers of people participating. Without solidarity among oppressed people, resistances to the dominant social order are dispersed and weakened.

However, the politics of solidarity has often neglected the politics of difference by reflecting in their own organizations and culture the very forms of domination and exclusion that existed in the wider society (Leonard 1995). Marxism, for example, has often overlooked other forms of oppression, such as patriarchy and racism, and has tended to view the working class as a homogeneous group whose members possess a fixed identity (i.e., an exploited and alienated worker) and who are all equally exploited, not recognizing stratification, ethnicity, gender, and other types of differences among them. Similarly, early second-wave feminism also called for solidarity and unity among oppressed 'sisters' without regard to differences in race, social position, and so on and without recognizing or acknowledging other forms of oppression experienced by many women. These examples demonstrate the need to reject the notion of an essential subjectivity (e.g., women, workers) and to substitute the concept of 'fractured identities' to refer to individual diverse subjects. The notion of fractured identities also helps us in anti-oppressive work to avoid the common practice of identifying and classifying people as either oppressors or oppressed. Everyone in society occupies both roles (identities) at various points in time, although one's principal status will tend to be one or the other. This notion of fractured or multiple identities and the multiplicity of oppression (and domination) are the subjects of Chapter 7.

Postmodernism has been especially important in acknowledging the multiple forms of 'otherness' as they emerge from differences in subjectivity, gender, class, race, and the like. It is this aspect of postmodernism that Stephen Leonard (1990) says gives it a radical edge. Postmodernism helps the anti-oppressive worker to develop a new politics of solidarity—one that pursues the idea of fractured identities in which differences within particular oppressed groups 'are always given attention, contextualized with reference to their specific geographical location in the world, their class position, and their places within the structures of race and ethnicity . . . age, sexuality, and differences of ability' (P. Leonard 1995, 7). As an early writer on oppression argued, identities are social constructions whereby 'the minority situation is more a matter of social definition than of social difference' (Adam 1978, 10). Traits such as gender, skin colour, sexuality, and class are seized upon as bases for inequality. Differences of skin colour, class, gender, and age are today's social realities, but how we deal with these differences is one of the great issues of the day. So far, we (Western society) have tended to use them to rationalize situations and practices of oppression and social inequality. In sum, solidarity within and among oppressed groups is crucial in the struggle for emancipation, but to avoid various forms of oppressive inclusions and exclusions that have occurred in the past, it must incorporate a progressive politics of difference (to be discussed in subsequent chapters). Peter Leonard (2001, 5) underscores this belief:

> Neither a belief in interdependence nor a belief in difference can, I believe, stand alone. Exclusive emphasis on interdependency, on solidarity, can lead to the smothering subordination of the diverse Other as the earlier history of Left politics demonstrates. Exclusive emphasis on difference, on the other hand, can lead to continuous fragmentation into smaller, and perhaps increasingly excluding, communities of identity, eventually ending in new forms of individualism.
>
> When we try to anticipate a future for critical social work, I think that these beliefs, in a dialectical tension with each other, are likely to prove valuable in working out where we might want to head.

Conclusion

In this chapter, I have emphasized the need for clear theoretical frameworks of explanation in which to locate good (informed and well-articulated) social work practice. Without analytically and rigorously developed social work theories, practitioners are left with their own personally constructed theories that reflect only the individual worker's particular experiences, social position, and associated biases. The specific school of social theory adopted in this book is critical social theory informed by postmodern, post-structural, feminist, and post-colonial insights. As opposed to the victim-blaming assumptions inherent in the order perspective of society, critical social theory is consistent with the conflict perspective, which locates social problems in systems of dominant–subordinate relationships. Critical social theory is concerned with people who are oppressed, informed by critical analysis of oppression, and driven by a goal of emancipation from oppression.

Although the book follows the critical social theory tradition of advancing our knowledge and understanding of the world of oppression in order to change it, it moves beyond the critical theory that belongs to a historical period known as modernity. It makes no claims to universality, reason, and order—claims that in the past have often masked the interests of those making them. Rather, the book is consistent with the 'critical postmodernist' approach that was adopted and developed in the 1990s by several social theorists and social work theorists. This approach represents an attempt to revitalize critical social theory, using some of the insights of postmodernism, post-structuralism, post-colonialism, and cultural studies.

Critical Questions for Discussion

1. How would you respond to a politician or editor of a newspaper who is calling for social work positions to be filled by people who have no formal social work education, claiming that all you need to do social work is to possess common sense and be a good people person (i.e., like people and have people skills)?

2. How would you respond to fellow students who say that they get all their satisfaction in their field placement because that is where their real learning occurs and the theory presented in the classroom has nothing to do with the real world?

3. How would you explain the existence of the following problems, using each of the seven theoretical perspectives presented in this chapter: poverty, unemployment, domestic violence, mental illness, racism, drug abuse, child abuse?

4. Looking at Table 1.2, how do you think a social worker can combine (i.e., use simultaneously) a conventional social work theory/perspective with a progressive approach?

5. What is an invisible structure of oppression and how does it work?

6. Can you think of a few subtle 'acts of resistance' to classroom material or to an instructor that students can carry out in the classroom that minimize the risk of retaliation?

Further Readings

Agger, Ben (2006). *Critical Social Theories: An Introduction*, 2nd edition. Boulder, CO: Westview Press. One of the leading critical theorists in North America, Agger provides a cogent and accessible explanation of critical social theory. Students are introduced to social and cultural theories such as the Frankfurt School, feminist theory, postmodernism, cultural studies, theories of multiculturalism and difference, and communication theory. Agger argues for an integration of these theories.

Lundy, Colleen (2004). *Social Work and Social Justice: A Structural Approach*. Peterborough, ON: Broadview Press. This book situates the Canadian welfare state and social work within the historical context of the globalized capitalist economy. An analysis of the structural forces that cause social problems is presented, along with practice skills and strategies for working with individuals, groups, and families that at the same time present a process of social change based on empowerment, critical consciousness, and provision of material resources.

Mullaly, Bob (2007). *The New Structural Social Work*. Don Mills, ON: Oxford University Press. This book reveals the shortcomings of traditional mainstream social work, which accepts and participates in the present social order rather than addressing the systemic social problems and oppressive relationships that result in privilege for a minority at the expense of the majority.

Payne, Malcolm (2005). *Modern Social Work Theory*, 3rd edition. Chicago, IL: Lyceum Books. The most comprehensive book on the market on social work theory. The author poses general questions about the definition of theory, its uses, and how it is put into practice. Current debates about social work theory are presented, as are individual schools of theory in terms of their major themes and applications, ranging from psychodynamic approaches to radical and critical perspectives, including anti-oppressive social work.

Rubington, Earl, and S. Martin Weinberg, eds. (2002). *The Study of Social Problems*, 6th edition. New York: Oxford University Press. This critically acclaimed book has long been a standard in its field. It presents seven perspectives used to examine social problems—social pathology, social disorganization, value conflict, deviant behaviour, labelling, the critical perspective, and social constructionism.

Chapter 2

Oppression: An Overview

All things are subject to interpretation. Whichever interpretation prevails at a given time is a function of power and not truth.

—Friedrich Nietzche

Diversity, Difference, and Oppression

The basis of oppression is difference (Preston-Shoot 1995; Stainton and Swift 1996; Thompson 2002)—not the fact or reality of difference but how we respond or do not respond to it. Society is characterized by immense variation, not only across such social groups as class, race, gender, sexual orientation, age, religion, and ability/ disability but within them as well (Thompson 2002). Michael Preston-Shoot (1995) has defined oppression as the exploitation of difference by a dominant group, whereas G. Singh (1996) has defined it as the denial of difference. In the former case, the dominant group uses difference to maintain and solidify its privileged position, and in the latter case, by denying difference, the dominant group also denies different levels of power and oppression in society, thus maintaining its privileged position in society. Oppression, of course, can occur from either the exploitation or denial of difference. Johnson (2006, 16) argues that the difficulties we encounter with respect to diversity or difference is that we have 'a world organized in ways that encourage people to use difference to include or exclude, reward or punish, credit or discredit, elevate or oppress, value or devalue, leave alone or harass.'

Rather than exploiting or denying difference, a society may actually promote, affirm, and even celebrate the diversity that exists within it. This approach is sometimes called 'the diversity approach' (Thompson 2002) or the 'politics of difference' (Young 1990). Historically, however, those regarded as different have been ignored, devalued, blamed, and dehumanized, with their difference used to justify such treatment (Preston-Shoot 1995). Most people who experience social problems and are served by social workers are members of groups different from the dominant group. Central to this is the power of some individuals and groups over others to define relationships and impose beliefs (Hugman 1991, cited in Preston-Shoot 1995).

The 'diversity' or 'politics of difference' approach to difference is based on the belief that the existence of diverse populations is a good thing in itself rather than a problem needing attention. However, because diversity is based on difference, there is always a possibility of difference leading to discrimination in a negative and unfair way rather than to a celebration. Thompson (2002, 43) argues that 'discrimination is not simply unfair in a narrow ethical sense, but [is] also a major source of disadvantage, pain, suffering and degradation—in short, oppression.' Although the concept of difference is widely used today in academic and everyday discourse, its meaning is not at all clear. In a very perceptive article looking at the concept of difference and how it does and should relate to social work curricula, Stainton and Swift (1996) review three separate theories of 'difference': (1) difference as value-neutral empirical phenomena; (2) difference as value-neutral but socially constructed; and (3) difference as a value-driven socially constructed approach.

Although it is beyond the scope of this chapter to present a complete overview of each theory, a brief summary of Stainton and Swift's critique is included here. They reject the 'difference as value-neutral empirical phenomena' theory on a number of grounds, including the fact that there is much literature suggesting that an objective, empirical realm lying outside the social realm is, if not impossible, at best ineffable (e.g., Berger and Luckmann 1966; Featherstone and Fawcett 1994; Foucault 1978). Also, Foucault (1978) has argued that knowledge is produced by discourse and is a social product rather than the articulation of some kind of empirical fact or universal truth. Stainton and Swift reiterate Noel's (1994) contention that one of the most effective means of oppression has been the reification of social phenomena as 'natural facts.' Examples of oppression based on claims of objective differences are women's traditional exclusion from the public sphere on the basis of their natural association with the private realm (Pateman 1989, cited in Stainton and Swift 1996) and black people being considered genetically inferior to white people, as reflected in the immigration policies of Canada, the US, Britain, and Australia during the nineteenth and early twentieth centuries. On these bases, Stainton and Swift (1996) reject the value-neutral concept of difference. The acceptance of objective knowledge as the basis of difference would conceal the power of the dominant group and allow it to retain a claim to truth, thus ensuring its power and control over subordinate groups—in the name of truth.

The second theory of difference presented by Stainton and Swift (1996) is the 'value-neutral but socially constructed view.' Although the theory presents ideas as socially constructed, this construction suggests neither an imbalance of power nor the existence of a dominant group. This view is part of the larger liberal ideology (see Mullaly 2007 for a detailed overview of the liberal paradigm and its influence on social work), which has been dominant in North America since the Second World War and influential in varying degrees in most other Anglo democracies. It minimizes social, economic, and political differences and subscribes to a belief in 'equal opportunity' as the solution to significant or unacceptable levels of inequality in society. In other words, inequality may exist in society, but if people work hard, play by the rules, and take advantage of opportunities available to them, then differences can be overcome or at least modified to the point that they are not problematic. This liberal view of society tends to overemphasize 'sameness'—deep down, we are all the same, and because we all have the same opportunities for development and success in life, then we should not interfere with this arrangement, which means that everyone should be treated the same way. Both social work and the social welfare systems in North America developed within a liberal paradigm, and as such, both reflect liberal values and beliefs, such as ignoring diversity and difference and developing social policies that provide superficial equality. An example of the latter would be the development of human rights legislation in Canada. Every province has the equivalent of a human rights commission to deal with instances of persons having their human rights violated (e.g., housing, employment, or public services denied to them on the basis of race, creed, gender, and so on). However, these commissions tend to deal with individuals only, and they focus on acts of 'discrimination' (i.e., violations of human rights legislation), which are much more restrictive than many acts and forms of 'oppression.' As pointed out by Preston-Shoot (1995), 'discrimination' is a legal term (with legal remedies), whereas 'oppression' is a social term (much of which has no legal remedies, such as the attitudes and acts of aversion and avoidance discussed in Chapter 3). In effect, by virtue of being part of the liberal paradigm, traditional social work and the welfare state have tended to reinforce the power and privilege of the dominant group in North American society.

Not only is the focus on 'sameness' problematic, so too is an overemphasis on 'difference.' This approach subjugates the individual to the group of which he or she is a member through both reductionist and an essentialist processes. With respect to the former, the overemphasis on difference serves to confine the individual to roles predetermined by dominant groups, such as 'a black person,' 'a poor person,' 'a disabled person.' In this way, the dominant group defines the *other* in ways that mask differences within the subordinate group. (This is one of the main criticisms of multiculturalism, which will be discussed in Chapter 5). The essentialist view is premised on the idea that all members of any particular subordinate group possess an innate essence, such as considering all women natural caregivers or all poor persons work-shy or all gay persons perverts. In effect, overemphasis on difference can lead to a justification of stereotypes as part of an identification of subordinate group members by the dominant group (Stainton and Swift 1996). And on a more personal level, an overemphasis on group differences interferes with the individual's ability to define the self just as much as the imposition of sameness by the dominant group on subordinate groups does.

Given the above critique of the two value-neutral theories, Stainton and Swift reject them and choose instead the 'difference as a value-driven and socially constructed theory.' This theory rejects both versions of the 'neutral' approach to difference and instead defines it as the exercise of power by a dominant group, which, as will be discussed below, often remains unintentional and invisible. In this way, difference always entails an *other* and always implies power and oppression. Dominelli (2002) points out that identity formation (to be discussed in Chapter 3) uses difference to mark one individual or group from another in an evaluative sense by setting up binary opposites, which allows one trait to be identified as superior or more desirable than another. 'These differences can emanate from a number of sources including the physical, psychological and sociological terrains' (2002, 37). Only by viewing difference in terms of oppression can we begin to unmask the dominant *one* and identify the dynamics and mechanisms of oppression, which is necessary to develop processes of emancipation (Stainton and Swift 1996).

Also, 'when the mechanisms of oppression and emancipation become the focus of analysis, rather than particular identity features creating difference, we have a means of encouraging solidarity rather than fostering competing claims' (Stainton and Swift 1996, 80). In other words, the 'value-driven approach' permits an analysis of social relationships that retains 'otherness' without accepting the dominant construction of an identity defined as 'different.'

Social Work Approaches to Difference

As noted above, mainstream social work, or what Dominelli (2002) calls the (social) maintenance school of social work, developed within the liberal paradigm and therefore tends to reflect liberal values and beliefs. It has emphasized 'sameness' in dealing with different groups, as evidenced by its stated belief in such value positions as impartiality, colour-blindness, equal opportunity, equal treatment, universal knowledge, unitary theory, and objective and value-neutral practice. Peter Leonard (2001, 1) criticizes the notion of 'sameness' on a societal level when he says,

> The emancipatory narrative of Western modernity has been shown to be based on claims to universal, objective knowledge, supported by a linear view of history whereby the West assumed the role in bringing development to the rest of the world—the steady march of Civilization. The ethnocentric arrogance of these claims leads to a profound inability to respond creatively to difference, and results in the suppression of the voices of the Other.

Mainstream social work in its liberal and modernist traditions is part of this 'ethnocentric arrogance.' It has attempted to deal with difference by accepting the dominant group as the norm and any differences to be the result of deviance, with the treatment plan being to restore the deviant individual or group to (dominant group) 'normalcy.' And mainstream social work education has traditionally taught from the voice of the dominant or oppressor group (Stainton and Swift 1996).

Over the past two decades or so, social work education and practice have extended their focus to include particular subordinate groups such as women, people of colour, and Aboriginal persons. Unfortunately, this development has been uneven and more than a little politicized. Stainton and Swift (1996) suggest that it has gone to the other extreme of sameness by overemphasizing difference, thus obscuring the commonalities across oppressed groups. The proliferation of different groups all demanding a 'course of their own' in social work curricula contributes to this phenomenon. Stainton and

Swift refer to it as an 'identity' model. These authors also express concern about a further ghettoization, prompting competition among subordinate groups for teaching resources and attention in the curriculum. As with any competition, there are winners and losers, with groups closest to the dominant group having their issues addressed while others are ignored. For example, the survey of social work curricula carried out by Stainton and Swift (1996) revealed that the curriculum content reflected the social power of each particular identity group such that courses on women were the most numerous while courses on gay and lesbian issues were the most rare. Another concern with the 'identity model' is that specialized courses may address the concerns of groups that are closest to the dominant group—women, for example—but ignore not only other subordinate groups but more marginalized subgroups of women such as women of colour, lesbians, and women with disabilities. A couple of other limitations to an 'identity model' is that it overlooks the fact that groups of oppressed people are not homogeneous but have much diversity within them and most oppressed people are oppressed in more than one way—that is, they are multiple-oppressed (e.g., a woman of colour is oppressed along both gender and racial lines). The advantages of a theory centred on difference itself is that it actively promotes an examination of both the dynamics and the techniques of oppression and emancipation and includes difference within subordinate groups along with multiple or intersectional oppression in its explorations. It is this approach to difference, oppression, and privilege that this book adopts. This is not to say that such an approach is problem-free. For example, Williams (1999) warns of two interrelated concerns around the concept of 'difference.' First, how do we connect specific positions that identity groups hold within a frame of larger social movements for equality? And second, how do we acknowledge differences within groups without losing the potential to mobilize around commonalities? These are among the issues discussed in Chapter 7.

The Nature of Oppression

Oppression is generally understood as the domination of subordinate groups in society by a powerful (politically, economically, socially, and culturally) group. It entails the various ways that this domination occurs, including how both structural arrangements and a ruling culture (i.e., the culture of the dominant group) favour the dominant over the subordinate group. However, 'oppression' as a term is not wholly satisfactory, because it implies, for some people (e.g., Lerner 1986), forceful subordination or evil intent on the part of oppressors. It also assumes a 'fixed identity' on the part of both oppressors and oppressed—that the world is divided into two groups and people belong to either one or the other but never to both. This dichotomy between oppressors and oppressed and the interaction between the two is the traditional view of oppression. 'Useful as these insights into oppression are, they are inadequate for painting a full picture of oppression: how it works; how it is experienced; how it is reproduced; and how it might be resisted and eradicated' (Dominelli 2002, 7). A major purpose of this book is to move beyond the limited concept of oppression as a binary relationship between people and to theorize and analyze oppression in ways that illuminate many of its complexities and facilitate effective forms of anti-oppressive social work practice. I agree with Lena Dominelli (2002) when she suggests that it is not enough for social workers to believe in social justice and equality. They must also understand oppression and the dynamics that (re)produce it. Otherwise, they run the risk of further oppressing members of subordinate groups directly and indirectly when trying to help them become part of the broader society and/or assume more control over their lives.

The position taken here is similar to that of Caroline Ramazanoglu (1989), who argues that although a single term is limited, 'oppression' is a relatively loose concept that can be qualified in different situations or at different historical moments. It does not need to entail, for example, evil intent on the part of men, with women as passive victims. Nor does it necessarily deny that persons can be both oppressors and oppressed (the subject of Chapter 7). For example, poor people over the course of history have been exploited and oppressed by affluent persons, yet poor people do not comprise a homogeneous group, as evidenced by the fact that there are 'working' and 'non-working' subgroups of poor people. Although both subgroups are dominated by affluent groups and are oppressed in the form of classism, the working poor also oppress the non-working poor in that they have been among the most vocal critics of the non-working poor and the welfare benefits that go to them. And, of course, in addition to these two subgroups of poor people, there are also other subgroups such as poor women, poor older persons, poor people of colour, poor persons with physical and mental disabilities, and poor white males. It is worth noting as well that members of the latter group may be oppressed as poor people but can also be oppressors in their role as white males.

Oppression, then, is not a static concept but a dynamic, multi-dimensional, and relational one. Dominelli (2002) points out that although oppression involves relations of domination that divide people into superior and inferior groups, these relations occur as interactions between people not only at the interpersonal level but at the cultural and institutional levels as well. Gil (1998, 11) argues that once oppression is 'integrated into a society's institutional order and culture, and into the individual consciousness of its people through socialization, oppressive tendencies come to permeate almost all relations.' He points out, however, that the intensity of oppression is not constant but varies over time as a result of acts of resistance and the emergence of liberation movements based on solidarity to overcome oppression (Freire 1994 [1970], cited in Gil 1998). Dominelli (2002, 9) agrees with this position:

> . . . oppression is socially constructed through people's actions with and behaviors towards others. Its interactive nature means that oppressive relations are not deterministic forces with preordained outcomes. . . . Thus, resistance to oppression can always take place . . . [and] can be undertaken both by individuals and through groups.

To understand what oppression is, it is necessary to know what oppression is not. As discussed in Chapter 1, no one in society is free from social structures. Such structures consist of boundaries, barriers, expectations, and regulations. One could make a loose argument that everyone in society is oppressed because one's choices or freedoms are restricted by the facts of social structures. For example, when a person drives an automobile, she or he is obliged to buckle the seat belt, drive on one particular side of the road, and obey all traffic laws and regulations. These restrictions on our freedom cannot be regarded as oppressive. Not everything that frustrates or limits or hurts a person is oppressive. So if one wishes to distinguish between what oppression is and is not, one has to look at the social context of a particular restriction, limit, or injury (Frye 1983).

Everyone suffers frustrations, restrictions, and hurt. What determines oppression is when a person is blocked from opportunities to self-development, is excluded from full participation in society, does not have certain rights that the dominant group takes for granted, or is assigned a second-class citizenship, not because of individual talent, merit, or failure, but because of his or her membership in a particular group or category of people. Examples of such groups in Western society are people of colour, women, poor people, and gay and lesbian persons. 'If an individual is oppressed, it is by virtue of being a member of a group or category of people that is systematically reduced, molded, immobilized. Thus, to recognize a person as oppressed, one has to see that individual as belonging to a group of a certain sort' (Frye 1983, 8).

What Is Oppression?

A group of social work students were overheard one day discussing the 'oppressive actions' of their faculty. 'They have all the power and they abuse it. They expect us to read all kinds of material, write papers, attend classes, participate in discussions, and they evaluate everything we do. On top of this, they are always asking us what areas we want to focus on, what methods of evaluation we should have, what our learning objectives should be, and what we think about everything. Jeez, they want us to do their job for them. There is just too much pressure on students in this program. It is so oppressive!' At another school, a group of social work students were overheard discussing the oppressive actions of their faculty. 'They never ask what we want to learn or how we can learn it or what ways of evaluation we think would be most valuable and helpful. They have rules and policies for everything and if we don't follow them—watch out! They never ask our opinions. They think just because they are the faculty that they know everything and that students have nothing to offer. It's so oppressive in this program!'

Arguably, not all groups in society are oppressed. Nor are all oppressed groups equally oppressed. Those in the dominant mainstream of society are less likely to be oppressed and more likely to be among the oppressors. Women are more likely to be oppressed (by men) as women. Men are less likely to be oppressed as men. People of colour are more likely to be oppressed (by white people) as people of colour. White people are less likely to be oppressed as white people. Gay, lesbian, and bisexual persons are more likely to be oppressed (by heterosexuals) as gay, lesbian, and bisexual persons. Heterosexual persons are less likely to be oppressed as heterosexual persons. This is not to say that oppression is a simple matter of dividing society into two groups: bad people (i.e., the oppressors) and victimized people (i.e., the oppressed). It is much more complex. As indicated above, given the relational nature of oppression, people may be oppressed in some relations and oppressors in others, while some relations may involve mutual oppression (Gil 1998). These issues are addressed in some detail in Chapter 7.

There is also a danger in presenting oppression as based on a singular group characteristic. Postmodernism cautions us against reducing oppression to monocausal structural explanations (Agger 1998), for as Lyotard (1988) points out, such explanations simplify the complexities and varieties of social reality by not acknowledging the incredible diversity inherent in people's differing gender, class, race, age, and sexuality positions. So although women may be oppressed as women, for example, there is great diversity among women that will result in more or less oppression. Yes, all women are oppressed by patriarchy (although there is no agreement among feminists as to how much), but many women are also oppressed by race, class, age, sexuality, standards of beauty, and so on. And many women may assume the role of oppressor along these same lines. Oppression is a complex and multifaceted social phenomenon.

In addition to the fact that oppression is group-based (i.e., dominant groups tend to be the oppressors of groups outside the mainstream), another feature of oppression is that it is not accidental (nor is it usually intentional).

> The experience of oppressed people is that the living of one's life is confined and shaped
> by forces and barriers which are not accidental or occasional and hence avoidable, but
> are systematically related to each other in such a way as to catch one between and
> among them and restrict or penalize motion in any direction [Albert et al. 1986, 19].

Given that oppression is perpetrated and perpetuated by dominant groups and is systematic and continuous in its application, a logical question is: why does it occur? Freire (1994 [1970]) argues that oppression occurs because it benefits the dominant group. It protects a kind of citizenship that is superior to that of oppressed groups. It protects the oppressors' access to a wider range of better-paying and higher-status work as well as preferential access to and treatment from our social institutions. Oppressed people serve as a ready supply of labour to carry out the menial and dangerous jobs in society, and they also serve as scapegoats for the dominant group during difficult times, often blamed for inflation, government deficits, crime, recessions, social disruptions, and so forth. In short, oppression carries out certain social or political functions for the dominant group, ensuring that society reproduces itself and maintains the same dominant–subordinate relationships.

The dominant group in society probably does not subscribe to the idea that it uses oppressive behaviour as a means of protecting its favourable position. Most people would not consider themselves as oppressors. In fact, most people would probably believe that oppressive behaviour should not be a part of a democratic society. Why, then, do they engage in oppressive practices? Paulo Freire (1994 [1970], 45) eloquently answers this question:

> The oppressors do not perceive their monopoly on having more as a privilege which dehumanizes others and themselves. . . . For them, having more is an inalienable right, a right they acquired through their own 'effort,' with their 'courage to take risks.' If others do not have more, it is because they are incompetent and lazy, and worst of all is their unjustifiable ingratitude towards the 'generous gestures' of the dominant class. Precisely because they are 'ungrateful' and 'envious,' the oppressed are regarded as potential enemies who must be watched.

Thus, the view that many oppressors tend to hold of oppressed groups is that they constitute potentially dangerous classes that must be controlled for the good of the whole society. This view is underpinned by a number of myths detailed by Bishop (1994) and summarized below. These myths are part of a larger ideology of oppression that rationalizes it as necessary for the preservation of society.

- Myth of scarcity: There is not enough to go around, which deflects attention from the fact that a small minority owns most of the world's resources.
- Myth of objective information: It is possible for one group (mainly white, Anglo-Saxon, bourgeois males) to observe humanity objectively, thus becoming the authoritative knower.
- Myth of might is right: The majority rules even if it means tyranny of the minority.
- Stereotyping: All members of a group are the same.
- Blaming the victim: People are responsible for their own oppression.
- Separation, competition, hierarchy: Human beings are competitive by nature and aspire to be ahead/above others.

To this set of myths that supports oppression, Haney (1989) adds two others:

- Myth of supremacy: The dominant educational system, with its emphasis on Western civilization, leads to a belief in the supremacy of a white, Western, male culture.

- Myth of class: Most people belong to the middle class, which lives in harmony with a 'higher' (superior) class—this belief mandates and then sanctions a dominant class and a subordinate class.

I would add one more myth to the above list—the myth that underpins liberal ideology: the myth of equal opportunity (or meritocracy). Because civil and political rights have been equalized under the law, it is believed that if one works hard and takes advantage of the opportunities (in education and on the job market, for example) available to all, one can succeed in life. If a person fails, the judgment is that the person did not take advantage of available opportunities (and therefore should not be helped). This myth overlooks or does not recognize the fact that not all people are in the same position to take advantage of so-called opportunities, since social position and resources will give some people preferred access to these so-called 'equal' opportunities. And, of course, since the majority of the people who 'fail' are disproportionately from historically disadvantaged and subordinate groups, the notion of superior/inferior groups is reinforced—an example of a process that Ryan (1976) calls 'blaming the victim' (outlined in the previous chapter).

Dominant–subordinate relations form part of a social hierarchy marked by differences in power, status, and resources. A hierarchy is often shaped as a pyramid, with small numbers (a privileged elite) near the top and large numbers (less privileged subordinate people) near the bottom (McGregor 1997; Moane 1999). Most major systems in Western societies are hierarchically organized and male-dominated— politics, economics, religion, art, culture, health, and education (Seager 1997). However, this male domination is more prevalent in some countries (e.g., France, Portugal, and Greece) and less prevalent in others—the Scandinavian countries have the highest number of women in the top positions of these hierarchies (Karl 1995). Also, the males at the top of the hierarchies are primarily of a particular race (white), religion (Christian), class (bourgeois), and sexual orientation (heterosexual) and tend to be able-bodied (Moane 1999). It must be noted here that hierarchies also exist within subordinate groups themselves (Walkerdine 1996; Wineman 1984), a theme that will be explored in Chapter 7.

When a hierarchy becomes established, a dynamic of superiority-inferiority or domination-subordination is inevitable, and there is difficulty maintaining the conceptualization of the lesser (inferior) person having as much intrinsic worth or value as the superior person (Miller 1986). Once a group is defined as inferior, the label tends to become permanent (Gil 1998). The superior group judges members of inferior groups as incapable of performing roles or functions that the dominant group values and therefore assigns them roles and functions that are poorly valued (such as providing unpaid or ill-paid services). Dominelli (2002) and Miller (1986) remind us that superior-inferior relations are socially constructed by the dominant group and that the socially constructed inferior capacities of members of subordinate groups are considered innate or natural and immutable. For example, many men consider women biologically inferior and emotionally weak but also natural caregivers. Therefore, it is believed, the best place for a woman is in the home (of a man), looking after it and (his) children—functions that are not valued. Such stereotypes reinforce, in the dominant group's eyes, the need for hierarchies, because they reflect normal and natural social divisions and relations.

Using anthropological studies, Gil (1998) shows that relations of domination, subordination, and exploitation within and among human societies were never, nor are they now, normal, natural, and inevitable. Rather, they were and are the results of human choices and actions. An essentialist argument is sometimes made that domination and subordination are natural and inevitable outcomes of our human nature because the evidence is all around that we naturally compete and try to gain dominance over others and pursue our own individual interests in almost all activities. However, 'human nature' is a slippery concept. Gil (1976b) contends that you can make an argument that human nature is whatever you want it to be by the use of selective evidence. A counter-argument, for example, is that a preponderance of evidence shows it is natural for people to co-operate with each other and work towards the collective good of society. In other words, it may be human nature (if there is a human nature) to be both competitive and co-operative, and the society will emphasize one or the other. That is, human nature is socially constructed or produced and changeable, not universal, innate, and essential. Gil (1998) also argues against the inevitability thesis of oppression by referring to (1) societies in the past that were not characterized by oppression and inequality and (2) liberation movements throughout history that have emerged to challenge and overcome oppression and injustice.

Oppression as a Social Justice Issue

David Gil (1994, 98) makes the point that although social work professional codes of ethics require social workers to 'promote social justice,' these codes do not specify the meaning of social justice, instead treating it as if it were self-evident. Yet social justice cannot be promoted unless its meaning is first clarified, and we must also examine its relationship to oppression/anti-oppression.

In *Justice and the Politics of Difference*, Iris Marion Young presents a concept of social justice that goes beyond mere distributive/redistributive notions of social justice. Because it encapsulates such elements of oppression as social practices and processes that cause inequitable distributions in the first place, I believe that Young's concept of social justice has much more potential for understanding oppression than any distributive notion of social justice. In defining social justice as 'the elimination of institutionalized domination and oppression,' Young (1990, 15) contends that contemporary philosophical theories of justice do not conceive justice so broadly. Instead, they restrict themselves to an interpretation of social justice as the morally proper distribution (or redistribution) of benefits and burdens among all of society's members. The benefits to be distributed would include both material resources, such as wealth and income, and non-material social goods, such as rights, opportunities, and power. Issues of distributional justice are analogous to persons dividing a stock of goods and comparing the amount or size of the portions individuals have. Injustice, according to this distributive notion of social justice, would be defined as a situation in which one group has a monopoly over a particular good. Even explicitly socialist discussions of social justice fall within the distributional theory, since the principles of distribution (need versus market) are considered paramount in social justice. What distinguishes the distributive perspective of social justice, then, is the tendency to see social justice and distribution as co-extensive concepts.

Welfare capitalism and conventional social work have also adopted the distributional concept of social justice in that the focus has been on the distribution and redistribution of income and other resources (often defined in terms of some kind of social minimum). Discussion has tended to centre on inequalities of wealth and income and the extent to which the state can or should alleviate the suffering of the poor and disadvantaged. Even progressive social work and social welfare writers tend to equate social justice with a redistribution of goods and services. An example is Lena Dominelli, who has written landmark books on feminist social work (Dominelli and McLeod 1989), on anti-racist social work (Dominelli 1988), and on anti-oppressive social work (2002). She contends that 'those endorsing an emancipatory approach to social work have an explicit commitment to social justice' (2002, 4). She then criticizes the law as limited in pursuing social justice: 'Its [the law's] tendency to individualise collective problems can only mean that *redistributive justice* remains beyond its scope. Yet it is precisely *this form of justice* which black activists, women, and other oppressed groups are demanding' (1988, 14; emphasis added). It may be that some oppressed groups are demanding this form of justice, but again, it is limited justice because it does nothing to alter the processes and practices that allow for an unjust share of society's resources to go to one group in the first place.

Obviously, the immediate provision of basic goods and services for people suffering severe deprivation must be a first priority for any group or program seeking social justice. Any conception of justice must take into account the vast differences in the amount of material goods that exist in our society, in which thousands starve and live on the streets while others can have anything they want (Young 1990). From an anti-oppressive perspective, Young identifies a major limitation of the distributional notion of social justice. Equating the scope of social justice with distribution only is misleading in two ways: (1) the social structures, processes, and practices that caused the maldistribution in the first place are ignored, and (2) the limits of the logic of extending the notion of distribution to such non-material goods and resources as rights and opportunities are not recognized. Let us examine these two limitations.

1. *Ignoring social structures, processes, and practices.* Young notes that the distributional view of justice assumes a social atomist or individualist perspective of people in that they are externally related to the goods they possess and only related to one another in

terms of a comparison of the amount of goods they possess. The institutional contexts within which distribution occurs are ignored. These institutional contexts go beyond a narrow Marxist account of the mode of production and include all social structures, processes, and practices, the rules and norms that guide them, and the language and symbols that mediate social interactions within them. It is this institutional context that affects distribution—what is distributed, how it gets distributed, who distributes it, who receives it, and what the outcome is. An example presented by Young is economic inequality. Distributive discussions often omit the decision-making structures that determine economic relations in society. Young writes:

> Economic domination in our society occurs not simply because persons have more wealth and income than others, as important as this is. Economic domination derives at least as much from the corporate and legal structures and procedures that give some persons the power to make decisions about investment, production, marketing, employment, interest rates, and wages that affect millions of other people. Not all who make these decisions are wealthy or even privileged, *but the decision-making structure operates to reproduce distributive inequality and the unjust constraints on people's lives* [1990, 23; emphasis added].

2. *Limits of extending the notion of distribution to non-material goods and resources.* Advocates of the distributive theory of justice claim that any issue of justice, including such non-material goods as rights and opportunities, may be treated as some thing or aggregate of things to be possessed and/or distributed and redistributed. Young argues that such treatment produces a misleading conception of the issues of justice involved because it reifies aspects of social life that are better understood as functions of rules, relations, and processes than as things.

Because rights and opportunities are not possessions, distributing or redistributing rights and opportunities is not the same as distributing or redistributing income. Some groups may have rights and opportunities that other groups do not, but extending them to the groups that do not have them does not entail the formerly privileged group surrendering some of its rights and/or opportunities, as it does with a redistribution of income. Rights are not things but relationships, institutionally defined rules specifying what people can do in relation to others. 'Rights refer to doing more than having, to social relationships that enable or constrain action' (Young 1990, 25). Given that the dominant group does not lose any of its rights by extending the same rights or opportunities to others, it would seem that such social changes would be relatively acceptable and straightforward. However, the infamous Proposition 8 passed in the November 2008 election by the voters of California changed the state constitution so that it now restricts the definition of marriage to a union between a man and woman, thus eliminating the right of same-sex couples to marry. In effect, a dominant (heterosexual) group has a right that the subordinate (gay and lesbian) group does not have. Furthermore, if the right to marry were extended to same-sex couples, it would not interfere with the right of heterosexual couples to marry. This differential treatment was rationalized by the dominant group on the belief that same-sex marriage would damage society, threaten the sanctity of traditional marriage, fly in the face of religious teachings and scripture, and legitimate sexual promiscuity and perversion. Support for Proposition 8 is a clear example of the dominant group using a socially constructed negative view of a subordinate group to oppress it.

It should be noted here that even when certain rights are extended to subordinate or oppressed groups, there is no guarantee that the subordinate group members will be able to exercise these rights. In other words, people may be given certain rights but still be unable to exercise them because of particular social constraints based on class, gender, race, and so on. For example, a person living in poverty may have a right to a fair trial but be financially unable to hire proper legal counsel.

Similarly, opportunity connotes doing rather than having. It is a condition of enablement rather than possession, which usually involves a system of social rules and social relations as well as an individual's skills and abilities. Having opportunities may lead to securing material goods such as food, shelter, and a job, but it is no guarantee that these goods and services will be secured. Just as people may have certain rights but are unable to exercise them, so too might people have certain opportunities but because of particular social conditions and practices be constrained from using them. For example, in Australia or in North America, we may say that Aboriginal persons have the opportunity to obtain an education, but education occurs in a complex context of social relations. Aboriginal communities tend to have inferior schools, fewer material resources, and less access to tutors and computers. As well, Aboriginal children often experience a degree of culture shock in schools outside Aboriginal communities. This is not to say that distribution is irrelevant to educational opportunities, but opportunity has a wider scope than distribution (Young 1990).

The above discussion of the distributive theory of social justice shows that it contains a major limitation. By focusing on something that must be identifiable and assignable, it reifies social relations and processes and institutional rules. It gives primacy to substance over relations, rules, and processes by conceiving of people as social atoms, which fails to appreciate that individual identity and capacities are themselves the products of social relations and processes (Taylor 1985, cited in Young 1990). Such an atomistic social ontology ignores or obscures the importance of institutional contexts and rules and social relations and processes for understanding issues of social justice. An adequate conception of social justice must enable an understanding and evaluation of these social phenomena as well as the substance of distribution.

Heller (1987) suggests a conception of justice that includes the above social phenomena that are absent from the distributional concept. She views justice as primarily the virtue of citizenship wherein persons collectively deliberate about problems and issues facing them within their institutions and actions, under conditions free from oppression and domination, with reciprocity and mutual tolerance[1] of differences. Young argues that this conception of justice shifts the focus from distribution issues to procedural issues of participation in deliberation and decision making. A norm would be just or fair only if people who follow it had an effective voice in its consideration and acceptance. A social condition would be just only if it enabled all people to meet their needs and exercise their freedoms. A social process would be just only if it were an inclusive process with respect to different social groupings. A social practice would be just only if it were in accordance with the way that people carrying it out would like to be treated themselves. Social injustice from this perspective entails not only an unfair distribution of goods and resources but includes any norm, social condition, social process, or social practice that interferes with or constrains one from fully participating in society—that is, from becoming a full citizen.

This concept of social justice is empowering because it goes beyond a concern with distribution to include the institutional conditions necessary for the development and exercise of individual capacities and collective communication and co-operation (Young 1990). Oppression consists of institutional conditions that inhibit or prevent one from becoming a full participant in society. A society may be evaluated as just to the degree that it contains and supports the institutional conditions necessary for the promotion of the universal value that everyone has equal intrinsic worth. For all those concerned with developing an adequate conception of social justice and for those committed to social justice in practice, oppression must be a central concern.

The Genealogy of Modern-Day Oppression and the Politics of Identity

As pointed out above, most members of a dominant group would not consider themselves oppressors. Rather, their oppressive and exploitative behaviours, policies, and practices make sense to them because they are largely compatible with the pursuit of socially sanctioned goals and with the internal logic of established social institutions. Gil (1998, 233–234) asks, 'how and why did human societies evolve ways of life in which oppression and injustice came to be taken for granted and considered legitimate, and appropriate?' Looking for a single, universal causal explanation for oppression is of course futile, given its complexity and its historical and contextual variability. However, a number of writers have attempted to develop genealogies of oppression. A review of a few of them increases our understanding of oppression as a social phenomenon.

Using anthropological, historical, and archaeological sources, Gil (1998) contends that oppression is not inevitable, since it only became firmly established in human societies within the past 10 000 years (out of a history of 300 000 years) following the development and spread of agriculture, animal husbandry, and crafts, which gradually generated a stable economic surplus. These new conditions facilitated the emergence of complex divisions of work, social castes, and the spatial and social differentiation of societies into rural and urban areas—all of which set the conditions for oppression and injustice. Using comparative cultural studies, Sidanius and Pratto (1999) argue that before economic systems began to produce and sustain surpluses and wealth, social structures were relatively flat, with the exception of gender and age hierarchies that they claim are essentially universal across all known societies. 'As soon as a society can produce an economic surplus, this surplus facilitates the development of role specialization, coalition formation among males, and the creation of an arbitrarily-set hierarchy' (1999, 299). Arbitrarily set hierarchies include such social characteristics as class, race, ethnicity, tribe, and nation. Haney (1989) presents another historical analysis of oppression. She cites four formative events between the fourteenth and nineteenth centuries in Europe and England that shaped contemporary patterns of racism, sexism, classism, and other expressions of oppression: (1) the slave trade; (2) the 'enclosure movement' whereby men with money began to regard land as a commodity to make more money; (3) the rise of the modern family and 'invention of childhood' whereby patriarchy became entrenched and the home became the private, intimate space—the king's castle; and (4) the period during which nature became increasingly viewed as an object to be subdued and mastered rather than simply understood or lived with—leading to an image of nature as penetrated and raped (i.e., nature became feminized).

Whatever genealogical account of oppression is presented, there is agreement in the anti-oppression literature, especially among feminist writers, that oppression today was most influenced by post-Renaissance 'man,' his science, and his theories (Weedon 1997). Modern-day forms of oppression are not superstitious carry-overs from the Dark Ages. On the contrary, Young (1990) states that nineteenth- and early twentieth-century scientific and philosophical discourse explicitly proposed and legitimated formal theories of race, sex, age, and national superiority. She also contends that the methods of science and the attributes of the scientist have in part contributed to the formulation of these theories of superiority/inferiority.

The social construction of a white, bourgeois male as a superior being should not be surprising. In Western thought, the philosopher and the scientist (that is, the knower and the producer of knowledge) came from the same social context—from bourgeois and male-dominated European families. Only children of bourgeois or aristocratic families had the resources to pursue education and scholarship (among other opportunities, such as politics, commerce, or leadership of the armed forces). Garner (2000), in her overview of the development of Western social theory, points out that by the end of the nineteenth century, many social theorists taught at universities and every major theorist was a man of European background. She states that

> [W]omen did not enter organized scholarly intellectual life till the turn of the
> [twentieth] century; they published books of travel observations and insightful
> memoirs, but were simply not included in the more abstract, ongoing conversations
> about the nature of society that formed the heart of social theory. Equally excluded
> were all people in colonized societies and in regions outside of the western, Christian
> world. Most workers and peasants, wherever they lived, were excluded because they

were unlikely to obtain the education needed to enter intellectual and academic life. Elites in the Americas and eastern and southern Europe were marginally included in modern, western intellectual life if they spoke English, French, or German, and appeared like western Europeans in looks and culture, but both distance and western European prejudices kept them at the edge of academic and intellectual life [2000, 3–4].

Thus, the group of aristocratic white males not only controlled the economy, the political system, the army, and the culture but also controlled the production of ideas and knowledge. And as will be argued below, the ideas and knowledge they produced under the banner of science both reflected and reinforced their claims of superiority and their positions of power and dominance.

There has been much criticism of modern scientific reason by critical theorists, feminists, and postmodernists. These criticisms, summarized in the previous chapter, have in part punctured the authority of modern scientific reason. A major aspect of the criticism has been directed at the construction of the scientist and philosopher as a knower or subject standing outside the objects of knowledge—autonomous, objective, and neutral. The subject is a socially detached observer, standing in the immediate presence of reality but without any involvement in it. Moreover, as Foucault (1977) notes, these observations are not mere passing looks but normalizing gazes that assess their object according to some hierarchical standard. Some of the particulars or attributes of the object are then defined as deviant or are devalued in comparison to the norm.

Closely related to Garner's work (noted above) on how Western scholarship developed a Eurocentric, male bias, Young (1990) cites other scholarship revealing the bourgeois, male, and European biases that have been attached to the notion of rationality. That is, the virtues of science have also become the virtues of masculinity—detachment, careful measurement and the manipulation of instruments, comprehensive generalizing and reasoning, and authoritative speech supported by evidence (Keller 1986 and Merchant 1978, both cited in Young 1990). Those articulating and carrying out the code of modern scientific reason were white, bourgeois males speaking for themselves and unmindful that there might be other positions. In other words, not only did they become the knowers or truth-seeking subjects, they also became the standards against which all other groups (objects) were measured. This already privileged group assumed the privilege of the authoritative subject of knowledge, and groups they defined differently became the objects of their distancing and mastering observations.

The imposition of scientific reason's dichotomy between subject and object on hierarchical relations of race, gender, class, and nationality . . . has deep and abiding consequences for the structuring of privilege and oppression. The privileged groups lose their particularity; in assuming the position of the scientific subject they become . . . agents of a universal view from nowhere. The oppressed groups, on the other hand, are locked in their objectified bodies, blind, dumb, and passive. The normalizing gaze of science focused on the objectified bodies of women, Blacks, Jews, homosexuals, old people, the mad and feeble-minded. From its observations emerged theories of sexual, racial, age, and mental or moral superiority [Young 1990, 127].

This superior/inferior, normal/abnormal, good/bad distinction did not guarantee respectability and superiority for all white bourgeois men, however, because even they were subject to disease and deviance, especially if they succumbed to sexual impulse. The nineteenth-century medical and moral literature is replete with male fears of becoming effeminate. Therefore, manly men had to protect their health and beauty (i.e., their manly virtues) by exercising control over sexual urges. Bishop (1994) contends that every oppressed group has been assigned at least one negative sexual myth, usually that the oppressed group is sexually out of control, immoral, or perverted. All women secretly want to be raped. Gays and lesbians are perverts who engage in unnatural sex acts and want to seduce children. Poor people breed like rabbits. Black men want to rape white women. Black women are sexier than white women. Aboriginal women cannot say no. Disabled and old persons have no sexuality. These stereotyped attributes, of course, reinforced the socially constructed and scientifically legitimated belief that groups other than young, white, bourgeois males were inferior and degenerate.

Scientific legitimation of inequality along lines of gender, class, race, and other social divisions is by no means an artifact of the nineteenth century. The past few decades have seen a resurgence of attempts to define human nature as the product of biological inevitability and assertions that biology determines destiny—including capitalist competition, gender roles, race relations, national and international antagonisms, and so on (Rose 1982). 'Biological determinism' is an attempt at a total explanation of human social existence based on two principles: (1) social phenomena are the direct results of the behaviours of individuals, and (2) individual behaviours are the direct results of inborn physical characteristics (Lewontin, Rose, and Kamin 1984). Biological determinism has been adopted as a social theory by some sociologists and is known as sociobiology. It has provided the dominant group in general, and the New Right in particular, with a reductionist theory of human nature that ascribes all inequality or social differences to perceived physical differences such as gender, skin colour, and class. However, there is nothing biologically intrinsic in being, for example, black, Jewish, gay or lesbian, or poor. In addition, biological determinism is more than a theory. It is politics as well, for if social inequalities are the result of our biologies, then no social intervention can significantly alter social structures or the positions of people within them. Indeed, we should not even try, because differences among human beings are biologically determined and therefore natural and fixed.

Lewontin, Rose, and Kamin (1984) cite some examples of studies in which policy-makers used biological explanations of social phenomena to reject or terminate social programs. The difference in IQ scores between black and white persons was attributed in one American study (Jensen 1969) to the genetic inferiority of black people (not to any cultural or linguistic biases of the instruments) and suggested that they would be better served if they were educated for the mechanical tasks to which their genes predisposed them. This claim of genetic inferiority was extended from black people to the working class in general in a subsequent study by psychologist Richard Herrnstein (1971). The Nixon administration in the United States seized upon these genetic arguments to make cuts in education and welfare. In the 1970s, claims of intellectual inferiority associated with (non-white) race by a psychologist (Eysenck 1971; 1973) in the UK became an integral part of the campaign against Asian and black immigration in order to curb demands on the welfare system. Claims of basic biological differences between men and women with respect to temperament, cognitive ability, and 'natural' social roles (i.e., claims for the immutability of male supremacy by such academic biologists as E.O. Wilson) contributed to the rejection of the Equal Rights Amendment to the constitution of the United States in the mid-1970s. In spite of being discredited time and again, biological determinism is still used by dominant groups and their allies to legitimate domination and social inequality.

Biological determinism or sociobiology is really an ideology of oppression, or what Rose (1998) calls 'ultra-Darwinism,' rather than science. Feminists and post-modernists, among others, have shown us that social categories are by no means self-evident and unproblematic. The production of social identity changes for any group over time with respect to its defined membership, its relationship to the mainstream, and its position of privilege or punishment (Adam 1978). In addition, the essentialism of biological explanations implies that there are no differences within social categories—all women are the same, all black people are the same, and so on. Social inequality requires the means to distinguish between sameness and difference, self and other, among people. And biological determinism helps to provide such means.

In a pre-figurative work to postmodernism, Adam (1978, 10) stated:

> A moment's reflection will reveal the extraordinary triviality of traits per se by which disqualification from social opportunities is achieved. A momentous world of meanings accrues about, for example, gender, skin tone, erotic preference [sexual orientation], etc., as these qualities are seized upon as bases for social inequality. The minority [subordinate] situation is more a matter of social definition than of social difference.

Once a social definition is constructed, various social practices and psychological responses come into play to contribute to its institutionalization. In effect, an aggregate of differentiated individuals are categorized (constructed) as a distinct group and consequently share a common status assigned to them by others and are subject to categorical treatment. They become united only by a negative identity.

The Dynamics of Oppression

As argued above, racial, gender, class, mental, and other theories of superiority generated by biological determinism and by nineteenth-century scientific reason have been discredited by twentieth-century research and social movements. There is now a considerable number of pieces of social legislation and social rules in the form recognition of civil, political, and human rights and affirmative action and employment equity programs that express a commitment to equality among social groups. Ideologies of natural superiority and group domination no longer seem to hold the influence they once did in our society. Nonetheless, various forms of oppression are still rooted in contemporary society, but they appear in different manifestations, having both continuities and discontinuities with past structures.

In its current form, oppression does not mean the exercise of tyranny by a ruling group (at least not in democratic societies). Oppression does not usually occur today through some coercive rule of law (although sometimes it does, as in cases of anti-union legislation) or because of the evil intentions of a dominant group. It mostly occurs through the systemic constraints on subordinate groups, which take the form of unquestioned norms, behaviours, and symbols, and in the underlying assumptions of institutional rules. Young (1990, 41) contends that people suffer disadvantage and injustice 'not because a tyrannical power coerces them, but because of the everyday practices of a well-intentioned liberal society.' Oppression is more effective in achieving its apparent function of maintaining the privileged position of the dominant group when both victims and perpetrators are unaware of the dynamics of oppression. When people perceive their situation as natural and inevitable and there is an illusion of freedom and opportunity, no other weapons are necessary to defend and legitimate unjust ways of life that benefit the privileged groups at the expense of the oppressed groups.

Much of modern day oppression in Western democracies is structurally systemic, covert or hidden, and unintentional.

> In this extended structural sense oppression refers to the vast and deep injustices some groups suffer as a consequence of often unconscious assumptions and reactions of well-meaning people in ordinary interactions, media and cultural stereotypes, and structural features of bureaucratic hierarchies and market mechanisms, in short, the normal processes of everyday life. We cannot eliminate this structural oppression by getting rid of the rulers or making new laws, because oppressions are systematically reproduced in major economic, political, and cultural institutions [Young 1990, 41].

For us to understand the meaning and practice of oppression, Foucault (1977) suggests that we go beyond viewing oppression as the conscious and intentional acts of one group against another. Instead, oppression is often found in such areas as education, the production and distribution of goods and services, public administration, the delivery of health and social services, and the like. In other words, many people contribute to maintaining and reproducing oppression in carrying out many of their day-to-day activities, but they do not understand themselves to be agents of oppression. This is not to say that members of oppressed groups are never intentionally harmed, as evidenced by the rape of women, physical attacks on gay men, locked-out workers, and the harassment of people of colour. Nor does it mean that members of oppressed groups never oppress others, as indicated by the verbal attacks of the working poor on the non-working poor, by physical attacks of youth gang members belonging to one oppressed group against youth belonging to another oppressed group, or by attacks on members belonging to the same oppressed group. In spite of these acts of intentional oppression, the contention here is that most oppression today is systemic and unintentional because it is built into our social institutions and carried out unconsciously in our day-to-day activities.

'I Have Never Been Oppressed'

One day in a class on anti-oppressive social work, a discussion was taking place on gender oppression. Fiona, a young, single, upper-middle-class, white student exclaimed in an animated tone, 'I think all this talk on how women today are downtrodden is grossly exaggerated. I can honestly say that I have *never* experienced oppression. I had all the things I needed while growing up. No one has ever told me that because I am a woman I could not do whatever I wanted. I am in university today and will be a professional social worker when I am finished. This is not to say that some women don't have it hard, but so do other people. To say that society oppresses women today is a "crock".' The instructor asked the other women in the class if they agreed with Fiona. A lively and awareness-raising discussion ensued.

What are some of the systemic and unintentional daily activities that contribute to oppression in today's society? Bishop (1994) outlines several components that appear to be common to all forms or sources of oppression and help to maintain oppression. First, a position of supremacy is held by the dominant group, and it is backed by 'power over' others. This power can include greater material resources, physical strength, weapons, information, decision-making, and control of the media. Both groups internalize this hierarchy and act it out, thus reproducing the hierarchy with minimal resistance. Second, all social groups incur stereotypes. Although stereotypes can be positive, they are most often hurtful and used in a damaging way against subordinate groups. The more powerful groups in society cannot be hurt by stereotypes as much as those with little power. Third, all oppressed groups are susceptible to violence or its threat in society. Beatings, threats, vandalism, and harassment are activities sometimes perpetrated on subordinate groups to keep them in their place whenever they step out of it or think of doing so. Fourth, as mentioned above, all oppressed groups have been assigned at least one negative characteristic about their sexuality. Usually it is a belief that members of the oppressed groups are sexually out of control, perverted, or immoral. Fifth, subordinate groups are at greater risk of being separated from their children than are members of the dominant group. Poor people, Aboriginals, single mothers, blacks, gays and lesbians, and immigrants are all suspect in terms of their ability to care properly for their children, and consequently they experience more surveillance and intrusions and have less protection of their rights than those in the dominant group. Fear of losing one's children is, of course, a powerful social control mechanism for obtaining compliance or conformity from subordinate group members.

Forms of Oppression

Although all oppressed groups experience some obstacles to developing their capacities and to participating fully in society, it is impossible to give one essential or universal definition of oppression. Iris Young (1990) has developed a set of five categories or forms of oppression (summarized below) that encompass both distributive issues of injustice and social structures, relations, and practices that go beyond distribution. The first three forms or 'faces' of oppression emerge from the social division of labour, the fourth from culture, and the fifth from violence. Although not all oppressed groups experience all five forms of oppression, they do experience at least one of them and usually more than one.

1. Exploitation

As a form of oppression, exploitation refers to the social processes whereby the dominant group is able to accumulate and maintain status, power, and assets from the energy and labour expended by subordinate groups. Exploitation is primarily experienced by working-class persons, women, and people of colour. With respect to workers, capitalism systematically transfers powers from workers through the private ownership of the means of production and through markets that allocate labour and the ability to buy goods. As well, the powers of workers are diminished by more than the amount transferred, because workers also suffer material deprivation and a loss of control over their work, which results in a loss of self-respect.

The injustice of class division goes beyond the fact that a few people have enormous wealth while many people have little. Exploitation is realized through a structural relationship between the have and have-not groups. Social rules about what work is, who works for whom, how work is to be compensated, and how the results of work are to be distributed and used all operate through a systematic process to produce and reproduce relations of power and inequality.

Women are exploited not only in the Marxist sense that they are wage workers or that their domestic labour is covered by the wages a family receives but also in terms of their sexual labour, nurturing, caring, and smoothing over workplace tensions (Alexander 1987; Young 1990). These tasks, which are often unnoticed and unacknowledged, involve women expending energy in jobs to enhance the wealth, status, or comfort of others, usually men who are released to carry out what is often considered more important and creative work. In other words, the power, freedom, and status of men is often attributable to women who work for them, which constitutes a systematic and unreciprocated transfer of power and energy from women to men (Young 1990).

Along with class and gender, Young argues that there is also a race-specific form of exploitation resulting from members of non-white groups performing menial labour tasks for white people. Wherever there is racism in a predominantly white society, there is an expectation that members of non-white groups will carry out servant roles for the dominant group—domestics, bellhops, maids, non-professional nannies, porters, busboys, janitors, dishwashers, and the like. In addition to servile, unskilled, minimum-wage, and low-status work with little autonomy, these jobs involve a transfer of energy whereby the servers enhance the status of the served.

Besides Young's contention that menial labour constitutes a form of exploitation, dangerous work can also be considered exploitative. During times of war, it is usually poor white and black workingmen who are on the front lines of the battle, while white bourgeois males—high-ranking officers and officials in departments of defence—direct operations far from the front lines and take credit for victory. Aboriginal men are often recruited as construction workers on skyscrapers and bridges. Female workers are subject to sexual harassment on the job, a type of corporate violence to which men are not typically exposed. Many female workers who earn a living by making repetitive wrist, arm, and back movements, such as secretaries and other keyboard operators, are subject to repetitive strain injuries such as tendonitis and carpal tunnel syndrome (Dekeseredy and Hinch 1991).

The above forms of exploitation cannot be eliminated by a redistribution of material resources. As long as current structural relations and institutionalized practices remain unaltered, the process of transferring energy and labour from the exploited to the dominant group will reproduce an unequal distribution of goods and benefits. 'Bringing about justice where there is exploitation requires reorganization of institutions and practices of decision-making, alteration of the division of labour, and similar measures of institutional, structural, and cultural change' (Young 1990, 53).

2. Marginalization

Marginalization primarily affects people of colour, old and young persons, many single mothers and their children, physically and mentally disabled people, unskilled workers, and Aboriginal people. These groups constitute a growing underclass permanently confined to the margins of society because the labour market cannot or will not accommodate them.

Young suggests that marginalization is perhaps the most dangerous form of oppression because it excludes whole groups of people from useful and meaningful participation in society and this in turn may lead to severe material deprivation. Even though advanced capitalist societies have put modern welfare systems in place to deal with the material deprivation, in Anglo democracies, at least, welfare redistribution has not eliminated large-scale suffering, and in the present political climate there is no assurance that the welfare state will continue. As well, the welfare state in liberal democracies has been criticized for denying those who become dependent on it of certain rights and freedoms that others take for granted (Galper 1975; 1980). Welfare bureaucracies have often treated poor people, elderly persons, and disabled individuals who rely on them for support and services with punitive, demeaning, patronizing, and arbitrary policies and regulations that interfere with their basic rights to privacy, respect, and autonomy.

Even when material deprivation is not present, marginalization may still occur. Many old people, for example, have the material means to live comfortable lives, but they are excluded from meaningful social participation and cannot exercise their capacities in socially defined and recognized ways. Most of society's productive and recognized activities are age- and work-related. Thus, older people are often subject to marginality in the form of feelings of uselessness, boredom, and a lack of self-respect. Marginalization constitutes a basic feature of injustice and oppression. To overcome it requires both restructuring productive activity to address a right of participation within the wage system and establishing some socially productive activity outside the wage system.

3. Powerlessness

Powerlessness consists of inhibitions against the development of one's capacities, a lack of decision-making power in one's working life, and exposure to disrespectful treatment because of the status one occupies. It primarily affects non-professional workers but to a lesser extent affects people of colour and women as well. Powerlessness is based on the social division of labour but is more complex than the traditional Marxist model of class exploitation in that it recognizes the distinction between the 'middle class' and the 'working class' as a social division of labour between professionals and non-professionals.

Most workplaces in advanced capitalist societies are organized hierarchically so that direct participation of workers is rare and decisions (in both the private and public sectors) are imposed on workers and citizens. However, this decision-making power is often mediated by agents who may have no say in the decision but do exercise power and authority over others in carrying out decisions and policies. The powerless are those who do not have power or authority even in this mediated sense; they 'exercise little creativity or judgement in their work, have no technical expertise or authority, ... and do not command respect' (Young 1990, 58–59). Non-professionals suffer this type of oppression; professionals (white males at least) do not.

The status privilege of professionals has three aspects (Sennett and Cobb 1972, cited in Young 1990). First, a professional develops her or his capacities and gains recognition by obtaining a university education and through subsequent professional advancement with an accompanying rise in status. Second, professionals have considerable work autonomy relative to non-professionals and usually have some authority over others, whether subordinate workers or clients. Third, the privileges of the professional extend beyond the workplace to a whole way of life or culture associated with respectability. The norms of respectability in our society—in terms of dress, speech, tastes, and demeanour—are those of a professional culture. If one wishes to make a good impression, whether seeking a bank loan or applying for a job or appearing in court, one will often try to look 'professional' or 'respectable' as part of his or her efforts. Typically, professionals receive more respectful treatment in our society than non-professionals do.

Allies or Enemies?

Carolyn and Heather, although from different geographical locations, have similar backgrounds. Both were raised in poverty and were exposed to abuse and alcoholism in their families. They and their families received constant visits from child and family services workers, police, and representatives of other regulatory agencies. They were victims of harsh and discriminatory treatment at their respective schools. Both also worked hard, struggled to get an education, received a few breaks, and eventually graduated from social work programs. Here the similarities end. Heather would bend over backwards for the service users with whom she worked, especially if they came from conditions of poverty. She had tremendous empathy for them and a keen understanding of their situations. Carolyn, on the other hand, became one of the most punitive and moralistic social workers in the agency, especially towards those who were poor. She also treated the clerical staff and others in subservient positions in the agency in an overbearing and heavy-handed manner. It is easy to understand Heather's position as an ally and advocate for poor people, but what about Carolyn's?

The power and respectability aspects that accompany the privileged status of the professional also involve racist and sexist dynamics. People of colour and women who are professionals must prove their respectability again and again. When their status as professionals is not known, they are often not treated with respect or deference, but when their status as, for example, a university teacher or a business executive is revealed, they often do receive respect. Conversely, working-class white men are often accorded respect until their non-professional, working-class status becomes known.

The injustices of powerlessness are fundamentally issues of the division of labour and bring into question the social status of those who make decisions and those who carry out these decisions. This social division of labour provides a plausible explanation for why so many social workers are co-opted by our present social system, which oppresses many people. As professionals, social workers can exercise their capacities through their university training and the professional development that they experience throughout their careers. In addition, they are in a position to exercise considerable power over others and receive the respect that goes with the privilege of professionalism. It requires considerable commitment as well as energy to work at transforming the society that has given the social worker some degree of power and privilege.

4. Cultural Imperialism

Exploitation, marginalization, and powerlessness all refer to relations of oppression that occur through the social division of work. Feminists, post-colonial and cultural theorists, and black liberation philosophers, among others, have identified a different form of oppression—cultural imperialism. This form of oppression comes about when the dominant group universalizes its experience and culture and uses them as the norm. Through a process of ethnocentrism, the dominant group, most often without realizing it, projects its experience and culture as representative of all humanity. Our social institutions are based on the culture and experiences of the dominant group, and our educational system, the media, the entertainment industry, literature, and advertising reinforce this notion of a universal culture. We are socialized into this ethnocentric view of the world. Cultural imperialism is experienced in varying degrees by all oppressed groups.

The dominant group reinforces its position by measuring other groups according to the dominant norms (which are the dominant group's own norms). Thus, the differences between women and men; between black people or Aboriginal persons and white people; between Jews and Christians; between gay men, lesbians, and bisexual people and heterosexuals; and between workers and professionals become largely constructed as deviance and inferiority. These 'Other' groups experience a double and paradoxical oppression. Stereotypes are used to mark them at the same time that their own experiences and perspectives are rendered invisible.

The stereotypes applied to the culturally imperialized, which brand them as deviant and inferior, are so pervasive in society that they are seldom questioned. Examples are that Aboriginal persons are alcoholic and lazy, gay men are promiscuous and perverted, women are good with children, black people are drug addicts and criminals. The fact that culturally dominated groups tend to be defined from the outside not only renders their own experiences and perspectives invisible to the dominant group but forces oppressed groups to look at themselves through the eyes of a dominant group that views them with contempt and amusement (Du Bois 1969, cited in Young 1990). This, then, is the injustice of cultural imperialism: that the oppressed group's own experience and interpretation of social life finds little expression that touches the dominant culture, while the same culture imposes on the oppressed group its experience and interpretation of social life' (Young 1990, 60). To overcome cultural imperialism, it would seem that a necessary step would be for culturally oppressed groups to take over the definition of themselves and assert a positive sense of group difference. This and other matters related to cultural imperialism are the subjects of Chapter 4.

5. Violence

Almost all oppressed groups suffer systematic violence simply because they are subordinate in the social pecking order. Violence includes not just physical attack but harassment, ridicule, and intimidation, all of which serve the purpose of stigmatizing group members. The oppression of violence lies not only in direct victimization but in the constant fear that violence may occur solely on the basis of one's group identity.

Women have reason to fear rape, people of colour have reason to fear harassment, gays and lesbians have reason to fear unprovoked assaults, striking workers have reason to fear attacks by police or strike-breakers. Violence is structural when it is tolerated, accepted, or found unsurprising by the dominant group, when perpetrators receive little or no punishment, or when structural inequalities lead to morbidity and mortality (this last point is discussed in Chapter 5). Violence is a social practice when people from the dominant group set out looking for people from oppressed groups to beat up, rape, or harass or when members of a subordinate group carry out acts of violence on other members of the same group. This latter form of violence is called 'horizontal violence.' To reform institutions and social practices that encourage, tolerate, or enable violence against members of specific groups will require a change in cultural images, stereotypes, and the day-to-day reproduction of dominance and aversion. Strategies for such change are outlined in Chapters 8 and 9.

Young's (1990) five faces of oppression, summarized above, avoid the problems associated with either a unified (i.e., there is one form of oppression that is dominant over all others) or a pluralistic (i.e., there are a number of oppressions that run parallel to one another) account of oppression. The former tends either to omit groups that even the theorist thinks oppressed or to leave out important ways in which groups are oppressed. The latter fails to accommodate the similarities and overlaps in the oppressions of groups on the one hand and falsely represents the situation of all group members as being the same on the other.

Young's framework avoids these reductions and exclusions. Rather than representing a full theory of oppression, the five forms of oppression function as objective criteria for determining whether or not individuals and groups are oppressed. Each criterion can be operationalized and applied through the assessment of observable behaviour, status relationships, distributions, texts, and culture. Although the presence of any one of these five conditions is sufficient for considering a group oppressed, different oppressed groups exhibit different combinations of them, as do different individuals within these groups. Comparisons can be made of the ways that a particular form of oppression occurs in different groups or of the combinations of oppressions that groups experience. Obviously, the framework has significant potential for helping social workers better understand the oppressions of people with whom they work in their professional practice.

Some writers have presented sets of control factors or mechanisms (some of which overlap Young's five forms of oppression) that they believe are characteristic of systems of domination and oppression. For example, Bartky (1990) argues that stereotyping, cultural domination, and sexual objectification are central to maintaining oppression, and Ruth (1988, 438) refers to 'circles of control'—economic control, cultural control, and psychological control (the latter is manifested in internalized oppression, which is the subject of Chapter 6). Geraldine Moane (1999) proposes six mechanisms of control that she argues are characteristic of oppression and have important implications for psychological functioning: violence, exclusion from power, economic exploitation, sexual exploitation, control of culture, and fragmentation or 'divide and conquer.' All of these mechanisms are addressed and discussed in various sections of this book.

Personal, Cultural, and Structural Levels of Oppression

Since at least 1972, writers have identified specific forms of oppression, such as racism (Bromley and Longino 1972; Dominelli 1997), violence (Galtung 1990), and oppression or discrimination in general (Thompson 1997, 1998, 2001; Sisneros et al. 2008), as occurring at three levels: the personal or individual level, the cultural level, and the institutional or structural level. These three levels or locations of oppression are in dynamic interaction with one another, with each level supporting, reinforcing, and influencing oppression on the other two levels and in turn being supported, reinforced, and influenced by the other two levels. Thompson (1997) has termed this multi-dimensional perspective as the PCS model of analysis (P for personal, C for cultural, and S for structural). As stated by Thompson (2002, 44–5) 'The basis of PCS analysis is that any approaches to the questions of discrimination and oppression which do not take into account all three of these levels, and their inter-relationships, is in danger of oversimplifying a very complex set of issues.' This model, which extends oppression beyond the individual to individual interactions or the practitioner-to-service-user encounters, is adopted here as the working model of oppression/anti-oppression.

In some respects, the PCS model of analysis is an elaboration of 'the personal is political' analysis by feminists, social activists, and progressive social workers (Mullaly 2007). It retains the 'personal' and the 'political' because it recognizes that social problems are political or structural by nature and that they cause personal difficulties for many people. Furthermore, just as structural forces affect people, so too do people affect structures. This insight is behind all social change movements, ranging from small acts of resistance or protest on an individual level to large social movements such as the civil rights and environmental movements. What the PCS model adds to this perspective is an intermediary level—the cultural level. Culture (values, norms, and shared patterns of thought) tended to be lumped in with other structural forces in the 'personal is political' model. However, thanks to the relatively recent emergence of cultural studies (discussed in Chapter 4), we now have greater understanding of how, by endorsing the idea of a superior culture, the dominant culture of a society reflects and reinforces oppression on the other two levels. Cultural imperialism was outlined above as one of Young's five forms of oppression.

The individual or personal level is located within both the cultural and structural contexts of society, and the cultural level is located within the structural context (see Figure 2.1). Thus, although we may examine oppression at only the personal level or at one of the other levels, it will be an incomplete examination because one's thoughts, attitudes, and actions can only be understood in the larger context(s) with an awareness that the three levels continuously interact with one another.

Oppression at the personal level comprises the thoughts, attitudes, and behaviours that depict a negative prejudgment of a particular subordinate social group. It is usually based on stereotypes and may be overt or covert. Without institutional or structural backing, these negative thoughts, attitudes, and behaviours constitute prejudice (Dominelli 1997; Thompson 1998). Thompson (2002) issues a warning that personal prejudice or oppression is part of the complex web of oppression and therefore we should be wary of overemphasizing its importance and thus underemphasizing the significance of cultural and structural factors. Oppression at the personal level and the responses of individual oppressed persons to their oppression are the subjects of Chapter 3.

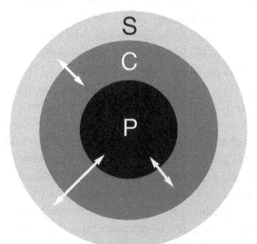

Figure 2.1   PCS Levels of Oppression

Oppression at the cultural level consists of the values, norms, and shared patterns of seeing, thinking, and acting, along with an assumed consensus about what is right and normal, that taken together endorse the belief in a superior culture. It refers to the ways and discursive practices used by the dominant group to portray subordinate groups in history, literature, the media, stories, movies, humour, stereotypes, and popular culture. It acts as a vehicle for transmitting and presenting the dominant culture as the norm, the message being that everyone should conform to it. Ultimately, it can lead to ethnocentrism—that is, to a narrow view of the world only from within the narrow confines of one culture (Thompson 1998). It is the cement of cultural oppression that reinforces the personal and structural oppression (Dominelli 1997). Unfortunately, social work has tended to equate culture with ethnicity in developing practices of cultural awareness and sensitivity and has overlooked a broader view of culture, one that is related to everything we see, hear, believe, and do. Even social work writers who profess social justice ideals and approaches, such as Baines (2007) and Dominelli (2002), tend to lump culture in with structural variables. Not only do they miss out on what Agger (1992) considers the most exciting development in critical theory today (i.e., cultural studies), but they underplay how the dominant group in a pluralistic society maintains hierarchical divisions of class, race, gender, age, and so on and how it promotes, imposes, and universalizes its own culture while repressing others. Oppression at the cultural level is crucial to understanding how oppression works and in developing strategies of liberation. Oppression at the cultural level is the subject of Chapter 4.

Oppression at the structural level refers to the means by which oppression is institutionalized in society. It consists of the ways that social institutions, laws, policies, social processes and practices, and the economic and political systems all work together primarily in favour of the dominant group at the expense of subordinate groups. At this level, oppression is often given its formal legitimation. An analysis of how social structures produce oppression, including structural violence, is the subject of Chapter 5.

Conclusion

This chapter has examined the concept of oppression along several dimensions. Oppression was described as a second-class citizenship that is assigned to people not on the basis of failure or lack of merit but because of one's membership in a particular group or category of people. Oppression exists because it carries out a number of positive functions for the dominant group at the expense of subordinate groups. A number of myths that rationalize oppression as necessary for the preservation of society were presented. It was argued that the (re)distributional concept of social justice that has historically underpinned social welfare and social work practice only compensates victims of oppression. It does nothing to alter the social processes and practices that produce and reproduce inequality. A few competing accounts of the genealogy of oppression were presented, the common element among them being that although oppression is remarkably stable and resistant to change once it is established, it is not a fixed, essentialist, or natural social condition.

Although there are different forms, sources, levels of severity, and experiences of oppression, there is a common set of dynamics between dominant and subordinate groups. Iris Marion Young's five categories of oppression, of which all oppressed groups experience at least one (and usually more), were presented. This categorization is adopted here because it encompasses both distributive issues of social injustice and practices that go beyond distribution. Finally, a model of oppression that locates oppression at three levels—personal, cultural, and structural or institutional—was outlined. The next three chapters offer a more in-depth look at oppression at each of these levels.

Critical Questions for Discussion

1. Most oppressors would never think of themselves as oppressors. Why are they oppressors, and why don't they realize it?

2. Some authors (e.g., Thompson 1997; 2001) refer to 'anti-discriminatory social work' instead of 'anti-oppressive social work.' What is the difference between discrimination and oppression and between anti-discriminatory social work and anti-oppressive social work? Can you give some examples?

3. If we are equal before the law and all have the same rights, which are protected under human rights legislation and Canada's Charter of Rights and Freedoms, isn't this enough equality? What are some examples of rights that the dominant group has and various oppressed groups do not have?

4. How is 'difference' treated in the curriculum of your social work program? That is, which subordinate groups have *more* than one course (half course or full course) devoted entirely to their issues? Which have one course devoted entirely to them? Which have no courses devoted entirely to them but are a significant part of at least one course? Which receive only passing reference in the curriculum? And which are not even mentioned in the curriculum? How do you account for these variations?

5. Given that we all have multiple identities, most of us belong to at least one oppressed group. Using Young's five faces of oppression, can you think of instances in your own life when you experienced any of these five forms of oppression (exploitation, marginalization, powerlessness, cultural imperialism, or violence) because of your membership in a particular subordinate group?

6. Take any source or form of oppression, such as poverty, sexism, racism, heterosexism, ageism, religion, and so on, and give some examples of how it occurs at the personal level, the cultural level, and the structural level.

7. Is the gender division of labour natural? Why or why not?

Further Readings

Baines, Donna, ed. (2007). *Doing Anti-oppressive Practice: Building Transformative Politicized Social Work*. Halifax: Fernwood. This book focuses on integrating anti-oppressive theory into politicized, transformative social work practice. Using practice vignettes, personal experiences, and case work examples, the contributing authors focus on social work practice in a variety of settings and suggest ways that social work on the front lines can resist oppression and challenge injustice while at the same time transforming larger systems.

Dominelli, Lena (2002). *Anti-oppressive Social Work Theory and Practice*. Basingstoke, UK: Palgrave Macmillan. This book, written by one of the leading theorists in the field of progressive or critical social work, focuses on how social workers can assist individuals, groups, organizations, communities, and society at large to challenge and transcend the many sources and forms of oppression (e.g., poverty, racism, sexism, disability, mental illness) that disempower them. It explores the limitations of traditional mainstream social work in dealing with the complexity of the range of levels at which oppression occurs and argues that these models be replaced with social justice–oriented approaches such as anti-oppressive social work.

Gil, David (1998). *Confronting Injustice and Oppression: Concepts and Strategies for Social Workers*. New York: Columbia University Press. The author presents perspectives and strategies to transform unjust and oppressive institutions into alternatives that are conducive to human development, empowerment, and liberation. The book explores the meanings, sources, and dynamics of injustice and oppression and calls for social workers to embrace the core values of progressive social work—equality, liberty, co-operation, and affirmation of community. In Gil's view, anti-oppressive social workers must be overtly political, advocate human rights, facilitate critical consciousness through dialogue, and build social movements through activism.

Shera, Wes, ed. (2003). *Emerging Perspectives on Anti-oppressive Practice*. Toronto: Canadian Scholars Press. This book contains 27 chapters, each developed from a paper originally presented at a conference held by the Canadian Association of Schools of Social Work on anti-oppressive social work practice. These papers address a number of themes or areas of anti-oppressive social work, including theory, fields of practice, critical issues, social work education, and future challenges. The chapters in this book laid much of the groundwork for anti-oppressive social work scholarship and practice today.

Thompson, Neil (2001). *Anti-discriminatory Practice*, 3rd edition. Basingstoke, UK: Palgrave Macmillan. This book explores each of the main areas of discrimination and considers the practice implications of developing an anti-oppressive approach to social work. The author presents a clearly articulated theory base—the PCS model (personal, cultural, structural), which has been used by a number of leading theorists in the development of anti-oppressive and social justice approaches to social work. Written in an extremely clear and accessible manner.

Young, Iris Marion (1990). *Justice and the Politics of Difference*. Princeton, NJ: Princeton University Press. A seminal book in a number of scholarly and professional areas, including social justice and anti-oppression. The author makes probably the most convincing case for the emancipatory implications of postmodernism. The book presents a critical analysis of different theories of justice and finds them lacking in that they do not contain the claims of excluded groups with respect to decision-making, cultural expression, and division of labour. By assuming a homogeneous public, traditional theories of justice (including distributive or redistributive justice) fail to consider institutional arrangements for including people not culturally identified with white European male norms of reason and respectability. Young identifies concepts of domination and subordination to cover issues not included in the distributional model and argues for a principle of group representation in democratic decision-making.

Chapter 3

Oppression at the Personal Level

An injustice to one is a menace to all.
—Montesquieu

Normalizing Gaze and Objectified Bodies

In the previous chapter, it was pointed out that the scientific discourse of the nineteenth century gave legitimation to a white, male, bourgeois, body type and facial features as the norm or hierarchical standard against which all other groups were measured (Young 1990). Using this measuring stick, the autonomous, neutral, and objective subject of knowledge, who typically fit these characteristics, observed by way of normalizing gazes (Foucault 1977) that all other bodies were degenerate or less developed. Whole groups of people came to be defined as 'different'—as the Other—and members of these groups became locked or imprisoned in their bodies. This concept of 'difference' was presented in the previous chapter as the basis of oppression.

In addition to a superior body type, the nineteenth-century ideal of health and beauty was primarily an ideal of manly virtue[1]—a strong, self-controlled rational man distanced from sexuality, emotion, and everything disorderly or disturbing (Mosse 1985; Young 1990). The groups of people referred to above—such as people of colour, Jewish persons, and women—came to be defined as the Other because they did not possess the ideal body type and they also were assumed (by white bourgeois males) not to possess these manly virtues, which affirmed their degeneracy. The notion of whiteness was associated with reason, while blackness was associated with body (Kovel 1984). This allowed people who were white to identify themselves as possessing reason and therefore to be the subject of knowledge and to identify people of colour as the objects of knowledge (Said 1978). Nineteenth-century discourse often extended the concept of black to depict Jews and gays and lesbians.[2] A new discourse on old age also occurred at this time, shifting it from an association with wisdom and endurance to an identification with frailty, incontinence, and senility (Cole 1986, cited in Young 1990). All groups that did not meet the norm of the young, white, strong, self-controlled, rational, bourgeois man were objectified (in varying degrees) as the degenerate Others.

Subordinate groups were given negative identities by the dominant group on the basis of bodily characteristics (ugly, dirty, smelly, defiled, impure, contaminated, weak, disfigured, sick, and so on) and on the basis of inferior intellect and character (lazy, irrational, intellectually underdeveloped, mentally childlike, hypersexual or asexual, brutish, uncivilized, overly visible, criminal, and so on). This is not to say that all subordinate groups endure the same composite stereotypes (though many do), but all groups have some of these negative characteristics assigned to them by the dominant group.

Acts of Oppression at the Personal Level

As outlined in the previous chapter, oppression at the personal level consists of thoughts, attitudes, and behaviours that depict negative prejudgments of subordinate groups. Oppression at the personal level is usually based on stereotypes and may be manifest in conscious acts of aggression and/or hatred, but today it tends to be in the form of unconscious acts of aversion and avoidance. Let us look at both types of oppression.

Conscious Acts of Aggression and/or Hatred

Many acts of oppression at the personal level reflect the notion of an inferior and/or ugly body type. African North Americans have experienced a number of derogatory names imposed on them by white people in reference to the colour of their skin—nigger, coon, spade, darky, smokey, shadow. Similarly, North American First Nations people have been subject to the names redskin or savage or chief; people of Asian origin to the degrading labels of Japs, gooks, chinks, or slanty-eyes; and physically challenged persons to crip or spaz (the former is an abbreviation of cripple and the latter an abbreviation of spastic). It is still common to hear males address or talk about women in vulgar versions of their sexual characteristics. This insulting type of labelling may be applied verbally to a specific member of a subordinate group or it may be found in locker-room humour or in graffiti. Whatever form it takes, name-calling devalues members of subordinate groups by accentuating differences between the dominant and subordinate groups in a negative way. It reflects the belief that the characteristics of the dominant group (skin colour, eye shape, male body) represent the norm or universal standard and that anything not meeting the standard is open to ridicule and insult. The message to the subordinate group is that they are inferior because they do not meet these standards or norms.

Although legislation today aims to protect people from harassment and codes of behaviour make these actions socially unacceptable, they still occur too often. One need only visit the men's washrooms in any university to find some of the most extreme racist, sexist, homophobic, and anti-Semitic sentiments written on the lavatory walls and doors. These anonymous expressions of hatred towards persons who are defined as different and as having ugly or fearful bodies constitute clear evidence that such thoughts, beliefs, and attitudes, which portray a negative prejudgment of subordinate groups, still exist today in spite of a discursive commitment to equal respect and consideration for all.

Objectified and socially constructed ugly and degenerate bodies are not the only objects of conscious acts of oppression; after all, nineteenth-century biological and medical science held that the superior body type directly determines the intellectual and character superiority of persons in this group (West 1982). Conversely, the inferior body type was seen as directly determining the intellectual and character inferiority of persons in other groups. With the rational, strong, self-controlled, and autonomous white, bourgeois male as the universal standard, whole groups of people were and are classified as intellectually and morally degenerate (Young 1990). For example, women were considered physically delicate and weak because of the specific constitution of their bodies and therefore subject to madness, irrationality, and childlike behaviour (Astbury 1996).

The Iron Lady

A common response in the US in the 1970s and 1980s to the question of whether or not a woman ever could or should become president was 'No, because at the first indication of a war, a woman president would likely start to cry' (rather than exercise the manly virtues of decisive, strong, and strategic leadership). There are exceptions to this gender-exclusive rule, however. Margaret Thatcher, former prime minister of the United Kingdom, was often portrayed as 'male-like' or 'a pseudo male' (e.g., possessing strength, reason and able to make the hard decisions), as evidenced by the label 'the iron lady' that was given to her. This label marked her not only as a strong leader but also as an exception to the rule. There would be no need to label a strong male prime minister as 'the iron man' because his power would be assumed. Power appears natural in a male but unusual and even problematic in a female (Johnson 2006).

Other characteristics often assigned to members of subordinate groups include sexual licentiousness or promiscuity (women and people of colour), sexual degeneracy or depravity (gay and lesbian persons), asexuality (older persons and disabled people), childlike stupidity (people of colour, women, older persons), irresponsibility (most subordinate groups), laziness (most subordinate groups), criminality (most subordinate groups), and intellectual deficiencies (most subordinate groups).

These and other characteristics, defined by the dominant group as part of the identity of subordinate groups, are used in the same way as derogatory names—to harass, ridicule, defame, intimidate, and in effect remind subordinate populations of their second-class status. At the same time, the definition of subordinate groups as degenerate and intellectually and morally inferior provides a convenient rationale for reserving most of life's opportunities for the dominant group. Decent income and jobs, education, good health, supportive networks, social and political inclusion, and adequate housing in nice neighbourhoods ought to go to members of the dominant group, who are considered more deserving and worthy. Otherwise, opportunities would only be squandered. Members of the dominant class will often point to the vandalizing of public housing as evidence of a lazy, irresponsible, and ungrateful group of people.

The most extreme form of a conscious act of aggression and hatred is violence against members of oppressed groups. The fear and loathing of socially constructed ugly bodies, in concert with cultural stereotypes, have much to do with harassment and physical violence perpetrated on members of oppressed groups. The previous chapter presented an overview of violence as one of Young's (1990) five forms or faces of oppression. Young notes that violence is: (1) systemic when it is directed at members of a subordinate group just because they are members of that group; (2) a social practice when members of a subordinate group are sought out to be beaten up, raped, or taunted; (3) legitimized when it is tolerated or found to be unsurprising because it happens frequently or when perpetrators receive light or no punishment; (4) mostly irrational and xenophobic; and (5) a form of injustice that a theory of distributive justice does not capture.

A Racialized Space

From 'Racialized policing,' an opinion piece by Elizabeth Comack, professor of sociology at the University of Manitoba and a research associate with the Canadian Centre for Policy Alternatives (Manitoba), *Winnipeg Free Press*, 17 December 2008, p. A15.

From the very first day of the inquest into the shooting death of Matthew Dumas (an Aboriginal male) by a Winnipeg police officer, lawyer Robert Tapper took pains to emphasize that race had nothing to do with Matthew's death. In her recently released report, provincial court judge Mary Curtis agreed, concluding that Matthew died as a result of his own actions, not because of police racism.

Many might take solace in Judge Curtis's conclusion, seeing it as affirming that the problem of Aboriginal-police relations in our city is really a problem 'of' Aboriginal people. But too many Aboriginal people in Winnipeg know otherwise.

For the past five months I have been engaged in a research project that has involved interviewing Aboriginal people about their experiences with the police. The initial plan was to conduct 30 interviews but more and more people kept coming forward, wanting to tell their experiences. We eventually stopped at 79 interviews.

A Racialized Space (*continued*)

What I have learned from these interviews is disturbing. Racist stereotypes and racialized practices were starkly evident in people's accounts. Aboriginal men who live in the inner city are regularly questioned by police. When asked 'what did I do wrong?' police typically respond, 'you fit the description.' As one young man remarked, 'Look at me. I look pretty much like every other male who lives in the North End.' Sometimes the men are taken to the police station several miles away, and then left to find their own way home upon release. Aboriginal women reported that they cannot even walk to the grocery store without being stopped by police, who assume they are prostitutes.

In this respect, the inner city is a 'racialized space.' Just being present—and Aboriginal—within that space makes you suspect. . . .

Other reports of racialized practices are even more troubling. Accounts of the so-called 'phone book treatment' came up regularly in the interviews. Apparently, when hit with a phone book, no visible bruises are left on the surface of the skin. The police seem to use this strategy—sometimes in the elevator of the Public Safety Building—to extract information from people.

Another disturbing practice involves the police driving Aboriginal people to the outskirts of Winnipeg and leaving them there—often in bitterly cold weather—to find their way back home. We know from Justice Wright's inquiry in Saskatchewan into the death of Neil Stonechild that such practices occurred in that province. Manitoba appears to be no exception.

All members of subordinate groups must live with the fear of random and unprovoked physical attacks on their person, family, or property. African-Americans may not fear lynching and public whipping to the extent they once did, but they still experience a high incidence of racial violence, including beatings and rape by on-duty police officers. Gay-bashing is common today, as is the physical abuse of children and the elderly. Physical violence (beatings, sexual assault, murder) against women continues at epidemic levels. Ethnic violence is prevalent against Jews, as is government-sanctioned violence by police against striking workers on picket lines. The terrorist attacks of 11 September 2001 in the United States have resulted in wide-scale violence in many Western countries against people of Middle Eastern extraction and persons of the Islamic faith, with public harassment, damage to and destruction of mosques, beatings, and even murders reported in the media. Even when there is no violence, the threat is ever present, and this threat and the accompanying fear rob oppressed people of freedom, dignity, and peace of mind.

Ungrateful or Unjust?

John, a 14-year-old boy, and his family lived in a relatively new public housing neighbourhood. It seemed to John that as soon as the parents of friends he made outside his neighbourhood learned where he lived, he was not invited back to their homes. He had also applied for a number of part-time jobs, but whenever the person taking his application noticed John's address, the tone of the interview changed, and John never received a call to come to work, although others outside the neighbourhood did. At school he did not seem to receive the same favourable treatment from certain teachers that other children did. One day he overheard one of his teachers referring to 'the troublemakers who come from that welfare neighbourhood.' It seemed to John that his home address caused him a lot of problems. He soon became a willing and regular participant in vandalizing the property and grounds of the public housing estate.

Unconscious Acts of Aversion and Avoidance

It is probably true today that theories and ideologies of superiority do not exercise the influence in society that they once did. After much struggle on the part of all sub-ordinate groups, there is a formal commitment in most Western democracies to some sense of equality, as evidenced by civil rights and human rights codes and legislation regarding affirmative action, equal pay, and other policies of equal treatment. And as Young (1990, 132) notes:

> Commitment to formal equality for all persons tends also to support a public etiquette that disapproves of speech and behavior calling attention in public settings to a person's sex, race, sexual orientation, class status, religion, and the like. . . . The ideal promoted by current social etiquette is that these group differences should not matter in our everyday encounters with one another.

This is not to say that committed racists, sexists, and so on are relics of the past, but such people must be more careful today of how and when and where they exhibit overt acts of oppression and prejudice. Many (maybe most) acts of oppression at the personal level today are not of the open and aggressive type but occur as aversive behaviour that emerges in everyday interactions between persons in dominant and subordinate groups. In other words, much oppressive behaviour at the personal level has gone underground. Hostility, fear, avoidance, and feelings of superiority are expressed by dominant group members in mundane contexts of interaction in terms of their gestures, speech, tone of voice, and body movements (Brittan and Maynard 1984). For example, dominant group members may show that they are uncomfortable or nervous around persons of a subordinate group by avoiding eye contact, increasing the physical distance between them, using kinetic gestures of defence and aversion, or going out of their way to avoid interaction or sharing the same approximate space.

It is not uncommon, for example, for men to be nervous around a group of women or for white people to cross the street when they see two or more black males coming down the street towards them. It is not unusual for a loving heterosexual couple to recoil in horror upon seeing a gay or lesbian couple displaying the very same affectionate behaviour that they themselves display, or for a black person to be followed around a store by security people, or for people to shout at and talk in baby terms to an older person, or for the noise level in a room of white people to diminish when a person of colour enters, or for a salesperson to look at and address the male partner of a couple, asking the woman only what she thinks about the colour of the car or the kitchen in a house that is being shown to them.

Rather than overt sexism, racism, and so on, the above are examples of covert acts of oppression or of oppression having gone underground. Many members of the dominant group exhibiting these aversive and unconscious acts would deny that they are prejudiced or that they acted in an oppressive way. In fact, many of these same people may be consciously committed to equality and respect for members of all social groups. This shows how entrenched sexism, racism, ageism, classism, and the like are in our individual, collective, and cultural psyches and why unconscious oppression is so difficult to counteract and eradicate. Unlike explicit acts of aggression and exclusion, acts of aversion and avoidance cannot be legislated against. There is no legal or policy remedy for this kind of oppression.

Effects of Oppression on the Individual

Thus far, this chapter has looked at acts of oppression that occur at the personal level—that is, acts of aversion or avoidance directed specifically (though not necessarily intentionally) at subordinate group members personally by dominant group members. The remainder of the chapter discusses the impact and effects of oppression on the individual who is oppressed. Of course, oppression at any level (personal, cultural, or structural) is felt eventually by subordinate persons at the individual level. In effect, what exists is a three-headed monster (i.e., personal, cultural, and structural forms of oppression) that treats subordinate groups in an inhumane, unjust, and discriminatory manner. The oppressed person experiences the full impact of multiple-level oppression every day. Therefore, questions to be addressed here include: How does oppression affect one's identity or sense of self? How does it affect one's sense of location in society? And what effect does it have on the individual's self-esteem and other facets of the personal psyche?

Impact on Identity

Oppression at the personal level reinforces the privileged social position of the dominant group and the disadvantaged position of the subordinate group in a number of ways. First, the group identity of the subordinate group is defined or socially constructed by the dominant group, and subordinate group members have no say in this definition or construction (though they may protest it, resist it, and try to change it). It is imposed on them, marking them as different and inferior—as the Other—and there is no escape from it, because the behaviour and reactions of members of the dominant group and other subordinate groups (and members of one's own identity group in some cases) are constant reminders of it. Conversely, dominant groups have no need to think about their group identity because they occupy an unmarked, neutral, normative, and universal position (Young 1990). The dominant group depicts the socially constructed inferior status of subordinate groups as natural and immutable or fixed (Dominelli 2002). The identity as inferior that is imposed on subordinate groups on a personal level is reinforced by the ways they are portrayed in the dominant culture, through the media, the education system, advertising, literature, movies, and so on, as will be discussed in the next chapter, and the way they are treated by social institutions, policies, and practices, as will be discussed in Chapter 5.

When members of subordinate groups experience aversive and avoidance behaviour from the dominant group, they are reminded of their group identity and feel either marked (when the behaviour is aversive) or invisible (when the behaviour is avoidance) or not taken seriously or demeaned. This presents a double bind for them. They can either protest aversive or avoidance behaviour or they can suffer its humiliation in silence. Because we live in a society in which an aspect of the dominant culture is to avoid conflict and confrontation, it tends to be seen as tactless and in poor taste to draw attention to covert and often unintentional acts of racism, sexism, ageism, and so on. If a member of a subordinate group protests against such acts, it could lead to his or her exclusion from public or social events. As well, anyone who does protest against this kind of oppression is often accused of being too sensitive, or making something out of nothing, or overreacting. Thus, when experiencing oppressive behaviour, the subordinate group member is left with the choice of either suffering it in silence or protesting such behaviour and then made to feel as though he or she has acted inappropriately.

The above, of course, prompts the questions: what is identity, what are its functions, and why is it so important? 'Identity' is one of those loose and slippery terms, with no universal agreement on its precise meaning. Breakwell (1986) says that what one theorist calls 'identity' another will call the 'self,' even though both are attempting to understand the same fundamental phenomenon. Some writers view identity as one of a set (along with character, self-concept, personality, status) of social, psychological, and behavioural characteristics that differentiate one person from another. Breakwell points out that one's theoretical orientation will largely determine the meaning one gives to identity. For example, in the psychoanalytic tradition, identity is a global awareness (i.e., awareness of oneself in relation to others) achieved through crisis and sequential identifications in social relations; the behaviourist talks in terms of personality; the symbolic interactionist might talk of the self-concept; and to the role theorist, identity is any label applied consistently to a person. The concept of identity adopted here is social-psychological and links socio-political with intrapsychic phenomena in the belief that both contribute to the establishment of or changes to one's identity or identities. In other words, this concept of identity focuses on the dialectical relationship between social context and personal psychology (i.e., the personal is political and vice versa) and considers how they both contribute to a person's identity.

There is a voluminous psychological literature on identity, and no attempt will be made here to summarize it. Instead, a selection of ideas consistent with a social-psychological perspective of identity will be presented. It is hoped that these ideas will contribute to an understanding of what an identity is, how oppression affects identity, some of the negative intrapersonal and interpersonal consequences of having a negative identity for oppressed persons, and how they might respond on intrapersonal, interpersonal, and inter-group levels.

Structure of Identity

In its simplest terms, identity refers to the conditions or distinguishing features that mark or characterize or identify an individual. A person may be identified by his or her name, history, present social status, gender, race, personality, age, appearance (e.g., height, weight), religion, and so on. Some of these identity characteristics are obviously associated with one's physical being; others are invisible (e.g., sexual orientation, religion); still others are psychological (e.g., personality); and yet others are social characteristics (e.g., class) or social roles (e.g., parent, academic). The politicization of differences among these identity characteristics involves privileging the attribute(s) of one group at the expense of others. This creates various sets of binary oppositions, which in turn, sets up a 'we–they' division among people (Dominelli 2002). If individuals do not possess the characteristics considered of value or desirable (e.g., whiteness, affluence), they become socially excluded and subject to discrimination and marginalization. And it is 'these dynamics [that] underpin the social construction of oppression' (Dominelli 2002, 38).

Obviously, many factors contribute to identity. In fact, 'identity' is probably an inaccurate or incorrect term, since each of us has many identities. Each of the above markers or identity characteristics may constitute an identity in itself. For example, part of my identity for those who know me or know of me is that of a male. However, for people who do not know me but just see me on the street, my *total* identity may be that of a male, or at least a white male. This point touches on the legitimate concern of postmodernists—that we should not assume that individuals have only one identity. Each component of identity may be considered an identity in itself, or what some writers refer to as a 'sub-identity.' These characteristics or defining properties of identity (or sub-identities) are known in the literature as the content of identity (Dominelli 2002).

Even though many of these characteristics are shared by other people, the particular constellation or configuration attached to a person makes that person distinctive and gives him or her a unique overall identity. It should be noted that the contents of identity are not static. They will shift in relation to each other according to the context in which the identity is located.

My Shifting Identity

While living in Australia, I found myself emphasizing my Canadianness more than I ever did living in Canada. I did this in part because Canadians are, on average, well-regarded by Australians, and this part of my identity gave me a good deal of positive attention and value. Similarly, but for a different purpose, when I was attending university in Toronto in the late 1970s and early 1980s, many faculty and students were 'Toronto-centric,' holding views of Maritimers such as me as a backwater and inferior group of people. In response to this negative identity imposed on Canadians living in Atlantic Canada, I emphasized (some would say overemphasized) my 'Atlantic Canadianness' in an 'in-your-face' kind of way in an effort to decentre the negative prejudgments made of me simply because I was not from the 'centre-of-the-universe' (i.e., Toronto).[3] Waddell and Cairns (1986) explain such shifts in emphasis as being determined by different situations or contexts. That is, identity components (or sub-identities) will be highly relevant or emphasized and valued in one context (e.g., my being Canadian in Australia) and irrelevant or inappropriate to emphasize in other contexts (e.g., my being Canadian in Canada). Certain identity components can also be used in acts of resistance, as in my reaction as an Atlantic Canadian in Toronto. Resisting negative views and stereotypes will be further discussed in subsequent chapters.

In addition to the contents of identity not being static, Breakwell points out that the organization of the contents are not static either. Some people have a relatively fixed hierarchy of identity components, while others have no level of fixed connectedness among the characteristics of their identities. Although it is not known exactly what causes this variation, to some extent the organization of components must depend on the value attached to them. The content dimension is one part of the structure of identity. The value dimension is the other. A positive or negative value attached to each component of identity is based on current social beliefs and values in interaction with previously established value codes (Breakwell 1986). And, of course, components that have a positive value attached to them correspond highly with the identity characteristics of the dominant group, whereas the negatively valued identity components tend to be associated with subordinate groups. Although the value attached to various contents of identity is socially determined, the powerful and dominant group largely determines the value, and as argued in Chapter 2, they do this in a way that protects and reproduces their privileged social position.

The individual learns his or her social and personal worth through interactions with others in the context of dominant ideologies. And as Tajfel (1981) reminds us, the determination of self-worth or social worth cannot occur free of stereotypes. This is not to say that an absolute systems determination of values occurs, for self-reflection and evaluation may lead to a rejection of current dominant social values. There should be no assumption that identity is without agency—an important point for anti-oppressive practice. However, the tendency is for dominant ideologies to influence the individual's choice of personal values and beliefs about his or her identity and its value. For example, persons receiving welfare and single-parent women have been socially constructed as inferior persons and therefore are held in low esteem in a society in which the dominant ideology is neo-conservative or neo-liberal. The dominant discourse of neo-conservatism/liberalism portrays lone-parent women and welfare recipients as work-shy, abusers of the public purse, and, in the case of single-parent women, of bearing children to get on the welfare rolls.

Any viable exploration of identity must differentiate between personal identity and social identity. The latter is that part of the self-concept derived from group associations, interpersonal relationships, and social position or status, whereas the former is free of such role or relationship determinants (Breakwell 1986). There is considerable disagreement in the psychological literature about the relationship between these two concepts and whether or not the person does experience or can differentiate between the two types or aspects of identity. The position taken here is that personal identity is the way the person views himself or herself, whereas social identity is the way society or the world surrounding the person views him or her (recognizing that each will influence the other). As mentioned above and argued in more detail below, the way society views (and responds to) the individual will have an effect on, but not necessarily totally determine, the way the individual views himself or herself. With respect to the question of whether or not the individual experiences both types of identity and/or can differentiate between them, the history of oppression and oppressed persons answers this question in the affirmative. Dominelli (2002) argues that an understanding of these two aspects of identity (i.e., people's sense of themselves and what others think of them) are crucial for anti-oppressive social work, which is aimed at creating new, non-oppressive social relations. It does this, in part, by being involved in a process of contesting identities in which established truths about identity are challenged and the identity claims of subordinate groups asserted.

Oppressed persons learn early in life how society views and treats them, and throughout their lives this learning is reinforced. The (dominant or subordinate) individual actively accommodates to and assimilates portraits of the self supplied by the social world. When one's personal identity matches the negative portrait or social identity provided by the social world, then we have a case of internalized oppression.

When there is incongruence between the personal identity and social identity of a subordinate person, there is potential for resistance and change. In the case of incongruence within and between both sets of identities, however, the oppressed person is likely to experience uncertainty, insecurity, guilt, and anguish—and these feelings must be confronted before any efforts at social change can occur.

Processes of Identity Formation

Consistent with the social-psychological approach (and with phenomenological and historical materialist philosophies and critical social theory), identity is the process and product of an individual's interactions with influences in the physical and social worlds. These influences include, among others, one's history, one's family, and the dominant ideology at the particular point of history in which the individual is going through the process of identity formation. For example, many people who experienced the Great Depression of the 1930s are still influenced by this event in their current lives, as evidenced by an extreme caution and frugality with money and purchases. Part of our identity is our history and culture—who we are, where we came from, the social status and other characteristics of our family and/or social group. The family is a significant determinant of identity because it is the actual location in which people are socialized in the first instance and learn about their place in the world, how to behave in it, and what to expect from it based on personal and family characteristics. The dominant ideology of a society, which is transmitted to the individual through interactions with others and through the dominant culture (see Chapter 4), identifies and legitimates an individual's position of dominance or subordination in society according to the person's class, gender, race, age, sexuality, and so on. Persons develop and internalize a picture of themselves, in large part, according to how society views them, which in turn is determined largely by ideology, stereotypes, myths, and ethnocentrism.

The notion that identity may be totally a product of dominant ideologies is, of course, overly simplistic and crudely deterministic. At any one time, the social context contains many competing ideologies or explanations of social events, conditions, relationships, and dynamics. In other words, the individual is presented with many competing and contradictory explanations and interpretations of social reality. There is no doubt that the dominant ideology will significantly influence the formation of one's identity, but it will not necessarily be the sole determinant. The individual is not without agency. For Peter Leonard (1984), these contradictions provide the individual with choices, and it is these choices that form part of the dialectic between the individual and the social order. The individual, on the one hand, is shaped, influenced, and penetrated by the social order—its institutions, ideologies, and social practices. On the other hand, the individual will mediate the conflicting messages and ideologies and engage in acts of resistance (often unconsciously) to the dominant ideology and attempt to change the social order. The individual both shapes and is shaped by the social order. Identity is both a social product and a social process. Dominelli (2002, 39) argues that identity is a 'site for struggle' as the groups who have inferior identities imposed on them by the dominant group 'seek to establish their own grounds for defining who and what they are.'

Unfortunately, there is no satisfactory or comprehensive explanation or theory of how choices among competing ideologies and contradictory messages are made by persons and incorporated into their structure of identity. Breakwell (1986) proposes three goals that are inherent in the identity process and give it purpose and direction. The identity processes work to produce: (1) uniqueness or distinctiveness of identity for the individual; (2) continuity of identity across time and context; and (3) a feeling of personal worth and social value. Little is known about how these three relate to each other, and it is obvious that there will be occasions when they conflict with one another. Apter (1983) would add a fourth goal to identity formation, which would also guide the processes of identity—the desire for autonomy. These goals suggest that a healthy identity is one that at a minimum has its own distinct nature and character, is relatively stable over time and in different social contexts, reflects a positive self-image on the part of the person and a sense of value to society, and allows the person to be self-determining and able to act with purpose on his or her own behalf.

It has already been argued that many or most members of subordinate or oppressed groups will not have healthy identities as defined by the above criteria. To be viewed and treated as second-class, subhuman, expendable, and the like, and to have an identity imposed by another group based on stereotypes and Eurocentric ideas and sentiments of an inferior Other, does not facilitate the development of a healthy identity. In other words, oppression interferes with the development or maintenance of a healthy identity—and a healthy or strong sense of identity would seem to be essential for tackling one's oppression and oppressors. Building and strengthening identity would seem to be essential activities in an anti-oppressive social work practice.

Obviously, identity is a complex and multifaceted concept. A complete coverage is well beyond this book (or any other book). However, given its crucial relationship to oppression and in turn to anti-oppressive social work, we should examine a number of salient features of identity, as summarized in Table 3.1.

Coping with Threats to Identity

As mentioned above, oppression presents a serious threat to the development or to the existence of a healthy identity. Because a healthy identity is part of what it is to be an autonomous and self-directing human, the individual will develop and employ coping strategies to protect his or her identity. A coping strategy is any action the individual believes will protect the self (i.e., physical, psychological, or social self). Breakwell (1986) outlines a number of coping mechanisms that operate at the intrapersonal or intrapsychic, interpersonal, and group (inter and intra) levels, with strategies at one level having repercussions for events at the other levels. These mechanisms may be recognized and intentional on the part of the individual, or they may be employed unconsciously. They can have as their targets: (1) the removal of certain (material or ideological) aspects of the social context that contain threat; (2) the movement of the

Table 3.1   Selected Features of Identity

- Identity refers to the conditions or distinguishing features that mark or characterize or identify an individual.
- A person's identity may be based on his or her name, social status, gender, race, personality, age, appearance, religion, geographical origin, etc.
- A person's identity is formed through interactions with others in a number of different domains simultaneously.
- Because many factors and many groups have a role in forming a person's identity, each of us has many identities. These identities intersect and overlap with one another, giving us privilege in some areas and oppression in others.
- The politicization of difference by the dominant group gives privilege to those attributes that it possesses at the expense of other groups and the means to maintain this privilege across all domains of society (i.e., across social, political, cultural, and economic realms).
- One of the ways that the dominant group maintains its privilege is that it is able to define subordinate groups in negative ways as different and inferior (i.e., the Other) and impose this identity on them. This identity of difference and inferiority is reinforced in the media, the education system, the political system, the church, literature, and other social institutions, which are all controlled by the dominant group.
- A contest is entered into with the dominant group attempting to maintain its privileged position and subordinate groups attempting to (re)claim their self-defined identity and sense of self, to become full-fledged citizens, and to achieve a society marked by social equality.
- The subordinate individual is not without power or agency. Because everyone has multiple identities, subordinate groups have alternative identities different from the ones imposed on them, some of which may be privileged. These privileged identities can be used for political purposes, such as affirming positive self-identities and deconstructing dominant categories of identity to neutralize their hegemonic potential.

person into a different social position that is not as threatening; and (3) the revision of the content or value dimensions of identity structure. Although an overview of each coping mechanism is well beyond the scope of this book, a brief overview of the levels at which these coping mechanisms occur is presented below.

Intrapsychic coping mechanisms operate at the cognitive and emotional levels rather than at the action level, although they have implications for action. There are a number of groups of intrapsychic strategies: (1) those that deflect the implications of the threats to identity; (2) those that accept the threat as real and attempt to modify parts of one's identity to escape from or reduce it; and (3) those that re-evaluate and change (excising part of or adding to) the contents of identity because one or more aspects of the identity may engender threats. Interpersonal coping strategies rely on changing relationships with others to cope with threats. Examples are isolating oneself from others and its opposite strategy, negativism, whereby the person confronts anyone who threatens his or her identity structure. Group coping strategies include joining a number of different groups simultaneously to ameliorate the threat or stigma of being a member of one's identity group only. Another group strategy is to come together with others who are experiencing the same threat or form of oppression (either as an information-exchange group or a self-help group). The following sub-section presents a different version of some of these coping mechanisms.

Effects of Oppression on the Psychological Functioning of the Oppressed Person

Moane (1999), in reviewing a series of studies, found that oppression negatively affects psychological functioning because it leads to a loss of personal identity (discussed above), a sense of inferiority or low self-esteem, fear, powerlessness, suppression of anger, alienation and isolation, and guilt or ambivalence. Some of these effects of oppression are discussed in the following paragraphs.

Positivist psychological literature claims that self-esteem is positively related to one's identity as a dominant group member and negatively related to one's identity as a subordinate group member. However, Adam (1978) points out a number of problems with such findings. First, measures of 'general self-esteem' often run aground in a conceptual fog. All assume a universal absolute standard of esteem and anxiety and ignore the general level of anxiety tolerance of the group of which the individual is a member. Heightened insecurity may be normal in a particular context. For example, one study (Powell 1973, cited in Adam 1978) found higher self-esteem among black citizens in a southern US city with a large black population, a historically black university, a militant student population, and an active desegregation program than among a small ghettoized black population in a northern city with a conservative Protestant majority and an apathetic city administration. Second, exclusive focus on psychological states incorrectly equalizes their macro-social conditions. For example, McCarthy and Yancey (1971) and Rosenberg and Simmons (1971) found that many of the studies carried out in the 1960s, which compared black and white levels of self-esteem, ignored the white hegemony of earning a living, going to school, reading, watching television, participating in the consumer society, and so on. Finally, such measures ignore the situationality of the phenomenon because they are based on the concept of a unitary, fixed, or essential identity. A black person's personal self-esteem and his or her racial self-esteem, for example, may differ dramatically, and the self-esteem among black people ranges from high to low levels.

What the self-esteem studies are likely reflecting is the fact that a subordinate person's social environment is one in which insecurity is normal. Lack of control over one's destiny and the unpredictability of one's world contribute to a general insecurity, anxiety, fear, and restlessness. Black children, for example, perceive their environments as more threatening than white children do (Baughman 1971, cited in Adam 1978). The gay or lesbian person does not know what to expect from family, friends, and workmates if and when he or she 'comes out.' The verbal bashing of poor people and social assistance programs by bourgeois politicians and the mainstream media contributes to unrest and worry among people receiving financial assistance. The objective insecurity of members of subordinate groups is often mirrored in a heightened sense of personal insecurity and anxiety (Adam 1978). This may lead to lowered self-esteem, but it may not. And if it does, it may not mean lower self-esteem in every area of the subordinate person's psyche.

Another psychological effect of oppression is that members of subordinate groups often assume ambivalence or guilt for the systemically constricted life chances available to them. The post-colonial revolutionary and writer Frantz Fanon (1967, 139) says, 'All those white men in a group, guns in their hands, cannot be wrong. I am guilty. I do not know of what, but I know that I am no good.' Oppressed persons might ask themselves, 'What have I (or my identity group) done to attract the hostilities of society?' In the absence of anything obviously responsible for the oppressive situation, coupled with the continuous message from the dominant group that they and similar people are ugly, degenerate, and morally inferior, subordinate persons often blame themselves. Women who are sexually assaulted might ask, 'What did I do to bring on this assault?' Black parents might teach their children not to do anything to attract negative attention and then berate them when they are harassed or beaten even if the attacks were unprovoked. Concentration camp victims often experienced profound guilt about events completely beyond their control. Gay and lesbian persons may suffer enormous guilt (especially for disappointing their parents), given religious teachings that homosexuality is an abomination and until recently its classification by the medical establishment as a mental illness (Greenberg 1988). Suffering, it seems, can lead to the growth of guilt. Suffering may be experienced as 'guilt anxiety' rather than social injustice. Over time it develops a logic of its own in that it emerges as an ingrained, reflexive mechanism to cope with oppression (Adam 1978). Sometimes it is easier to accept blame and punish oneself for something one did (but in reality did not do) than to believe that the hostile environment one faces stems from who one is and is thus beyond one's control. In this way, social order is maintained.

Alienation is another outcome of oppression. In fact, Bulhan (1985, 186) argues that it is the key to understanding oppression: 'there is hardly a concept as pertinent to the situation of oppression as alienation.' The concept has a long history and has gone through many reformulations, most notably by Rousseau, Hegel, and Marx. Bulhan argues that it is a dynamic concept with synthesizing power. It not only relates experience to social conditions but also entails a critique. And consistent with critical social theory, this critique implies a solution. Marx's concept of alienation is probably the best known. He argued that capitalism resulted in the alienation of the worker and that this alienation had four aspects. The first was the worker's alienation from the product of his or her labour, which, according to Meszaros (1970), meant alienation from that which mediates the worker's relationship to the external world and hence to the objects of nature. The second aspect of Marx's concept of alienation was the worker's alienation from himself or herself because he or she is coerced, controlled, and regimented and therefore derives no intrinsic satisfaction from work activities. The worker is alienated from his or her own activity, and that also means alienation from his or her body, mind, and spirit, which taken together constitute the self. The third aspect refers to alienation from human essence as the worker is denied realization of his or her inherent human potential through work activity. The final aspect of Marx's concept of alienation is alienation from other people in that capitalism divides society into antagonistic classes (owners and workers) to the point where degradation and violence ensue (Bulhan 1985).

Obviously, Marx's concept of alienation is that of 'alienated labour,' and his focus was on economic and class oppression. Fanon (1967), the black Algerian psychiatrist, revolutionary, and intellectual, adopted alienation as a central and synthesizing concept. Bulhan, in his book on Fanon and his ideas, points out that although Fanon was greatly influenced by the Marxian formulation of alienation, as a psychiatrist he was interested in a psychological perspective of the concept. As well, his exposure to existentialism (he was a personal friend of Jean-Paul Sartre), phenomenology, and psychoanalysis enriched his perspective on alienation. His reformulation of the concept of alienation, which occurred in a developmental way over years of observing and experiencing colonization first-hand and gathering clinical data, emphasized some variables (i.e., cultural and psychological) more than others (i.e., economic and class).

Bulhan outlines Fanon's concept of alienation, which contains five aspects: (1) alienation from the 'self' or from one's corporality and personal identity; (2) alienation from 'significant others'—that is, from one's family and group; (3) alienation from the 'general other,' illustrated by the violence and paranoia characterizing relations between the white colonizers and black colonized; (4) alienation from one's 'culture' or from one's language and history; and (5) alienation from 'creative praxis,' which involves the denial and/or abdication of self-determined, socialized, and organized activity. Fanon's concept of alienation obviously contains more relevance for more groups of oppressed people than Marx's concept does, since it extends alienation beyond class and economics. Fanon himself emphasized alienation from self and alienation from culture as the most significant aspects of alienation.

The following section looks at how oppressed persons might respond to oppression and its effects. The role of an anti-oppressive social worker in dealing with the effects of oppression will be covered in the final two chapters.

Surviving Oppression: Responses of Oppressed People at the Personal Level

Frantz Fanon (1967; 1968) proposed a theory of identity development among oppressed people. He presented three models of psychological defence and identity development under conditions of prolonged oppression: the first involved a pattern of compromise; the second, flight; and the third, fight. Bulhan (1985) developed these three models into stages of colonization (although they have relevance for most oppressed groups). Although the notion of stages is fraught with practical difficulties because it implies a linear track of progress (see the discussion in Chapter 8 on the limitations and dangers of adopting linear developmental models), Bulhan's model sheds some light on the shifting relationship between oppressed people and their oppressors. The first stage (capitulation) involves an identification on the part of the oppressed with the oppressor, which results in increased assimilation into the dominant culture along with a simultaneous rejection of one's own culture. The second stage (revitalization) sees a reactive repudiation of the dominant culture and a defensive romanticization of the subordinate (or indigenous culture in post-colonial terms). The third stage (radicalization) is characterized by synthesis and an unambiguous commitment to radical change. In a not dissimilar fashion, Dominelli (2002) identifies three possible courses of action for oppressed people in response to their oppression: acceptance, accommodation, and rejection. She contends that any one individual or group may use any one of these in a strategic or tactical manner to achieve a particular goal and may move from one to the other in no particular sequence.

Adam (1978) outlines a similar model of responses to oppression. He presents two major sets of responses that oppressed people may make with respect to their lived oppression: (1) accommodation and compliance through a process of accepting one's externally imposed inferior status or (2) rejection through a process of collective resistance and a politics of difference (Adam 1978; Young 1990). Although presented here in binary form, some oppressed persons may adopt both sets of responses and shift from one to the other depending on the context. Accommodative responses are discussed below, while rejection of inferior status and resistance are considered in Chapters 5 and 8. It should be noted that although the responses that seem to reflect a sense of inferiority on the part of subordinate persons are outlined here, the concept of 'internalized oppression' and various theories or explanations of it will be covered in detail in Chapter 6.

As noted earlier, members of oppressed groups are defined by the dominant group in ways that often devalue, objectify, and stereotype them as different, deviant, or inferior. Expressions of their own experiences and interpretation of social life have little place in the dominant culture (Young 1990). Because they find themselves reflected in literature, the media, formal education, and so forth either not at all or in a highly distorted fashion, they often suffer an impoverished identity (Adam 1978). The paradox of this situation for oppressed populations is that at the same time that they are rendered invisible by the dominant group, they are also marked as different.

The lack of a strong self-identity can, in many cases, lead to an internalization of the dominant group's stereotyped and inferiorized images of subordinate populations (Young 1990). This internalized oppression, in turn, causes some oppressed people to act in ways that affirm the dominant group's view of them as inferior people and consequently leads to a process of inferiorized persons reproducing their own oppression. Through a process of cultural and ideological hegemony, many oppressed people believe that if they cannot make it in our society, that if they are experiencing problems, it is their own fault because they are personally incapable of taking advantage of the opportunities that the dominant group says are available to everyone. It is, as Paulo Freire (1994 [1970]) said, as though the oppressor gets into the head of the oppressed. People come to understand their interests in ways that reflect the interests of the dominant group.

When people internalize their oppression, blaming themselves for their troubled circumstances, they often contribute to their own oppression by considering it unique, unchangeable, deserved, or temporary (Adam 1978), or they may blame other significant people in their lives, such as parents or other family members. Oppressed persons often also contribute to their own oppression by psychologically or socially withdrawing or engaging in self-destructive behaviours, which leads to their rejection by others. This rejection in turn confirms the low image they may have of themselves (Moreau and Leonard 1989). The radical psychiatric movement of the 1970s considered all alienation as the result of oppression that has mystified or deceived oppressed people. That is, the oppressed person is led to believe either that he or she is not oppressed or that there are good reasons for his or her oppression (Agel 1971).

Paulo Freire (1994 [1970]) discusses several positions that oppressed people may adopt that either reinforce or contribute to their own oppression. Fatalism may be expressed by the oppressed about their situation—'there is nothing I can do about it' and 'it is God's will' are common expressions of fatalism. However, the oppressor often interprets this fatalistic attitude as docility or apathy, which reinforces the dominant group's view of the oppressed as lazy, inferior, and getting no more than they deserve. Horizontal violence often occurs among oppressed people—an Aboriginal person, for example, might strike out at another for petty reasons—which again reinforces the negative images of subordinate groups held by the dominant class. Self-deprecation also occurs when a group hears so often that they are good for nothing that in the end they become convinced of their own unfitness. Moreau and Leonard (1989) and Adam (1978) call this process 'inferiorization.' Another characteristic of some oppressed persons is that they feel an irresistible attraction towards the oppressor and his or her way of life, which is rather similar to the Stockholm Syndrome whereby hostages over time often come to feel affection and even admiration for their captors. This affirms, of course, the belief that oppression is legitimate and that it is more desirable to oppress than to be oppressed.

It must be noted that such responses on the part of the oppressed persons who use them are not irrational. Although they may appear to be peculiar, unnatural, or neurotic, they are actually rational coping mechanisms employed in everyday life to lessen the suffering of oppression. Their irrationality lies in the fact that they also function to sustain domination. Adam (1978) identified seven such responses, as follows.

1. *Mimesis.* One response to oppression is for a member of a particular oppressed group to mimic or imitate the behaviours and attitudes that the dominant group displays towards that group in an attempt to gain a slightly more privileged status. For

example, the harshest critics of the non-working poor often are the working poor (who repeat all the punitive and moralistic accusations expressed by the dominant group), even though both groups suffer the oppression associated with poverty. Similarly, an organized women's group in Canada called REAL Women has been unrelenting in its attack on the efforts of the women's movement to obtain more gender equality in society, and 'Uncle Tom' black persons who are given positions of authority over other black persons not infrequently treat their subordinates as inferiors rather than as compatriots.

Each oppressed group has a small class of converts and apologists who assist the dominant group in the preservation of the status quo by conforming to the values of their 'masters.' Impressed with the small privileges that go with their 'borrowed status,' they savour these privileges and often defend them by instilling fear and employing harshness. Over time, the converts often come to identify more with the dominant group than with their own community, thus presenting it with a chronic threat or destabilizing force from within.

2. *Escape from identity.* To avoid or ease the burdens of oppression, some inferiorized persons attempt to escape from the 'composite portrait' (with its accompanying range of social penalties) used by the dominant group to define their particular place in society. Although this behaviour may be regarded as neurotic in that one cannot escape from what one is (or is constructed to be), the person attempting to flee from his or her identity views escape as an attempt to move into another social category— one with fewer social penalties attached to it. However, escaping one's identity isolates the individual from others in the same subordinate group because it means denying or not recognizing that one is a member of that group. Examples are Jews who convert to Christianity solely to escape their primary identity, gay and lesbian persons who enter into heterosexual marriages in order to be socially accepted, and women who associate exclusively with men.

Escape from identity, like other inferiorized responses to oppression, functions as a form of false consciousness that subordinates the person to the rationality of oppression. As well, it successfully isolates the person from others who share the same form of oppression. This false consciousness and fragmentation of oppressed people serve to maintain the status quo with respect to dominant–subordinate relations in society.

3. *Psychological withdrawal.* Oppressed persons may adopt a cautious, low-profile conservatism as a way of decreasing their visibility (and social penalties) and compensating for a disfavoured identity. Overly visible behaviour (even though it may sometimes be deliberate acts of resistance to oppression) by fellow members may be strongly condemned because it gives the rest a bad name (for example, the 'loud-mouthed' black, the 'pushy' Jew, or the 'swish' homosexual). Reducing the hazards of a high-risk environment seems to outweigh the value of active resistance. This coping effort is often manifested in psychological responses such as passivity, lethargy, and submission. African-Americans during the period of slavery and Jews in Nazi

concentration camps often exhibited these psychological characteristics. Obviously, psychological withdrawal reinforces rather than threatens the oppressive order.

4. *Guilt-expiation rituals.* Sacrifice is classically conceived as the destruction of a victim for purposes of maintaining or correcting a relationship with the 'sacred' order. Some oppressed persons see the dominant order as sacred and immutable, and to atone for their guilt for not being able to become full-fledged members, they may engage in certain conscious or unwitting guilt-expiation rituals. These rituals become manifest in certain self-mutilating alterations, such as black people straightening their hair and lightening their skin, gay men acquiescing to aversive therapy such as extended electroshock treatment to atone for their imputed transgressions, and the ultimate self-sacrifice of suicide by Aboriginal persons (and others) as a guilt-ridden response to oppression.

5. *Magical ideologies.* Some oppressed people see their situation with respect to the dominant group as so immutable that they look to supernatural means as a way out of their oppressed condition, such as astrology, various superstitious beliefs, messianism, and even gambling. They appeal to someone or something full of power and authority to fix what is wrong. Internal blinders shield the person from confronting the real menace causing his or her inferiorized situation and lead him or her on a search for a magical solution. For example, reading the astrology section of the daily newspaper may be an interesting and harmless pastime for many people, but some people may avoid taking action on troublesome life situations because they believe their destiny is determined solely by the stars. So why even try? They can do nothing about their oppression, because their destiny rests with a force greater than themselves. Every day begins a new search (in an astrological chart) for a sign that their travails will be (magically) alleviated or eliminated. This kind of fatalism is also manifest among the many people who believe that everything in life is in God's hands and that no amount of human endeavour can change what Divine Providence has in store for them. Because people believe that their problems are determined by magical means or supernatural beings, then only a magical or supernatural solution can resolve them.

6. *In-group hostility.* Hierarchies provide a self-perpetuating dynamic that allows the dominated to console themselves by comparing themselves to even more degraded people. This tactic constructs what Adam (1978) calls a 'poor person's snobbery' that sets up a superior-inferior relationship among oppressed groups similar to that between dominant and subordinate groups. It can occur on an inter-group basis, as in the case of members of the white working class oppressing black people, or within an oppressed group, such as closet gay people ridiculing homosexuals or light-skinned black people treating their more dark-skinned compatriots with disdain. In this way, the dynamics of oppression are reproduced by dominated groups themselves.

7. *Social withdrawal.* Social withdrawal is a coping strategy in which the oppressed person externalizes identity conflict into the immediate social environment. The oppressed person may develop repertoires of behaviours for different audiences. That is, he or she will behave in one way when in contact with the dominant group

(usually assuming a low profile to escape attention) and another way when in contact with their own subordinated community (in a way that affirms with others their true identity). Social withdrawal does not challenge or negate the dominant view of the oppressed group, since it is a means of placating the powerful other. For example, black parents may advise their children to avoid (withdraw from) confrontation with the dominant white society as a means of coping with harassment. In effect, this behaviour contributes to a strategy of invisibility, but it also supports the dominant view that black people are by nature servile and passive.

The other side of social withdrawal is that it permits the first move towards reconciliation with other members of one's subordinate group. As oppressed individuals withdraw from the dominant group by acts of compliance and enter into communication with other members of the subordinated community, they may discover their identity with them. That is, they become acquainted with their identity as defined by their own group, as opposed to the identity that has been defined and imposed by the dominant group. A dialectical movement towards integration occurs as community members discover each other and in the process discover themselves. Although the discovery of self and community requires some degree of social withdrawal from an inhospitable social environment controlled by the dominant group, the danger is that it may lead to ghettoization, which, though safe from the dominant group, is also stifling and confining for oppressed persons. The ghetto or haven is a response to oppression and potentially a first assertion of community. It has the potential to stimulate the development of a more genuine identity—a sense of community, solidarity, and confidence—so that members are able to assert their authentic identity and differences in ways that contravene the prevailing rationality of the dominant group.

Social withdrawal opens up the possibility of resistance to dominating power. As noted in Chapter 1, Foucault (1988) argued that power and resistance are implicated in each other—that power and oppression are never exercised without insubordination and obstinacy—that is, without resistance. Resistance is the inevitable and pervasive counterpart of oppression. It can occur on an individual or a collective basis. As such, social withdrawal holds the potential for consciousness-raising, community-building, and mobilization against oppressive structures, cultures, and practices. Chapter 8 further discusses using acts of resistance as strategies to confront and challenge oppression.

Critical Social Theory and Personal Oppression

As observed in Chapter 1, the treatment of oppression and anti-oppression in this book is grounded in critical social theory in general and in the conflict perspective of society in particular. Such theory explains social problems as the result of contests or conflicts between various social groups, with a dominant group controlling most of society's resources and possessing most of the economic and political power. Society is organized for the benefit of this group (mainly bourgeois males of European descent) and is held together not by consensus but by the differential control of resources and power. Social structures, processes, and practices are established by the dominant group and favour its members while oppressing others along lines of class, race, gender, age, sexuality, and so on. In other words, dominant groups enjoy their privilege at the expense of subordinate groups by way of a set of unjust social conditions and a system of oppressive social relations (Gil 1998).

But how is modern-day oppression carried out and sustained? Critical social theory answers this question in general terms by arguing that oppression is relational, cultural, and structural—that people's everyday lives are affected by interactions with others, politics, economics, culture, discourse, social practices, gender, race, and so on. It also argues that structures of oppression are reproduced through the internalization (by both oppressors and oppressed) of dominant–subordinate relations. The practical mission of critical social theory is to translate its developed understandings of domination, exploitation, and oppression into a political (anti-oppressive) practice of social transformation whereby society is freed from these phenomena. Thus, a crucial task for critical social theory is to locate actual practices of domination wherever they occur—that is, at the personal, cultural, and structural levels.

Conclusion

This chapter has critiqued dominant–subordinate relations at the personal level and attempted to locate the social practices of oppression that occur in everyday personal interactions between members of dominant and subordinate groups. The dominant group is able to mark the body of the Other as ugly and degenerate. Furthermore, this inferior body type becomes an indication of an intellectually and morally inferior character. These socially constructed differences are then used by the dominant group as the bases and rationale not only for appropriating most of society's resources and political influence but for carrying out acts of prejudice and discrimination against subordinate group members. Such acts can be either conscious and aggressive or, more likely today, unconscious and aversive. Unconscious and aversive acts of oppression are much more difficult to contravene, since given their nature, they can seldom be legislated against.

The effects of these acts of oppression on oppressed people at the personal level include the imposition of an identity by the dominant group that is often stereotyped, essentialist, and inferior. The subordinate group had no say in the development or definition of this identity. On the surface, there appears to be no escape from this negative identity—subordinate group members are reminded of it in their interactions with the dominant group on a daily basis, and a heightened sense of insecurity and anxiety invariably accompanies it. Even if subordinate group members avoid interactions with the dominant group, they see and hear about their negative identities every day in the media, through the education system, advertising, literature, movies, and so on. The politics of identity include a tendency to accept and internalize this socially constructed and imposed identity and to act in ways that reinforce the stereotypical identity in the eyes of the dominant group.

However, oppressed people can and do respond to their oppression. Some are compliant with and accommodating to their subordinate status while others resist oppression, yet it is not always a simple matter of distinguishing between the two. What may appear to be compliant behaviour to the observer may actually be a coping mechanism on the part of the subordinate person to protect himself or herself from some of the hurt that all oppressed people often experience in their daily interactions with dominant group members. Or it may be an act that resists the image or identity that the dominant group has defined and instead is a preliminary step towards defining one's own identity.

Critical social theory provides a useful framework for understanding oppression in all its complexity. However, to paraphrase Marx, it is not enough to understand an oppressive society—the task is to change it. And as noted in Chapter 1, critical social theory has a practical or political component. One must be able to translate the critical analysis of a subject into a transformative political practice. The implications of this chapter's analysis of dominant–subordinate relations at the personal level for anti-oppressive social work practice are presented in Chapter 8.

Critical Questions for Discussion

1. Have you ever experienced an act of unconscious aggression or aversion directed at you because of some subordinate group identity you may have? What was the act directed at you? How did you feel and what did you think when it happened? Compare what you did at the time with what you really wanted to do. How do you usually cope with these acts of unconscious aggression or avoidance that you experience?

2. Have you ever committed an act of unconscious aggression or aversion in your role as a member of a dominant group? If you can recall such an event, did you do it alone or in conjunction with other members of your identity group? Given your current understanding of unconscious acts of aggression or avoidance, would you do anything differently if the situation were to arise again? If so, what?

3. Make a list of your identities that have a positive value attached to them by society (e.g., white, male). Make a list of your identities that have a negative value attached to them by society (e.g., homosexual, resource-poor). What do you consider your master (most prominent) identity? Why?

4. Make a list of the privileges you enjoy that are associated with each positive identity. (See Peggy McIntosh's celebrated article, 'White privilege'). Make a list

of negative experiences you have had that are attached to each negative identity. Which list was the most difficult to compile—positives or negatives? Why?

5. If you are a member of a subordinate group, how do you usually cope with the negative treatment you receive because of your perceived inferior identity? For example, do you discuss it with your family or other members of your group? Do you grit your teeth and say nothing until the experience passes? Do you use humour to deal with it? Do you strike out verbally or some other way?

6. If you are a member of a dominant group, how do you think you would respond if you received the same negative treatment that members of subordinate groups experience every day simply because of their membership in a subordinate group?

7. When some members of dominant groups are asked about their privilege or are asked a question such as number 6 above, they grow defensive and start talking about the hard times they have experienced and that they worked hard for their privileges and so on. What do you think lies behind this kind of defensiveness and denial of privilege?

Further Readings

Adam, Barry D. (1978). *The Survival of Domination: Inferiorization and Everyday Life.* New York: Elsevier. This book was written well ahead of its time. It remains one of the most insightful and incisive assessments of how domination survives and an inequitable social order is reproduced. It examines the dialectic of inferiorization and responses to inferiorization by presenting a phenomenology of everyday life that comprehends the choices made by people within the material and practical constraints of their subordination, which then recreate or alter that subordination. The responses of resistance, accommodation, and compliance are examined in detail, and strategies to resist domination are presented.

Bulhan, Hussein A. (1985). *Frantz Fanon and the Psychology of Oppression.* New York: Plenum Press. This book, written by an African-American psychologist, presents and extends many of the ideas and theories of the African psychiatrist and revolutionary Frantz Fanon—the father of post-colonialism. Bulhan developed Fanon's three models of psychological defence and identity among colonized/oppressed people (i.e., compromise, flight, and fight) into stages of colonization that have relevance for all oppressed groups—capitulation (assimilation into dominant culture) is the first stage, followed by revitalization (repudiation of the dominant culture), and finally, radicalization (a commitment to radical change). Following Fanon's lead, Bulhan includes culture in psychological theory and practice and further develops a 'black' psychology.

Dominelli, Lena (2002). *Anti-oppressive Social Work Theory and Practice*. Basingstoke, UK: Palgrave Macmillan. This book, written by one of the leading theorists in the field of progressive or critical social work, focuses on how social workers can assist individuals, groups, organizations, communities, and the larger societal context to challenge and transcend the many sources and forms of oppression (e.g., poverty, racism, sexism, disability, mental illness, and so on) that disempower them. A significant focus of the book is that of 'identity' as a central feature of oppression. This is so because identity is intricately bound up with people's sense of who they are and who others are in relation to themselves. Dominelli spells out concepts such as identity politics, identity formation and exclusionary processes, identity in social work, and othering—all from an anti-oppressive framework.

Fanon, Frantz (1994). *Black Skin, White Masks*. New York: Grove Press. This book has been and continues to be a major influence on civil rights, anti-colonial, and black consciousness movements around the world. It is the unsurpassed study of the black psyche in a white world. Fanon presents his thesis that the inferiority complex of a subjugated people and the alienation of some of them from their own identity group results in their wish to be identified with and to imitate their European colonizers. This book is recommended reading for those who wish to understand more about the effect of colonialism on the colonized and their varying reactions to this oppressive menace.

Chapter 4

Oppression at the Cultural Level

The question is not 'is there life after death?' but rather 'is there life after birth?'
—Saul Alinsky

Introduction

In Chapter 2, it was pointed out that culture in the broad sense is often absent in the social work literature. Mainstream writers tend to associate it with ethnicity, and progressive writers tend to lump it in with structural variables. This is unfortunate, given that culture is ubiquitous in everyday life, that everyone participates in cultural practices, and that many of these practices contribute to or maintain relationships of domination and subordination. Culture is not just something to be studied—it is a lived phenomenon. There is a culture associated with every group in society, including professionals such as social workers. The eminent critical social theorist Ben Agger (1992; 2006) contends that the interdisciplinary field of 'cultural studies' (described by progressives of all sorts as a major academic revolution as we start the new millennium) is one of the most important contemporary theoretical movements, drawing on a variety of interrelated sources including the work of Marxist sociologists of culture, the Frankfurt School, feminist theorists, and postmodernists. He argues (2006) that cultural studies has transformed the humanities in two ways. First, it has challenged the canon—that is, the pieces of literature that were thought to convey indispensable Western knowledge and values (i.e., knowledge and values associated with a bourgeois, Eurocentric male living in a capitalist society)—and broadened it to include work done by women, minority groups, and non-Western artists and writers. Second, it has broadened the meaning of culture to include popular culture as a legitimate area for cultural analysis and criticism. Agger also argues that what he calls the new scholarship in the humanities, of which cultural studies is a part (as is feminist studies, queer theory, critical race theory, postmodernism, post-structuralism, and post-colonialism), has informed critical social science in that it views cultural discourses and practices as ideological and commodified and has helped to formulate more general theoretical understandings of society. Thus, cultural studies is truly inter-disciplinary, with no discipline (including social work) falling outside its purview. Table 4.1 highlights some of the main characteristics of cultural studies, which show that it is obviously a critical social theory as defined in Chapter 1.

Table 4.1 Selected Characteristics of Cultural Studies

- Cultural studies aims to examine its subject matter in terms of *cultural practices* and their *relation to power*. Its constant goal is to expose power relationships and examine how these relationships influence and shape cultural practices.
- Cultural studies does not view culture as a discrete entity divorced from its social and political context. Its objective is to understand culture in all its complex forms and to analyze the *social and political context* within which it manifests itself.
- Culture in cultural studies always performs two functions: it is both the *object* of study and the *location* of political criticism and action. Cultural studies aims to be both an intellectual and a pragmatic enterprise.
- Cultural studies attempts to *expose and reconcile the division of knowledge*, to overcome the split between tacit (i.e., intuitive knowledge based on local cultures) and objective (so-called universal) forms of knowledge. It assumes a common identity and common interest between the knower and the known, between the observer and what is observed.
- Cultural studies is committed to a moral evaluation of modern society and to a radical line of political action. The tradition of cultural studies is not one of value-free scholarship but of social reconstruction by critical political involvement. Thus, cultural studies aims to *understand and change* the structures of domination everywhere but in industrial capitalist societies in particular.

Source: Sardar and Van Loon 2004, 9.

For all the above reasons, I followed the lead of Neil Thompson (1997; 2002) and included culture in the first edition of this book in 2002 (informed by 'cultural studies') as one area or level where oppression, resistance, and anti-oppressive practice can occur. Since that time, although lip service has been paid, little serious treatment of culture from a critical perspective has appeared in the literature on anti-oppressive social work practice in Canada or the UK or the US. Yes, books and articles have been written on multicultural social work, culturally sensitive and culturally competent social work practice, and social work practice with diverse populations, but as will be discussed below, these approaches tend to equate culture with race (except for the white race) and/or ethnicity (for example, see *Multicultural Social Work in Canada*, edited by Alean Al-Krenawi and John Graham, 2003) and contribute very little to anti-oppressive practice (see Nelson and McPherson 2003 for an insightful analysis on this point). Seldom is there any discussion of dominant, subordinate, and alternative cultures, or oppressive stereotypes and how to confront them, or dominant discourses and counter-discourses, or cultural issues outside of racial or ethnic groups. Nor is there any discussion of Western culture (Nelson and McPherson 2003). Where is the discussion on class culture, disability culture, non-heterosexist cultures, or on cultures related to primary language spoken, religion, country of birth/adoption, age, or on the multi-dimensional nature of culture and the intersections of various cultures? And where can you find any mention of the scholarship and contributions from the revolutionary academic field of 'cultural studies' that straddle the intellectual and academic landscape from old established disciplines to new political movements, intellectual practices, and modes of inquiry, such as Marxism, post-colonialism, feminism, and post-structuralism? Instead of adhering to tired old social maintenance 'theories' such as systems and ecological approaches (which are not even theories) and treating culture as the 'poor cousin' in social work theory and practice, I believe that we should turn to cultural studies as an activity of critical theory that challenges accounts of mainstream culture that legitimate power, wealth, and elitism (Agger 1992). In my view, treating culture in a narrow way and ignoring scholarship from the field of cultural studies have been serious impediments to the development of anti-oppressive social work theory and practice, especially at the cultural level.

This is not to say that no work has been done in the area of analyzing culture from a critical perspective and incorporating it into emancipatory social work and social welfare practices. Peter Leonard's work (e.g., 1997; 2001) in developing a critical postmodern social work approach is an example. As well, two recent books by American social work authors that focus on cultural social work hold some promise for bringing culture out of its 'poor cousin' status in anti-oppressive social work. *Critical Multicultural Social Work* (2008) by Jose Sisneros et al. is written from a critical perspective and focuses on cultural oppression and privilege. And *Diversity, Oppression and Change: Culturally Grounded Social Work* (2009) by Marsiglia and Kulis, also written from a critical perspective although not as critical as the work of Sisneros et al., avoids the laundry list approach of reviewing all cultural groups and their identities one by one and presents instead a 'culturally grounded perspective' that advances an understanding of the concept of intersectionality.

This chapter presents a critical analysis of culture as a site of oppression, resistance, and anti-oppressive practice. I take as my point of departure the contemporary meaning of culture and how it differs from traditional anthropological and other views. I will argue that because there are always multiple cultures that conflict with one another, culture is highly political and there will always be a dominant culture that helps to maintain the privileged position of the dominant group. The dominant culture does this by promoting, imposing, and universalizing itself while repressing, suppressing, and oppressing other cultures. The chapter also presents an analysis of the oppressive features of 'pop (popular) culture,' along with an overview of different critical theories or perspectives of culture, beginning with Marx and including such notables as Lukács (reification), Gramsci (hegemony), the Frankfurt School (the culture industry), the Birmingham Centre for Contemporary Cultural Studies (counter-hegemony), Baudrillard's postmodern perspective on culture (hyper-reality and the simulation society), and the feminist perspective on culture (feminist cultural politics to create a non-misogynist and gender-equal society). The concept of stereotypes as a form of cultural oppression will be analyzed, as will the role of language and discourse in keeping subordinate groups subservient to the dominant group. Finally, social work as a profession will be examined with respect to the danger that it could become an oppressive force in society instead of a liberating force.

Culture (the 'Poor Cousin' in Social Work)

In Chapter 2, culture was defined as a common set of values and norms, including shared patterns of seeing, thinking, and acting, that a group holds. However, there is no accepted universal definition or unitary notion of culture today. In fact, communication—the 'ways and means' of sharing culture (linguistic, nonverbal, symbolic)—is itself part of culture. For example, the terms 'popular culture' and 'mass culture' are used to refer to the electronic and print media that distribute cultural messages in the form of music, television, novels, movies, and so on. Peter Leonard (1997) identifies three common meanings of culture: (1) high culture—the traditional hierarchical conception in which only the products evaluated positively by elites are counted as culture (e.g., classical music, the arts); (2) popular or mass culture in which the emphasis is on mass-produced cultural forms such as pulp fiction, genre novels, television shows, movies, and videos; and (3) as the objects of ethnographic study—cultures as ways of life of specific societies. Leonard then proceeds to deconstruct these notions in a way that opens up cultural analysis to all sorts of interpretive possibilities.

Proponents of postmodernism, post-structuralism, and cultural studies talk about multiple cultures that often intersect with one another (e.g., cultures of class, gender, race, nation). Indeed, as Agger (1992, 9) notes, 'cultural politics is [today] considered an important auxiliary of traditional class politics, more narrowly defined in economic terms.' Like Leonard, he argues that the concept of culture today is much broader than the received high culture of various literary and philosophical canons. He claims that much of the credit or momentum for expanding the notion of culture is due to the sweeping transformations in information technology after World War II and that a good deal of the momentum of cultural studies is attributable to the post-structural turn in anthropology with its reflexive focus on the impact of anthropological discourse on the cultures and peoples studied by anthropologists. Both Leonard and Agger point out that the earlier modernist notions of culture are problematic because they contain essentialist ideas about culture, making truth claims about the accuracy of descriptions and analyses of 'other' cultures and universalizing cultural domination rather than cultural pluralism.

To explore and present the complexities and various meanings of culture, along with the competing theoretical, political, and methodological treatments and critiques of culture, is well beyond the scope of this book.[1] The best I can do at this point is to outline the concept of culture as it is used here in an attempt to further our understanding of oppression and anti-oppression. I view culture in the broad anthropological sense as any expressive activity that contributes to social learning. This view is similar to that of the Birmingham School of Cultural Studies (discussed in a subsequent section of this chapter). Members of the Birmingham School contend that not all culture is institutionalized, because in the broadest sense, culture refers to the language we use, along with the meanings, symbols, and interpretations of social reality. It includes ideologies, religious faiths, and the texts and representations of social communication that we (as a society) produce. Seidman (1998, 200) articulates this broad view of culture: 'Culture is less the sort of thing we associate with museums, galleries, and prize-winning literature than the meanings—norms, values, beliefs, ideals—that make up the stuff of everyday life.' Culture is what makes us human. It provides the filters through which people look at their lives and the lives of others in their social environments (Marsiglia and Kulis 2009). Culture enables people to find connections and solidarity as they view and interpret the world around them (Takaki 1993, cited in Marsiglia and Kulis 2009). However, these ideas and beliefs change over time because culture is always evolving in its social and political context. As well, not all persons respond in the same way to their common culture, since they have different levels of adherence to the collective norms and different interpretations of the cultural worlds they inhabit. Therefore, although it is important that social workers understand culture and its impact on individuals (i.e., cultural sensitivity and literacy), they should be aware of potential individual differences within a culture to avoid essentialist conclusions and group stereotypes (Takaki 1993, cited in Marsiglia and Kulis 2009).

As suggested above, society is saturated with culture. And because culture involves social learning, it is inherently political, since social learning both communicates and reproduces the social order. Williams (1981, 13) underscores this political function when he defines culture as 'the signifying system through which necessarily (though among other means) a social order is communicated, reproduced, experienced and explored.' Thus, culture as a system of signifiers not only provides a sense of location for individuals and communities, it also provides a location of conflict—an important insight for anti-oppressive practice. Cultural social work writers such as Marsiglia and Kulis (2009) point out that an individual's culture is the outcome of a number of factors such as class, gender, race, age, sexual orientation, and religion intersecting with each other. Cultures also have a history and carry a story about their origins and how they became what they are today. For these reasons, it is important to examine the oppression of cultural groups from historical and sociological perspectives. 'Every individual is a complex collection of identities that draw from many different types of heritages and from membership in different social groups, and the individual plays a role in how these identities are brought together' (Marsiglia and Kulis 2009, xviii).

In Western, pluralistic society, there are always multiple cultures that often conflict with one another, but usually one culture dominates and a number of cultures are subordinate. Consistent with critical postmodern thought, the dominant culture attempts to remain dominant through the suppression of difference and multiplicity inherent in a pluralistic society. In other words, one of the ways the dominant group is able to maintain hierarchical divisions of class, gender, race, age, sexual orientation, and the like is by promoting, imposing, and universalizing its own culture while repressing or suppressing other cultures. This is not to say that culture is simply imposed on people from without; rather, as the post-structuralists suggest, it is lived practice. In other words, culture is not only received by people as consumers, but it is also produced and reproduced by the same people in everyday life. However, before we explore how the dominant culture remains dominant, we first must consider some of the elements of the dominant culture.

The Dominant Culture

Adam (1978, 30) states that 'Educational institutions, churches, the mass media, the publishing industry, and other [cultural] agents serve as conduits of cultural reconstitution, by continually reproducing the language and symbolic universe of a society.' But what is it exactly that is reconstituted or reproduced? In a nutshell, the dominant cultural messages, images, or products are those that present a world view or define reality in ways that privilege males over females, affluent people over poor people, white persons over persons of colour, heterosexual people over homosexual or bisexual people, young adults over children and older adults, Christians over non-Christians, able persons over persons with disabilities, anglophones over non-anglophones, employed people over unemployed people, two-parent families over other forms of families, North (industrialized countries) over South (industrializing countries), Western societies over Eastern societies, liberal democracies over social or socialist democracies, and capitalism over other economic systems. What we have is a totalizing culture with inclusions and exclusions. Most people would fall within some of the above categories of the dominant culture, but most people would also fall outside many of the categories. A white woman, for example, is a member of the dominant group with respect to race or colour but is a subordinate member with respect to gender. A loose argument could be that the more dominant characteristics one has, the more privileged one tends to be. Also, the fact that almost everyone is a member of at least one dominant group makes it difficult to challenge the dominant culture, since everyone has at least a little stake in preserving it (this point is pursued in Chapter 7).

Advertising, the news, entertainment, and other mass media forms produce and distribute images and products that depict the dominant groups or social systems as the norm—the 'official definition of reality' (Adam 1978). Every day, dominant group members see their identity groups, their religion, their social systems, their language, and so on presented as the norm in the mass media, in their government bodies, in advertising, and in other cultural arenas. In effect, they see themselves seamlessly reflected in the 'official culture' of society. As Young (1990, 59) notes, 'the dominant cultural products of the society, that is, those most widely disseminated, express the experience, values, goals, and achievements of these [dominant] groups.'

In contradistinction to the dominant groups, members of subordinate groups discover themselves as symbols of the Other, manipulated in the transmission of the dominant culture. Frantz Fanon (1986; 1989) argued that members of indigenous populations in colonized countries characteristically feel inferior if they do not conform to the cultural values imposed by the colonizers and that when their own culture is not validated, they become resentful and withdrawn (cited in Hopton 1997). The systematic selection of particular characteristics of subordinate group members for public presentation by agents of cultural transmission constructs an image that rationalizes an inferior or fearful status for subordinate groups. For example, even before the events of 11 September 2001, people from the Middle East were constantly presented in American movies, television, and novels over the past decade as swarthy, unshaven, sinister, fanatical terrorists who were hell-bent on bringing the United States to its knees. Conversely, those fighting the evil terrorists tended to be portrayed as youthful, white (sometimes with a token African-American), English-speaking, Christian, and macho males—an American cultural and stereotypical ideal.

Studies and analyses of the cultural products and messages transmitted by the media (in North America, at least) have shown that the dominant group and the status quo consistently receive favourable treatment and, conversely, that subordinate groups and their efforts to obtain social justice consistently receive negative treatment (see, for example, Gitlin 1980). In an excellent chapter on community organizing and the media, Biklen (1983) presents an overview of how and why the media protect the status quo and undermine the legitimate aspirations and social change activities of subordinate groups. Biklen looks at the news and entertainment functions of the media separately (he does not look at advertising). He argues that both areas legitimate the status quo by defining social reality in narrow terms that are more in accordance with the lived reality of the dominant group than that of subordinate groups. The media limit audiences' viewing and reading choices to events and interpretations that fall within the prevailing institutional order. For example, crime is defined as most devastating (i.e., front-page news) when a member of the upper socio-economic group is the victim and least devastating (i.e., back-page or no coverage) when the victim is a subordinate group member. The media define politics in terms of political leaders and treat social movements, which are also political events, as one status step above crime. Similarly, they define power as something that a small group possesses but do not suggest that this power is enjoyed by a few at the expense of others (usually subordinate groups). Not only do the media treat power, politics, and crime narrowly (and consistent with corporate values), but they do the same with regard to social problems and other critical social phenomena. Biklen states as well that they treat subordinate group members and social activists who attempt to change the status quo and their issues as 'marginal, deviant, and not in the preordained set of legitimate choices' (1983, 157).

Biklen argues that the pure entertainment part of the mass media includes many of the characteristics of the news side. For example, television entertainment often presents a stylized and/or stereotypical portrait of North America, which defines the public's sense of reality and the nature of social conditions, social change, and viable solutions to social problems in narrow terms that do not threaten the privileged position of the dominant group. Using one of Todd Gitlin's (1979) critiques of television, Biklen (1983, 163) says of its treatment of difference:

> Television treats difference (for example, poverty, homosexuality, aging) romantic- ally, as a vehicle for humour, individualistically, or not at all. Situation comedies portray poverty in a romantic, humorous light. Productions that deal with human tragedy tend to treat genuine differences as individual problems with individual solutions. Even when television ventures out to deal with controversial topics such as racism, prejudice is often shown as laughable. The audience is largely protected from the painful hurt and suffering that attend real-life prejudice. In more realistic shows, we usually learn that social problems and personal differences rarely can ever be solved adequately.

Many subordinate group activists find themselves presented by the media as irresponsible and incompetent militants rather than as people who have suffered first-hand from systemic and systematic discrimination, prejudice, and exploitation. Biklen also makes the point that even when the media recognize the legitimacy of a subordinate person, it is done in a way to suggest that the person is unusual or an exception—not like the others. The media treat social movements in much the same way that they do crime—overly concerned with its effects on the dominant group and tending to sensationalize it. Rather than examining the issues central to public protests and demonstrations, the media tend to focus on the dress, decorum, and size of the group.

The experiences related in the box opposite are but a few examples of one way society controls its dissidents, aided and abetted by the media—kill or defame the messenger and you effectively kill or discredit the message. Fortunately, there have been many instances in which the media have been used to promote the interests of subordinate groups and to bring about social change. However, given the nature of the media and the people who either own or largely control it, any attempt to use them to promote the legitimate causes of subordinate groups requires careful planning to prevent having the message twisted or subverted. Biklen provides some helpful sug- gestions on how to use (and avoid being used by) the media.[2] Any practice of anti- oppressive social work cannot ignore the fact that the mass media reach more people more often than any other mode of communication.

The ethnocentric phenomenon of universalizing the dominant culture as the norm and marginalizing subordinate cultures—as the media invariably do—was identified as 'cultural imperialism' in Chapter 2. All people are socialized, to varying degrees, into the dominant culture, and all social institutions are based on the culture of the dominant group. Conversely, all 'other' cultures are measured against the yardstick of the dominant culture, and the more they deviate from the dominant culture, the more they are judged to be deviant and inferior cultures. But how is this domination, along with its social reproduction and social control functions, actually carried

Media Bias against Social Protest

In the mid-1980s, I was involved in a number of peaceful social protests in my home province of New Brunswick. The media reporting of one demonstration (outside the legislative buildings) against cuts in health, education, and social services gave prominence to the flowerbeds trampled by the 'rowdy demonstrators.' (In fact, they were trampled by the rowdy reporters trying to get photos of or interviews with the leaders of the protest.) Another demonstration, which I helped to organize, had one of the largest turnouts in recent memory in Fredericton, the capital of New Brunswick. In spite of the large turnout, the main question asked of me was how I could account for the lower than predicted turnout. Somehow, an inflated number of expected crowd size had floated around before the demonstration. That became the issue (and the headline)—not the concerns and suffering that had led to the demonstration in the first place or even that it was the largest demonstration in recent years. Some of my Aboriginal colleagues in New Brunswick have told me that it is not unusual during their protests for the media to attempt to elicit a comment from them about the possibility of violence or for reporters to look through the windows of their vehicles for firearms and/or liquor bottles. Of course, such actions by the media are based on the stereotype of drunken, violent, irresponsible 'Indians,' a stereotype often reflected in the news reports.

out? And what are the cultural means whereby dominant cultures are universalized and subordinate cultures repressed and suppressed? In an attempt to answer these questions, we will examine the following four areas with respect to their contributions to maintaining oppression at the cultural level: popular or mass culture; humour and stereotypes; language and discourse; and the culture of (social work) professionalism and respectability.

Popular/Mass Culture

As noted above, popular or mass culture refers to cultural forms that are either mechanically or electronically mass-produced, such as movies, television shows, popular fiction, and popular music. Several writers or schools of writers have looked critically at the role of mass culture in reproducing dominant–subordinate relationships. Although each of their theories or analyses is an incomplete explanation of cultural oppression by itself, cumulatively they help us to better understand how the role of social reproduction is carried out. As a corollary to understanding the social control and social reproduction functions of mass culture, we also develop means of political resistance to dominant cultures and overall social change.

American critical social theorist Ben Agger (1992; 2006) has written extensively in the area of cultural studies as a form of critical theory. It is mainly from his work that I draw the following overviews of the contributions made by various critical theorists to understanding oppression at the cultural level.

Critical Social Theories of Culture

Marx and Ideology

Karl Marx (arguably the founder of critical social theory) produced the earliest critical social theory. Central to Marx's critique of capitalism and the culture of capitalism is the notion of 'ideology.' Whereas the common meaning of ideology today is a world view or a consistent set of social, economic, and political beliefs (Mullaly 2007), Marx used the term to refer to a system of mystifications that invert and distort reality and create falsehoods to protect the capitalist status quo. Much of his critique of capitalism identified ideas that justified (and mystified) its exploitative and oppressive social relations and/or obscured more egalitarian social relations. Such ideas as 'capitalism is necessary' and 'it has a life of its own' were used by the early capitalists (and are repeated by contemporary capitalists) to alleviate class-consciousness and to prevent the working class from seeking alternative economic arrangements.

Marx and Engels (1978) argued that the ruling (i.e., dominant) ideas in a given society are those of the ruling (i.e., dominant) classes and that these ideas, although presented in ways that make them seem to be in everyone's best interests, actually support the interests and privilege of the dominant class. Kellner (1990) notes that ideas such as competition and the right to accumulate unlimited property and wealth, which serve the interests of the capitalist class, are presented as universally valid ideas that serve the interests of everyone.

An example of how Marx engaged in a critique of capitalist ideology may help to clarify this discussion. Marx identified religion (a form of culture) as part of the ideological apparatus of capitalism and referred to it as 'the opiate of the masses.' By this he meant that because religion promised relief from suffering and misery in the hereafter (by admission to heaven), it helped to console and pacify people and reconcile them to material deprivation and occupational servitude here on Earth. In this way, religion acted as an ephemeral narcotic. Marx was much more concerned about the material conditions of 'life after birth' than he was with a spiritual concern of 'life after death,' and he saw the latter as a diversion from the former. He perceived religious teachings such as 'Blessed are the meek, for they shall inherit the earth' as false claims about society that only serve to convince people that radical change is undesirable. Similarly, he perceived messages that capitalism was both inevitable and a rational social and economic system as false claims to divert workers away from the socialist revolution detailed in *The Communist Manifesto* that Marx and Engels produced in 1848 (Marx and Engels 1967). The effects of these false (ideological) claims were to divert people from their alienation and portray the existing society as rational and necessary.

Of course, Marx wrote in the period of early capitalism when the primary concern of many in the working class was to put food on the table. Marx tended to identify culture as a mere reflection and extension of the economic base of capitalism; in other words, his view of culture was that it simply extolled and reflected the values of capitalism as doctrine. Most critical social theorists today believe that culture in late capitalism or global capitalism is much more subtle, complex, and pervasive than the way Marx perceived it more than 160 years ago. Rather than simply reflecting the economy or operating independently of it, culture today is seen by theorists as necessarily appearing to operate independently of the economy—otherwise, it would not so effectively maintain and celebrate the status quo. Thus, ideology continues to be an important concept in the study and understanding of culture and cultural domination, but Marxist cultural theorists have reformulated Marx's original concept in light of the limitations noted above.

As well as being narrow and underdeveloped, the ideology of capitalism in Marx's time was clear and visible because it was contained in books (e.g., the Bible) or in stated assertions by capitalists. Because this ideology was conveyed in a visible and audible form, it seemed relatively easy to address and refute clear-cut claims that oppression and suffering in this world will be overcome in the next world (in heaven) by counter-factual claims that, for example, there is no afterlife. However, this early Marxist view of ideology overlooks the facts that ideology (1) is not always conveyed in the form of a clear-cut text but is often concealed and thus difficult to refute and (2) is not simply something that is read or received through ideological indoctrination but is experienced in our everyday lives in which subtle and subliminal messages are conveyed in ways that are so tied into cultural discourses, practices, and experiences that we lose the distinction between what is real and what is illusory. To account for these broader notions of ideology and culture, we must turn to other critical social theorists.

Reification and Hegemony

Two early twentieth-century theorists who attempted to update, reformulate, and expand Marxist theory are Georg Lukács and Antonio Gramsci. Although it was not their central focus, both addressed the concepts of ideology and culture. Lukács was among the first Marxists to give serious attention to culture in a way that suggested that in the form of art and literature (i.e., high culture), it was an important realm in and of itself for social and political investigation. In effect, he helped to free culture from its Marxist 'economistic' straitjacket (Agger 1992).

Lukács's main goal was to explain why the socialist revolution that Marx had prophesied did not occur. As part of his explanation, Lukács (1971) argued that as capitalism advanced from its early form in the nineteenth century to a technological form in the twentieth, workers did not face the same dire material conditions as existed earlier and began to accept capitalism as an inevitable and workable social and economic system. According to Lukács, this is exactly the image of capitalism that the capitalists wanted to nurture, and they increasingly manipulated class-consciousness to convince people that radical social change was impossible. Lukács called this claim 'reification'—the reduction of social relations, culture, and ideas to inert processes that, like nature, appear frozen and hence unchangeable (Agger 2006). In other words, reification supported the view of society as an immutable part of nature. Conservative religious doctrine, evolutionary biology, and 'laws' (*sic*) of bourgeois economics were used to rationalize this status quo position. Also, the development of state intervention (including the welfare state) and the emergence and growth of the middle class served to dampen any revolutionary fervour that may have previously existed among the working class. Although Lukács made a significant contribution to understanding how social relations under capitalism were reproduced in everyday life, his analysis was predominantly a class analysis.

Antonio Gramsci, an Italian Marxist, extended the cultural critique beyond ideas associated with a class-based ideology or cultural political economy. He perceived culture as a relatively autonomous area of experience and practice with respect to the economic system and analyzed culture to examine the conventional wisdom of a society promoted in everyday life through various sources of hegemony (Gramsci 1971). In Gramsci's writings, hegemony refers to the unquestioned dominance of all conformist ideas that support the interests of the group promoting them. These ideas embody social structures and lead to a reproduction of society. The following is a good summary of the meaning of hegemony.

> As part of a continuous historical process, through control of the education system, religious institutions, the mass media, and internationally, through economic and cultural imperialism, those at the top of the [social] hierarchy can produce and promote ideologies that help to justify their position at the top, justifying the power and privileges that this position brings. It is necessary for the dominant group to promote the belief that the social hierarchy is necessary for the well-being of society as a whole and that the current social structure is inevitable and natural [McDonald and Coleman 1999, 22].

Hegemony goes beyond clear-cut texts that contain falsehoods or indoctrination about the necessity for and rationality of the present society. It also refers to the ways in which domination is produced not only from outside everyday life (through the structures of capitalism) but also from within everyday life by people who are resigned to their subordinate positions and are often supportive and enthusiastic about the 'goods' society. In fact, Gramsci and subsequent critical social theorists have made the point that the most effective hegemonic messages are those concealed in various discourses of popular culture and in people's everyday experiences and activities.

Kellner (1990) distinguishes between hegemony and propaganda. Whereas propaganda has the connotation of deliberate, planned, heavy-handed, and coercive manipulation, hegemony suggests a subtle process of incorporating persons into particular patterns of belief and behaviour. Hegemony functions in ways that divert people from their alienation by suggesting such relief as watching television or shopping and subtly depict current society as rational, inevitable, and necessary. This concept of hegemony goes a long way towards explaining how culture is a crucial factor in maintaining dominance and exploitation, although not necessarily in any deliberate or conspiratorial way.

Gramsci is important in another way as well. His view of society went beyond the simplistic monolithic model of a belief that social institutions are merely instruments of class or group domination. He recognized that in any society there is a competition over which assumptions, ideas, beliefs, and positions are dominant. In his view, hegemony is never established for all time but is always open to negotiation and/or contestation—by efforts to establish counter-hegemony on behalf of subordinate groups (Kellner 1990). The idea of developing counter-hegemony and contributing to a crisis of the dominant hegemony, in my view, contains enormous potential for anti-oppressive practice.

The Culture Industry

The Frankfurt School theorists—Theodor Adorno, Herbert Marcuse, and Max Horkheimer and their heir apparent, Jürgen Habermas—have made sophisticated revisions to Marx's original works and have contributed enormously to the development of critical social theory (see Jay 1973 for an overview of the Frankfurt School). They addressed a 'later' late stage of capitalism than did Lukács. One of their contributions was the development of the concept of the 'culture industry' to explain ideological manipulation and cultural domination. Horkheimer and Adorno used the term 'culture industry' to refer to the ways by which entertainment and the mass media became industries in post–World War II capitalism that distributed cultural commodities and manipulated people's consciousness. The culture industry thesis helps to explain how the commodification of culture in late capitalism contributes to both profits and social control. In effect, they argued that it is impossible to separate the economic system from the ideological or cultural dimensions of capitalism, an argument that gave critical social theory its own dialectical methodology of analyzing society at both the economic and cultural levels simultaneously (Agger 1992).

The Frankfurt theorists viewed mass culture as a late capitalist mode of ideology that acted much like Marx's notion of religion (as ideology) in anaesthetizing the masses. Instead of presenting clear texts about the necessity for and rationality of the present society, mass culture diverts people's attention away from their personal problems and the irrationality of the present system by idealizing the present and making it appear pleasurable (Agger 1998). Watching movies or television occupies people's time, takes their minds off their troubles, and suggests that they ought to solve their problems by the same means and in the same world as the people they are viewing—that is, in ways that do not involve radical social change. And even if viewers are unable to overcome problems in the same way, they can vicariously enjoy the problem resolution of others by identifying with the people on the screen.

Not only does the culture industry make a profit from movies, magazines, and television shows, it also remedies our alienation through the processes of diversion and identification. And as Agger (1998) points out, although the culture industry may operate in the same way that religion does, it is not a structured document like the Bible or the Koran that can be studied and criticized. Nor does it offer relief in the distant hereafter as religion does; rather, it offers immediate relief. The Frankfurt theorists argued that the culture industry of late capitalism has rendered culture part of our everyday existence. Culture is not separate from us. It *is* us. This makes it much more difficult to critique than when it was a realm apart.

Another argument coming from the culture industry thesis is that mass culture is relatively undifferentiated because all classes and groups in society are exposed to the same advertising and entertainment. Thus, all classes and groups develop the same or similar consumer aspirations, as well as a common world view characterized by individualism, consumerism, and other capitalist values. In this way, mass culture appears to level class differences, which in effect actually protects them.

The culture industry thesis also argues that mass culture, by way of advertising, creates or manufactures certain false or manipulated needs and desires in order to ensure that mass consumption matches mass production. These needs or desires are not arrived at through autonomous or rational thought; they are imposed on us. As well, the images that bombard us through the mass media not only stimulate consumption, they also deflect critical thought because people tend to identify themselves primarily with their leisure and consumer lifestyles. In this way, according to the Frankfurt School, the reproduction of capitalism is guaranteed.

The Birmingham Centre for Contemporary Cultural Studies

The ideas of the above Marxist cultural theories and theorists set the stage for more recent critical theories of culture. Gramsci's writings on hegemony and counter-hegemony, as well as his notion of the 'organic intellectual' (Gramsci 1971), are central to most schools of cultural studies today. The term 'cultural studies' was popularized by the Birmingham Centre for Contemporary Cultural Studies, which was established in 1964. This group of interdisciplinary scholars has developed a highly original body of literature indebted to Marxist theory, but they have gone beyond Marxist approaches to culture to synthesize such diverse intellectual and political influences as critical social theory, postmodernism, post-structuralism, post-colonialism, and feminism. The work of the Birmingham School was particularly influenced by its confrontations with Margaret Thatcher and her policies attacking intellectuals, the Left, and the working class (see, for example, Hall 1988). Thus, much of their work, carried out closer to everyday politics and social movements, has been more concrete than that of the members of the

Frankfurt School, whose theorizing reflects a certain social distance and aloofness. For example, empirical studies have been carried out by various Birmingham scholars on working-class and youth culture (see, for example, Brake 1980; Clarke 1990; Hebdige 1979, 1988; Willis 1977, 1978) and women's culture (McRobbie 1981; Radway 1984).

The Birmingham cultural theorists have been able to maintain theoretical integrity in their work while grounding it in political critique. Using Gramsci's theory of cultural hegemony, their studies analyze hegemony[3] at the level of everyday cultural practices with the intent of developing counter-hegemonic practices—alternative formulations of culture and everyday life that counter dominant formulations. This, of course, takes cultural studies away from being a mere academic activity and gives it a political purpose and practice. It also differentiates the Birmingham School from the Frankfurt School—the latter, for the most part, gave up on the politics of everyday life (i.e., attempting to achieve social transformation), which reflects historical differences in the contexts of the two schools more than theoretical differences.

Among the many contributions that the Birmingham School has made to the study of culture is that by insisting that working-class culture should receive attention, it has helped to broaden the study of culture to include work done by women, minorities, and non-Western writers and artists. Conversely, it has contributed to the rejection within the cultural studies movement of the values conveyed by the white, male, bourgeois, Eurocentric canon—notably capitalism, Christianity, and male supremacy. This again reflects the political or social change dimension of the Birmingham Centre for Contemporary Cultural Studies. I will look more carefully at some of their political practices in Chapter 8 when I discuss anti-oppressive social work practice at the cultural level.

Postmodern Perspective on Culture

The postmodern theory of Baudrillard (1983) makes a significant contribution to our understanding of how today's mass culture helps to maintain the status quo. His concepts of the 'simulation society' and 'hyper-reality' show how the process of power associated with Marx's notion of the mode of production has tended to be replaced by the process of power coming from electronic means of information and entertainment. Baudrillard argues that in postmodernity (what he calls hyper-reality), we lose all distinction between reality and 'simulations' of reality that come from advertising, journalism, and entertainment.

In an age of hyper-reality, texts written to reveal reality, such as Marx's *Capital*, lose their capacity to educate, anger, and stimulate people to engage in social change because they are not distinguished from, nor are they as popular as, magazines and tabloids found on racks at grocery store checkouts. Agger (1998) contends that the most efficacious social texts of our times are popular magazines (e.g., *People, Seventeen*), movies, and advertisements for clothing, beer, and other consumer products because they embody everyday discourses that make simulation more real than reality. Few books today are intended to be read slowly and critically. Of this, Agger says:

Simulated Family Life Today

The example of simulated family life most cited in the literature focuses on television and the family. Instead of sitting at the dinner table discussing each others' day at work, school, or home and thus bonding together, it is commonplace today for families either to eat (often fast foods) quickly and rush to the television or to eat their evening meal in front of the television to watch/consume a simulation of family life. And usually, these simulations present an idealized happy, harmonious, traditional, and successful problem-solving family image—at a time when the family is undergoing changes in form and structure, when it is experiencing attacks in the form of domestic violence, desertion, careerism, and unattainable materialism, and when members are looking for understanding and satisfying relationships that are not available to them in the workplace or at school. Thus, television (in this case) provides a simulated family life to those experiencing an impoverished or oppressive family life.

Textuality loses the character of considered argument, to be perused in a sense out-side of reality, and becomes a simulation, representation, reproduction, photograph, and figure, thus subtly presenting itself to readers as reality itself (and not an authored text promoting one version of reality among many possible versions) [1998, 141].

This line of reasoning is similar to that of the Frankfurt School, but it gives deeper meaning to how domination is maintained by the narcotic and vicarious effects of the mass media. It is not just a matter of escaping or having people's attention diverted from social problems by popular culture, as asserted by the Frankfurt theorists; it is also the substitution of imagery for reality. This imagery is not just about selling a product either; it is about selling a lifestyle. Beer advertisements, for example, not only promote a particular brand of beer; they (all) promote a particular lifestyle as well—a youthful, physically attractive, popular, and affluent culture. Anyone can be a (simulated) member of this culture by simply purchasing and consuming the product, thus achieving contact with the imagery in the commercial.

The loss of distinction between reality and simulations of reality is an important insight in understanding how the dominant culture reproduces itself. In addition, Agger (1998) claims that the interpretive deconstruction methods of postmodern-ists are useful in (1) revealing the political positioning of various 'social texts,' which comprise 'old-fashioned' doctrinal texts and various discursive practices from academia to advertising and (2) suggesting reformulations of oppressive discursive practices. This will be considered further when we come to language and discourse.

Feminist Perspectives on Culture

Since the women's movement in the 1960s, feminists have sought to empower women to speak in their own voices about their own experiences in order to form their own images of themselves. This has led to a feminist cultural politics that seeks to create a feminist, non-misogynist culture. Agger (1998) contends that all feminists—liberal, socialist, radical, cultural, Marxist, and visible minority—emphasize the following three goals of feminist cultural politics, although each school of feminism conceptualizes these goals differently and accords different explanatory power to each.

Feminist cultural politics seeks to (1) make the invisible visible by drawing theoretical and critical attention to cultural works by and about women, (2) unmask and oppose the sexual objectification of women in culture, particularly through feminist film theory and a critique of pornography, both of which challenge conventional representations of women that distort their real experiences, and (3) address issues of how femininity and masculinity are constructed through culture by raising the question of engendered cultural works and interpretation. These three goals show how contemporary feminism has thoroughly integrated its political and cultural concerns and how it has engaged in a feminist practice in a culture in which women are either invisible or sexually objectified. An anti-oppressive practice at the cultural level has much to learn from feminist cultural studies about self-identification and developing cultural theory, politics, and practices that are in opposition to the dominant culture.

In sum, there is much to be learned from the above critical theories and perspectives on how popular or mass culture promotes, produces, and reproduces the dominant culture. Marx's concept of ideology is helpful in understanding the way we are told lies about the rationality of and necessity for capitalism and then made false promises to the effect that if we accept our fate within capitalism, we will be rewarded by the system or in the hereafter. Lukács's concept of reification is a useful contribution because it reveals how the dominant group forestalls attempts at fundamental social change by convincing us that the system is inevitable, workable, and intractable. Gramsci's theory of hegemony extends the notion of culture beyond a narrow economic interpretation to include all conformist ideas that are internalized and become part of people's everyday lives and practices, ultimately leading to the reproduction of society. The Frankfurt School's identification of the (mass) culture industry as a major means of manipulating people's consciousness by anaesthetizing the masses and diverting their attention away from their troubles is another major contribution to understanding cultural oppression. The cultural studies of the Birmingham School show us how the ruling hegemony is carried out at the level of everyday cultural practices—practices that support a white, male, bourgeois, Eurocentric domination. Baudrillard helps us to see how strategies for social or political change are thwarted in a society in which the distinctions between reality and simulations of reality are blurred and imagery promotes a lifestyle more consistent with that of dominant groups than of subordinate groups. Finally, feminist cultural studies help us to see how one subordinate group has integrated analysis, theory, and practice into a politics of empowerment and emancipation. Taken together, the insights of these theories, analyses, and perspectives help us to develop anti-oppressive practices at the cultural level and to inform our anti-oppressive practices at other levels.

Stereotypes as Cultural Expressions of Oppression

One major way by which the dominant group reinforces its position of power and privilege and, coincidentally, oppresses subordinate groups is through the use of stereotypes. A stereotype is a biased, oversimplified, universal, and inflexible conception of a social group. Although stereotypes may be positive, such as the brave soldier or the smart businessman (who avoids taxation) or the polite and friendly Canadian or the respectable doctor or clergyperson, most stereotypes are harmful and destructive. It is no accident that most negative stereotypes are applied to subordinate groups, since they are powerful tools of ideology that help to maintain oppression. Every oppressed group is undermined by stereotypes that have been imposed on them by the dominant group. It is part of the process of the social identity of subordinate groups being determined mainly by the dominant group rather than by themselves, as noted in the previous two chapters.

As discussed in Chapter 2, the dominant group projects its own experiences and culture as representative of humanity, often without realizing it. Because encounters with other groups have the potential to challenge this claim to universality, the dominant group reinforces its position by measuring (i.e., contrasting) other groups along the lines of dominant group characteristics. As a result, the differences between women and men, non-Christians and Christians, and homosexual and heterosexual persons become reconstructed as largely deviant and inferior (Young 1990). These groups become the Other and are marked by negative stereotypes that in effect reinforce notions of dominant-group superiority. The stereotypes permeate society and become so ingrained that they are seldom questioned by members of the dominant group or by some members of the subordinate groups (to be discussed in Chapter 6). Some examples of seldom-questioned stereotypes are that Atlantic Canadians have developed a culture of dependence on federal aid (so said Stephen Harper before he became prime minister of Canada), all Aboriginal people are alcoholics, all unemployed people are afraid to work, all gay men are perverse pedophiles, all women are natural caregivers, and all black people lack any sense of sexual control. On the other hand, white, bourgeois, heterosexual males tend to escape such group stereotypes and are free to be individuals (Young 1990).

Thompson (1997; 1998) maintains that stereotypes are part of the dominant culture and that all stereotypes have three characteristics. First, they defy logic or evidence because they are based on ideology and therefore are resistant to challenge and change. Second, they are often unduly negative and thus hurtful and potentially oppressive. Third, they become so ingrained that we are often unaware that they affect our perceptions and actions. It should be noted that Thompson's first characteristic is debatable to a certain extent. Bishop (1994, 67) argues that stereotypes do not 'come out of the blue'—that is, they are usually built on a real observation of another culture and contain a kernel of truth. Bishop notes, for example, that in North America, Jewish mothers have been the subject of some cruel humour that combines sexism and anti-Semitism in that they are portrayed as simple-minded, overbearing, and possessive. This negative stereotype is based on the love, care, and concern that many women give to their children in the generally highly valued family structure of the Jewish community (which is the kernel of truth about the stereotype). In addition to interpreting a positive characteristic in a negative way outside the culture, the stereotype overlooks the fact that this group comprises millions of scientists, artists, and great minds, as well as women struggling with addiction and poverty and adhering to every conceivable type of child-rearing belief and practice. Thus, I would add another two characteristics of stereotypes to Thompson's list: (1) a stereotype represents a perceived essential nature of members of the subordinate group (e.g., poor people are naturally lazy, women are naturally good with children), and (2) the group is homogenized within a stereotype in that it applies to all members without exception (e.g., all Aboriginals are alcoholic, all black men are violent).

Although each oppressed group may be characterized in a unique stereotypical way (e.g., Jews are greedy and cunning; black people are lazy and sexually promiscuous; poor persons are irresponsible and drink too much), Adam (1978) and Dominelli (1997) argue that all subordinate groups are constructed as problematic for the dominant society. And because they are problematic, they must be watched and controlled for the good of society. Stereotypes help to reinforce the notion of the problematic and the need for surveillance and control. Stereotypes also make prejudice, oppression, and even violence at the personal level more acceptable. For example, if there is a culture of oppression and homosexuality is seen by the dominant group as perverse, deviant, and sinful, it is likely that a degree of gay-bashing on an individual level would be tolerated.

Focusing on Jews, black persons, and gay and lesbian people, Adam (1978) discusses a 'composite portrait' that the three share because of the stereotypes imposed on them, a portrait that calls for surveillance and control. For example, all three groups have been categorized as subhuman at various times throughout history. Black slaves were sold without regard for family ties because it was believed that black sexuality could not include love. Hitler wrote in *Mein Kampf* of discovering a Jewish smell (smell is a marker of lower races and base animals in modern Western civilization) following his reading of anti-Semitic pamphlets. In the not too distant past, psychiatric ideologies denied the possibility of gay or lesbian love and echoed popular opinions that homosexual people are given to 'mindless animal promiscuity' (Hodges and Hutter 1974, cited in Adam 1978). Similarly, all three groups have historically been characterized as exhibiting 'uncivilized behaviour'—unrefined, ill-mannered, unscrupulous, unethical, unclean, and deceitful. Adam shows how all three groups have a history of being stereotyped by the dominant group as hyper-sexual, as heretics and conspirators (religious and sexual heretics; conspiring to take over the world or our culture or our children), and as 'in-your-face' and overly visible (loud, pushy, aggressive, or offensively flamboyant).

Although it is beyond the scope of this book to present a comprehensive and detailed overview of the stereotypes associated with each form and source of oppression, a few additional examples may help to illustrate the hurtful and oppressive consequences of stereotyping. Poor persons are often presented in the mass media, cartoons, social and political commentary, and all types of literature as a lazy, degenerate, irresponsible, unclean class of people who cheat on their welfare and breed 'like rabbits.' This portrait leads the dominant group to believe that poor people represent a dangerous class who must be constantly watched and monitored because they cannot be trusted and they pose a threat to law, order, and the economy. Questions of need among poor people are seldom considered because they are portrayed as the architects of their own fate; indeed, because it is believed that they cannot look after themselves properly, some claim that they should have no say in any form of public decision-making. They should be grateful for any meagre assistance (public or private) rendered to them and should, in return, allow themselves to be exploited by taking low-wage, menial (or dangerous) dead-end jobs; by participating in workfare programs that do not lead to jobs; by fighting wars; by accepting blame for government deficits; and by serving as an example to others of what can happen if one does not conform to the dominant group's rules and expectations. Dominelli (1997, 96) presents an overview of the racial stereotyping of black families:

> Common stereotypes of the black family, particularly of African or Afro-Caribbean descent, cover the sexual prowess of black men; the lack of sexual morality amongst black women, as evidenced by a high ratio of single parenthood; the absence of a stable family tradition; the lack of family bonds between family members; and the power of strong domineering matriarchs complemented by weak black men incapable of sustaining stable relationships [*Ebony* 1986 and Staples 1988, both cited in Dominelli 1997].

This stereotype not only problematizes 'the black family' and reinforces white cultural supremacy, it arrogantly presents the notion that there is a universal black family, when in fact there is a rich and diverse variety of black family forms, each with its own specific set of relationships, obligations, and networks. However, it is the myth or stereotype of the black family as deviant and unstable that permeates society and is often used to establish social policy and social work practice (Ahmed 1991; Dominelli 1997).

Carlen and Worral (1987, 3) describe a gendered stereotype of the 'normal woman':

> Being a normal woman means coping, caring, nurturing and sacrificing self-interest to the needs of others. It also means being intuitively sensitive to those needs without them being actively spelt out. It means being more than man, in order to support and

An Inadequate Mother or Oppressive Expectations?

Susie, a young married woman, had three children under school age. Her husband Brian worked long hours, which meant that Susie was the full-time caregiver for the children. Brian's work required them to move to another province, halfway across the country, far from friends and family. Susie found after a while that she was not coping very well with her children and sought help from a (male) social worker. The social worker did not question the 'woman as the natural caregiver of children' stereotype and referred Susie for help with 'parenting skills.' No consideration was given to the likelihood that the full-time care of three small children was too big a job for one person.

dependence. Being a normal woman means needing protection. . . . It means being childlike, incapable, fragile and capricious. It is being less than man in order to serve and defer to Man [cited in Thompson 1997, 43].

This concept of normality is, of course, grounded in a patriarchy that takes for granted certain stereotypical expectations of men and women. For example, women are considered natural nurturers and caregivers, which makes them primarily responsible for child care (and elder care). In turn, it makes them responsible when things go wrong with respect to such care. The focus in dangerous families, where children are at risk, is on dangerous mothers (Parton and Parton 1989), and even if the mother is not the abuser, she is still held culpable because she failed to protect the child (Beagley 1989). Consistent with this patriarchal stereotype, parenting is equated with mothering, and bad parenting is equated with bad mothering (Thompson 1997).

Cultural stereotypes such as those outlined above carry out several political functions for the dominant group including the following:

- They internalize a feeling of inferiority on the part of members of subordinate groups (Adam 1978; Young 1990), which in turn reduces any questioning, challenging, or resisting of the dominant culture.
- They justify the surveillance, control, and exploitation of subordinate groups and rationalize inattention to their expressed and unexpressed needs.
- By characterizing members of subordinate groups as 'bad' and their cultures as 'inferior,' stereotypes dialectically convince the dominant group of its own identity as 'good' and its culture as 'superior' (Adam 1978). This occurs without any examination or analysis by the dominant group of its privilege and power. If black people did not exist, for example, then they would have to be invented by white people.

- Negative images and stereotypes deflect attention away from the structural causes of inequality, blocked opportunities, and differential treatment and focus attention on the perceived personal deficits, liabilities, and weaknesses of the individuals who are stereotyped. In other words, stereotypes aid and abet victim-blaming.

Language and Discourse as Mechanisms of Oppression (and Anti-oppression)

Two important concepts for understanding and analyzing oppression and for developing anti-oppressive practices are language and discourse. At the most basic level, culture is transmitted through language and discourse—parents speaking to children, individuals speaking to peers, educational institutions and churches communicating to their students and parishioners, messages from texts and the mass media, the reading of literature, and so on.

Language

Through language we become members of a human community (Spender 1990). Language helps us to make sense of the world and to communicate and interact with others (Thompson 1998). Everyone is immersed in language, and no one is independent of it (Howe 1994). However, language is never politically neutral. It does not simply describe or reflect the reality of inequality and oppression in our society; it is also used to construct and maintain oppression and may be used to resist and challenge it.

One of the cornerstones of postmodernism is its emphasis on the relationship between language and power. Howe (1994, 522) summarizes this relationship: 'Those with power can control the language of the discourse and can therefore influence how the world is to be seen and what it will mean. Language promotes some possibilities and excludes others; it constrains what we see and what we do not see.' The postmodernists have emphasized that language does not possess the properties of absolute truth but is historically, socially, and culturally contextualized and largely reflects the interests and world views (including the culture) of dominant groups (Agger 1989).

Language may be oppressive simply by the choice of words used in communication. And some words that reflect and maintain oppression are so well established that their usage is taken for granted and their oppressive connotations are not recognized. For example, 'man' is often used as a prefix or suffix or a stand-alone word: chairman, manpower, man is the centre of the universe. This sexist or gendered and exclusive use of language contributes to the invisibility of women and therefore to a continuation of their subordination to men. 'Black' is a word often used to portray evil (e.g., it was a black day when President Kennedy was assassinated) or is contrasted with white to refer to right (white) and wrong (black) factors, which reinforces the notion of white superiority. Terms such as 'the poor' and 'the elderly' reflect a view of people that is depersonalized and dehumanized because the words used are impersonal adjectives or descriptors. It is similar to negative medical terminology whereby people are categorized and referred to in terms of their particular ailments (e.g., the gall bladder in Room 202 or the head injury in Emergency) rather than in human terms. A number of words, as noted in the previous chapter, constitute overt oppression (e.g., nigger, spaz, queer) because they refer to members of subordinate groups in hurtful and harmful prejudicial terms.

Even if a person using oppressive words or language does so in good faith without any intention to hurt or insult the group involved, it is still harmful and hurtful and therefore is always unacceptable. Language reflects culture, particularly the dominant culture, and if the culture is oppressive, then one of the ways of changing it is to avoid words or language that reflect and/or reinforce the oppressive elements of that culture.

Discourse

Language and its relationship to oppression are much more complex than a simple list of taboo words. Language is part of a larger framework of thought, meaning, and knowledge, or what Foucault (1976; 1980) has called a 'discourse.' Leonard (1997, 2) describes discourses as 'linguistic systems of statements through which we speak of ourselves and our social world.' A 'linguistic system of statements' is not restricted only to statements, however, because a discourse also includes the unwritten rules (based mainly on ideology and culture) of what will be included and excluded in the statements. A discourse frames the knowledge that is formulated from within it and is similar to Kuhn's (1970) notion of a 'paradigm,' although Foucault makes more use of ordinary language and everyday experience to establish the parameters of a discourse (Agger 1991). Although discourse can occur between two people, it also includes other forms of cultural expression, such as advertising, academic journal articles, and the representation of women and other subordinate groups in literary and visual culture.

An Unconscious Act of Oppression

One of my colleagues at Victoria University in Melbourne, a strong advocate for Aboriginal rights, related to me a poignant experience she had had. She was telling an Aboriginal friend about her recent trip to Britain. She said that after weeks of visiting ancient buildings, she felt that Australians had no history. Her Aboriginal friend pointed out that because she saw history as being mainly about buildings, she had just ignored more than 40,000 years of her (Aboriginal) history and culture.

Discourses are not politically neutral but are related to power. They are delivery systems for political assumptions about the world that largely reflect the interests of dominant groups such as white people, bourgeois males, and Christians and that assist in the reproduction of existing class, race, gender, and other inequalities (Agger 1989). This reproduction occurs through the promotion of ideas that support the current socio-political order and, conversely, through the suppression and/or marginalization of ideas that seek to challenge and transform it. Foucault (1963; 1976) notes that when particular discourses are adopted by members of the dominant group, they are given legitimacy, whereas alternative discourses are discounted (Hopton 1997). This can be seen in the media, which promote particular discourses of the dominant group, and even in the professional social work literature. For example, progressive or critical social work scholarship is frequently excluded from social work textbooks or treated in a manner that neutralizes its political impact and transformative potential under the pretext that it lacks objectivity or reality (Wachholz and Mullaly 2000). Thus, what social work students learn from textbooks is a discourse (attitudes and scholarship) that teaches personal reform and/or limited social reform rather than social transformation as the means to deal with oppression and inequality. This ensures that the structures and cultures of oppression remain relatively untouched.

The postmodernists and social constructionists have helped to move us away from the idea that there is objective, unitary, absolute, and verifiable knowledge about the human condition and the social world that can be gathered by using scientific methods and principles. There is general agreement today in the social sciences and humanities that there is usually more than one version or interpretation or explanation of an event, a social condition, and so on. A number of alternative or competing explanations are available to us through the language of alternative and competing discourses. Each of these discourses will tell a different story about the event or the condition because each has a different way of representing the world and how it operates (Burr 1995). In Chapter 1, we examined different explanations or theories of social problems and saw that each social problem perspective has its foundation in a particular discourse in which some variables are included and others excluded. For example, the social pathology explanation for social problems includes individual characteristics (e.g., deviance, personal deficiencies) and excludes structural factors (e.g., patriarchy, cultural racism).

As in Kuhn's (1970) version of a dominant paradigm (e.g., capitalism) existing among a number of competing paradigms (socialism, communitarianism), one dominant discourse always exists among a set of alternative discourses. Not surprisingly, the dominant discourse belongs to and represents the interests of the dominant social group. In order to protect its privilege and power, the dominant group must present its view of the world (i.e., its discourse) in such a way that subordinate groups either agree with it and endorse it or find it imperfect but the only viable alternative and therefore must live with it. For example, the dominant economic discourse today is that the 'laws of the market' must prevail and that the requirements of global capitalism demand less government involvement in social, economic, human, and environmental affairs. In spite of what neo-conservative politicians, right-wing economists, mainstream journalists, and self-interested business leaders say, there are no laws in any social science, including economics. There are only theories or perspectives or discourses. But if the dominant group can convince the public that there is no viable alternative to its view, then its position of power and privilege is consolidated. Furthermore, because the alliance between big business and bourgeois governments controls the major means of transmitting culture (e.g., the mass media, educational institutions), they are able to present their economic messages and views (i.e., their discourse) in a favourable light while ridiculing and dismissing any alternative economic discourse as unreasonable, unrealistic, and/or socialist. In other words, those with power can control the discourse, thus influencing how the world is to be seen and how it should work.

A dominant discourse is potentially much more powerful as a social control mechanism than an army, police force, or legislation. If subordinate group members concur with the world view and social and political practices of the dominant group, there is no need for acts of resistance or strategies for social change. However, history has shown that discourses, which contain claims to reason, order, and universality, often mask the interests of those making them. Smith (1993, 31) underscores this point:

> Imperialist nations, ruling classes, males, whites, heterosexuals, doctors, psychiatrists and criminologists have all claimed that their perspective defines a universal and rational outlook. By doing so they have effectively silenced other nations, other classes, other genders, other races, those of other sexual orientation, patients, the mad and prisoners.

Dominant discourses, then, cover up and/or contradict the interests of all subordinate groups: a discourse of patriarchy contributes to the oppression of women; a discourse of white supremacy contributes to the oppression of people of colour; a discourse of capitalism contributes to the oppression of working-class persons; a discourse of heterosexuality contributes to the oppression of gay, lesbian, and bisexual persons. Dominant discourses not only reflect dominant–subordinate relationships based on social divisions such as class, race, and gender but relationships in occupations as well. For example, professions—including social work—often contribute to oppression by controlling the discourses of their practices through pathological, diagnostic, and professional vocabularies that exclude and disempower the service user.

Dominant discourses also negatively affect social welfare. Peter Leonard (1997) points out that the dominant welfare discourse today is that of 'welfare dependency,' which emanates from a 'culture of poverty' discourse. This discourse, which is transmitted in the mass media on an almost daily basis, pathologizes people in need of financial assistance by portraying them in stereotypical fashion as dependent, inadequate, moral failures. Any alternative discourse, such as viewing welfare as an aspect of 'interdependency,' is covered up by the dominant ideological illusion of individual independence, even though interdependency is our inescapable experience as human beings living in association with and depending on each other.

Although dominant discourses tend to be oppressive, the notion of a discourse itself is helpful in developing anti-oppressive practice in two major ways. First, to understand discourses as contested sites of power and conflict, as Foucault does, is very important in making sense of the covert, almost invisible nature of ideology today. This allows postmodern insights and interpretive techniques (i.e., deconstructionism) to be used to unpack a discourse and bring its hidden assumptions and arguments to light (Agger 1998). In this way, we can make more sense of the dominant culture's current hegemony. Second, deconstructing a dominant discourse and bringing its oppressive underpinnings to light makes it easier to develop a fully articulated counter-discourse, one that critiques the ruling discourse and points the way towards more egalitarian social relations, practices, and processes. Feminism and anti-racism, for example, have been powerful counter-discourses to the dominant patriarchal and white supremacist discourses. More will be said in Chapter 8 about incorporating counter-discourses into an anti-oppressive practice.

Social Work and Cultural Oppression

Social work is an occupation in which most of its members are university-educated, experience a similar socialization process, share a set of common values and ethics, and organize themselves along the lines of a 'professional association' model. However, it would be a mistake to assume that social work is a monolith in which all its members practise in the same way or share the same goals or hold the same explanations for the occurrence of social problems or even agree on the merits of professionalism.[4] Elsewhere, I have presented four distinct theories and practices of social work, each of which is determined by the particular ideology held (consciously or unconsciously) by the social worker (Mullaly 2007). It is, of course, an oversimplification to suggest that social workers fall into one or another of the four approaches outlined in my book *The New Structural Social Work*, since most operate across more than one approach. Given that social work theory and practice may take different forms, however, an important question is: How can one avoid oppressive social work practices and carry out anti-oppressive practices? To answer this question, it is necessary to understand the ways that social work has operated and does operate to maintain and reinforce the dominant culture. We should also be mindful that there is a professional culture attached to social work, that social work was developed in the Western world by bourgeois, white, privileged persons, and that it is the culture of the latter group that has provided the foundation for social work ideas, values, methods, explanations for social problems, and so on. In other words, social work originated and developed in a culture marked by inequality, male dominance, and the supremacy of anything European. The very perspectives and tools and methods it uses to analyze difference and social problems are culturally specific, patriarchal, and rooted in a European perspective. To work effectively with other cultures, we must be familiar with our own social work culture. I agree with Marsiglia and Kulis (2009, xvi) that up until recently at least, social work approaches to cultural diversity relied 'on an implicit Westernized belief that there can be and should be a mainstream, standardized, and culturally neutral form of practice and that focus on the materialistic and individual aspects of human beings.' Dominelli (2002, 122) reminds us that our track record with respect to cultural differences has been anything but emancipatory:

> The history of the profession is littered with examples of social workers oppressing women, black people, indigenous people, disabled people, people with mental ill health—the list can easily be extended—with the aim of making them 'fit' more readily into the existing social order. This has occurred because social workers have uncritically accepted their role as 'normalisers' promoting the interests of those advocating dominant discourses.

It is not my intention here to 'bash' social workers for carrying out practices of oppression, social control, or victim-blaming. Most social workers I know are concerned about the horrendous living conditions that affect so many people today in both capitalist countries and non-industrialized societies, and they want to do something about them. However, social workers, like everyone else in our society, are socialized into the dominant culture and may unwittingly (or otherwise) carry out oppressive acts. As well, social agencies tend to view social problems narrowly and to define them in terms of personal deficiencies, dysfunctional families, and inferior cultures, and they expect their social work employees to treat and reform their service users rather than transform society (Rose and Black 1985; Mullaly 2007). Some social work scholars have suggested that the 'object' (i.e., the service user) of social work was originally determined by a patriarchal bourgeois commitment to the regulation of poor people, who were considered to be the 'dangerous classes' (Leonard 1994; Margolin 1997). This dangerous class (or working class) needed to be reformed in order to reduce deviance, disease, and chaos and to advance civilization. Reformation attempts would include charitable devices contingent on socialization into bourgeois culture and moral conversion into Christian culture. A voluminous literature comprising critical or radical social work, feminist social work, anti-racist social work, postmodern social work, and other forms of progressive social work attests to various oppressive thought structures, attitudes, practice forms, and approaches that permeate and underpin much social work theory and practice of yesteryear and today. In other words, although social work is regarded by many as a progressive profession, it has a culture dating back to the charity organization days of social control (of subordinate populations) and oppression.

Professionalism is a contradictory and problematic concept for social work. On the one hand, as noted by Thompson (1998), social work professionalism is committed to a (progressive) set of values, to high standards of practice, to accountability, and to the development and use of a knowledge base acquired by research and reflective practice. On the other hand, professionalism has been criticized for emphasizing the technical aspects of helping (e.g., impartiality, emotional neutrality, apolitical service) when social problems are political and moral issues; for organizing into an exclusive group based on academic credentials, which divides social workers from other workers and from the persons they serve and thus creates elitist social and occupational hierarchies; for creating the illusion that the best source of help rests with the 'expert' social worker; for treating social problems as individual misfortunes, which detracts from their structural causes (and solutions); and for ignoring the experience of all older professions in which professionalism has primarily benefited the professionals themselves (i.e., the obtaining of personal, social, economic, and political power) rather than service users (Mullaly 2007). Many progressive social work writers have argued that the 'culture of professionalism' is conservative, self-interested, and oriented towards the status quo. In effect, professionalism is for professionals, not for service users (Carniol 2000; Galper 1980; Hardy 1981a; Laursen 1975; Mullaly 2007; Wagner and Cohen 1978).

Table 4.2   12-Step Recovery Program for Professionals

My name is _____ and I am a recovering professional.
              (fill in your name)

1. I admit to believing that I had no useful skills or knowledge—unless I called myself a 'professional.'

2. I came to believe that as a 'professional,' I could fix people and solve their problems.

3. I came to believe that 'professionalism' was not a way to distance myself from service users.

4. I admit to calling myself a 'professional' in an attempt to cover up my insecurities and self-doubts.

5. I came to believe that the 'professional relationship' is not hierarchical. Just because I am the expert doesn't mean that we're not equals.

6. I came to convince myself that wearing expensive clothes and driving a fancy car did not separate me from my resource-poor service users. After all, we're all just people.

7. I admit to adding my professional credentials to everything I wrote or signed.

8. I admit to sending a memo (with my name and credentials) to people rather than bothering to talk to them.

9. I admit to using my voice mail to screen certain difficult people.

10. I admit to saying, 'Call me, and we'll do lunch.'

11. I admit to using professional jargon, acronyms, discourse, and my prolific propensity for elite, exclusionary vocabulary to impress, overpower, intimidate, and distance people.

12. I admit to embracing 'professionalism' without taking into account its undermining effects on my stated beliefs in social justice, egalitarianism, and other social work values and ideals.

Social Work Reproduces Gender and Racial Oppression

Social work is a profession or semi-profession that has always had many more female members than male members. Social work is also a profession committed to such values as social equality and social justice. In spite of this, white males are still disproportionately represented in positions of power and privilege within social work, since directors of large agencies and social work educational programs are overwhelmingly white and male. Conversely, most front-line workers caring directly for victims of oppression are women. In this way, social work is reproducing relationships and roles of oppression along gender (and racial) lines by which women and people of colour remain in subordinate positions and continue to carry out their traditional roles of caring for others. White males also remain in their traditional roles of leading, directing, and dominating others.

Professionalism contains elements of oppression not only for service users but also for the profession as a whole and for particular groups of social workers in particular. An example may help to clarify this. Recall the discussion in Chapter 2 of 'powerlessness,' one of Young's (1990) five faces of oppression. It was noted that the norms of respectability in our society are associated with a professional culture—professional dress, speech, tastes, and demeanour. It was also noted that professional respectability tends to be associated with white males, who dominate the professions. White males are still overrepresented in the traditional professions of medicine, law, and engineering. And it is not just a matter of domination by numbers but also a matter of domination in terms of those who hold the powerful positions in professions.

Earlier in this chapter, it was argued that language and discourse contain political messages and that these messages tend to reinforce the dominant culture and the privileged position of the dominant group. Here, I analyze a current social work discourse on culture to show that even what appears to be a progressive concept can actually contribute to social relations of domination and subordination. I refer to the concepts of cultural sensitivity or cultural literacy or cultural competency, since it is these concepts that mark much of social work's contemporary approach to the study of cultural diversity. Most social work programs today in Canada, the US, the UK, and Australia require students to take courses that examine cultural diversity, oppression, ethnicity, and race. Students often learn about different cultures by reading literature, by listening to representatives from marginalized groups who have been asked to come into the classroom and speak to them, and by participating in bridging activities, which introduce students to other cultures through the four Fs—fairs, food, festivals, and folktales (Kanpol 1997, cited in Sisneros et al. 2008) or what

Sardar and Van Loon (2004, 123) call 'the saris, samosas and steel bands syndrome.' Marsiglia and Kulis (2009) call this approach to diversity 'the cultural orientation paradigm,' and Clarke (2003) calls it 'the cultural literacy or knowledge' approach. This paradigm or perspective is based on the assumption that cultural differences exist and that becoming familiar with these differences will prevent or undo any inter-group misunderstandings. Problems occur because of misunderstanding or a lack of affinity between groups (especially between dominant and subordinate groups) and not necessarily because of discrimination or oppression. The solution to problems based on misunderstandings among cultures is to (1) become aware of the different sets of norms governing various cultural groups, (2) set aside ethnocentric ideas, and (3) learn each other's cultural rules and standards (Marsiglia and Kulis 2009). In other words, social workers would study the history, background, characteristic traits, and so on as a way of understanding the life world of other persons or groups. This approach to diversity training has become quite common in corporate North America and in social work education.

The limitations of this approach are that it puts the social worker in the position of expert/knower, ignores the heterogeneity within the group, and overlooks the socio-political context (Clarke 2003). Similarly, the approach does not necessarily account for social and historical oppression—that is, the experience of difference is not put into its social, historical, and political context (Marsiglia and Kulis 2009). The danger then of this approach for social workers is that although they will become aware of differences between and among cultures, they will not learn about 'the subtle and often hidden processes that sustain and perpetuate the privilege of certain groups and the processes that undermine the efforts of groups marginalized by class, race, gender and sex, sexual orientation, and ability status' (Sisneros et al. 2008, 7). I believe that knowledge and appreciation of different cultures is a prerequisite to anti-oppressive social work at the cultural level. But by itself, it contains all the limitations mentioned above. Alternatives that move beyond cultural awareness are the experiential-phenomenological approach in which the worker seeks understanding of the person's lived experience through 'experiential-phenomenological inquiry' (Clarke 2003), 'the culturally grounded approach' that sees difference as a political phenomenon with power as its central factor and the experience of oppression as a major force that shapes people's lives (Marsiglia and Kulis 2009), and 'the critical multicultural approach' that involves an analysis of the systems that maintain and perpetuate inequality, with the presumption of a commitment to egalitarianism through action (Sisneros et al. 2008). These three cultural social work approaches that move beyond a cultural knowledge and appreciation model are obviously consistent with the anti-oppressive framework that underpins this book. More will be said about them in Chapter 8.

Although social work is a profession committed to progressive values, social change, and social justice, its members are still susceptible to oppressive practices and to reproducing dominant–subordinate relations—not only with the people they serve but also with each other along lines of gender and race (and other social divisions).

This shows how difficult it is to work and practice in a way that confronts, resists, and attempts to change the larger culture. An anti-oppressive social work practice is not restricted to working with people experiencing social problems. It must include social workers working with each other in ways that (1) do not reproduce the inequalities of the larger society, (2) challenge attitudes and agency cultures that moralize social problems and blame their victims, (3) do not ascribe all social problems to individual deficiency (Mullaly 2007), and (4) avoid the pursuit of a professional culture of respectability gained at the expense of others.

Conclusion

This chapter has focused on oppression at the cultural level. It has adopted a broad view of culture—the norms, values, beliefs, and ideals that make up 'the stuff of everyday life.' Culture is pervasive in our society and is related to everything we see, hear, believe, and do. The culture of the dominant group (i.e., the dominant culture) privileges that group at the same time that it carries out cultural imperialism by suppressing and/or repressing all subordinate cultures. The dominant culture is presented and promoted as the universal cultural norm (i.e., the official culture) by the dominant group. It is continually produced and reproduced by such cultural agents as the mass media, the entertainment industry, and our social institutions.

In an effort to better understand how cultural oppression is actually carried out (as a prerequisite to developing anti-oppressive strategies), we examined a number of critical social theories. The people who developed these theories focused, for the most part, on arguably the most influential and powerful form of culture—mass or popular culture. Several functions that mass culture carries out to protect and enhance the privileged position of the dominant group were extracted from these theories.

Two other major cultural expressions of oppression examined in this chapter were stereotyping and language and discourse. Stereotypes are biased, oversimplified, universal, and essentialist depictions of social groups. Every subordinate group has, as part of the identity imposed on its members by the dominant group, at least one stereotype that defies logic, is unduly negative and hurtful, and is so ingrained as to be seldom questioned. Stereotypes fulfill several political functions for the dominant group. Similarly, language does more than simply describe or reflect social phenomena; it can also be used to construct and maintain oppression. Language and discourse are related to power in that they are both delivery systems for political assumptions about the world, and dominant discourses largely reflect the interests of dominant groups. Finally, certain oppressive features are inherent in the culture of professionalism, and the profession of social work is no exception in this regard.

Any serious attempts at formulating and/or practising anti-oppressive social work must incorporate the concept of culture, which means being informed by research and literature from cultural studies. As mentioned at the beginning of this chapter, cultural studies has been described by the noted critical social theorist Ben Agger (1998, 122) as 'one of the most important contemporary theoretical movements' and 'one of the best examples of an interdisciplinary critical theory.' To date, social work has tended to treat culture in narrow ways in that it is often associated with differences based on race or ethnicity, as illustrated by the literature on multicultural social work, or else it is lumped in as part of the larger social environment (i.e., a structural force) that extends beyond individuals or families. Such conceptualizations fail to take into account that culture is more than a context or a particular tradition or set of ideas. Culture is also an everyday practice by which the ruling hegemony is carried out. No one in society is free from participating in everyday cultural practices—practices that support the position of the dominant group. Social workers are quick to say that the personal is political (and the political is personal). However, this stated relationship is overly simplistic because culture mediates between the personal and the political. The relationship between the personal and the political is not a direct relationship but an indirect one. The dominant cultural messages invariably legitimize such political effects on individuals as conformity and oppression, and the dominant culture must be demystified and exposed for individuals to see the need for structural or political change. I believe that social work must take up the critical view of culture and of cultural social work. Otherwise, it will continue to be a conveyor of the dominant culture and a force for maintaining the status quo. In this regard, Dominelli (2002, 28) reminds us that our record has been one in which '[S]ocial Work has been implicated in oppressive forces by fostering relations of dominance that are consistent with supporting the status quo.'

Critical Questions for Discussion

1. How would you respond to a social worker who says that his or her practice is based on the social work principle of 'impartiality'—that is, he or she does not discriminate? He or she claims to treat everyone the same way—it doesn't matter whether the service user is Aboriginal or white, male or female, a poor person or a middle-class person. 'We are all people, and no one should be treated differently,' says the social worker. 'When I'm working with people, I am colour-blind, gender-blind, and blind to any other difference. I am completely neutral.'

2. How would you respond to a white male friend who says to you, 'I am sick and tired of all these people saying how oppressed they are. I'm oppressed too. Lots of jobs I have applied for were given to women or visible minority persons under some kind of employment equity policy. It's just not fair!'

3. What are the differences between race and ethnicity and culture?

4. Can a man be a feminist? Why or why not?

5. If there is no such thing as a black race because race is a social construction, why do we have racism?

6. How would you respond to a person who asks, 'How can I be pro-black without being anti-white?'

7. How would you describe 'white culture'?

8. Have you ever 'vegged out' by turning on the television just to get your mind off your troubles or worries? Did it work? Culture theorists would say that this is participating in an escape that they would categorize as an 'opiate of the masses.' Explain.

Further Readings

Agger, Ben (1992). *Cultural Studies as Critical Theory*. London: Falmer Press. This book examines the growing field of cultural studies and argues for its relevance in addressing the enormous impact of culture, including popular culture, on society today. Among the perspectives analyzed are Marxist theories of culture, the Frankfurt School's concept of the 'culture industry,' the Birmingham School of Cultural Studies based on Gramsci's earlier works, postmodern and post-structural perspectives, and feminist cultural studies. Agger focuses on the political grounding and political functions of culture.

Gramsci, Antonio (1971). *Selections from the Prison Notebooks*. London: Lawrence and Wishart. The insights contained in this book marked a turning point in Marxist thinking because it offers a cogent explanation for the fall of Marxism in late capitalism. Gramsci's theory of 'hegemony,' which is a crucial concept in understanding dominant–subordinate relationships and for anti-oppressive social work, is fully presented. Gramsci analyzes how oppression is maintained through ideological conditioning that occurs through the school system, the media, the legal system, and other social institutions.

Marsiglia, Flavio Francisco, and Stephen Kulis (2009). *Diversity, Oppression, and Change: Culturally Grounded Social Work*. Chicago: Lyceum Books. This book explores the relationship between cultural diversity, oppression, and social change and their implications for social work. The culturally grounded perspective developed by the authors describes specific ways of helping and integrates these methods into social work practice, policy, and research. The book moves beyond a limited cultural awareness approach to social work practice with diverse groups.

Sardar, Ziauddin, and Borin Van Loon (2004). *Introducing Cultural Studies*. Thriplow, Royston, UK: Icon Books. This primer presents an overview of the origins, main ideas and concepts, international treatment, and leading theorists in cultural studies.

Sisneros, Jose, et al. (2008). *Critical Multicultural Social Work*. Chicago: Lyceum Books. This book explores multicultural social work from a critical perspective and emphasizes critical reflection on the part of the social worker. It examines oppression and diversity across multiple dimensions and presents a mechanism for viewing the intersectionality of multiple oppressions.

Chapter 5

Oppression at the Structural Level

Social injustice is killing people on a grand scale.
—Excerpt from a report by the World Health Organization, 2008

Introduction

In 1845, Fredrich Engels coined the term 'social murder'[1] to describe the horrific effects of a new economic and social system (i.e., capitalism) on the living conditions of workers and their families. Given an economic policy of laissez-faire and a social policy in the form of the 1834 revised Poor Law, which was more punitive and more restrictive than its predecessor, Engels provided a detailed account in his book, *The Condition of the Working Class in England in 1844* (1987 [1845]), of the misery and death from starvation and disease experienced by the working class. He laid responsibility for this social murder at the doorstep of the social system that had come to dominate the social and natural environment. He argued that just as when a person knowingly inflicts an injury on another so that death results and we call it murder, so too is it murder when society places working people under conditions in which they can neither retain health nor live long. It is argued in this chapter that what Engels called 'social murder' in 1845 (and what I call 'social terrorism' today) still exists in all societies that are characterized by dominant–subordinate relations.

Social work has always professed to be on the side of those who are hurt by social and economic conditions beyond their control. Today, social work's concern has extended from its original but narrow preoccupation with (working) class to include all forms and sources of oppression. In spite of this progressive development, however, the evidence is clear that all oppressed groups still experience higher rates and more severe forms of illness and higher incidences of premature morbidity than the dominant group does. This occurs in large part because of the socially sanctioned ways that social institutions, laws, social policies, and social practices all work together to benefit the dominant group at the expense of subordinate groups. For example, society disproportionately allocates good jobs, adequate health care, decent housing, and so on to dominant group members and unemployment or underemployment, inadequate health care, homelessness, starvation, incarceration, low social status, and so on to members of subordinate groups. If social work only helps subordinate group members to cope with, adjust to, or fit back into a social system that injured them in the first place, then we are complicit in the social murder or social terrorism that oppressed or subordinate groups experience every day of their lives. It will be shown in this chapter that the social inequalities that are part of oppression often have violent effects or outcomes. And just as Engels argued that adverse social conditions resulted in social murder, it will be argued here that social inequalities are actually socially sanctioned forms of physical and psychological violence, which over time lead to slow, agonizing, premature, and unpunished death for countless numbers of subordinated people all over the world on a daily basis.

In Chapter 2, oppression at the structural level was defined as the means by which oppression is institutionalized in society. It consists of the ways that social divisions, practices, and processes, along with social institutions, laws, policies, and the economic and political systems, all work together to benefit the dominant group at the expense of subordinate groups. This chapter will examine the social, economic, and political systems in terms of how each contributes to overall oppression at the structural level. Although we will look at these three spheres individually, they cannot be separated in reality. A symbiotic relationship exists among them, with each sphere constantly acting upon and influencing the other two. At the same time, each sphere is acted upon and influenced by the other two spheres. Taken together, all three are responsible for the social terrorism and structural violence experienced by millions of marginalized people in Canada alone and hundreds of millions of oppressed people all over the world.

Social Relations and Oppression

We have already discussed how social divisions based on class, gender, race, age, and so on engender oppression. I have also argued that most people today would not overtly subscribe to or condone acts of oppression, as evidenced by the existence of considerable legislation and policies to combat prejudice and discrimination, such as equal rights and human rights laws. Among the potential ways or policies that might be adopted to deal with the negative effects of social divisions or 'difference,' two are particularly noteworthy—assimilation (or monoculturalism) and multiculturalism. The former, a modernist and liberal humanist approach, accords equal social status and treatment to everyone, regardless of class, gender, age, race, and so on, according to the same principles, rules, and standards. The latter, a politically engaged postmodern approach, is based on the belief that people's differences are more important than their similarities. Obviously, these two approaches are diametrically opposed: assimilation tends to adopt a blind approach to difference, and multiculturalism tends to adopt a blind approach to commonalities or similarities. Proponents of each claim their particular approach is best at combating the hierarchical sets of dominant–subordinate relationships that characterize our pluralistic and heterogeneous social system.

Assimilation

Wasserton (1980) outlines three reasons for choosing assimilation as a solution to group-based oppression. First, by imagining a society in which class, race, gender, and so forth have no special social significance, one sees more clearly how these categories unnecessarily limit possibilities and opportunities for some people. Second, a clear and unambiguous standard of equality and justice for all is promised, and any group-related differentiation or discrimination would be suspect. That is, any social benefits distributed differentially according to group membership would be viewed as unjust. Third, assimilation eliminates the situation of group differences resulting in social differences. Thus, people would be free to develop themselves as individuals. In sum, assimilation promises subordinate groups a 'deal' in which their identities, culture, and values are to be surrendered in return for the promise or opportunity of improved life chances. Submission to the social rules of the dominant group supposedly mitigates the barriers confining subordinate groups (Adam 1978).

Many writers (e.g., Young 1990; Adam 1978) have criticized assimilation as an unacceptable goal for liberation politics. Today in most Western democracies, there is widespread agreement that no person should be excluded from political, economic, or social activities because of ascribed characteristics. However, group differences continue to exist, and certain groups continue to be advantaged. Although some persons from disadvantaged groups have succeeded in improving their overall life chances, the overall scheme of allocating privilege and resources has remained unchanged (Adam 1978).

Young (1990) outlines three ways that assimilation, by ignoring group differences, has oppressive consequences. First, assimilation entails bringing formerly excluded groups into the mainstream, but this means coming into the game after the rules and standards have already been established and having to prove oneself according to these rules and standards. The privileged group defines the standards against which all will be measured. And because their privilege involves not recognizing these standards as culturally and experientially specific, they are perceived as the ideal of a common, universal, and neutral humanity in which all can participate regardless of differences and inherent disadvantage to some. Because these standards are in fact specific to the dominant class, they place subordinate groups at a disadvantage in trying to measure up to them. For that reason, assimilation policies perpetuate their disadvantage.

Second, the notion of a universal humanity devoid of group differences allows dominant groups to overlook or not recognize their own group specificity. The assimilationist's blindness to difference perpetuates cultural imperialism because it is the subordinate groups who must surrender their respective cultures and adopt the dominant culture, which is presented as a common, universal humanity.

Third, assimilation often produces an internalized devaluation by members of subordinate groups. To participate in the assimilationist project involves accepting an identity other than one's own and being reminded by others and by oneself of one's true but now submerged identity. As a result, for example, children of non-English-speaking groups are often ashamed of the accents of their parents, women seek to control their tendency to cry, and gay and lesbian couples avoid displaying affection towards each other in public.

Because it has historically operated within the liberal humanist paradigm, conventional social work has (unwittingly for the most part) supported assimilation (Wachholz and Mullaly 2000; Potocky 1998).[2] By de-emphasizing differences (as discussed in Chapter 2), by developing approaches and interventions that help people to cope with and adjust to the dominant culture, by emphasizing impartiality as a principle of practice (i.e., treat everyone the same), by advocating for equal rights legislation (without the legal or financial resources to utilize it), and by privileging expert knowledge and dominant Eurocentric discourses, conventional social work has contributed to the subordination and homogenization of oppressed populations to the logic of capitalism and the dominant culture (Leonard 1994).

Multiculturalism

Multiculturalism[3] is a North American offshoot of postmodernism (Agger 2006). It reflects concern that any overarching theory of oppression may omit or de-emphasize the unique and specific expression of each oppressive construct and context (e.g., see hooks 1990; West 1993). Multiculturalism posits a sharp break (a great divide) between modernity and postmodernity and emphasizes a theoretical logic based initially on the trinity of class, gender, and race as separate and co-equal dimensions of oppression and liberation (Agger 2006). This trinity has been extended to include age, disability, and other forms and sources of oppression, thus embracing a politics of identity (Arnowitz 1992) or what Wineman (1984) calls 'parallel oppressions.' Separating different forms of oppression from each other leads to a conservative brand of politics that militates against any notion of solidarity among groups or uniting different groups into common causes to begin to change oppressive social structures. Instead, a competition for resources, media attention, and public support among various subordinate groups occurs—a competition that obviously benefits the dominant group.

Given their emphasis on individualism, liberalism, and the politics of identity, along with their rejection of social change theories, how do multiculturalists deal with oppression, which, as discussed in Chapter 2, is a group-based phenomenon? Because each form and/or source of oppression is considered unique by multiculturalists, they believe that each oppressed group should be encouraged to 'narrate' its own experience of oppression and that only members of the oppressed group can tell their story (Healey 1995). Others from outside the group cannot understand or appreciate another's experience or know what it is like to be 'them.' The political purpose of these narratives is to allow members of oppressed groups to formulate coherent personal identities based on their membership in these groups—in other words, to remake the self aided by hearing and reading narratives of other like-group members

Attending Multicultural Celebrations

I have had the good fortune of having lived in Toronto, Canada, and Melbourne, Australia, two cities that pride themselves on their multicultural character. However, in both cities I have been struck by the number of people who equate multiculturalism with annual ethnic celebrations featuring traditional rituals, interesting entertainment, colourful dress, and wonderful food—what Kanpol (1997) calls the four Fs: fairs, food, festivals, and folktales; Sardar and Van Loon (2004) call the three Ss: saris, samosas, and steel bands syndrome; and Harris (2001) calls a 'boutique multiculturalism.' In other words, multiculturalist adherents tend to focus on superficial manifestations of culture and make them exotic. Although they may enjoy these exotic festivities and food, many of these people show little interest in or knowledge of the struggles, blocked opportunities, and second-class citizenship that members of these (subordinate) cultures experience on a daily basis. Indeed, many multiculturalists view cultures in terms of how different they are from the dominant Eurocentric culture, not on their own terms (Sardar and Van Loon 2004). Although difference may be acknowledged, issues of power and domination are not. Participating in a smudge or a sweat, for example, may be a good first step in learning about First Nations' cultural practices, but there is a lot more involved in understanding colonization and its ongoing effects on Aboriginal persons.

consciousness-raising of critical social theory, which uses it as a means to political action, the remaking of one's identity is an end in itself. What one does with this remade identity is, of course, an individual choice.

Colin Powell, the African-American former chief of staff of the American armed forces and one-time secretary of state in the George W. Bush government, and Condoleezza Rice, an African-American woman who succeeded Colin Powell as secretary of state, are both examples of the postmodern politics of identity. They both identify themselves as African-Americans and in their speeches often tell stories or narratives about their own lives that do not deny their identities as African-Americans. In fact, their narratives often express and enhance their respective identities, subjectivity, and personhood. To the multiculturalist, the achievement of such selfhood is effective social change. Powell and Rice have succeeded in enhancing their personal identities as major players in the American mosaic (a multicultural goal) rather than as change agents against a culture and institutions that oppress African-Americans (and others).

> Multiculturalism is the common notion that describes diverse races living in pluralistic harmony. It sees diversity as plurality of identities and as 'a condition of human existence.' Within this pluralist framework, identity is regarded as the product of an assemblage of customs, practices and meanings, an enduring heritage and a set of shared traits and experiences [Sardar and Van Loon 2004, 123].

As an approach to understanding diversity, multiculturalism has come under a great deal of severe criticism. The following is a summary of the critique of multiculturalism made for the most part by Marsiglia and Kulis (2009). They acknowledge that the multicultural approach can be the basis for promoting tolerance as a means of transcending differences between people (although I believe there is a significant difference between tolerance of difference and celebration of difference) and that many multiculturalists reject the idea that Western society is superior to other traditions. However, it must be noted that although multiculturalism rejects Eurocentrism, it has developed almost exclusively from theoretical models within the European tradition. Thus, it has been criticized for lacking a vision of how to address differences in power and status among different cultural groups because the very tools it uses to analyze difference are culturally specific, patriarchal, and rooted in European tradition. Critics of multiculturalism argue that this imposes limitations on understanding groups that have been oppressed and excluded because of the cultural and social privilege of its leading theorists. Proponents of this view accuse multiculturalism of actually perpetuating inequality by focusing attention on the heterogeneity of cultural groups but disregarding or overlooking their differences in status and power (McKerl 2007, cited in Marsiglia and Kulis 2009). Nelson and McPherson (2003) make the same point when they criticize a multicultural approach to social work for seeking universalistic knowledge within cultures and focusing on differences among cultures. This approach compartmentalizes culture into distinct differences, which are then presented as knowledge that is essential for communication with a particular culture (i.e., universalism within diversity). Nelson and McPherson argue that instead of only learning differences, social work should focus on the interface of cultures, given that cultural knowledge is relational, not representational. We should reflect more on how the dominant culture oppresses and suppresses other cultures than on differences among cultures, since historically, social work has tended to view differences as pathologies to be treated, thus normalizing personal prejudice.

Interestingly, an anonymous reviewer of the first edition of my book made an argument that there was a difference between Canadian and American approaches to multiculturalism and criticized me for saying that multiculturalism does not seem to possess much potential for anti-oppressive social work. The reviewer argued that Canada has a system of federally legislated policies, which although not perfect have been introduced to recognize cultural differences and *perhaps* (reviewer's term) to privilege these differences in order to close the gap between diverse and mainstream groups. I find this very naive and uninformed, and I stand by my statement that multiculturalism does not seem to hold much potential for anti-oppressive social work. Let me elaborate on this belief. First, I do believe that a multicultural approach is a prerequisite to changing dominant–subordinate cultural relations because it does acknowledge the importance of cultural differences and group identity. However, I still believe that multiculturalism is a limited perspective and by itself does not do much to alter the relationship between the dominant culture and subordinate cultures. I agree with Marsiglia and Kulis (2009) that multiculturalism may be unable to recognize its own constraints. For example, we only have to look at how religious symbols vary in terms of legitimacy, power, and authority in Canadian and similar societies. In Canada during the summer of 2008, a great deal of publicity followed a couple of incidents involving young Muslim girls being prevented from wearing the hijab (headscarf), a religious practice, while playing soccer, even though Christian children were allowed to wear crucifixes around their necks (a religious practice), Jewish children were allowed to wear the Star of David around their necks (a religious practice), and Jewish boys were allowed (or encouraged) to wear a kippah (skull cap) while playing soccer (or any other game). Thus, we have in 'multicultural' Canada a different standard for the wearing of religious symbols, with the dominant religious group (Judeo-Christians) given religious privilege and a subordinate group (Muslims) having a religious belief and practice banned or outlawed. Similarly, Muslim women are often harassed for wearing veils—another religious practice of a subordinate group. Racial profiling (a form of cultural profiling) is common at points of security in airports, in retail stores, and in police behaviours in Canada. The ongoing treatment of Aboriginal people by our federal government under the Indian Act whereby many live in Third World conditions is another example of a group with few human rights relative to the dominant culture. Similarly, Canadian society has a welfare system that tends to pathologize and criminalize poor people, who represent another subordinate culture. Hate crimes are seldom perpetrated on members of the dominant culture in Canada (or elsewhere). Same-sex couples in Canada are still refused many of the rights held by heterosexual couples. Later in this chapter, I show how subordinate cultures experience structural violence and social terrorism in Canada on a daily basis. So the argument that by virtue of being a multicultural nation, Canada is committed to undoing all privileges of the dominant culture is a bit suspect, I believe.

The reviewer mentioned above argues that Canada is seeking to repair the damage experienced from decades of inequality by putting in place an institutional system of rights. I have already argued the point that rights are useless unless an individual has the resources to exercise such rights. The reviewer cites a few writers who 'argue for a "recognition of differences" in which diverse identities are both recognized and protected in a way that works to strengthen the overall national identity of a country' (reviewer's words). I agree with these authors, and I think they agree with me. The salient point is that what they call for (and what I call for) has not happened in spite of a policy of multiculturalism and a number of other similar federal policies. I think the reviewer does not look critically enough at the social policies the federal (and provincial) governments have put in place. We know that social policies are not necessarily based on altruism or adopted with the needs of subordinate groups as the main motivation. To follow the reviewer's logic, we would have to say that we have a welfare system (in place since the end of the Second World War) to end poverty and promote social equality among Canadian classes. Such a claim flies in the face of everything we know about the welfare state and the social control functions that it carries out for the dominant group, such as keeping the 'dangerous classes' in their place. I believe that what Harris (1991, 152) says about multiculturalism in Britain applies just as much to multiculturalism in Canada:

> Contrary to popular belief Britain is not a multi-cultural society. A mere aggregation of cultures does not constitute a multi-cultural society. . . . Britain will become a multi-cultural society when the insights, mores, and habits of the subordinate cultures are accorded equal value and become incorporated into the legal and social structures of British society.

Since the reviewer gratuitously referred me to a few sources on multiculturalism in Canada, let me refer him or her to a couple of books on Canada's multicultural policy: Himani Bannerji's *The Dark Side of the Nation: Essays on Multiculturalism, Nationalism and Gender* (2000) and Richard Day's *Multiculturalism and the History of Canadian Diversity* (2000). The latter concludes, after analyzing Canada's state policy of multiculturalism, that it was created to manage and control diversity, not to encourage it, let alone celebrate it. The policy of multiculturalism is the Canadian government's way of protecting its national identity as it deals with the problem of the French, the immigrant, and the Aboriginal person.

A concept that is often used in the multicultural discourse is that of 'social inclusion' or its opposite, 'social exclusion.' Social inclusion has been a goal of the Commission of the European communities since the late 1980s and of New Labour in the UK since the 1990s (Garrett 2002), and along with social exclusion, it has become the dominant discourse with respect to social policy and poverty issues in Canada since the 1990s (Sin and Yan 2003). Social exclusion is presented by its adherents as a more comprehensive and relevant concept than the traditional concept of people experiencing poverty and deprivation. That is, the groups oppressed in society extend beyond people living in poverty, and these groups should be recognized both in the social work and social welfare areas and in the government social policy field. The goal of government policy should be to bring in or include the currently excluded or subordinate groups in society so that they can become full citizens with all the rights and responsibilities currently held by the 'in' (i.e., dominant) group. This, of course, is a multicultural approach in that the goal is to extend rights and benefits held by the dominant group to all subordinate groups, and because it is a multicultural approach, it suffers from the limitations outlined above. For example, it deals only with the fact of social exclusion and not the socio-political reasons for social exclusion. Certain rights may be extended to subordinate groups, but there is no guarantee that these groups will be able to exercise these rights. This is similar to the 'myth of equal opportunity' that I presented in Chapter 2—the belief (perpetrated by the dominant group) that we all have the same opportunities in society to succeed and if we do not succeed, it must be our fault for not taking advantage of available opportunities. I may have a right to a fair trial, but if I cannot afford the expensive legal help that members of the dominant group can, my right to a fair trial is essentially useless to me. I may have the right to participate in the political process, but if I do not have sufficient resources, then members of the dominant group will continue to control the political process, political decisions (that favour them), and political parties (that cater to them). I may have the right to a decent education, but if I am living in an Aboriginal community or in an inner-city neighbourhood, my education will be inferior to that received by children of the dominant group, who can put pressure on school boards and politicians for adequate school funding. The social inclusion strategy is satisfied if people have a right to run for a school board position or have the right to ask the school board or local politicians for adequate resources. This is the Achilles heel of the social inclusion approach, however, since it assumes a level playing field once all groups have the same rights accorded to them.

Other limitations of using social exclusion as the dominant discourse in dealing with cultural inequalities, as noted by Sin and Yan (2003) are: (1) although it centres on nurturing individual skills and capabilities, it does not address structural inequalities of material resources; (2) the concept is used as a totalizing concept in which the goal is to bring excluded groups towards the centre of the dominant culture, which in effect mainstreams them; and (3) the concept imposes social goals defined by the dominant group—such as common aspirations—common good, and common life, on the excluded groups without dialogue or negotiation on these goals. In other words, excluded groups are required to accept or adopt mainstream beliefs, goals, and values—which in effect assimilates them into the dominant culture.

A number of writers criticize the use of 'social exclusion/inclusion' because it depoliticizes disadvantage and oppression (e.g., Baines 2002). Garrett (2002) points out that even though poverty is more prevalent today than it was a couple of decades ago (in most Western countries)—that more people are living in poverty, and that the extent of poverty and the gap between poor and non-poor is greater—the term 'poverty' has been all but dropped from social work and social welfare discourses and replaced by 'social exclusion,' which now dominates the conceptualization of and responses to poverty (Prescott 2002, cited in Garrett 2002). Garrett argues that use of the term 'social exclusion' masks or covers over poverty and related questions of income and wealth distribution. Levitas (2001) critiques the use of social inclusion in that it erases issues connected to low wages because the goal of social inclusion is to bring unemployed people into the job market. It does not deal with low pay or employment rights (Lister 1999), and it does little to assist the social workers who on a daily basis work with people excluded from the labour market because of illness, disability, caring responsibilities, or discriminatory employment practices (Garrett

2002). With respect to the current employment model, aimed at bringing unemployed people into the labour market whatever the rates of pay or lack of employment benefits, Ferguson (2008) argues that it has replaced wealth redistribution as a social policy goal of the Labour government in the UK and that low pay, not unemployment, is largely responsible for child poverty. To the Labour government, social exclusion primarily means exclusion from paid work, which has led to the implementation of welfare-to-work strategies and the exclusion of social work from such welfare initiatives because it was not considered suited for the tough economic role these initiatives demanded (Jordan and Jordan 2000). Ferguson (2008) also contends that the Labour government's concern has shifted from reducing inequality to getting more people out of poverty and letting the rich keep their wealth. In other words, greed and exorbitant levels of inequality are fine as long as people are not living in absolute poverty (i.e., relative poverty is acceptable). Sanctioning social inequality is contrary to the goals of anti-oppressive social work. Parallels between the effects of Third Way policies of the Labour government in the UK and the situation in several Canadian provinces that have implemented similar policies should make all social workers committed to social justice wary of such concepts as social inclusion/exclusion that serve to cover over and depoliticize problems associated with social inequalities.

Given the above critique of multiculturalism, I will repeat myself here: *multicultural-ism does not seem to possess much potential for anti-oppressive work*. It may go a step further than assimilation in that it acknowledges the importance of group identity in formulating personal selfhood, but it also produces a status quo political agenda. By simply attempting to improve the well-being of individuals within various multicultural fractions, it leaves the structures of society intact. That is, multiculturalism may attempt to make adjustments so that subordinate cultures have a place in society, but it does nothing to undo the hierarchy of dominant–subordinate (superior–inferior) cultures. It views multicultural narratives as ends in themselves rather than as springboards to radical or structural change. It also denies oppressed groups the possibility of entering into coalitions or alliances with other such groups. Furthermore, joint action on the part of members of a particular oppressed group is diluted by the fact that the major concern is to produce narratives that express and enhance victims' selfhood or identity. Finally, multiculturalism's acceptance of individualism and liberal capitalism makes it difficult to foster a commitment to social change.

The Politics of Difference

Because a policy of assimilation leads to oppressive consequences and a policy of multiculturalism to a ghettoization of subordinate groups, something else is needed to combat oppression at the structural level. As an alternative to assimilation, Barry Adam argues for collective resistance to oppression on the part of subordinated groups. He emphasizes the importance of community for developing self-identity, solidarity, and resistance to domination. Communication among members of a subordinate group over time engenders social networks and language that nurture collectivization and a new understanding of their life situation—one defined by the group itself.

> Shared experiences identify effective strategies for coping with social limitations, methods of survival and self-betterment, sources of freedom and joy. Brotherhood or sisterhood is not the simple correlate of, for example, physical resemblances; it is the mutual creation . . . of each member by the other [Adam 1978, 122].

Although this process of group solidarity and self-identity is crucial to maintaining one's culture, it could, if unchecked, lead to a situation of ghetto-like communities of oppressed groups separated from the dominant culture and from each other. To overcome this possibility, Young (1990) proposes a 'politics of difference.' She elaborates on Adam's notion of community as the means of overcoming oppression. Rather than attempting to transcend group differences, as the assimilationist approach would do, the politics of difference seeks equality among all socially and culturally differentiated groups whereby mutual respect and affirmation of their differences would occur. Group differences would be considered as positive and desirable rather than as a liability or disadvantage. The positivity of group difference would be liberating and empowering in that the identity the dominant group has taught them to despise would be reclaimed, affirmed, and celebrated. This positive view of one's specific culture and experience would make it increasingly difficult for the dominant group to parade its values and norms as universal and neutral.

It might seem at this point that there is not much difference between multiculturalism and a politics of difference, since both advocate that different subordinate groups establish separate organizations that exclude all other groups. However, there is a crucial difference between the two in terms of the purposes of establishing exclusionary organizations. Multiculturalists view separate organizations as an end in themselves—a place where members can meet and tell their stories. Proponents of a politics of difference view them as a means to an end—that is, a means to full participation and first-class (equal) citizenship in society. The politics of group difference would promote a notion of group solidarity against the individualism of liberal humanism because it is recognized that a positive view of one's specific group would require separate organizations that exclude others. However, this would not eliminate the need for coalitions among groups or the need for oppressed groups to combat other types of oppression (e.g., white people against racism or men against sexism)—an impossibility of the multicultural approach. Group autonomy is an important vehicle for empowerment and the development of a group-specific voice and perspective (Young 1990), but it does not by itself eliminate practices of oppression by the dominant group.

Young (1990) notes that many people fear that asserting group differences will lead to a justification of subordination. However, she contends that a politics of difference confronts this fear by presenting group difference not as essentialist, otherness, or exclusive opposition but as ambiguous, relational, and shifting, marked by specificity and variation. In this way, group differences are conceived as relational rather than defined by substantive categories and attributes (Minow 1985, 1987; Ng 1993). A relational view of difference does not focus on the attributes of groups as the measure of difference but on the interaction of groups with institutions (Littleton 1987, cited in Young 1990; Ng 1993).

With this relational view, the meaning of difference becomes contextualized (Ng 1993; Scott 1988, cited in Young 1990). Group differences are conspicuous, depending on the groups compared, the purposes of the comparison, and the point of view of those making the comparison. Such contextualized understandings of difference undermine essentialist assumptions. Young provides the following example to underscore this point. Wheelchair-bound persons are different from other people in terms of athletics, health care, and social service support, but they are not different in many other respects. At one time, disabled persons were excluded and segregated from society because the differences between able-bodied and disabled persons were conceptualized as extending to all or most capacities.

A relational understanding of group difference rejects social exclusion. Differences among groups do not mean the groups or their members are different in all respects. Overlapping experiences, common goals, and shared attributes are recognized. The assumption that oppositional categorization is inherent in group differences must always be challenged. A relational and contextualized understanding of difference also undermines the notion of an essential individual identity. Persons have many different identities because they tend to be members of many affinity groups, not just one. Black persons, for example, may be poor, rich, old, or gay. These differences produce different identities as well as potential conflicts with other black people and affinities with some white people. Thus, contextualizing the meanings of difference and identity helps us to see the differences that may exist within affinity groups. Oppressed persons are seldom oppressed along one dimension only. They tend to be multiply oppressed. 'In our complex, plural society, every social group has group differences cutting across it, which are potential sources of wisdom, excitement, conflict, and oppression' (Young 1990; 172–173). This intersectional nature or multiplicity of oppression is the subject of Chapter 7.

A politics of difference, of course, has serious implications for policy-making. A goal of social justice (and anti-oppressive social work) is social equality. As discussed in Chapter 2, social equality refers both to an equitable distribution of social goods and to full participation by everyone in society's major institutions, and this must involve the socially supported opportunity for all to develop and exercise their inherent capacities. Although formal legal equality for most groups exists in Canada and in many other Western societies, these societies are still marked by extreme social inequality. Instead of policies that are universally formulated and thus blind to differences of class, race, gender, age, and so forth, a politics of difference would require policies that reflect the specific situations of oppressed groups. 'Groups cannot be socially equal unless their specific experience, culture, and social contributions are publicly affirmed and recognized' (Young 1990, 174).

A politics of difference would require a dual system of rights: a general system of rights for all and a more specific system of group-conscious rights and policies (Young 1990, 174). We already have a precedent for such a system in the form of civil, political, and human rights for all citizens, as well as affirmative action and employment equity programs for some groups (e.g., women, people of colour) who have been historically disadvantaged in our society. To extend this dual system of rights to the point that there would be effective recognition and representation of the voices and perspectives of oppressed groups (as opposed to interest groups), Young proposes the implementation of institutional mechanisms and public resources to support the following: (1) the self-organization of subordinate groups whereby group members could achieve collective empowerment and a reflective understanding of their collective experiences and interests in the context of society; (2) group analysis and generation of policy proposals in institutionalized settings whereby decision makers are obliged to demonstrate that their deliberations have taken relevant group perspectives into consideration; and (3) group veto power regarding specific policies and decisions that affect a group directly, such as land use for Aboriginal communities or reproductive rights for women. Such institutional mechanisms would go a long way towards combating oppression at the structural level.

Economic Relations and Oppression

Capitalism is one of the structures that maintains hierarchical social divisions. In the previous chapter, we looked at capitalism as a totalizing culture (Leonard 1997) that produces and maintains dominant–subordinate relationships in all areas of society. And in Chapter 2, we saw that three of Young's five faces of oppression (exploitation, marginalization, and powerlessness) are related to the social divisions of work inherent in the capitalist economic system. Here we will look at how capitalism as an economic system has changed its form over the past few decades (but not its oppressive function), along with the contemporary and related discourses of capitalism and welfare.

That the face of capitalism has changed since the mid-1970s is now a matter of record. Although seldom steady and never free from tensions and conflict, postwar capitalism managed to maintain an economic boom from 1945 until 1973. This long boom raised material living standards for much of the population in advanced capitalist countries and provided a relatively stable environment for corporate profit-making. The assumption underpinning this model of capitalism was infinite economic growth. The production and consumption of more and more products would be followed by more and more jobs, increased profits, higher wages, and more government revenue for an ever-expanding welfare state.[4] Although cracks had already begun to appear in the postwar capitalist economy (Harvey 1989), the sharp recession of 1973, combined with the oil crisis of that year (which saw a quadrupling in the price of oil) and the inflationary impact of the Vietnam War, set in motion a whole set of processes that undermined the postwar capitalist model. Beginning in the mid 1970s, we witnessed the transformation of capitalism from its postwar form, where its location tended to be within the nation-state, to a global form of capitalism spearheaded by the corporate sector. Technological change, automation, downsizing, mergers, acceleration of capital turnover, and moves to countries with cheaper and more manageable labour became the strategies for corporate survival (Harvey 1989).

Governments also felt the effects of the 1970s crisis in capitalism and its subsequent transformation. Faced with shrinking revenues because of economic decline and growing numbers of people in need, most governments chose to reduce expenditures rather than increase taxes and targeted the welfare state as a major area of cost containment. Fisher and Karger (1997) point out that capital mobility has eroded the power of nation-states to control their own economic and social matters.

These changes in capitalism have occurred in all Western advanced capitalist countries. Although given different labels—Thatcherism in Britain, Reaganomics in the US, neo-conservatism in Canada, and economic rationalism in Australia and New Zealand—the changes in the economic, social, and political environment of the new capitalism have re-emphasized the vulnerability of historically disadvantaged groups, particularly women, children, immigrants, visible minorities, poor people, and workers in less developed countries. These changes have also weakened the trade union movement, since it has lost core, full-time members in the face of the transition to a flexible (i.e., part-time, subcontracted, temporary) labour force. Trade unions have also experienced legislative curbs on their power and the relocation (and the threat of relocation) of many manufacturing businesses to underdeveloped countries. And class-consciousness has diminished because struggling against exploitation in a large factory or plant is very different from struggling against a small subcontracting business or against a father or uncle or other 'godfather' who runs a home- or sweatshop-based business.

Along with a transformed capitalist economic system comes a discourse that justifies this new global capitalism—a discourse of economic determinism. The central messages of this discourse on the new economy, or what Ferguson, Lavalette, and Mooney (2002) call 'the globalization thesis,' are as follows:

- Globalization represents the triumph of capitalism over socialist ideas.
- Neo-conservatism is the driving ideological force underpinning globalization.
- The dominant discourse of globalization is that it is normal, inevitable, and irreversible and therefore should not be resisted or interfered with.
- Nobody (or no group) is in charge of globalization; only the natural laws of the market regulate it.
- The spread of globalization would change dictatorships into democracies.
- Increased trade would spread prosperity across the globe; globalization benefits everyone.

- Nation-states would surrender much of their political and economic sovereignty to global markets.
- The welfare state is both unaffordable and the cause of many economic and social problems.
- The economy must be deregulated and labour unions regulated.

The dominant discourse on the new economy also speaks of the joys of entrepreneurial innovation and the economic need for worker adjustment (Leonard 1997). At the same time, it is made to appear imperative that any resistance to desired changes in the labour processes or to new forms of production must be overcome by whatever means are at hand (Head 1996).

The discourse of globalization uses Darwinian and Hobbesian language to urge us to accept that competitive life, although nasty and brutish, is necessary for survival in the global economy (Leonard 1997). We are told that we must accept the negative consequences of the development of globalization on employment, unemployment, wages, community, and class relations because the consequences would be even worse if we did not compete successfully in the global market. Worsening poverty is deemed unsolvable because it is the product of an 'underclass' subculture (Fisher and Karger 1997). Economic development is part of the discourse applied to exploitation of the developing world by corporate capitalism, yet the developing world continues to provide cheap resources just as it did in the days of colonial rule. Needless to say, such a system maximizes profits for global corporations while contributing to global poverty.

A significant part of the discourse on the new economy is to present the market and social investment as a contradiction. That is, how can a lean economy that must compete in the global market support a welfare state? The predictable answer, of course, is that it cannot. Leonard (1997, 113) comments on this position:

> the old ideas which ruled the modern welfare state—universality, full employment, increasing equality—are proclaimed to be a hindrance to survival. They are castigated as ideas which have outlived their usefulness: they are no longer appropriate to the conditions of a global capitalist economy.

Ironically, while many ideas associated with the modern welfare state are presented as irrelevant and outmoded in the discourse of the new economy, old ideas about work are given a renewed emphasis. The notion of work is that of waged work (without regard to the level of wages or employment benefits, as discussed above) and is framed as a moral obligation (reinforced by the emphasis on the Protestant work ethic during the stages of early and middle capitalism), which in effect subordinates individual needs and capacities to the imperatives of accumulation, profit, and social regulation (Leonard 1997). The social paradox this creates is that in the face of increasing poverty among both traditionally and non-traditionally poor groups, there is diminished social spending as governments roll back social gains made by working populations.

The caring and empowering aspects of the welfare state are reduced at the same time that its regulating and controlling functions are enhanced. 'Need' is no longer the absolute criterion for assistance, as evidenced by compulsory work-for-welfare schemes and the recent program of the Ontario government in Canada for mandatory drug-testing of all welfare recipients (those who test positive must seek help for their alleged addiction or lose their welfare assistance). Those in need are vilified in the new dominant discourse as being afraid to work, dependent, immoral, and a drain on the public purse.

Hopeful Economic Signs

In the 2007 edition of my book *The New Structural Social Work*, I included a section on 'hopeful signs' that were in place after three decades of doom and gloom messages about inevitability that were part of the globalization thesis and discourse. These hopeful signs were (1) the success of the anti-globalization movement, (2) the 'collapse of the globalization thesis,' and (3) the changing economic situation of the government of Canada. Here I will summarize and update these three areas.

1. *Anti-globalization movement*. Cracks were already appearing in the globalization movement in 1999 when the opponents of globalization began their concerted and well-orchestrated series of international demonstrations to protest meetings of the organizations and groups (e.g., the World Trade Organization [WTO], the International Monetary Fund [IMF], the World Bank, and the G8 leaders) that were leading the globalization movement. The eclectic alliance of anti-globalists comprised more than 700 organizations and groups that included student organizations, labour unions, environmental groups, human rights proponents, consumer activists, feminists organizations, anti-racist groups, animal rights organizations, church groups, advocates of Third World debt relief, and social justice groups, among others. They protested the WTO's neo-conservative position on agriculture, multilateral investments, and intellectual property rights, along with the massive wealth accumulation by the leaders of globalization that came at the expense of reduced health care, education, social services, and decent jobs for many in both the developed and the developing worlds.

These and other demonstrations stunned the architects and true believers of globalization in that they could be publicly humiliated by non-professionals (Steger 2003). They also changed the discourse of the proponents of globalization from enthusiastic optimism and inevitability to negativity and defensiveness (Saul 2005). Leaders of the IMF were suddenly astonished to find themselves and their ideology blamed for the myriad of social problems that accompanied the globalization process, and they issued a call for attention to be paid to the negative social outcomes of globalization and for international standards of human rights to be met. The protesters were no longer seen as disconnected from reality as evidenced by this response, and they successfully challenged many aspects of both the ideology and the laissez-faire process of globalization. The anti-globalization movement continues to be active today.

2. *The collapse of the globalization thesis.* In his recent book *The Collapse of Globalism and the Reinvention of the World* (2005), the Canadian historian and philosopher John Ralston Saul makes a compelling case that although many of its effects (both positive and negative) are still with us, globalization as it was originally conceived and predicted by its supporters is now dead. He bases his arguments on numerous events and occurrences that contradict and negate the globalization orthodoxy or globalization thesis outlined above. First, although globalization was to result in nation-states losing autonomy and power to the global economic inevitability that the international institutions (WTO, IMF, World Bank) set up to regulate international trade and other global forces, nationalism and the nation-state are stronger now than they were before globalization began. Second, in Latin America, after governments followed the neo-conservative prescriptions of the international lending institutions for a few years, even greater economic collapse occurred. Many Latin American countries no longer believe in globalization and are now designing their own economic solutions. Third, two gigantic developing countries—India (a socialist country) and China (a communist country)—are leading the world in economic growth by *not* following the economic principles of globalization but by putting controls on capital and various limitations on movements and investments. Fourth, in 1999, after 15 years of fully embracing the ideology of globalization, New Zealand declared the economic doctrine of globalization a failure and voted in a strongly interventionist government. Fifth, in 1998, in the face of an economic meltdown in Asia, Malaysia refused to continue down the masochistic road of globalization and went about breaking most of the rules of the economic doctrine of globalization. Investments grew and production and exports increased, which showed that nation-states were capable of making their own choices and succeeding through unconventional actions. And sixth, one of the correlates of globalization has been the rise of a culture of corporate greed, especially among the executives of the largest corporations. Deregulation and the establishment of self-serving corporate regulations have been used to normalize the most basic forms of corruption. At one time, we would not question the integrity of our corporate masters. However, beginning in the mid-1990s, there has been a backlash against corporate greed that in many cases spilled over into fraud. Several corporate executives who were also leaders of the globalization movement are now in jail, including Canada's own Conrad Black. The fall of many corporate leaders from public trust and respect has cast doubt on the globalization project itself.

3. *From deficit to surplus (to deficit).* The third hopeful economic sign discussed in my 2007 book was the fact that after years of experiencing huge deficits and using them as the rationale for cutting back on the welfare state (health, education, and welfare), the Canadian government started to accrue large surpluses in 1997/98. From that year until this past fiscal year (2007/08), there have been successive surpluses. I argued in 2007 that these surpluses represented a different context with respect to the Canadian welfare state because governments could no longer rationalize cuts as a necessary evil to deal with deficits as they did for decades before 1997. During the

federal election campaign of 2006, all political parties, to varying degrees, promised new social programs or extensions to existing social programs. None of the parties talked about cutbacks, because there was no economic reason for doing so. This was the hopeful sign I noted in my previous book—that a surplus situation is more hopeful than a deficit situation with respect to devising and/or developing health, education, income maintenance, housing, and other systems that are responsive to human need. However, this hopeful sign seemed to disappear when a worldwide recession, worse than any since the Great Depression, emerged full-blown in 2008. All countries were negatively affected by this recession, with the Canadian government stating that Canada would experience a deficit for the year 2008/09, the first since 1996/97, and that this deficit situation would continue for a short while (?) into the future.

Although the return to deficit financing may be seen as a setback to the development of the welfare state, I believe a few new hopeful signs have accompanied the international financial crisis. The most hopeful sign is that unlike the economic crisis that began in the mid 1970s, governments do not seem to be cutting back on their spending to deal with deficits or surrendering their economies to the corporate sector. In fact, the governments of most of the major economies (e.g., the US, the UK, Canada, France, Italy, Germany, Japan) have all developed plans to confront the economic crisis that include a major increase in government spending as a way of increasing economic activity. Proponents call this strategy a stimulus package, and opponents call it a bailout. Most economists of all political stripes seem to support the idea of a stimulus, differing only on details. US President Barack Obama has implemented the largest stimulus package in the history of that country. The irony (and a hopeful sign) is that the US, which represents the purest form of a capitalist nation, is leading the way in terms of government intervention in the face of the global economic crisis. And opponents of the strategy are only a small minority who, in the view of many, are free market ideologues whose only plan is to let industries, companies, and individuals go bankrupt regardless of the social outcomes.

A second hopeful sign is the demand from the public for greater regulation of financial markets and the economy, and politicians across the world have promised to respond to this demand. A third hopeful sign is that the public has also demanded that the greed that was part of the corporate culture be terminated—cases of fraud are now being prosecuted, excessive bonuses and other perks for corporate executives are currently being reined in, and there is a general call for more accountability from the banking and investment sectors. A fourth hopeful sign is that the election of Barack Obama would seem to signal a major potential step towards social justice policies and practices in the US in particular and throughout the world in general. Here I am talking about Obama's call for combating climate change and promoting a green economy, ending the war in Iraq and closing down Guantonamo Bay, rebuilding the infrastructure of American cities, helping to rescue the North American auto industry, attending to the mortgage crisis, and so on. And it seems that the whole world waits in anticipation for him to resolve (or at least make a major step towards resolving) the global economic crisis.

A fifth hopeful sign, for Canada at least, is the fact that in December 2008, the Harper Conservative government very nearly brought the entire federal political system into crisis because it had not included a strategy to deal with the economic crisis in its economic statement in late November. This, along with a few partisan elements in the statement, so enraged the opposition parties that they entered into a coalition to replace the minority Conservative government. Only the decision of the governor general to prorogue Parliament saved the government, which then responded more appropriately to the economic crisis in its late-January budget. The hopeful sign is that even a right-wing Conservative government recognized the need for a stimulus package rather than leaving the economy to the vagaries of the free market.

Chapter 9 addresses what can be done through an anti-oppressive framework to deal with the discursive practices of globalization. At this point, however, it is sufficient to note that the global economy has already shown cracks and that a crisis of legitimacy has occurred. The growing economic crisis, increased rates of poverty, and the discrepancy in material and living conditions between rich and poor cannot be tolerated indefinitely, nor can the growing number of people in need at the same time that the welfare state is being cut back. The doctrine that unfettered capitalist development on a global scale is necessary for economic survival must continue to be challenged by efforts to show that such development has occurred because of decisions and actions made by a relatively small group of people (corporate power and its government allies). What was made by people can be unmade and/or remade. Hopefully, we have already started.

Political Relations and Oppression

Politics refers to the activities carried out through which people govern themselves—that is, how they determine what they will do collectively, how they will live together, and what they want in the future (Pitkin 1981). This decision-making can occur at a small group level (e.g., work unit or family or interest group) or at a macro level (e.g., provincial or state or national government). The focus here is on the latter—how decisions are made in the public arena, who makes them, and who benefits from them. In Chapter 1, we looked at the consensus and conflict views of the nature of society. In contrast to the consensus view, the conflict perspective holds that many groups in society have conflicting interests and that political decisions are made on the basis of economic and political power. In other words, the powerful or dominant groups are able to exercise their power at the political level to have legislation or policies enacted that protect their interests and domination, often at the expense of subordinate groups. But how does this happen in democratic societies such as the Anglo-American nations?

Politics and governance in most liberal or neo-liberal market societies today are couched within a discourse on democracy or democratic participation. However, as

Peter Leonard (1997) points out, there is a contradiction between the social ideal of democracy required for the legitimation of our current political system and certain social practices, such as centralized hierarchical decision-making, that are necessary for the continuation of the system. While acknowledging that some democratic gains, historically, have been made through political struggle by a bourgeoisie in pursuit of its class and gender interests, he argues that embedded within the dominant discourse on democracy are bourgeois and patriarchal assumptions about representation, leadership, majority rule, dissent, and diversity. These assumptions underpin how our current democracy operates to protect the interests of the dominant group under the guise of a free and participatory political system.

Social work subscribes to democratic ideals such as self-determination, participation, and an equal distribution of political power. In fact, much of social work practice is directed towards individuals and groups, helping them gain or regain autonomy and control over their lives. However, there are basically two methods by which democracy can be practised: representative democracy and participatory democracy. We are all used to the representative form of democracy because it is the model practised in most Anglo-American nations today. Let us briefly examine the dominant discourse on representative democracy before discussing participatory democracy.

Representative Democracy Discourse

Although there are elements of other political philosophies (e.g., conservatism and social democracy) within most Anglo-American nations, by and large, liberal values, ideals, and beliefs have formed the basis of their political systems since World War II (Marchak 1981; Mullaly 2007). The fundamental political beliefs of liberalism lie in representative democracy (Marchak 1981) and pluralism (Sills 1968). Liberal democrats would argue that direct participation in the day-to-day business of government by the electorate is impossible. Rather, the essence of modern-day democracy rests in the popular control of elected representatives. Control is exercised through the competition of people running for office, selection by the people of representatives in periodic elections, limitations on the power elected representatives can exercise while in office, and removal of the incumbent representatives if they fail to perform to the people's satisfaction. In sum, liberals contend that the ultimate control within a representative democracy rests with the people who elect and hold accountable a representative government.

According to liberals, universal suffrage has led to a transformation of political systems in Western democracies from the institutionalized ruling-class governments of the eighteenth and nineteenth centuries to open and democratic structures in which the ordinary citizen now has direct and immediate access to his or her elected representative. However, 'modern society has become considerably more complex during the twentieth century and "political power" has become more "diffused" and more "corporate"' (Pritchard and Taylor 1978, 93). In other words, governments are more involved in a whole range of issues and areas, and numerous competing interest and pressure groups have emerged whose purposes are to influence the decisions of elected representatives.

The second fundamental political belief of liberals is that in a representative (liberal) democracy, political power is divided among competing interest groups so that no one group dominates another, let alone dominates the government. This view of political power is called pluralism. The government acts as an independent arbitrator (umpire) of these competing interest groups, controlling their activities by a set of rules—the law—through which it acts as the guardian of the public interest and of individual rights. Thus, it is claimed, no government can fail to respond to the wishes of its citizens because the individual is heard through his or her membership in particular interest groups and at election time.

Critique of Representative Democracy

The discourse or ideal of representative democracy is very different from its actual practice. Although this model of democracy may be relatively efficient in terms of the time it takes to make decisions, its weaknesses have been well documented in the literature (e.g., Galper 1975; Hardy 1981b; Lees 1972; Marchak 1981; Pateman 1970). For example:

- Political elites at times make decisions that are not responsive to the wishes of the electorate.
- Interest groups may gain some sectional advantage at the expense of more general welfare.
- Unorganized sections of society may be ignored or exploited by powerful, organized sections.
- The right to vote every few years is inconsistent with the notion of democracy.
- Such a system promotes and relies on a considerable degree of passivity in the majority of people.
- In the absence of participatory principles, those who make decisions will be those who have been most successful in getting to the top, which is an individualistic and not an egalitarian practice.

As Lees (1972, 39) observed, 'Though democratic in the way it is chosen, representative government has been shown to be elitist in the way that it operates.'

A major concern with the pluralistic nature of representative government is that it reflects the Darwinian notion of competition that characterizes the capitalist economic system. Competition permeates not only the way the governing party assumes power (i.e., by winning an election) but how political decisions are made. Various interest groups (including dominant and subordinate groups) compete with one another to gain the attention of legislators and government officials, have their needs and interests recognized, and have legislation and policies enacted to help meet these needs and interests. And, of course, in any competition there are winners and losers. Furthermore, the dominant groups have more financial resources and political connections to help them better make their needs and interests known. Thus, the system is biased in their favour. One does not win by persuading the public that one's cause is just (Young 1990). In a system of interest-group pluralism, no distinction is made between the assertion of selfish interests (e.g., a plea by the wealthy for a tax break) and normative claims to justice or rights (e.g., a plea by gay and lesbian couples for same-sex family benefits). The winner in a pluralistic political system will most likely be the group able to mount the most effective campaign, which of course will be largely determined by the size of the group along with the financial and political resources available to it.

To be sure, politicians and their close advisers directly decide on public policy, but who are these decision-makers in terms of their social and economic characteristics? Since the system is based on the notion that an elected government represents all the people in society, do politicians reflect the makeup of society in terms of class, gender, race, and other social variables? Addressing the Canadian situation, which does not appear to be significantly different from that of other Anglo parliamentary democracies, Wharf and Cossom (1987) make two important observations. First, the number of people making political decisions (i.e., proposing new policies and revising existing policies) in Canada at the federal and provincial levels are few in number—usually the prime minister (or premier) and a few powerful cabinet ministers and their senior advisers. Second, these few decision-makers are relatively homogeneous. For the most part, they are middle-aged white men with a business or professional background who have benefited and prospered from the existing social, economic, and political arrangements. Because they are 'successful,' they have little personal commitment to change any aspect of Canadian society in a fundamental way.

While the rhetoric or discourse of representative democracy is that elected representatives govern with the best interests of all people in mind, the reality is that elected officials will make decisions consistent with their world views, which in this instance have been shaped by their experiences as white, middle-aged, prosperous, and successful men. In effect, decisions that affect the quality of life and opportunities for development of members of subordinate groups are made by persons who are not members of those groups and in many cases have little understanding of the day-to-day realities faced by these group members. For example, poverty policy is made mostly by people who have never experienced poverty. Policies on Aboriginal issues are made by people who may never have visited an Aboriginal community. Housing policies are made by people who have never been without adequate housing, let alone no housing. And policies on race relations and human rights are made mainly by people who have never been turned down for a job or housing because of the colour of their skin. How can these people possibly represent the needs and best interests of marginalized and subordinate groups in any meaningful or constructive way—especially if it means changing society in ways that would erode their (the dominant group's) own social privileges and standing?

Two Societies

Fiona, the daughter of a business executive; Jill, the daughter of a newspaper publisher; and Roger, the son of a university professor, had similar experiences growing up. All had comfortable homes in crime-free and mostly white neighbourhoods. All attended the finest schools, had extra money from their parents when they needed it, wore the latest teen fashions, and belonged to the most popular clubs and organizations for adolescents. All went on overseas vacations with their families, which broadened their horizons and provided them with a certain sense of confident worldliness. All had their university education paid for by their parents and were able to make use of family connections to get good jobs after graduation. Conversely, Bill, the son of a seasonal worker in the Maritimes; Jim, one of five children in a lone-parent family; and Frances, daughter of parents in receipt of welfare, also had similar experiences growing up. They lived in neighbourhoods with inadequate housing, where heavy traffic and crime were problems. The schools they attended lacked resources, their parents could not provide extra help for them, and many of their clothes were bought at 'Sally Ann' stores. They could not afford to join clubs or organizations for teens or go on holiday trips and spent most of their spare time on the streets. There was always tension in their homes and a steady stream of bill collectors, police, and social services officials at their doors. There was no money for university and no family friends provided jobs. Whereas the former group saw and experienced a stable and orderly society full of opportunities, the latter saw and experienced a chaotic and crisis-ridden society with no opportunities.

At this point, a few words must be said about the theoretical incapacity of liberalism to explain certain social, economic, and political phenomena in a liberal society. Marchak (1981) provides an impressive amount of data that reveal some of the realities of Canadian society in particular but that could apply to any Anglo-American country. Liberalism does not explain why: there is poverty in the midst of affluence; there is evidence of interference in the political process by privately owned corporations; there are persistent divisions of the population along economic lines, which liberals refuse to recognize as class division or dominant–subordinate divisions; the decisions of large corporations affect the lives of people more profoundly than the actions of politicians do. These empirical facts of a liberal society are not accounted for within the liberal discourse.

Liberalism accounts for differences among individuals in terms of quality of life as the outcome of individual differences in talent or effort or of slight imperfections in a system that might not be perfect but which the discourse claims is the best there is (and therefore should be preserved). According to liberals, the consequences of the former can be alleviated, and the latter can be corrected or reformed. However, the evidence does not substantiate these beliefs but suggests instead that there are consistent and persistent differences among identifiable groups in Canada (and elsewhere) with respect to wealth; political power; and access to goods, services, and social institutions. The evidence also shows that these differences are attributable not to individual characteristics but to social characteristics such as ethnicity, gender, age, place of residence, and family of origin (Curtis et al. 1988; Marchak 1981). In other words, dominant–subordinate relations tend to be maintained and reproduced rather than reduced or eliminated under a liberal representative democracy. The major criticism of liberalism is that it has failed to reform the system to correct the causes of different levels of living and opportunities that exist among different social groupings. Writing on the Canadian situation, Marchak (1981, 42–43) articulates this criticism:

> Regional inequalities persist in spite of equalization payments; poverty persists in spite of a welfare system; the taxation system is finally unable to redress the considerable imbalances between the rich and the poor. These are puzzles that the liberal ideology, with its emphasis on individual achievement, equality of opportunity, a market-place for competing talents, and an openness to reform, cannot explain.

Participatory Democracy

By way of contrast, participatory democracy would produce a very different world (Hardy 1981b) from that of a liberal representative democracy. Aristotle associated citizenship with the rights of sharing in decisions (Berry 1986). Lees (1972) and Pateman (1970) contend that a participatory democracy would permit and encourage greater popular participation in such non-governmental arenas as industry, trade unions, political parties, corporations, schools, and universities. Pateman (1970) argues that this participation is educative and that a participatory system is self-sustaining because the qualities needed to support it are generated by the very act of participation itself.

Like Pateman, Bachrach (1969) believes that participation is both political and personal, for it recognizes the self-developmental nature of human beings and enables them to gain in self-esteem. In turn, this self-development will reveal to individuals their authentic identities (as opposed to the ones imposed on them by dominant groups) and what it is they really want (as opposed to manufactured wants and desires). Through participation, people may come to understand themselves as political beings capable of understanding issues that affect them and able to make decisions on these issues. This contrasts with the beliefs of such proponents of representative democracy (and critics of participatory democracy) as Joseph Schumpeter (1950) and Robert Dahl (1970) (cited in Berry 1986).[5] A participatory democracy would delegate a larger share of public power to local communities small enough to permit effective and meaningful general participation in decision-making. Lees (1972, 41) elaborates on this point:

> Participation in politics would provide individuals with opportunities to take part in making significant decisions about their everyday lives. It would build and consolidate a sense of genuine community that would serve as a solid foundation for government. The first and most important step is to recognize that personal self-development is the moral goal of democracy and that direct popular participation is the chief means of achieving it. When this is generally accepted, then society can get on with the largely technical job of thinking up new and better means for increasing popular participation.

With respect to thinking up new and better means for increasing political participation of subordinate or oppressed groups (as opposed to interest groups), the suggestions put forth by Young (1990) in her 'politics of difference' model would be good starting points. A dual system of rights, support for self-organization of subordinate groups, a political imperative of considering the perspectives of subordinate groups, and a group veto power over decisions that affect the group directly would go a long way towards reducing the 'tyranny of the minority' that often accompanies the 'rule of the majority' found in most representative democracies. Many participatory mechanisms and models found throughout the world could be considered to increase the political participation and power of oppressed groups. A first step, however, is to break free from a discourse that presents representative democracy as the only viable model of democracy.

Effects of Structural Oppression

Given the above discussions of how subordinate groups are excluded from or marginalized within or exploited by the three subsystems (i.e., social, economic, and political) of the structural level, this section addresses the question of what structural oppression means for dominated people with respect to their everyday living. What are the actual effects of maintaining group-based social hierarchy by structural means? Specifically, this section looks at the ways that social institutions, laws, policies, and practices disproportionately allocate goods and services with positive social value (e.g., good health care, decent housing, high social status) to dominant group members and disproportionately allocate goods and services with negative social value (e.g., inadequate housing, low social status, incarceration) to members of subordinate groups.

Most (but not all) structural oppression today in most Western democracies is covert. That is, unlike overt structural oppression, it does not openly and explicitly target particular social groups for differential treatment. Examples of overt structural oppression would be not allowing women or black persons to vote in elections (as was the case in many Western jurisdictions in the first half of the last century) or not allowing gay and lesbian persons to marry or to have other benefits, such as pension rights, that heterosexual couples have (as is often the case today). Many writers today argue that much of the overt structural discrimination or oppression of yesterday has been replaced by its 'covert shadow' (Sidanius and Pratto 1999, 128).

Covert oppression at the structural level is a powerful force in maintaining group-based hierarchies. First, it contradicts the spirit and intention of the civil and human rights legislation and the principles of liberty and equality that have been developed over the past 100 years to prohibit institutional discrimination and to extend citizenship status to previously excluded groups. Second, its hidden nature means that many dominant and subordinate group members do not recognize it, which, as will be seen in the next chapter, may result in subordinate group members blaming themselves for their own oppression (i.e., internalizing their oppression). Even if covert oppression is recognized, its hidden and subtle nature makes it very difficult for subordinate groups to employ collective action for change. The belief that modern Western democracies are largely free of discrimination and oppression at the structural level is not only held by the lay public but is widespread among political commentators, public intellectuals, and a number of scholars (Sidanius and Pratto 1999). However, the evidence overwhelmingly contradicts this belief. As will be seen below, rather than social equality and equal opportunity being of central importance in democratic societies, widespread institutional or structural oppression affects all the major areas of an individual's life—employment, housing, health, education, financial opportunities, and treatment by the criminal justice system. Structural oppression constitutes a total environment, or what Sidanius and Pratto (1999, 129) call a 'circle of oppression.'

Oppression as Structural Violence and Social Terrorism

In this section, I will argue that the term 'social or structural inequality' is part of an academic and professional discourse that reduces its political charge and impact by covering over the structural violence experienced by members of subordinate groups all over the world. Furthermore, by not including the violent consequences and correlates of social inequality in its discourse and practice, the profession of social work is in effect an unwitting agent in limiting healthy and productive living and causing death. It is part of a socially sanctioned process whereby people are tortured, maimed, and killed in ways that are unseen and unpunished. I call for all social workers to view social inequality as more than notions of deprivation, disadvantage, and redistribution. Social inequality is in fact a form of social terrorism perpetrated by privileged groups on subordinate groups at the structural level of society.

Violence, as defined in Chapter 2, includes both actions that result in physical injury and threats, intimidation, harassment, and bullying. When violence is systemic—that is, when it happens to someone because he or she is a member of a particular social group—then it is a form of oppression. Gil (1998), Bulhan (1985), and Fanon (1968) have argued convincingly that oppression at the structural or institutional level is a form of violence. Bulhan (1985, 135) provides a definition of violence that links it to structural oppression (as well as to oppression at the personal level): 'Violence is any relation, process, or condition by which an individual or a group violates the physical, social, and/or psychological integrity of another person or group.' From this perspective, Bulhan points out that violence negatively affects human growth and development, interferes with the inherent potential of individuals, limits productive living, and causes death.

Bulhan identifies five assumptions that underpin and flow from the above definition of violence. First, violence is not a simple random act but is any relation, condition, or process that negatively affects the well-being of its victim. Second, violence is not only moral or ethical but physical, psychological, and social as well. Third, violence in any of these three areas has repercussions for the other two areas (e.g., physical violence will have psychological and social effects). Fourth, violence occurs not only between individuals but also between groups and societies. And finally, the intention is less important than the consequence of most forms and acts of violence. This concept of violence also includes the vast array of legitimized or socially sanctioned forms of violence that create and maintain a condition of oppression. Some of these forms are presented below. Katherine van Wormer (2004, 152), a prominent American progressive social work writer, argues that such violence is ubiquitous in social work practice: '[S]ocial workers, whether engaged in individual practice or community organization work, deal on a daily basis with the personal and social problems that are rooted in structural or societal violence.'

Bulhan contends that violence at the personal level is relatively easy to detect and control because it usually involves direct action in which the act of violence and its consequences are observable. The perpetrator and the victim are normally distinguishable, and the purpose of the violence can be verified and its effects assessed. Structural violence is a much more complex and higher-order phenomenon. It is a feature of social structures and social institutions. The social processes, relations, and practices associated with social inequities often span generations. They are deeply ingrained in people and dominate everyday living. 'Structural violence involves more than the violation of fairness and justice. . . . [It] leads to hidden but lethal inequities, which can lead to the death of those who lack power or influence in the society' (van Wormer 2004, 136). Rather than a quick death by state execution or a personal act of lethal violence, structural oppression in the form of such inequities as inadequate income, substandard or no housing, unemployment, and lack of health care leads to a slow, agonizing, unpunished, and premature death for countless numbers of subordinated people all over the world on a daily basis.

Sidanius and Pratto (1999) present an impressive amount of empirical data and powerful evidence showing that covert structural oppression can be found in all the major areas of an individual's life in Western democratic nations.[6] These major areas include employment, financial opportunities, the housing and retail markets, education, health care, and the criminal justice system. An examination of the living situation of almost any subordinate group anywhere in the world is likely to show it experiencing oppression in all or most of these areas. That is, subordinate groups generally will suffer directly from lack of adequate employment, low income and poverty, inadequate housing, discrimination in the retail market, lack of educational opportunities, inferior health care, and an overrepresentation within the criminal justice system. These inequities are part of structural violence in that people who experience them in turn suffer from disproportionate levels and incidences of stress, anguish, frustration, alienation, exclusion, and so on that result in differential rates of mortality (i.e., lowered life expectancies), morbidity, incarceration, homicide, suicide, and infant mortality. There can be no doubt, as Bulhan (1985) argues and as Fanon (1968) did before him, that oppression at the structural level leads to violence at the personal level (e.g., suicide and self-mutilation), at the interpersonal level (e.g., homicide and domestic violence), and at the institutional level (premature death because of social inequalities). What makes this type of violence so insidious is the fact that no known perpetrator or intention can be identified as responsible for it.

Bulhan presents a litany of glaring examples of racial violence in its different forms as experienced in two countries, the United States and South Africa. A brief look at the American situation is presented here. Although the days of lynching, whipping, or castrating African-Americans may be over, structural violence has replaced much of this interpersonal violence. Bulhan cites studies showing that African-Americans suffer all the inequities discussed above. As a result, relative to the dominant white group, African-Americans have lower life expectancies; higher mortality rates (including infant mortality); and higher rates of heart disease (hypertensive heart disease), stroke, cancer, and homicide—all associated with social inequality. As well, African-Americans suffer high levels of chronic unemployment and are more likely to be hired for dangerous job assignments (including high-risk assignments in the military). Higher rates of African-Americans are incarcerated, and many more are on 'death row.' They also experience more severe sentencing and more unwarranted arrests. There is a much higher incidence of homicide among African-Americans than among white people and a higher incidence of violence within domestic and intimate contexts. Alcoholism and drug addiction are higher among African-Americans than among white persons, and the suicide rate has been rising faster than it has among white people (although white people still have a higher suicide rate). In sum, African-Americans bear an inordinate amount of the burden of violence in American society.

Subordinate groups in Canada have similar experiences to those of African-Americans with respect to structural violence.[7] Of all the oppressed groups in Canada, First Nations people, by all indicators, suffer most from social inequalities and therefore experience the most structural violence. Almost half of First Nations families live below the poverty line (Oberle 1993); the average life expectancy is 10 years less than that of Euro-Canadians (Health and Welfare Canada 1991a); and approximately 20 per cent of First Nations children are removed from their families by child welfare authorities (Clarke 1991). First Nations families have an infant mortality rate more than double the national average, and the suicide rate for Aboriginal adolescent girls is about seven times higher than the national rate and for Aboriginal adolescent boys about four times higher (Health Canada 1994). Incarceration rates for First Nations people are much higher than for the general population. In general, alcohol and drug abuse is higher among First Nations populations than in the general Canadian population (Health and Welfare Canada 1992), with 50 to 80 per cent of Aboriginal youth having abused alcohol (Round Lake Treatment Centre 1992). Chappell (1997) cites studies showing that family violence is disproportionately high among First Nations people; in fact, one study (Taylor 1991) suggests that as many as one in three Aboriginal women in the province of Manitoba has experienced spousal abuse.

Among other subordinate groups in Canada experiencing structural oppression and violence are older Canadians and women. Although Canadians on average are living longer these days, the high rate of mental health problems among the elderly cannot all be attributed to old age. Poverty, loneliness, and a sense of uselessness contribute to depression and exacerbate other mental disorders such as Alzheimer's and related dementias (Health and Welfare Canada 1991b). Suicide among elderly people is a major concern in Canada, with males over the age of 80 having the highest suicide rate of any age group in the nation (Health Canada 1994). Abuse of prescription drugs is also a major concern, with older Canadians consuming about 25 per cent of all prescription drugs in Canada (Health and Welfare Canada 1989).

The rate of violence against women is disturbingly high in Canada. One national study found that more than 51 per cent of Canadian women had been physically or sexually assaulted since age 16 and that out of 12 300 respondents, 29 per cent had been physically or sexually abused by a current or former partner (Statistics Canada 1993). Immigrant women and women with disabilities are particularly vulnerable to abuse. As well, the rate of poverty among single mothers has been growing steadily, reaching 57.3 per cent in 1994 (National Council of Welfare 1996). Discrimination against women has also been documented in the workplace with respect to wages, occupational segregation, training, and pensions (Canadian Advisory Council on the Status of Women 1990). This discrimination is an example of structural oppression, which of course makes women more vulnerable to structural violence.

Social Determinants of Health

Although the work dates back a couple of decades, a field of study and policy similar to the above perspective on the violent outcomes of social inequality has emerged in Canada and internationally since the mid-1990s. 'Population health promotion' or the 'social determinants of health movement' is an interdisciplinary movement that studies the factors associated with varying degrees of health and illness. It moves beyond the traditional determinants of health that are part of the health care system and includes social factors such as the ones mentioned in the following passage:

There is strong evidence indicating that factors outside the health care system significantly affect health. These 'determinants of health' include income and social status, social support networks, education, employment and working conditions, physical environments, biology and genetic endowment, personal health practices and coping skills, healthy child development, health services, gender and culture [Health Canada 1998, 1].

Similar to Health Canada's identification of the determinants of health, the Ottawa Charter for Health Promotion delineates the prerequisites for health as peace, shelter, education, food, income, a stable ecosystem, sustainable resources, social justice, and equity (World Health Organization 1986, cited in Raphael 2004). These prerequisites for health are concerned with the structural aspects of society and the organization and distribution of economic and social resources. One could easily substitute the terms 'structural violence' or 'social terrorism' for social determinants of health, since the determinants are the same. The organizers of the 2002 York University (in Canada) Conference on Social Determinants of Health arrived at 11 social determinants especially relevant to Canadians: Aboriginal status, early life, education, employment and working conditions, food security, health care services, housing, income and its distribution, social safety net, social exclusion, and unemployment and employment security. Others in the field (e.g., the 2002 Toronto Charter for a Healthy Canada) included Canadian women, Canadians of colour, and new Canadians as groups that are particularly vulnerable to the deleterious effects of all other social determinants—so much so that these groups represent social determinants of health in and of themselves.

The following box (taken from Raphael 2004, 13) highlights two approaches to better health care. The first approach, which is the traditional lifestyle approach, gives 10 tips for better health. It is individually oriented and assumes that individuals can control the factors that determine their health. The second approach, which is the social determinants approach, is societally oriented and assumes that the most important determinants of health are beyond the control of the individual. In spite of evidence in favour of the social determinants view, much of the Canadian public discourse on health and disease reflects the lifestyle approach to disease prevention (Raphael 2004).

The social determinants movement is more policy-focused than the anti-oppressive social work practice in the area of dealing with structural violence and therefore represents more of a liberal-humanist approach to social inequality as opposed to the critical approach of anti-oppressive social work. The former approach assumes that society can be reformed by way of enlightened social policies, and the latter assumes that the only way to achieve equal health outcomes for all groups in society is to transform it so that there is no dominant group. Nevertheless, the movement represents a significant advancement from the traditional medical perspective of looking only at health variables as relevant to health and illness. It recognizes that 'who' you are in society will largely determine your state of health and your risk of morbidity and premature mortality.

Which Tips for Better Health Are Consistent with Research Evidence?

The Traditional 10 Tips for Better Health
1. Don't smoke. If you can, stop. If you can't, cut down.
2. Follow a balanced diet with plenty of fruit and vegetables.
3. Keep physically active.
4. Manage stress by, for example, talking things through and making time to relax.
5. If you drink alcohol, do so in moderation.
6. Cover up in the sun, and protect children from sunburn.
7. Practise safer sex.
8. Take up cancer-screening opportunities.
9. Be safe on the roads: follow the highway code.
10. Learn the first aid ABCs: airways, breathing circulation. [Donaldson 1999, cited in Raphael 2004, 13]

The Social Determinants 10 Tips for Better Health
1. Don't be poor. If you can, stop. If you can't, try not to be poor for long.
2. Don't have poor parents.
3. Own a car.
4. Don't work in a stressful, low-paid manual job.
5. Don't live in damp, low-quality housing.
6. Be able to afford to go on a foreign holiday and sunbathe.
7. Practise not losing your job, and don't become unemployed.
8. Take up all benefits you are entitled to if you are unemployed, retired, or sick or disabled.
9. Don't live next to a busy major road or near a polluting factory.
10. Learn how to fill in the complex housing benefit/asylum application forms before you become homeless and destitute. [Gordon 1999, personal communication with Raphael, cited in Raphael 2004]

Conclusion

Oppression at the structural or institutional level is legally and socially sanctioned in that it is manifest in the ways our social institutions, public policies, laws, and the economic and political systems all work together to benefit the dominant group at the expense of subordinate groups. The nature of the relationship between dominant groups and subordinate groups was discussed with respect to their location within and treatment by society's social, economic, and political institutions. Assimilation and multiculturalism have been proposed and pursued as ways of dealing with difference, but both approaches have oppressive consequences. A 'politics of difference' offers a more viable anti-oppressive policy. The transformation of capitalism from a fixed and predominantly local or national basis to a global form, along with its legitimizing discourse of 'economic determinism,' has been presented by many in places of power and influence as an inevitable, normal, natural, and evolutionary process that should be embraced rather than resisted. This discourse dictates that to be successful in the global economy, we must accept for subordinate groups worsening poverty, greater social inequality, diminished social investment, and worker exploitation on a global scale. A number of hopeful signs that appear to be undermining the globalization phenomenon and discourse were presented. Alternative economic discourses that confront, resist, and challenge the globalization discourse must continue to be developed as one anti-oppressive strategy. With respect to people's relationship to the political system, subordinate groups are not well served by representative democracy. Most political leaders are members of the dominant group who benefit from our current sets of dominant–subordinate social, economic, and political relations and have no commitment to change. Participatory forms of democratic structures and decision-making are seen as alternatives to representative democracy.

Finally, structural inequalities often have violent effects or outcomes. Terms such as 'social inequality' and 'structural inequality' tend to cover up the violent outcomes that many people from subordinate groups experience. Structural inequalities are much more than one person or one group having a greater quantity of or more access to social goods, rights, and opportunities. They are more than violations of philosophical notions of fairness, equity, and justice. Structural inequalities are socially sanctioned forms of physical and psychological violence and terrorism, which over time will lead to hurtful discrimination and slow, agonizing, premature, and unpunished death. Structural inequalities torture, maim, mutilate, and kill members of oppressed groups. The terms 'social terrorism' and 'structural violence' and even Engels's use of 'social murder,' I contend, more accurately reflect the realities of oppressed persons. 'Social or structural inequality' is an abstract, technical, bourgeois, professional, and polite term that covers up its violent outcomes. We should call it what it is—socially sanctioned social terrorism. A brief overview of the social determinants of health movement was also presented because it is similar to the view of structural violence. Both perspectives regard structural inequality as the cause of premature death and disproportionate levels of ill-health. The major difference between the two is that the former aims at social reform as the solution while the latter holds that only social transformation will resolve the problem of social terrorism.

Critical Questions for Discussion

1. Why wouldn't people from a subordinate group want to be assimilated into the mainstream so they could enjoy the benefits of being full citizens and not be hassled because they chose to stay outside the mainstream? Is it easier for some groups to be assimilated? Why or why not?

2. Iris Marion Young, in her discussion of a 'politics of difference,' argues that we should view group differences as relational rather than defining them as categorical or based on attributes such as male/female, white/black, heterosexual/GLBT. What does this mean?

3. How do you make sense of the fact that governments of all political stripes (conservative, liberal, social democratic, Marxist) are all adopting similar responses to address the current worldwide economic crisis? Even the United States, with the purest form of capitalism on Earth, is engaging in massive government intervention into the economy, including the nationalization of some of its banks—which is a socialist strategy. Similarly, the Conservative government under Stephen Harper (arguably the most conservative prime minister Canada has had in decades) has adopted similar policies that seem to be the very antithesis of conservative ideology.

4. First Nations people have long advocated for and carried out a social movement for self-government. What does this mean, and how would it work in our present system of liberal democracy? How would it work within Iris Marion Young's 'politics of difference' model of governance?

5. In addition to the 11 social determinants of health adopted by many progressive health-oriented organizations in Canada and by Health Canada, the 2002 Toronto Charter for a Healthy Canada added three more determinants— Canadian women, Canadian people of colour, and new Canadians. How and why do these three groups represent determinants of health in and of themselves?

Further Readings

Leonard, Peter (1997). *Postmodern Welfare: Reconstructing an Emancipatory Project.* London: Sage. This book examines the future of the welfare state in the context of the dominance of global market capitalism and the rise of free-market welfare ideology. In particular, it surveys the debates and contradictions that frame the current social welfare discourse. From a critical theory perspective grounded in Marxism and feminism, the author uses elements of postmodernism to deconstruct and consider how we might rethink the present and the future of the welfare state.

Raphael, Dennis, ed. (2004). *Social Determinants of Health: Canadian Perspectives.* Toronto: Canadian Scholars Press. This book brings together a number of academics and high-profile experts in the area of the social determinants of health. The book summarizes how socio-economic factors affect the health of Canadians, surveys the current state of 11 social determinants of health across Canada, and provides an analysis of how these determinants affect Canadians' health. This perspective is the key to understanding patterns of health and illness in Canada today. These social determinants of health are also determinants of privilege and oppression.

Saul, John Ralston (2005). *The Collapse of Globalism and the Reinvention of the World.* Toronto: Viking Canada. The author argues that with its technocratic and technological determinism and its worship of the free market, globalization may have seen its best days. This book follows globalization from its promising beginnings in the 1970s through to the increasing deregulation of industry into the 1990s when regional economic collapses and concern for the environment and for the rights of workers led to disillusionment and widespread protest. In the wake of globalization's collapse, the nation-state is making a remarkable recovery of the best and worst sorts.

Sidanius, Jim, and Felicia Pratto (1999). *Social Dominance: An Intergroup Theory of Social Hierarchy and Oppression.* Cambridge: Cambridge University Press. The book attempts to dispel the notion that oppression and discrimination have been overcome in recent history or that they are only realities in despotic regimes. The authors present a compelling and well-documented account of dominant-group processes—how they work, how they are manifested, and why they are so resistant to change. The authors provide evidence to show that oppression remains omnipresent in all aspects of social life—in the workplace, educational settings, the judicial system, the retail marketplace, and health care systems.

Young, Iris Marion (1990). *Justice and the Politics of Difference.* Princeton, NJ: Princeton University Press. A seminal book in a number of scholarly and professional areas, including social justice and anti-oppression. The author makes probably the most convincing case for the emancipatory implications of postmodernism. The book presents a critical analysis of different theories of justice and finds them lacking in that they do not contain the claims of excluded groups with respect to decision-making, cultural expression, and division of labour. By assuming a homogeneous public, traditional theories of justice (including distributive or redistributive justice) fail to consider institutional arrangements for including people not culturally identified with white European male norms of reason and respectability. She identifies concepts of domination and subordination to cover issues not included in the distributional model and argues for a principle of group representation in democratic decision-making.

Chapter 6

Internalized Oppression and Domination

Q. If there is no natural hierarchy among humans, why are some cases of oppression so persistent?
A. Because of the coercive co-opting of the oppressed to join in their own oppression.
—Ann E. Cudd, *Analyzing Oppression*, 2006

Introduction

Most writers today agree that oppression is linked to social conditions and that the environment (social, cultural, political, and economic factors) plays an important role in influencing the individual psyche (Moane 1999). Conversely, there is broad agreement that the individual plays an active role in mediating the effects of these environmental factors. The basic dialectic of the psyche and society shaping each other is captured in many different theoretical perspectives—social constructionist, critical (social and psychological theory), interpretive, discursive, feminist, psychoanalytic. Because oppression is experienced differently by different people, it is impossible to construct a standard theory of oppression in general and internalized oppression in particular. Thus, the intention in this chapter is to present a general account of the nature, causes, and effects of internalized oppression.

Psychology of Oppression

In previous chapters, the focus has mainly been on social factors as they relate to oppression. The emphasis has been on the social dimensions and social relationships (gender, race, class, and so on) that constitute social hierarchies and on the social processes and practices that produce and maintain these hierarchies. Although psychological material was presented with respect to coping mechanisms and to some of the obvious consequences of oppression for the psyche, social theories, critical social analyses, and social science literature have so far dominated. However, any discussion of oppression would be grossly incomplete if psychological factors associated with oppression were omitted. A comprehensive treatment of the psychology of oppression is well beyond the scope of this book, but this section contains a synopsis of some of this material,[1] while subsequent sections cover the ideas of some writers on the subject.

Oppression and its associated social conditions of discrimination, powerlessness, subordination, exclusion, exploitation, scapegoating, low social status, and blocked opportunities are bound to have an impact on the psyche of dominated persons. The personal is political, and the political is personal. In other words, the psyche and society shape each other. The personal is influenced and shaped by the social, political, economic, and cultural context, and therefore, in order to understand the personal, one must understand the larger context.[2] This is one of the basic tenets of critical and liberation psychology and tends to separate them from more traditional individualistic schools of psychology that ignore broader social and cultural factors (for examples of psychological theorizing that includes social factors, see Bulhan 1985; Fox and Prilleltensky 1997; Moane 1999; and Wilkinson 1996). It is one of the fallacies of many models of psychology that it is possible to change the person without changing the social context (McLellan 1995). 'Psychological development and psychological change are not privatized individualized processes which happen regardless of social context, but are intrinsically and dynamically related to the individual's specific context' (Moane 1999, 7).

Bulhan (1985) links a psychological analysis of oppression with a systematic exploration of its links with psychological functioning in such areas as sexuality, identity, self-esteem, emotions, psychological distress, and interpersonal relationships. In a review of writers who discuss various psychological aspects of oppression derived from a number of oppressed groups (women, black women, colonized people, Aboriginal persons, and gay and lesbian people), Moane notes that oppression has a profound negative impact on psychological functioning. This impact includes loss of identity, powerlessness, fear, suppression of anger, isolation, ambivalence, and sense of inferiority. These (and other) psychological problems obviously will undermine the capacity of oppressed persons to resist domination and take action to bring about social change. Two of the psychological conditions brought about by oppression are a sense of inferiority and its correlate, internalized oppression. Internalized oppression is a theme found in writings on women, racism, colonialism, homophobia, and experiences of other forms of oppression. Moane points out that internalized oppression is associated with such psychological patterns as self-hatred, helplessness and despair, mutual distrust and hostility, feelings of inferiority, and psychological distress and madness. McDonald and Coleman (1999, 24) say of internalized oppression:

> . . . people who have been oppressed might consciously or unconsciously absorb the values and beliefs of their oppressors. This may lead to 'internalised oppression,' whereby members of oppressed groups may come to believe that the stereotypes, misinformation or propaganda being spread about their group are true (or partly true), so that they may develop low self-esteem, or they may behave in ways that are essentially consistent with their social stereotypes.

Both McDonald and Coleman (1999) and Kumsa (2007) warn that such internalized oppression can lead to competition among oppressed groups over which is most oppressed. Rather than uniting and fighting oppression, a hierarchy of oppression is created, with the oppressed groups fighting for the moral high ground. Internalized oppression is the subject of the remainder of this chapter.

Inferiority and Internalized Oppression

In *The Mass Psychology of Fascism*, Michael Reich (1975, 53) pointed out that 'what has to be explained is not the fact that the man [sic] who is hungry steals or the fact that the man [sic] who is exploited strikes, but why the majority of those who are hungry don't steal and why the majority of those who are exploited don't strike.' In the same vein, Rosen (1996) asks in his aptly titled *On Voluntary Servitude* why the majority of subordinated or oppressed people accept the rule of the minority elite, even when it is patently clear that it is against their interests to do so. Rosen makes the point that this is not a new question, referring to de la Boetie, who asked as far back as 1552 why some people accept their servitude voluntarily.

Reference has already been made in earlier chapters (especially Chapter 3) to the terms 'inferiorization' and 'internalized oppression.' Inferiorization denotes not only an acceptance of a second-class or inferior citizenship status in society by a member of an oppressed group but a belief that he or she and all members of that group are inferior to the dominant group. It is a belief that their oppression is deserved and unique, unchangeable or temporary (Adam 1978) and that their problems in living are due to their personal shortcomings (Shulman 1992). It is an acceptance of the negative identity defined by the larger society and of the stereotypes assigned to them. Inferiorization describes a situation in which oppressed persons often understand their interests in ways that reflect the interests of the dominant group (Freire 1994 [1970]).

Internalized oppression takes inferiorization a step further because it includes not only a belief that one's self and one's social group are inferior but also encompasses behaviours (discursive practices) that are self-harming and contribute to one's own oppression. These self-destructive behaviours on the part of some oppressed people, of course, reinforce the dominant group's view of them as inferior and lead to a rejection of them, which in turn often confirms the low image they may have of themselves (Moreau and Leonard 1989). Shulman (1992) points out that these self-perceptions can be reinforced by social workers who focus on personal pathology and ignore external or structural factors that create and reinforce this negative self-image.

Irish psychologist Sean Ruth (1988, 435) writes that 'the key to the maintenance of oppression . . . is what we call internalized oppression or internalized control. This is where people come to believe in their own inferiority and their powerlessness to change things.' Ruth links feelings of low self-esteem, inferiority, and powerlessness on the part of oppressed persons to a mistrust in their own thinking and intelligence, with the result that they pay scant attention or respect to each other and give much weight to the views of outsiders, particularly the dominant group. Mistrust in turn leads to divisiveness within the group. Marsiglia and Kulis (2009) give a couple of examples of this divisiveness that results in discrimination against other people in the same subordinate group. In schools with many immigrant students, those who already speak fluent English may ridicule more recent immigrants who do not. Or an immigrant mother may take her children to an Anglo dentist rather than an immigrant dentist because she believes that the immigrant dentist could not possibly be as competent as the Anglo dentist. This belief is a reflection of the prejudice she herself has experienced as an immigrant person. In addition to the divisiveness that internalized oppression creates within the group, Ruth identifies three other characteristics of oppressed people centring on power and authority that also emanate from internalized oppression: (1) they learn to behave in ways that do not provoke retaliation or draw attention; (2) they have ambivalent feelings about their own leaders, expecting much but not supporting them; and (3) they often oppress other oppressed groups to feel better about themselves (creating an oppressed person's snobbery) rather than attempting to change the system.

In Chapter 3, we examined a number of responses that oppressed people may adopt, which either reinforce or contribute to their oppression, including those identified by Freire (1994 [1970])—fatalism, horizontal violence, self-depreciation, attraction towards the oppressor and his or her way of life—and those discussed by Adam (1978)—mimesis, escape from identity, psychological withdrawal, guilt-expiation, magical ideologies, inter-group hostility, and social withdrawal. It was also pointed out in Chapter 3 that although these responses may appear to be peculiar, unnatural, or neurotic in that they function to sustain and reproduce oppression, they are more complex than that. Some of them may be acts of resistance to oppression (Kanuha 1999). As well, some of them function to reduce the everyday suffering of oppression experienced, which makes these responses or positions much more difficult to deal with from an anti-oppressive perspective. What follows is a more systematic exploration of some of the causes or explanations or correlates of internalized oppression as they exist in the literature with a view to developing a more inclusive and informed anti-oppressive social work practice.

The Master-Slave Paradigm

Lerner (1986) contends that the emergence of slavery is the most important development for tracing the history of domination because it serves as a model for other forms of domination-subordination at both the social and psychological levels. Moane (1999) notes that slavery involves the creation of a class of human beings who are deprived of freedom and forced against their will to labour for and serve another group of human beings. It requires the explicit development and institutionalization of a set of legal and social practices and processes that mark the enslaved group as different (the Other), excludes them from participation in society, and treats them as commodities to be bought and sold and exploited for their labour. These legal and social practices were the forerunners of the unwritten and silent rules, expectations, and practices that underpin oppression today.

As well as legal and social practices, psychological factors that originated with slavery characterize dominant–subordinate relations today. Lerner (1986, 100) writes of the stigma and internalized oppression associated with slavery, but she could just as well have been describing a part of the psychology of oppression as it exists in contemporary society:

> Stigma becomes a reinforcing factor which excuses and justifies the practice of enslavement in the minds of the dominant group and in the minds of the enslaved. If the stigma is fully internalized by the enslaved—a process which takes many generations and demands the intellectual isolation of the enslaved group— enslavement then becomes to be perceived as 'natural' and therefore acceptable.

Given that some of today's oppressive social and legal processes and practices and psychological conditions seem to have their origins in slavery, the 'master-slave' relationship would seem to be a useful concept in furthering our understanding of oppression. Hegel (1966 [1807]) wrote of this relationship in one of his works, *The Phenomenology of Mind*, a book that has had a profound effect on many subsequent writers, including Karl Marx and Jean-Paul Sartre, both of whom found in it ideas to understand, critique, and attempt to transform European society (Bulhan 1985). Hegel's discussion of the 'master and slave' dialectic, contained in this seminal work, has since informed intellectual discourse on oppression, particularly the psychology of oppression.

Hegel's philosophical argument was that the individual becomes conscious of himself or herself only through recognition by the Other. In order to achieve such recognition, a struggle or conflict occurs between two individuals. The winner becomes the master and attains recognition by the Other. The loser becomes the slave and does not attain recognition by the master. In addition to gaining recognition, the master also reduces the slave to an instrument of his or her will—to labour for and fulfill the needs of the master. (However, Hegel believed that the advantages accruing to the master actually compromised him or her and thwarted his or her self-actualization and thus the slave in the end became the real victor.)

Kojeve (1969) was able to extract deep and rich psychological meaning from Hegel's master-slave dialectic that helps to enhance our understanding of oppression. Kojeve's lectures on Hegel to the intellectual elite of Europe in the 1930s directly influenced the works of such intellectuals as the existentialist Jean-Paul Sartre and the postmodern psychoanalyst Jacques Lacan and indirectly influenced Frantz Fanon, the revolutionary black psychiatrist who fought against colonialism in Algeria (Bulhan 1985). Essentially, Kojeve (1969, as cited in Bulhan 1985) argued that Hegel's master-slave dialectic presupposes that people are fundamentally social, since recognition is possible only in the presence of and confrontation with the Other. The 'desire' for recognition leads to a search that involves the perilous struggle between two adversaries who attempt to force recognition one from the other, without reciprocating. Drawing from Hegel, Kojeve emphasized that the winner becomes the master and gains recognition by the Other (i.e., the slave), which confirms the master's self-worth, identity, and humanity. Kojeve further argued that because the master does not reciprocate a recognition of the slave, then the latter loses self-worth, identity, and humanity. The master is elevated to human life, and the slave is reduced to animal life. The former becomes autonomous and self-determining; the latter becomes dependent and determined. The master consumes and enjoys what the slave produces because the slave is only an extension of the master's will and body. This, according to Kojeve, is the foundation of human oppression.[3]

In his book *Frantz Fanon and the Psychology of Oppression* (1985), the African-American writer Hussein Bulhan traces the use of the concept of the master-slave dialectic in developing a psychology of oppression. He initially looks at and critiques Hegel's original notion of the concept along with Kojeve's interpretation and extension of Hegel's work. He then analyzes the use of the master-slave relationship in French psychoanalyst Mannoni's (1962) explanation of the origin and dynamics of colonialism. And finally, he reviews Fanon's development of Hegel's master-slave paradigm and the way he used it to analyze the relationship between contemporary white and black people. Bulhan notes that whereas Hegel and Mannoni directed most of their attention to the whys of oppression, Fanon (himself a descendant of slaves) explained how oppression dehumanizes all involved. Fanon reformulated and extended the abstract master-slave paradigm of Hegel and Mannoni so that he could apply it to concrete, lived experiences under slavery and colonialism.

Bulhan's book makes for fascinating reading on psychoanalytical and psychological interpretations of the minds of both oppressors/colonizers and oppressed/colonized people. Some of his conclusions about internalized oppression developed within the framework of the master-slave dialectic (particularly Fanon's version) are presented below.

- For a system of oppression to be effective, various forms of social control must pervade the life of the oppressed. They may include acts and the threat of physical harm, a narrow circle of tame ideas (ideological hegemony), infiltration of family and community to limit the capacity for bonding and trust, obliteration of the subordinate group's history and culture, and a system of rewards and punishment based on loyalty to the oppressor to foster competition among the oppressed.

- In situations of prolonged oppression, the oppressed group will internalize the oppressor 'without' by adopting the dominant group's guidelines and prohibitions and assimilating its image and social behaviours (see also Adam 1978). In this way, the oppressed group becomes the agent of its own oppression—an oppressor 'within.' Internalized oppression is highly resistant to change, since it would require a battle on two fronts: the oppressor within and the oppressor without.

- Patterson (1982) notes that a distinctive characteristic of the slave or oppressed person is his or her generalized condition of dishonour. In the oppressed person's eyes (and those of others), the person and status of the slave lack integrity, worth, and autonomy—all necessary characteristics for one to battle the master or oppressor group.

- The well-known inferiority complex of oppressed groups originates in the process of internalization, and the attendant but repressed rage causes some oppressed persons to act out, on each other, the very physical and/or psychological violence imposed on them. When oppressed persons engage in self-destructive behaviour, injuring themselves, their loved ones, or their neighbours, they often experience confounding ambivalence and guilt, which reinforce their sense of inferiority. Paulo Freire (1994 [1970]) refers to this type of violence as 'horizontal violence' (see page 170).

- There are two sets of contrasting attitudes and behaviours between a member of the oppressor group and a member of the oppressed group whenever they encounter each other. The former acts as a majority, demands more space and privilege, and exudes confidence and a sense of entitlement. The latter acts as a minority of one, settles for less, and displays self-doubt and a readiness to compromise. The dominant ideas, values, and rules of conduct serve the former and entrap the latter.

- Oppressed persons find everyday living a challenge. Being confined to another's rules, culture, expectations, and so on requires a marked degree of personal versatility and repression. Of this, Bulhan (1985, 123) says, 'The oppressed learn to wear many masks for different occasions; they develop skills to detect moods and wishes of those in authority, and learn to present acceptable public behaviours while repressing many incongruent personal feelings. . . . This pattern of adaptation no doubt entails a personal toll, an excessive use of energy, and a higher vulnerability for psychopathology.' It is not surprising, then, that social terrorism in the form of morbidity, mortality, incarceration, and psychiatric hospitalization rates are higher for oppressed groups than for oppressor groups.

The works of Fanon and Bulhan in particular give some important insights into the psyche of the oppressed person (i.e., the slave). The search for peace and harmony in conditions of oppression, the desire for personal safety and security in circumstances of social violence, and the wish for individual success at the expense of collective aspirations require few risks on the part of the oppressed person because such efforts accept the status quo. Emancipation, on the other hand, requires courage, vision, and a commitment full of risk. The dehumanizing master 'without' must be killed, at least psychologically, and the slave 'within' must be cast out. Both require organized action, and both risk a psychological crisis and even physical death (Bulhan 1985). However, none of us will escape physical death. There is also psychological, social, economic, and political death—all of which hasten physical death. Within the master-slave paradigm, this presents the oppressed person with a paradox. Out of fear of physical death, the slave will submit to the superiority of the master, but in so doing will suffer the other slower, tortuous, and agonizing deaths and likely will die at an earlier age (i.e., social murder).

Twenty-Seven Million Slaves

The master-slave relationship is not just a philosophical concept or an artifact of the past. Today, 150 years after the world's slave trade was abolished, as many as 27 million people (approximately the population of Canada) are living as slaves. Between 1.5 and 2 million children are bought and sold into lives of sexual slavery and exploitation. Up to 10 million children are believed to be working in bondage in India, including 300 000 in rug factories. In Pakistan, about 7.5 million of the country's estimated 20 million bonded labourers are said to be children. On cocoa farms in Ivory Coast, 15 000 to 20 000 children have been driven by hunger into working as slaves. Thousands of women have been trafficked by organized crime groups from the former Soviet Union to the streets of central and western Europe as prostitutes. Tens of millions of people are held in bonded labour, working up to 18 hours a day as domestic servants and farm and factory workers. One spokesperson for an American anti-slavery group remarked that 'Our global economy creates demand for cheap goods, and there is no cheaper labor than slave labor.' A correspondent writing for *The Age*, Melbourne's premier daily newspaper, refers to the slave trade as 'the dark underbelly of globalisation.' He comments further, 'While the world looks away, human lives are routinely being bought and sold for less than the price of a pair of shoes' (Riley 2001, 1, 13).

False Consciousness

In Chapter 1, it was pointed out that a key concept of critical social theory is 'false consciousness.' Marx originally used false consciousness to explain why a numerically superior working class seemed to accept capitalism as an economic system when clearly it exploited and alienated them by assigning them to a lifetime of horrendous working and living conditions. Simply defined, false consciousness is 'the holding of false or inaccurate beliefs that are contrary to one's own social interest and which thereby contribute to the maintenance of the disadvantaged position of the self or the group' (Jost 1995, 14). Eyerman (1981, 33) views false consciousness as 'the acceptance of an unreflected notion of the world as given, as it appears: as truth without mediation or interpretation, and thinking that this world cannot [be] or is not shaped through human action.'

False consciousness is a form of internalized oppression. It is associated with the concept of ideology (a consistent set of social, economic, and political beliefs) in that ideas, values, and beliefs of the dominant ideology may be internalized by subordinate group members because they are presented in ways that are consistent with reason, inevitability, and normalcy. False consciousness, however, is not just a simple matter of ideological indoctrination (or brainwashing) or the subjective realization of ideology. Rather than passively assimilating ideas and ideology from various organized sources such as the mass media and the school system, the individual actually participates in developing his or her world view and place in the world through everyday activities and interactions. In order for the individual to make sense of social conditions, social relations, and social interactions, they must be mediated through some theoretical framework. In the absence of a critical perspective, the interpretation and framework are usually that of the dominant group (Eyerman 1981). An individual not only sees himself or herself through the eyes of the dominant group and judges himself or herself on its values, but adopts them as his or her own, even when the interpretation serves other interests at the expense of the individual.

As discussed in Chapter 4, there are two primary means of maintaining dominance over subordinate groups: the threat or actual use of physical force and the control of ideas or what is known as 'ideological hegemony.' It was pointed out that the latter method is much more effective than the former because it does not involve a perceived injustice or exploitation that could be the catalyst for acts of resistance or insurgency. Subordinate groups are integrated into the established order through a process of socialization (or indoctrination) and ideological manipulation. False consciousness is one outcome of this process and is manifest when both dominant and subordinate groups are convinced of the purported fairness, justice, desirability, or inevitability of particular hierarchically organized social relations and the discourses that underpin them (Sidanius and Pratto 1999). Coercion is probably not enough to sustain oppression for any length of time; also needed to reproduce unequal societies and exploitative social relations is some degree of false consciousness.

Chapter 4 presented a number of theories of how the dominant culture is reinforced and reproduced through popular or mass culture. These theories of cultural hegemony attempt to explain how and why subordinate group members accept as their own the ideas, messages, and representations transmitted through mass culture that mainly serve the interests of the dominant group, often at the expense of themselves. Such concepts as Marx's ideology, Lukács's reification, Gramsci's hegemony, and the Frankfurt School's culture industry were discussed in terms of their attempts to explain how people exploited by such systems as capitalism, racism, and patriarchy come to accept, reproduce, and actually defend these systems that oppress them. Accepting, believing, or supporting any ideas or discourses associated with oppression is a form of false consciousness.

One example of a false conscious belief is 'fatalism,' the belief that nothing can be done to improve social conditions or one's lot in life. This belief is cultivated by the dominant ideology when it presents the status quo as normal, natural, inevitable, and consequently, that which ought to be accepted. A force or deity greater than humankind is often suggested as responsible for the way things are, and no one should tamper with them. Fatalism is often related to such religious beliefs as 'it (oppression) is God's will.' However, accepting or believing that a hierarchical society based on oppression for any reason—religious, political, philosophical—is the way that it is or has to be and that nothing can be done about it is a form of false consciousness in general and fatalism in particular.

'Life Would Be a Whole Lot Simpler'

Lest anyone minimize the impact or pervasiveness of 'fatalism' as a powerful mechanism of social control, one need only look at the profession of social work. Paradoxically, although much is written and said by social workers (including most social work academics) about the need for and approaches to social change, I have been told by many of these people throughout my career that my (and others') ideas about social change and my (and others') approaches to social work and social problems are unrealistic. Furthermore, my life, I have been told, would be a whole lot simpler if I would just accept the way things are or at least diminish my 'extreme' views and goals. In many ways, my life *would* be simpler and easier. Teaching a critical or political approach to social work is difficult work, and being labelled (i.e., defamed and marginalized) as an interesting but 'out-of-touch lefty radical' is often hurtful. This position, held and sometimes espoused by mainstream social workers, is, in my view, an example of fatalism and false consciousness. It does not recognize that the nature and form of the society we have today are the result of conscious decisions made by elite groups of people and that what has been made can be unmade and remade if we (social workers and others) can first shed some of our false beliefs.

Sidanius and Pratto (1999) report on the results of a 1997 public opinion study on race relations in the United States that contains another example of false consciousness. A large number of black and white people were asked whether or not they believed that both groups had the same chances to get any kind of a job, education, and housing. In spite of all the evidence to the contrary, the majority of both groups indicated their belief that there is equal opportunity between them in these three domains (although the belief was higher within the white group than within the black group—more than 80 per cent as opposed to 56 per cent). Obviously, there is little potential for or commitment to fundamental social change when both the dominant and subordinate groups believe that no socioeconomic advantage or disadvantage exists between them on account of race.

In his celebrated book *Pedagogy of the Oppressed* (1994 [1970]), Paulo Freire offers an explanation for why some members of oppressed groups commit violent acts against other members of their own group that is based in part on a false consciousness. Freire refers to such acts of violence as 'horizontal violence,' and the North American Native activist and writer Lee Maracle (1996) terms them 'lateral violence.' Freire (1994 [1970], 44) says that 'the oppressed feel an irresistible attraction towards the oppressor and his way of life. Sharing this way of life becomes an overpowering aspiration. In their alienation, the oppressed want at any cost to resemble the oppressors, to imitate them, to follow them.' This creates a dual (and false) consciousness within the oppressed person. On the one hand, he or she views the oppressor as omnipotent and invulnerable and would do anything to be like the oppressor, even to the point of acting like an oppressor. 'Their ideal is to be men; but for them, to be men is to be oppressors. This is their model of humanity' (1994 [1970], 27). On the other hand, they see themselves as their oppressors see them— ignorant, unproductive, and lazy. Given this dual consciousness, Freire says of them:

> the oppressed cannot perceive clearly the 'order' which serves the interests of the oppressors whose image they have internalized. Chafing under the restrictions of this order, they often manifest a type of horizontal violence, striking at their own comrades for the pettiest reasons. . . . Because the oppressor exists within their oppressed comrades, when they attack those comrades they are indirectly attacking the oppressor as well [1994 (1970), 44; emphasis added].

Similarly, Frantz Fanon (1968) speaks of horizontal violence among colonized people (particularly black people in North Africa) in *The Wretched of the Earth*, and Lee Maracle (1996) speaks of lateral violence among North American First Nations people and how it invades their intimate relationships and family life.

Agger (2006) contends that false consciousness today is promoted by positivist social sciences such as economics and quantitative schools of sociology that depict society as governed by intractable laws (e.g., law of supply and demand, any social change must be incremental and slow, collectivism is a threat to individual liberties). This depiction of society suggests that people ought to adjust to these allegedly fixed social, economic, and political patterns. Critical social theory and anti-oppressive social work attempt to pierce this kind of false consciousness by emphasizing the power of agency, both personal and collective, to transform society. Similarly, progressive or critical or liberation psychologists have criticized the fundamental individualism of psychology with its emphasis on adjustment and its neglect of powerlessness, inequality, and other social conditions as contributing factors to both external and internalized oppression (Bulhan 1985; Moane 1999; Starhawk 1987).

The notion of false consciousness is certainly not without its critics. Many interpretive theorists[4] (e.g., symbolic interactionists, ethnomethodologists, social phenomenologists, social constructionists, some schools of feminism) argue that it is arrogant and presumptuous on the part of social theorists and analysts to suppose that people have a false consciousness about their lives. Agger (1998) observes that rather than unduly claiming the right to decide whether or not someone's consciousness is true or false, interpretive theorists treat all narratives as having truth value, since they represent people's attempts to describe and make sense of their lives. In other words, to the interpretive theorist, one's consciousness is true for that person, and that is all that matters. Agger (2006, 7) goes further by arguing that '[w]ithout some kind of "true" consciousness of their own possible emancipation, people will only reproduce the present in their everyday behaviours.' Examples given by Agger are workers and women. If the former behave as though capitalism were eternal by acting out the subordinate roles prescribed for them by bourgeois economists, capitalism becomes eternal. By the same token, if women behave as though patriarchy were natural and everlasting, it becomes everlasting no matter how objectionable male supremacy is. If social work theorists and practitioners totally reject the concept of false consciousness and therefore the notion of true consciousness, they leave unchallenged the notion of 'social necessity,' which ignores human freedom.

In comparing and contrasting interpretive and critical social theories, Agger makes several other observations about how each views and/or treats false consciousness. First, although postmodern critical theorists and many feminists reject the polarity of true and false consciousness as presented by Marx, they do not accept the sheer relativism of many interpretive theorists who simply accept what people say about their own lives as true. Instead, postmodernists and feminists analyze the discourses (e.g., advertising, anti-welfare sentiments, free market imperative) of people's everyday lives as sources of power and control that people confront as inescapable structures of culture and consciousness. Foucault (1977), for example, did not adopt Marx's notion of false consciousness but understood certain discourses of criminality and sexuality to be agents of discipline and punishment that constrained people by restricting their views and experience of what is possible. In other words, people's narratives about their lives will reflect, to some extent, the definitions and discourses of reality that are given to them. And these definitions and discourses of reality are usually reflective and supportive of the interests of dominant groups.

Consciousness is not mechanically manipulated, as some structural Marxists believe, nor does it become established free of the influences of ideology and hegemony, as many interpretive theorists suggest. It 'develops in a dialectical interplay between experience and language that borrows from prevailing conceptions of reality and yet reflects people's own free imaginations' (Agger 1998, 33). An example of someone who builds on this dialectic is Norman Denzin (1991), who deals with people's narratives but in ways that show them to be simultaneously true and false. Their narratives about their lives reveal both how they have been socialized into accepting reality as defined for them by dominant ideologies and institutions and the ways by which they resist and transform these definitions (Agger 1998). Another example cited by Agger is the feminist theorist Patricia Clough (1994), who stresses that women tell important stories about their lives that contain both falsehood and truth, reflecting both their socialization and their feminist imagination.

Psychologists Jim Sidanius and Felicia Pratto also take exception to the true-false dichotomy implied in the concept of false consciousness. To them, the truth or falsity of legitimizing beliefs is not only difficult to ascertain but has nothing to do with their power to legitimize inequality. What in part gives power to beliefs that justify inequality is not their truth value 'but rather the degree to which people accept these beliefs as true, right, or just. The more firmly myths (beliefs) are tied to the basic values and points of view of their culture, the more difficult they will be to change' (Sidanius and Pratto 1999, 104).

Although capitalism has changed since Marx presented the notion of false consciousness, an understanding of the concept is still required to disabuse people of the belief that this is the best of all worlds in spite of its many imperfections. Ideology has not gone away but is found in venues not anticipated by Marx (e.g., the culture industry, the World Wide Web). It is much more pervasive and total than when Marx wrote. It is so tied into cultural discourses, practices, and representations that people often confuse what is real and what is illusory. Although the pervasiveness of ideology has increased since Marx's time, Agger (1998) contends that it conceals its representation of the world in order to increase its efficacy as 'silent argument.' That is, ideologies that appear polemical, doctrinal, or adversarial are viewed as old-fashioned by many and thus not to be taken seriously. This view, of course, serves by default to maintain the dominant ideology and discourse as unquestioned reality (i.e., a reality of hierarchy and oppression). It is also a prime example of false consciousness—a consciousness that must be pierced, exposed for its oppressive functions, resisted, and deconstructed so that liberating alternatives can be developed.

Other Perspectives on Internalized Oppression

Many writers have addressed 'internalized oppression' from a number of different perspectives but probably not as comprehensively as that contained in the master-slave dialectic or in the theory of false consciousness. It was mentioned at the beginning of this chapter that given different people's different experiences of and responses to oppression, it is impossible to develop a general theory of internalized oppression with universal applicability. Thus, the remainder of this chapter will present some observations and insights made by an array of writers from different disciplines who have addressed the phenomenon of internalized oppression. Although I present some of these observations and insights separately, it is important to note that in reality, many of them intersect with one another.

Internalized Labels

Albert Memmi (1963; 1967; 1968; 1973) has written extensively on his experiences both as a Jew and as a person living in Tunisia, a country colonized by the French. He (1968) identified several characteristics that the colonizer/oppressor tends to assign to colonized/oppressed people—lazy, stupid, backward, irresponsible, evil, brutish, cowardly, indulgent, uncivilized, unreliable, extravagant, unpredictable, mysterious, impulsive, and undisciplined. Moane (1999) identifies three consequences that this labelling process has for colonized people: (1) it stereotypes them as inferior in contrast to the colonizer, who is intelligent, brave, responsible, civilized, industrious, and so on; (2) it depersonalizes the colonized people, who are viewed as an undifferentiated mass; and (3) it objectifies colonized people in that their behaviour is attributed to their perceived negative characteristics rather than to social conditions. Of course, this labelling and its internalization justify the colonizer's privileged position and the dependent and inferior position of those who have been colonized.

Memmi (1963, 321–322) argues that oppressed persons come to accept the stereotypes imposed on them over time and tend to behave in ways that reinforce these stereotypes: 'The longer the oppression lasts, the more it profoundly affects him [i.e., the oppressed]. It ends by becoming so familiar to him that he believes it is part of his own constitution, that he accepts it, and could not imagine his recovery from it. *This acceptance is the crowning point of oppression*' (emphasis added). The only areas of autonomous action open to oppressed persons are their own community and family, and here feelings of rebellion, resentment, anger, and frustration are often acted out in forms of horizontal or lateral violence.

Socialization of Internalized Oppression

Chapter 4 presented some of the ways by which the dominant culture is transmitted through various social institutions and becomes internalized by both dominant and subordinate group members. A similar process occurs whereby individuals in a society learn the dominant ideas, rules, expectations, norms, culture, practices, and ideology of that society. The process of socialization is carried out by social institutions and authority figures and is learned in a variety of ways—through teaching, modelling, observation, experience, and identifying with and imitating role models and idealized persons. Not only do individuals learn these social phenomena, they internalize them as well—they become part of the self of the individual. Oppression is a learned and internalized social phenomenon. Although a number of writers allude or refer to internalized oppressive thoughts, attitudes, and behaviours being learned, two who discuss the socialization of internalized oppression are Gil (1998) and Bishop (1994; 2002). In a brief historical overview of oppression, Gil (1998, 44) contends that throughout history, 'dominant social groups succeeded in coercing and inducing dominated groups to internalize and accept as valid those social values which served the perceived needs and interests of the dominant groups, but affected adversely the needs and interests of dominated groups.' He points out that this internalization of social values was achieved initially by coercive means, but today coercion has been complemented, and often replaced, by socialization and social control rooted in such systems of ideas as ideology, mythology, and organized religion. For example, organized religion[5] has often taught that nonconformity to established values (e.g., women to honour their husbands; avoidance of masturbation, premarital sex, and birth control; performing an honest day's work even if exploited) would be severely punished, including through eternal damnation. Anne Bishop (1994, 35) talks about the consequences of internalized oppression for herself (as a lesbian and a woman) and others: 'To a certain extent we do keep ourselves and each other down. We reproduce the social, economic, and political system that formed us, again and again, by playing out our internalized oppression against ourselves and each other.' Bishop believes that internalized oppression begins in childhood as children suffer pain and powerlessness when they encounter racism, poverty, sexism, and discrimination based on language, geographic location, religion, and the like. This oppression, along with feelings that they lack the power to do anything about it, often results in fear, low self-esteem, and strategies for self-protection that are carried into adulthood.

Bishop contends that children learn to be afraid, distrustful, and watchful and to differentiate clearly between 'us' and 'them,' between safe and dangerous. They learn that they are part of a hierarchy based on deception and force, and they learn to judge the situation and make a decision (that faces all oppressed people) whether to go along with it or resist it. When children decide to resist or fight back, they learn to take every opportunity to grab a little power for themselves and to use that power to its limit. They develop a large repertoire of methods for manipulating, controlling, and disempowering others. On the other hand, when they decide to go along with the situation, they obey, conform, and remain silent. Bishop (1994, 50) elaborates on this point:

> Children learn to cozy up to those who can hurt them, say what the adults want them to say, please and protect adults, act on their behalf, disguise their own intelligence and power, and pretend to take pleasure in their own abuse. They learn to be afraid of what power they do have; they learn to deny it and see themselves as even more powerless than they really are. They also blame themselves for the situation and thereby reduce their self-esteem.

Bishop's argument then is that people learn in childhood to behave in ways that contribute to their own oppression. And, of course, the longer they employ these behaviour patterns, the more difficult it is to confront them, especially when they have been developed for survival. Survival also requires the suppression of feelings, because emotions can make a person with little power even more vulnerable. Miller (1980, cited in Bishop 1994) claims that the denial of feelings makes people obedient and adaptable and thus capable of being used for anything. At the same time, however, oppressed persons often misuse or abuse power because they have learned that we live in a hierarchical society and that power is something that must be exercised over another. Indeed, many oppressed people believe that if they can control the situation, they must do so, even if this involves the oppression of those less powerful, but if control is not possible, they must protect themselves by placating and obeying more powerful people. In other words, they have learned (from childhood) about hierarchy and their place in it. Bishop (1994, 55) sums it up well: 'We carry within us a blueprint of the culture's oppressive patterns to be reproduced wherever we have influence. The name for this is "internalized oppression."'

The Abject Other

Because of ideological and cultural hegemony, all people in society tend to identify with the subject view of the dominant group. Young contends that in the modern West, there is only one view or position—that of the unified, disembodied reason identified with the white bourgeois male. From this supposedly neutral subject position, all subordinate (inferior and deviant) groups are viewed and experienced as the abject Other. Thus, because members of subordinate groups tend to perceive the world through the lens of the dominant group, they will see themselves as inferior, deviant, lazy, irresponsible, and so on. In other words, they will see themselves as the abject Other and will 'often exhibit symptoms of fear, aversion, or devaluation toward members of their own groups and other oppressed groups' (Young 1990, 147). Some women will hold sexist views. Working poor people will often resent non-working (i.e., not attached to the labour force) poor people who, in their view (consistent with the dominant view), are getting a 'free ride' in society thanks to 'generous' welfare benefits. Some light-skinned black people will avoid contact with dark-skinned black people. Gay and lesbian people will sometimes exhibit homophobic behaviour. More common than intra-group oppression (i.e., oppression by members of the same oppressed group) is inter-group oppression whereby members of one oppressed group fear, despise, and oppress members of other oppressed groups. Some black people, for example, are hostile towards Asian people or towards gay, lesbian, and bisexual people. Some poor people hold sexist and racist views.

'I Made It without Help. Why Can't They?'

At a community meeting, a discussion ensued about allocating some of the community's resources to recently arrived families of refugees. A few residents, who had arrived from the same country a generation ago, argued strongly that refugee groups should not be assisted. One woman exclaimed, 'No one helped my family when we arrived. I had to work hard for my right to be here. They should do the same.'

Writing in the post-colonial East Indian context, Ashis Nandy presents a view similar to Young's 'abject Other' as the basis for internalized oppression. He sees the relationship between colonizer/oppressor and colonized/oppressed as complex and one in which a polarization (culture, lifestyle, status, power, and so on) between the two groups occurs. The colonized group internalizes the colonizer's culture, not vice versa. A splitting of the self occurs whereby part of the self, which relates positively to the dominant group and its culture in terms of accepting, desiring, and participating in it, is acknowledged and accepted. Conversely, that part of the self that relates to the subordinate group and its culture is often rejected (as is Young's 'abject Other'), but as suggested by Nandy (1983, 100, cited in Moane 1999), it is not rejected entirely. He observes that colonized people survive by 'overstressing those aspects of the self which they share with the powerful, and by protecting in the corner of their heart a secret defiance.' In this way, colonized people often reinforce colonial stereotypes of themselves, but resistance to colonialism always comes from their secret defiance (Gandhi 1998)—a defiance based on cunning and passivity (Moane 1999). This defiance provides some potential for anti-oppressive practice.

Service-to-Others Orientation

In her seminal work *Toward a New Psychology of Women* (1986), Jean Baker Miller talks about the interrelationship between particular social roles and psychological patterns of women that contribute to their subordination. Although focusing specifically on women, Miller contends that her observations and insights could apply to any person in a subordinate position or role, for 'anyone in a subordinate position must learn to be attuned to the vicissitudes of mood, pleasure and displeasure of the dominant group' (Miller 1986, 39). Subordinate persons may be more attuned to persons in the dominant group than they are to themselves, to the extent that they are unaware of their own needs. Consequently, they may act (and are expected to act) in ways that serve the interests of the dominant group but that negate their own interests.

Miller (1986, cited in Moane 1999) argues that the lack of self-knowledge that comes from a 'service-to-others orientation' means that subordinate persons tend to value themselves in terms of what they give to or do for the dominant group and obtain self-worth on the basis of how well they satisfy the needs of others. The 'self-sacrificing homemaker' is a common social role carried out by women even in contemporary society. Reinforcing this subordination (with its feelings of inferiority) is the fact that many of the activities of subordinate people (e.g., especially women's 'unpaid labour') are not valued by society and, therefore, they are often seen as not doing anything. Caring for others and fostering the advancement or careers of others, along with the emotional work that goes with it, is not seen as a work activity, because it is done (usually) for love and not money. It is invisible.

Miller identifies two other patterns of internalized oppression. First, subordinate persons often avoid direct action to serve their own interests because such actions may result in social ostracism, financial hardship, and even violence. Instead, they are forced to act in subtle and indirect ways, which are often perceived by dominant group members as manipulative (e.g., the conniving woman). This, of course, reinforces the negative image that those in the dominant group often hold of subordinate group persons. The second pattern of internalized oppression identified by Miller is that although subordinate persons are constantly in positions that elicit anger, they are not allowed to exhibit this emotion for fear of retaliation. Ideology makes it appear that subordinate people have no reason to be angry at the dominant group (only at themselves) and in the case of women, it is against their nature (gentle, feminine) and ascribed social role (caring, nurturing). Consequently, the anger of subordinate persons (in Miller's work, particularly women) becomes transformed into depression, ambivalence, or hysteria.

Nietzsche's Socratism

One final explanation for internalized oppression, which could be interpreted as a form of false consciousness but in my view deserves separate mention, is what Nietzsche (1967; 1969) called 'Socratism.' By Socratism Nietzsche means that there is a reason for everything, including suffering. He explains it in the following sentence: 'Man, the bravest of animals and the one most accustomed to suffering, does not repudiate suffering as such; he desires it, he even seeks it out, provided he is shown a meaning for it, a purpose of suffering' (1967, 162, cited in Rosen 1996). Although part of a much larger and more complex philosophical treatise, Socratism is basically part of the attempt to make the world acceptable by making it intelligible. Suffering oppression, then, must have a larger purpose. For Christians, the larger or higher reason for suffering was to enable one after death to enter the Kingdom of God where there would be no suffering. The more one suffered in life and lived according to certain (conforming) principles, the greater the likelihood of escaping eternal damnation and entering heaven.

Socratism is a search for justification about the nature of reality, a way of giving meaning to the world and of accommodating oneself within it intellectually (Rosen 1996). Obviously, this belief in a higher purpose for suffering has no limits with respect to applying non-rational beliefs as justification for suffering, whatever form that suffering might take—dispossessed groups suffering on Earth for the reward of heaven; university students putting up with a non-democratic, one-sided, authoritarian education for the prospect of a good job; small children accommodating all kinds of silly rules and wishes of adults so that Santa Claus will bring presents on Christmas Eve.

In sum, the above theories of internalized oppression shed light on a major aspect of oppression. It helps those of us who are concerned with developing anti-oppressive forms of social work practice to go beyond the notion that oppression is simply what one group does to another. It shows us why and how oppressed persons contribute to their own oppression. Internalized oppression has received increased attention in recent years, as evidenced by its inclusion in a psychology of liberation.

Psychology of Liberation

Many people within and outside social work view psychological approaches to social problems as at best unrealistic and at worst as contributing to the maintenance of social problems. Progressive social work has a long history of criticizing and accusing clinical or counselling social workers, psychologists, psychiatrists, and other helping professionals of selling out to the status quo by controlling and managing the 'dangerous (i.e., oppressed) classes,' attempting to cajole or coerce victims of social problems to adjust to the very systems that victimized them in the first place, diverting attention away from the real source of problems (i.e., an oppressive society), attempting to humanize an inhumane society, and promoting personal development through 12-step and other programs.

Kitzinger and Perkins represent those who reject psychology and psychiatry altogether. Concerned with women in general and lesbian women in particular, they criticize psychology for its obsessive preoccupation with the self and the quest for finding the real or inner self, which locks women into a perpetual cycle of self-discovery. Too often, they argue, have women entered therapy for depression, alienation, and exhaustion because of oppression only to focus on their childhood and endless analysis of their feelings. Psychotherapy and personal development have become substitutes for political action. According to Kitzinger and Perkins (1993, 198), American and British lesbians do not need psychology: 'Psychology is, and always will be, destructive of the lesbian/feminist enterprise.'

Such a radical position not only overlooks the obvious psychological consequences of oppression but also the psychology of both the oppressor and the oppressed, including the psychological process of internalized oppression. It is just as unacceptable to omit psychological phenomena as it is to omit social phenomena when analyzing oppression (or any other social or psychological phenomenon). In reality, one cannot separate the psychological (or the personal) from the social (or the political)—they constitute a symbiotic and dialectical relationship, with each acting upon and being acted upon by the other. The position of Kitzinger and Perkins tends to homogenize psychology and overlook the schools mentioned at the beginning of this chapter—critical and liberation psychologies, which also criticize mainstream psychology for its inattention to social variables. These schools of psychology start from the premise that psychological patterns can only be understood by analyzing the social context in which individuals live their lives.

Moane represents the critical and liberation schools of psychological thought. In *Gender and Colonialism: A Psychological Analysis of Oppression and Liberation*, she seeks 'to develop a political explanation of psychological phenomena, and to harness psychological insights for the purposes of political activism' (Moane 1999, 20). Along with the obstacles to political activism inherent in social, economic, cultural, and political forces, Moane includes internalized oppression. Her book outlines many psychological patterns associated with internalized oppression and presents a number of themes or elements of psychological processes for breaking out of internalized oppression and bringing about social change. She refers to this as a 'psychology of liberation.' This psychological approach is consistent with the anti-oppressive approach that is a major concern of this book, and many of Moane's ideas on the process(es) of liberation are presented in the section Anti-oppressive Social Work Practice at the Personal Level in Chapter 8. As Moane (1999, 182) says, 'Breaking out of oppression, whether at the psychological level or at the political level, requires changes in both psychological and social patterns.' Not attending to the need for social change means that social conditions associated with oppression continue to impinge on individuals and shape psychological functioning in oppressive ways. Not attending to the need for psychological change means that the attempt will be undermined by the negative psychological patterns (such as internalized oppression) associated with oppression.

Internalized Domination

Thus far, this chapter has presented the concept of internalized oppression, a concept that presents enormous challenges to the anti-oppressive social worker. It is not enough to understand that social conditions and forces lead to the oppression of many people; one must also understand how these oppressive forces affect subordinate persons both materially (i.e., socially, politically, culturally, and economically) and psychologically. To have a fuller understanding of domination and oppression, however, it is probably also important to be cognizant of the psyche of the oppressor and the dynamics of internalized domination. The final chapter in this book is devoted entirely to issues of privilege and domination.

In Chapter 2, we noted that much of oppression today is unintentional, non-conspiratorial, and covert and that the major reason it occurs is that it protects a privileged kind of citizenship for dominant group members. Members of the dominant group rationalize their monopoly on privilege as their earned right, which subordinate group members do not have because they are incompetent and lazy (Freire 1994 [1970]). Chapter 2 also presented several myths, which are part of a larger ideology of oppression (e.g., myths of scarcity and equal opportunity), and it was argued that these myths help to reinforce the dominant group's positive image of themselves and negative image of subordinate group members. All the evidence indicates that dominant–subordinate relations and oppressive behaviour are very difficult to change once they are established. We can begin to understand the persistence and tenacity of oppressive behaviour by dominant groups by examining the phenomenon of 'internalized domination.'

Just as a number of complementary and competing sets of theories or theoretical positions seek to explain internalized oppression, so too there are a number of explanations for internalized domination. Some theories attempt to explain both internalized domination and oppression. For example, socialization or social learning theory holds that both dominant group and oppressed group members are subject to the same dominant culture, messages, and so on. Thus, both groups will, to a large extent, internalize the dominant culture, because from early childhood, members of both groups have been socialized to feel and behave in certain ways. For dominant group members, the primary reason they exhibit hostile, discriminatory, and exploitative behaviours towards subordinate group members is socialization. Oppressive behaviours and attitudes towards others that are deemed appropriate are rewarded, while those considered inappropriate are punished and eventually disappear from the person's inventory. This theory of internalized oppression and domination may have some validity, but it does not explain the existence of variation in attitudes and behaviours among people (whether oppressors or oppressed) who grew up in the same society and were exposed to the same socialization process.

Paulo Freire has constructed a portrait of the oppressor in which he asserts that acts of exploitation of another and interference with another's pursuit of self-affirmation as a responsible person are situations of oppression. Even when sweetened by generosity or benevolence, such a situation constitutes violence because it interferes with the subordinate or oppressed person's ontological vocation of becoming more fully human. 'With the establishment of oppression, violence has already begun. . . . Violence is initiated by those who oppress, who exploit, who fail to recognize others as persons—not by those who are oppressed, exploited, and unrecognized. It is not the unloved who initiate disaffection, but those who cannot love because they love only themselves' (Freire 1994 [1970], 37). Paradoxically, the oppressed are always said to be violent, savage, deviant, or barbaric when they react to the violence of their oppressors. Consequently, the oppressed are seen as constituting the dangerous classes, and therefore they must be monitored, managed, and regulated so that they do not become violent against the dominant group.

Freire argued that for the oppressors, the term 'human beings' refers only to themselves and that all other people are 'things.' Oppressors have one primary right— their right to live in peace. However, they do concede (but not necessarily recognize) the right of oppressed persons to survive—but only because their existence is necessary for the existence of the oppressors. Any restriction on the oppressors' way of life is a profound violation of their individual rights, although they may have no respect for the pain, sorrow, misery, and despair of oppressed persons.

Their experience as a dominant class explains their way of understanding the world and their own oppressive behaviour. A climate of violence, both physical and structural, is perpetuated from generation to generation of oppressors. This climate creates in the oppressor a well-developed possessive consciousness, which in turn tends to turn everything around it into an object of possession and/or domination. Freire (1994 [1970], 40) says of this situation, 'For the oppressors, what is worthwhile is to have more—always more—even at the cost of the oppressed having less or having nothing.'

Even 'humanity' is a thing to be possessed by the oppressor as an exclusive right. The pursuit of their full humanity by subordinate persons, including the pursuit of freedom, is viewed by the oppressor as subversion. And the more that oppressors control oppressed people, the more they change them into inanimate objects or possessions. Freire, as well as Fromm (1966), contends that this tendency on the part of the oppressor to transform all things and all persons into inanimate possessions corresponds with a tendency towards sadism. By this they mean that as the oppressor blocks the oppressed person from pursuing full humanity and freedom, the action 'kills' the creative energy and power that characterize life. 'The oppressed as objects, as "things," have no purposes except those their oppressors prescribe for them' (Freire 1994 [1970], 42).

With respect to internalized domination, Freire presents an issue that is extremely relevant to anti-oppressive social work practice. Some members of the dominant or oppressor class inevitably join with a subordinate group in their struggle for liberation or emancipation. Freire argues that throughout the history of social struggle, oppressors who move to the side of the exploited always bring with them the markers of their internalized domination—that is, their prejudices, their stereotypes, and their lack of confidence in the ability of subordinate people to think, to organize, to strategize, and to mobilize. They often exhibit a type of generosity nourished by the unjust order, which must be preserved to justify that generosity. Accordingly, these dominant group members who sincerely wish to transform the unjust social order run the risk of becoming as paternalistic as the oppressors because they believe that they must be the executors of the transformation. Such a position, of course, is not liberating at all. Freire (1994 [1970], 46) says of this benevolent and paternalistic oppressor group that seeks to lead the struggle for social transformation: 'They talk about the people, but they do not trust them; *and trusting the people is the indispensable precondition for revolutionary change*' (emphasis added). More will be said on this theme in the final chapter.

Frantz Fanon (1968) developed a theory of internalized domination based on his experiences in French-colonized Algeria, where he witnessed and experienced the military and police violence that was necessary for the colonial domination of that country.[6] Central to Fanon's theory is the idea that a Manichean psychology underpins oppression and violence in all its forms (Bulhan 1985). A Manichean viewpoint is one that divides the world into compartments or categories and people into different species. This division is based on irreconcilable opposites or binary categories of 'either/or,' such as 'good versus bad,' 'intelligent versus stupid,' 'beautiful versus ugly,' 'white versus black,' 'us versus them,' and 'rich versus poor.' Although each of these categories constitutes a duality rather than a dialectic in which one of the terms is considered undesirable or unacceptable, in fact each duality of opposites is interdependent. This is so because each is defined in terms of its opposite, derives its identity from its opposite, and would have no meaning without its opposite. Even though each half of the duality is dependent on the other half, clear lines of division are necessary or else the Manichean psychology collapses. Oppression and violence create and require a Manichean psychology because such a view legitimates the favoured part of the duality to carry out any kind of action it deems necessary to keep the unfavoured part in check. And as has been argued throughout this book, the dominant group defines what is good and bad, beautiful and ugly, desirable and undesirable, and so on. That these definitions favour and privilege the dominant group while discriminating against and dehumanizing subordinate groups should be no surprise.

In oppressive situations, the Manichean psychology permeates the everyday lives of people. It is reflected in the living environment of people and how they are treated by social institutions. Bulhan presents an example in the form of the polarity of living conditions between dominant and subordinate groups. In the part of town where the oppressor resides, the houses are spacious and grand, the streets are tree-lined and well-lit at night, there is little litter, the residents are well-fed and well-dressed and friendly towards each other, and the police are both cordial to them and at their service. In the ghetto on the other side of town, people live in crowded and dilapidated buildings on streets that are ill-lit at night and have no trees, where garbage collection is sporadic and litter prevails. The residents are poorly clothed, not healthy-looking, and are friendly only to the few people they know and trust. The police are often suspicious and hostile towards them. In effect, two different species are living in different environments, one enjoying the good life and the other trying to survive while living on the edge.

From Social Leprosy to Social Respectability

I grew up in one of the oldest neighbourhoods in one of the oldest cities in Canada—Saint John, New Brunswick. At that time (the 1950s), this neighbourhood (the South End) had some of the worst slum housing in Canada. It jutted out into Courtney Bay, which was used by the city as a receptacle for raw sewage and where 'wharf rats' as big as cats bred and infiltrated some of the nearby housing. It had high rates of poverty, rental housing owned by absentee landlords, juvenile gang activity, and police brutality. There were many features of this neighbourhood that I loved—my friends; it was adjacent to the uptown area where all the action took place; it produced super-athletes, which I like to think included myself; and I managed to be part of a cohort that did well in school even though this was not valued by many of my age group in that neighbourhood. However, living there also caused me a certain amount of pain and resentment. The fact that I was from the South End meant that the parents of new or potentially new friends of mine would sometimes tell their sons not to hang around with me and their daughters not to go out with me. It also meant that the police who patrolled the South End would sometimes stop and interrogate me and others as to what we were up to, would take our names (for what purpose I could only guess), and on occasion would rough us up a bit. Just before I finished high school, my parents, with the help of Veterans' Affairs (my father was a World War II amputee), built a house on the outskirts of the city

From Social Leprosy to Social Respectability *(continued)*

in an up-and-coming middle-class area. The bus service to this area was not great in that the last bus left from town at midnight and if I missed it (which I often did), I would have to walk home (five or six kilometres, including a long, deserted road). The police would sometimes stop me as I was walking along the deserted road and ask me what I was doing and where I was going. When I told them I was walking home and where my home was, they often told me to hop in the police car, and they drove me home. I also stopped losing friends because of where I lived. I learned something then about a person's social respectability—that it was determined in large part (in my world) by where a person lived.

The Manichean psychology is also reflected in the prevailing or dominant values and beliefs of society. The oppressor or dominant group identifies itself in terms of goodness and beauty while portraying the subordinate group as ugly and evil. Members of the former group see themselves as the epitome of civilization and high values, and skin colour, habits, class, and all other markers of identification signify their superiority. Conversely, the characteristics of the oppressed or subordinate groups are despised because they personify filth, irresponsibility, and evil as opposed to ethical, civilized values. The duality here is that the dominant group puts itself beyond human attributes and reduces the subordinate group to subhuman status. Bulhan (1985, 142) speaks about the tenacity of the Manichean psychology:

> The Manichean psychology is hard to counteract once it takes root in people, the environment, and the culture. Those who live it rely on it for their individual and collective identity. On the surface, the oppressor benefits in the continuation of the Manichean psychology. His identity is more secure; his self-respect is maintained; his confidence seems firm; and he enjoys a relatively harmonious bond with his own kind. He has a sense of history, a measure of control over his destiny. All this is founded on the wreckage of and dehumanization of the other. Thus, the oppressed is full of self-doubt; he is made to feel inferior; his self-worth is undermined; his confidence and bond with others are weakened; his history is obliterated; he cannot control what happens to him; he feels victorious if he escapes an ever-present peril.

The concept of 'Other,' which is part of the Manichean psychology, has become a key concept in writings on post-colonialism to refer to colonized people, in some forms of feminism to refer to women, and in postmodernism to refer to all excluded groups. Both Fanon (1968) and Simone de Beauvoir (1961) used the idea of the Other to show how characteristics of the dominant group (men for Beauvoir, white colonizers for Fanon) become the norms while areas of weakness and vulnerability are imposed on women or colonized people. Beauvoir (1961, xvi, cited in Moane 1999, 28) says that woman is 'defined and differentiated with reference to man and not he with reference to her; she is the incidental, the inessential as opposed to the essential. He is the Subject, he is the Absolute—she is the Other.'

'Black Is Beautiful'

A key to understanding the psychology of domination or internalized domination is the notion of the 'Other.' All oppressed groups are defined in oppositional terms (i.e., as evil, ugly, subhuman, and so on) to the dominant group. This concept not only helps us to understand unjust and often violent acts of oppression, it also shows us an area where anti-oppressive practice might occur. African-Americans in the late 1960s and early 1970s built a whole social movement on the slogan 'Black is beautiful.' This slogan was developed to resist and overcome the dominant view of African-Americans (i.e., the Other) as ugly, inferior, dangerous. (Similarly, the lesbian, gay, bisexual, and transgender [LGBT] community built a social movement—'gay pride'—asserting that LGBT persons should be proud and not ashamed of their sexual orientation.) 'Black is beautiful' not only helped African-Americans reclaim part of their identity, it also started a cultural revolution in which in addition to skin colour, such cultural artifacts as black clothing, art, food, and hair texture became sources of pride to the black community rather than of shame and inferiority. This is an important lesson when we attempt to identify areas and strategies for overcoming oppression.

Conclusion

The basic question addressed in this chapter has been: 'Why do significant numbers of oppressed individuals comply with, participate in, and contribute to their own oppression?' To help answer this question, two concepts associated with the psychology of oppression—inferiorization and internalized oppression—are useful. A number of theories attempt to explain the existence and causes of these psychological states. The converse of internalized oppression—internalized domination—helps to explain why significant numbers of people from the dominant group seem to hold oppressive thoughts and exhibit oppressive behaviour but do not consider themselves oppressive.

The material in this chapter should assist the anti-oppressive worker to better understand the thoughts, attitudes, and behaviour of persons who have internalized their oppression and who as a result are behaving in ways that are destructive to themselves, to members of their own subordinate group, and to members of other subordinate groups. Similarly, the psyche of the oppressor must be better understood before anti-oppressive practice can succeed, for any strategy of anti-oppression must take into consideration not only internalized oppression but internalized domination as well. Because most people (including social workers) hold at least one subordinate identity in society, the material in this chapter should help to illuminate and explain any inferiorization or internalized oppression that may be associated with our own subordinate situations. Similarly, the concept of internalized domination should encourage all of us to reflect on the identities we may possess that make us part of the dominant group or dominant culture. This will help us to identify and expunge the prejudices, stereotypes, and behaviours that contribute to oppression. Interestingly (and sadly in my view), an anonymous reviewer of the first edition of this book suggested (without reasons) that this entire chapter be omitted in the second edition. Personally, I believe this is one of the most important chapters in the book for understanding oppression and for developing anti-oppressive social work. I endorse Cudd's (2006) explanation for the persistence of oppression—because the oppressor group has co-opted oppressed groups into participating in their own oppression. The implications of the material in this chapter for anti-oppressive social work practice will be outlined in Chapter 8 of this book.

Critical Questions for Discussion

1. A few statements reflecting internalized oppression with respect to women that are sometimes heard from women themselves are:
    'If she would just clean the house and be quiet, he wouldn't hit her.'
    'She needs to stand up for herself and quit being a victim.'
    'She was yelling at him. What did she expect?'
    Can you think of other examples of statements that reflect internalized oppression with respect to gender? Can you think of examples of statements that reflect internalized oppression with respect to race or sexuality or other subordinate group characteristics?

2. List as many reasons as you can why a woman might stay with a man who regularly abuses her.

3. What are some of the internalized oppressive beliefs that may be attached to: sexism, classism, racism, ableism, heterosexism, ageism?

4. What are some of the ways that we might help people (including ourselves) overcome their internalized oppression?

5. What are some of the ways that we might help people (including ourselves) overcome their internalized domination?

Further Readings

Fanon, Frantz (1968). *The Wretched of the Earth*. New York: Grove Press. Frantz Fanon (1925–1961) was a Martinique-born, black psychiatrist and anti-colonialist intellectual. He connects the effects of oppression on the psyche better than most writers do, in part because he experienced it. This book is considered by many to be one of the canonical books on the worldwide black liberation struggles of the 1960s. It analyses the role of class, race, national culture, and violence in the struggle for freedom. Within a Marxist framework, using a cutting and unsentimental writing style, Fanon draws upon his horrific experiences working in Algeria during its war of independence against France. He addresses the role of violence in decolonization and the challenges of political organization and the class collisions and questions of cultural hegemony in the creation and maintenance of a new country's national consciousness.

Fox, D.R. and I. Prilleltensky, eds. (1997). *Critical Psychology: An Introduction*. London: Sage. This book provides: (1) an overview of the values, history, methods, ethics, and practice of psychology from a critical viewpoint; (2) a critical examination of a wide set of subdisciplines of psychology, ranging from intelligence research through developmental and social psychology to cross-cultural, lesbian, gay, and political psychology; (3) major theoretical frameworks that have underpinned many critiques of the mainstream; and (4) reflections both on debates arising in the preceding chapters and on issues for the future of critical psychology. It is highly relevant to anti-oppressive social work, especially at the direct practice level.

Freire, Paulo (1994 [1970]). *Pedagogy of the Oppressed*, 2nd edition. New York: Continuum Publishing. This is a seminal book on liberation politics and practice. It presents Freire's theory of educating illiterate populations, which is based on the belief that every human being, no matter how oppressed, is capable of looking critically at his or her world in a dialogical encounter with others. In the book, Freire provides us with many tools and techniques for emancipatory social work with any population—including critical social analysis, consciousness-raising, empowerment, a critique of the banking concept of education, and dialogical relationships.

Memmi, Albert (1967). *The Colonizer and the Colonized*. Boston: Beacon Press. Albert Memmi wrote this study of the relationship and dynamics between the colonizer and the colonized many years ago, but the lessons he imparts to the reader are of great value to this day. Whether discussing racist, sexist, or politically oppressive conditions, Memmi manages to pinpoint the psychological and social impact on the individual. The book contributes towards greater understanding of the manner in which structural and institutional forces of other forms of oppression and inequality affect us today. A classic statement pertaining to the human condition and the potential for liberation.

Moane, Geraldine (1999). *Gender and Colonialism: A Psychological Analysis of Oppression and Liberation*. New York: St Martin's Press. Drawing on the writings of diverse authors, including Jean Baker Miller, bell hooks, Mary Daly, Frantz Fanon, Paulo Freire, and Ignacio Martin-Baro, as well as on women's experiences, this book sums up what writers on patriarchy, racism, and colonialism have said about the experience of oppression, identifies common themes and experiences, diagnoses the psychology involved, describes patterns associated with oppression such as sense of inferiority, self-doubt, fear, anger, shame, problems in relationships, and difficulties with direct action, and offers by way of synthesis an integrated approach to using liberation psychology to combat oppressive social forces.

Chapter 7

The 'Web': The Multiplicity, Intersectionality, and Heterogeneity of Oppression

Oh, what a tangled web we weave . . .
—Sir Walter Scott

Introduction

In Chapter 3, we saw that a person's identity is associated with physical, psychological, social, and cultural variables such as appearance, personality, social status or class, social roles, and race or ethnicity. One's identity is seldom if ever determined solely by one characteristic, although one characteristic may be a major marker of an individual or more prominent in most situations or contexts than others (e.g., one's gender or skin colour). These characteristics are termed 'contents' of identity by some writers, 'sub-identities' by others, and 'identities' by still others. Although the terms vary, they all have the same meaning in that they refer to the conditions or features that mark or characterize or identify an individual. The term used in this chapter is 'identity.' The individual does not possess a single identity but multiple identities that may shift and change over time and/or with changed contexts. This concept of identity is consistent with that of most post-structural, postmodern, and post-colonial writers.

The concept of multiple identities contains much potential for the development of anti-oppressive social work theory and practice. There has been a tendency in social work to focus on the specifics of particular oppressed groups (Langan and Day 1992) as they make their presence and needs known. Originally concerned with poverty and its victims, social work eventually turned its attention to issues of gender oppression and then racial oppression. Today, social work is concerned with many oppressed groups but still has the tendency to separate them for purposes of study, analysis, and intervention. A decade ago, with few exceptions (e.g., Day 1992; Baines 2001), even the social work writers who pointed out that oppression seldom occurs along a single line did not pursue this issue beyond saying that multiple oppression is more complex than a simple, singular form of oppression.[1] A typical example of multiple oppression found in the social work literature until recently was that of a black woman (sometimes mentioned as poor) who, it was pointed out, would experience sexism differently from a white woman. An explanation or analysis of this difference, however, was not pursued in any detail or depth in the literature. Some writers at that time, such as Thompson (1997), called for more research into multiple oppression, while Bishop (1994) lamented that no critical analysis of multiple oppression existed.

Fortunately, some contemporary social work writers go beyond simply saying that multiple oppression is more complex than a singular form and have attempted to develop models of multiple oppression. The first edition of this book outlined an intersectional model of multiple oppression that had been developed by Steven Wineman in 1984 and contrasted it with the single and parallel models of oppression. Given recent writings in this area, particularly by Marsiglia and Kulis (2009) and Sisneros et al. (2008), I will explore in this chapter some of the complexities of the multiplicity of oppression, including the concept of intersectionality and the fact of heterogeneity that is part of every oppressed group or category. Guided by the notions of multiple identities and multiple oppression, I will: (1) argue that multiple identities are a major influence on the production, persistence, and complexity of oppression; (2) present a tentative model of multiple oppressions; (3) analyze the concept of interacting or intersecting oppressions; and (4) present a brief overview of some selected forms and sources of oppression and domination with respect to the heterogeneity that exists within each of them.

Multiple Identities and the Persistence of Domination and Oppression

In Chapter 3, we noted that it is overly simplistic and incorrect to impose a singular identity on individuals because most people obviously belong to more than one social category. In other words, we have multiple identities that intersect and overlap with one another. The fact of multiple identities constitutes the basis of criticism of singular models of oppression and singular approaches to anti-oppressive work. A singular approach such as anti-racism or anti-sexism assumes a certain homogeneity that does not exist within and among a group oppressed by racism or sexism or any other form of oppression, and it reduces oppression to a singular cause and does not consider the intersectional nature of oppression. Any particular category of oppression is mediated by other identities. For example, all people of colour will not experience racism in the same way, nor will all women experience sexism in the same way. An affluent person of colour will not experience racism in the same way as a poor person of colour. Nor will a white woman experience sexism in the same way as a woman of colour. There is not one racism or sexism but many. For example, there is a black middle-class racism, a black lesbian racism, an Asian racism, an affluent Asian racism, and so on. Our intersecting identities will either help to buffer or exacerbate the oppression we experience because of a particular subordinate identity. A single standpoint anti-oppressive politics has the potential to create hierarchies of oppression in which oppressed groups compete with each other for resources, publicity, and so on, which is counterproductive to the achievement of equality (Williams 1999).

Initial Impressions of an Intake Worker

Linda, an intake worker, greeted her first appointment of the day—an Asian man who she assumed was middle-class, heterosexual, and Chinese. She asked him what part of China he was from, whether or not he was married, and if so, whether he had met his wife back home or in Canada. She was surprised by his reply. 'Actually, I am a gay man from Japan, and the company where I worked could not survive the current economic crisis and recently went bankrupt.' Part of his personal struggle was the fact that he felt pressure to define himself in accordance with society's rigid classifications of gender, race, sexual orientation, and socio-economic status. By listening to his stories, Linda was able to revise and/or eliminate some of the initial assumptions and labels she had imposed on him and to understand him and his situation better.

The concept of multiple identities is not restricted to the concept of multiple oppression; it also applies to persons who may be oppressed with respect to some of their identities and privileged in their other identities. Given the array of forms and sources of domination and oppression, most people obviously belong to more than one category. In fact, as stated by Anne Bishop (1994, 61), 'we are oppressors in some parts of our identity, and oppressed in others.' She suggests that it would be much easier to fight oppression if a line could be drawn between oppressors on one side and oppressed people on the other side, but there are probably only a few who would fall almost entirely on one side or the other. This position is also taken by Gil (1998, 11), who says that 'people . . . tend to be oppressed in some relations and oppressors in others, while some relations may involve mutual oppression.'[2] This means that most oppressed persons also have access to some form of superiority or domination. Thus, the experience of either superiority/domination or inferiority/subordination with any one form of oppression can induce people to seek or maintain positions of superiority or domination in other forms of oppression.

Because many people have at least one form of domination as part of their identity, it becomes very difficult to wage a campaign to extinguish oppression. Once oppression is integrated into people's consciousness and into society's culture and structural order, oppressive tendencies become a central part of almost all relations (Gil 1998). Individuals will likely want to maximize and enhance their life chances and opportunities, but this may come at the expense of others (Moane 1999). So although an individual may want to see the end of oppression with respect to the parts of his or her identity that are subordinate (e.g., old age, gay), he or she may be unwilling to surrender the power and privilege that come with the part of the personal identity that is dominant (e.g., affluent, white). And, of course, this unwillingness is reinforced by the larger oppressive tendencies that permeate a society characterized by inequality and by competition. In other words, people may agree to combat oppression as long as it does not affect their particular forms or sources of privilege and domination. For example, low-income working-class males often exhibit overt and extreme racism, sexism, and homophobia even though they are victims of similar attitudes and treatment by dominant groups.

Life chances and opportunities are not the only reasons for clinging to one's particular source of domination. Oppression may also give the oppressor a certain psychological value. As discussed in the previous chapter, oppressed persons often experience feelings of inferiority, powerlessness, uselessness, alienation, self-doubt, and self-hatred. One negative and counterproductive way of coping with these feelings is to take comfort in the belief that some people are even worse off. For example, poor working-class white men may support and participate in racist and sexist actions to compensate for their poverty and oppression (i.e., to feel better about themselves). Furthermore, they may believe that those who are worse off really deserve their fate and second-class treatment because they are lazy, deviant, irresponsible, and so on. In this way, worse-off groups receive the same value judgments from other oppressed groups that they receive from the dominant group. This phenomenon of oppression against one subordinate group by another subordinate group is known as a 'poor person's snobbery' in that the former believe that they are at a higher level than the latter in a perceived hierarchy of oppressed groups.

The net effect of protecting the parts of our identity that accord us relatively favourable treatment from society, as well as participating in and contributing to the oppression of others, is to keep the whole system of oppression and dominant–subordinate relations in place. As long as separation, competition, and hierarchy among subordinate groups exist, there is no potential for solidarity and collaborative action on the part of oppressed groups, which leaves the status quo preserved and protected. Only a complete and complex understanding of our own contradictory roles as oppressors and oppressed will allow us to recognize our shared interests and to resist rather than collude with oppression (Bishop 2002).

Models of Multiple Oppressions

Although the social work and anti-oppressive literature generally acknowledges that oppression is usually multi-faceted, no satisfactory conceptual representation or model depicts the multifarious nature of oppression. Donna Baines (2000, 6) argues that even the critical theorists who have sought to expose the bases of dominant–subordinate relations in society have failed 'to explicate the interrelations between and within the totality of oppressive relations' and that 'no one model exists which reveals how multi-oppressions continuously interact with, contest, and reinforce each other.' Other feminist and anti-racist writers (e.g., Anthias and Yuval-Davis 1992; Day 1992; George 2000) have argued in a similar vein and contend that existing theories and analyses of the complex relationships among class, race, gender, sexuality, and other forms of difference are still inconclusive. This section will discuss the intersections of oppression and present a modified version of Steven Wineman's (1984) 'intersectionist model' of multiple oppression as well as a couple of recent conceptualizations of intersecting multiple oppression (Marsiglia and Kulis 2009; Sisneros et al. 2008).

Single-Strand Model

The simplest model of oppression is the 'single-strand' model, which depicts one form or source of oppression as being fundamental to all others. For example, orthodox Marxists identify classism or exploitation of the working class as the primary source of all oppression and believe that all others are derived from and secondary to it. While recognizing sexism, racism, and other forms of oppression, conventional Marxists contend that these are secondary oppressions and that because these groups are more susceptible than others to oppression in a capitalist economy, they are oppressed not because they may be women or non-white and so on. In other words, they are oppressed because they are workers, and their gender or race only exacerbates rather than causes their oppression. Eliminate classism and you eliminate the root cause of all secondary oppressions. Early forms of radical or progressive social work were colour- and gender-blind and focused on class oppression only (e.g., Bailey and Brake 1975).

Other groups have argued against the centrality of class oppression but on the basis that some other form of oppression is primary. For example, some radical feminists have insisted that patriarchy or the exercise of male power is the central organizing category of oppression and that the basic class difference is between the sexes (Hartmann 1981). Similar positions have been adopted with respect to race. Black radicals and nationalists from different countries, such as Stokely Carmichael, Malcolm X, Louis Farrakhan, and Frantz Fanon, have all argued that racism is the oldest and most fundamental source of oppression. Even one of the foremost progressive social work writers today, Lena Dominelli, seems to argue from a single-strand position in *Anti-Racist Social Work* when she asserts that 'class and gender inequality will be included in the transformation resulting from the struggle against racism' (Dominelli 1997, 167).

Although single-strand models may contain a comforting sense of simplicity, they are also overly reductionist and simplistic. Complex social phenomena such as domination and subordination cannot be adequately understood on the basis of a solitary (no matter how fundamental) variable or category. The single-strand model does not account for the interconnections and intersections of oppression that exist.

For example, women of colour experience racism and sexism together (George 2000) and not separately, since one form of oppression is continuously mediated by the other(s) (Day 1992). Nor can the single-strand model account for the dynamic ways in which social relations complement and contradict or reinforce and undermine each other at different historical moments and in different contexts (Baines 2001).

In addition to its conceptual and explanatory limitations, the single-strand model holds little potential for social solidarity and joint action by oppressed individuals and groups. Wineman (1984, 163) states that 'it [a single fundamental source of oppression] at once fails to create a basis for unity which respects the dignity and felt experience of all the oppressed individuals and groups who are supposed to become unified, and it fails to generate a practical strategy and process which can . . . effectively challenge all forms of oppression.' Furthermore, a single-strand view does little to overcome the existing divisions and fragmentation that currently exist among oppressed groups. In fact, it may generate resentment as some groups are asked to submerge their 'secondary' interests and less-favoured forms of oppression until the 'root cause' of all oppression has been eliminated (Wineman 1984).

Parallel Model

A more pluralistic model of oppression, originally outlined by Wineman (1984) and used by many early progressive social workers such as the originator of structural social work in Canada, Maurice Moreau (1979; Moreau and Leonard 1989, cited in Carniol 1992), is the parallel-tracks depiction of oppression. Rather than adopting a model positing a single primary source of oppression, the parallel model depicts all forms and sources of oppression running alongside each other in a non-hierarchical, parallel fashion. Figure 7.1 presents a somewhat modified version of Wineman's 'parallel-tracks' perspective of multiple oppression. According to this perspective, different forms and sources of oppression all involve similar dynamics of dominant–subordinate relations, but each is caused and maintained by an autonomous set or configuration of social, economic, cultural, political, and historical factors. In addition, each form of oppression affects only a single distinct group of oppressed people (Wineman 1984). For example, sexism only oppresses women; class exploitation only oppresses working and poor people; homophobia only oppresses gay, lesbian, and bisexual persons; and racism only oppresses people of colour.

An obvious limitation of the parallel model is that it does not account for people who experience two or more sources of oppression—that is, it does not address how oppressions are relational and interact with each other. Nor does it account for persons who are oppressed in some areas of their lives and privileged in others. As noted above, Usha George (2000) makes the point that women of colour experience sexism and racism simultaneously, not as single or parallel strands of oppression. Wineman identifies another limitation to the parallel model. Although it does not claim that a separate solution to one form of oppression is the key to eliminating all forms of oppression (i.e., the single-strand belief), the parallel model offers little potential for solidarity and joint social action among oppressed groups. Because the causes, interests, and experiences associated with each form of oppression are seen to be distinct, requiring separate solutions, there may be occasions for ad hoc joint actions whereby one oppressed group supports another, but the emphasis is still on the 'single issue' of each group. In other words, the form of oppression experienced by a particular group is given particular emphasis by that group because it affects its members most deeply; in fact, the oppression is often used to promote internal solidarity and to strengthen group members psychologically and politically (Wineman 1984).

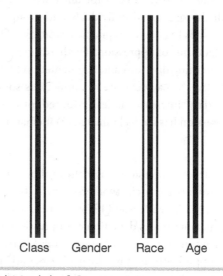

Class   Gender   Race   Age

Figure 7.1   Parallel Model of Oppression

Intersectional Model

Marsiglia and Kulis (2009, xvi) state that a major purpose of their book, *Diversity, Oppression, and Change: Culturally Grounded Social Work,* is 'to advance the concept of *intersectionality,* that is, the belief that humans form identities that are culturally multi-dimensional and beautifully complex.' They propose both a definition and a theory of intersectionality. 'The term "intersectionality" refers to the multidimensionality and complexity of the human cultural experience and describes the place where multiple identities come together, or intersect' (2009, 42). Their so-called theory of intersectionality does not go much beyond what already existed in the Canadian social work literature. (It is interesting to note that Sisneros et al. [2008] claim that the intersectional model was developed by radical social workers in Canada.) The major points contained in their theory of intersectionality are as follows:

- It was an earlier group of feminist writers such as bell hooks (1981) who first started to explore the multi-dimensional nature of oppression.

(Baines [2007] makes the same point in her book, as noted in the first end-note for this chapter.)

- It was Collins (1998) who described the intersection of race, gender, and social class as constituting a 'matrix of domination.' Within this matrix, individuals may experience oppression or privilege as a result of their combination of identities.

- Research on intersectionality has demonstrated that different systems of inequality are interconnected (Anderson and Collins 2004). For example, ethnic minority women may face 'double jeopardy' because of the combined disadvantages of their gender and ethnicity and may be relegated to the most menial and devalued jobs. African-Canadian lesbians would face 'triple jeopardy' on the basis of their gender, race, and sexual orientation. This latter group has often struggled for visibility and influence in the feminist, black, and lesbian and gay liberation movements.

- The social implications of intersectionality, like the systems of inequality they are based on, are constantly changing. Marsiglia and Kulis present 'affirmative action' in the US as a case in point. It was originally established to help over-come the historical disadvantage experienced by African-Americans with respect to employment, government contracting, and educational access, but in recent years there has been considerable social and legal debate on its current efficacy and fairness. Arguments against affirmative action have focused on middle-class African-Americans as beneficiaries when they do not need the help as much as poor African-Americans do. There has also been criticism of the exclusion of Asian-Americans from the policy. These criticisms highlight the considerable diversity that exists within and among racial categories.

- The intersectionality perspective is also useful for examining privilege. Those who enjoy dominant statuses such as whiteness, masculinity, heterosexuality, and socio-economic affluence not only enjoy the absence of oppression but reap the direct social and material benefits that accompany the intersection of those statuses (Bonilla-Silva 1997, cited in Marsiglia and Kulis 2009).

A model of oppression proposed by Wineman that accounts for intersecting, interlocking, and/or interacting oppressions is the intersectional model. Wineman asserts that although the different forms of oppression may be distinct in some ways, they are not unrelated. 'Different oppressions intersect at innumerable points in everyday life and are mutually reinforcing, creating a total system of oppression in which one continuum of stratification cannot be addressed in isolation from all the others' (Wineman 1984, 169). The model accounts for multiple identities in that an intersection is the location where a person's race, for example, will meet his or her class, age, or any other component of the person's identity. Figure 7.2 is a modified version of Wineman's intersectional perspective of multiple oppression. It shows that although there may be distinct categories of oppression, there is no oppression that creates a distinct group of oppressed people who are unaffected, one way or another, by other forms of oppression. Oppressed groups overlap each other—an important fact conceptually both for understanding the nature of oppression and for seeking alliances and coalitions of oppressed groups (the latter will be discussed in Chapter 8).

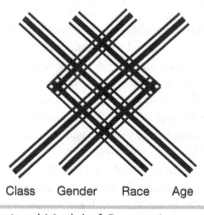

Class   Gender   Race   Age

Figure 7.2   Intersectional Model of Oppression

The intersectional model does not argue for hierarchies of oppression (i.e., 'my oppression is greater than yours'). This does not mean, however, that all oppressions are considered of equal severity or that they affect all oppressed persons in the same way. Similarly, as pointed out by Baines (2000), the model does not attempt to predict or define how different forms of oppression reinforce, contest, or complicate each other in different contexts. It must be remembered that the intersectional model is a model and not a theory or analysis. Models usually do not contain explanatory or predictive features. That is the job of analysis and theory. Models may identify or depict certain social realities, but they do not explain them. For example, general systems theory or an ecological model may be used to depict a family in its social context and identify the relationships among family members, but it does not account for power relationships within the family, nor does it explain conflict. It is a pictorial representation of the various subsystems that have a connection with a particular family (or other social system). It does not explain the nature of the family, the nature or causes of the problems being experienced by the family, the nature of the relationships pictured in the model, the extent of influence of various subsystems, and so on. No model (or theory) can account for or explain how individuals will experience oppression, because each experience is different, nor can it account for the ways in which different forms of oppression constantly change in relation to each other or how they vary in different contexts. The best we might hope for is to understand that the different forms, sources, and relations of oppression are continuous, contentious, dynamic, and mutually reinforcing social processes (Baines 2001). The contribution of the intersectional model of oppression is that it highlights the multiplicity of oppression. It reveals the complexity and multiple or intersecting nature of oppression. It also indicates areas for further analysis in our attempts to understand the multiplicity of oppression. Two of these areas, which will be explored below, are the nature of an intersection or interaction of oppression and the heterogeneity that exists within each category or form of oppression.

The Web of Oppression

Sisneros et al. (2008) have developed a model for conceptualizing an individual's position at the intersections of class, race, gender, and other social characteristics. This model, which they call the 'web of oppression' (see Figure 7.3), is based on the fact that each of us is positioned in a particular context with respect to our race/ethnicity, gender, class, ability, religion, sexual orientation, and so on. For the most part, this positioning is not a matter of choice. We do not have a choice of our parents or our social circumstances.

> One day we awake into a context—family, culture, language, ethnoracial identity, class status, country of birth and/or adoption, and sex, and physical and mental ability. . . . In each category there is a position that is considered normal. If one is not in this group, one is seen as the 'other' and is subject to the oppressions [i.e., Young's five faces of oppression] of marginalization, exploitation, powerlessness, cultural imperialism, and possibly violence [Sisneros et al. 2008, 70].

Our position along the continuum of each characteristic in the web of oppression is an indicator of our status or identity. Our positions can change over time with respect to some of the characteristics in the web, which would be accompanied by a change in our status or identity. For example, one's social and economic position can change, as can one's health status. Positions on the multi-dimensional spectrum influence social, economic, and political opportunities.

Although the web in Figure 7.3 was developed for an American readership, it also has relevance to other jurisdictions. The web is a model that allows us to examine the position of an individual at the intersections of class, gender, race, religion, ability, place of birth, language spoken, and sexual orientation. It goes further than Wineman's intersectional model because in addition to showing the areas of intersection, it also shows one's position or status within each area or social characteristic. This is its major contribution. The centre of the web represents access to resources, with persons at the centre of each wedge having institutionalized privilege and power with respect to that particular dimension. However, persons further away from the centre do not necessarily have less access to resources than those who are closer to the centre but still outside the ring of privilege. For example, Aboriginal persons (Native Americans in the US) are not necessarily more oppressed than African-Canadians or African-Americans. I believe that in most cases, though, the further one moves along one dimension from the centre, the more oppression one experiences. Of course, one's position on other dimensions will either buffer or exacerbate the experience of oppression along any

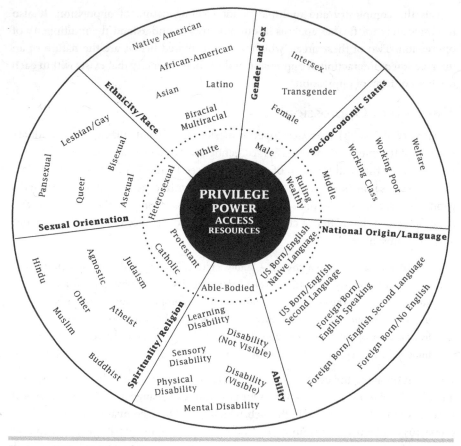

Figure 7.3   Web of Oppression

other dimension. It is impossible to consider only one dimension, since we have a total system of oppression with all dimensions related to and intersecting with each other. We have, in effect, a total system or web of oppression.

Intersections of Oppression: An Analysis

Most of the recent social work literature on anti-oppression emphasizes the importance of examining how various forms of oppression intersect or interact. The majority of radical, feminist, and anti-racist social work writers today go beyond the discrete, single-strand analysis of oppression, although they tend to restrict themselves to the trinity or triumvirate of race, class, and gender forms (e.g., Baines 2000; Day 1992; George and Ramkissoon 1998). They recognize, for example, that oppression based on patriarchy is not experienced in the same way by all women, since it will be mediated in some way by a woman's class position, race, sexuality, and so on. As well, one's oppression in one particular area will be mediated not only by other experienced forms of oppression but also by forms of domination (e.g., male, white) attached to an individual and by his or her psychological characteristics (e.g., sense of self, personality). In addition, the particular historical moment in which the oppression occurs and the surrounding social conditions or context in which it occurs will also affect the experience of oppression.

Multiple oppression is a very complex phenomenon. To understand its full effects would require a separate analysis of all the permutations and combinations of factors connected with each individual case of oppression. Such specificity would, of course, militate against any possibility for generalization or commonality (Nicholson 1990). This, in turn, would undermine identity, solidarity, and the capacity for political action (Brodribb 1992, cited in Moane 1999). Conversely, an overemphasis on commonality can lead to universalizing tendencies that ignore local conditions and impose inappropriate frameworks and patterns on particular oppressed groups or individuals. Making links between oppressions, therefore, requires the recognition of both commonalities and specificities across different forms and experiences of oppression (Moane 1999).

As was argued in previous chapters, much can be learned about the nature, dynamics, and processes of oppression without going into a case-by-case analysis of each instance of oppression. With respect to the multiplicity of oppression, one important area that is underdeveloped in the literature is the nature of an intersection of oppression. What does it mean when it is said that two forms of oppression intersect with each other? Or what does it mean when two intersecting forms of oppression mediate each other? Is it only forms of oppression that intersect? Or do forms of domination also intersect with forms of oppression and with other forms of domination as well?

Several writers (e.g., Moane 1999; Young 1990) make the point that multiple oppressions are not simply cumulative or additive. For example, the oppression experienced by a black woman goes beyond a simple summing of race and gender oppressions. Something else happens at the intersection of race and gender. In the language of statistics, a new variable is created. Not only does the black woman experience oppression as a woman and as a black person, but she also experiences oppression as a black woman. Her colour interacts with her gender. Interactive effects have long been recognized in social science research. In fact, the interactive effects of bringing two or more variables together are often measured statistically using multivariate analyses. This does not mean that oppression can be measured statistically in any meaningful way. Because much of oppression is qualitative in nature and currently not well understood, we do not have the conceptual knowledge or methodological tools to measure oppression quantitatively. Rather than positivist, the point I am making is conceptual. Whenever two or more independent social variables are combined (such as race and gender), the result is an effect on the dependent variable (such as oppression) that goes beyond a simple addition of the effect of both variables. The combinations (i.e., interactions) of variables also has an effect on the dependent variable. An analogy from chemistry may help. When sodium and chlorine are combined, a chemical reaction or interaction occurs producing a different substance—common table salt. Salt may result from combining two elements, but the result goes beyond simple additive effects in that salt is an autonomous substance with different properties and effects from those of either sodium or chlorine.

Let us look at a couple of examples in an effort to clarify this discussion of interactions. In the first example, we will consider two sources of oppression, race and gender. In Equation 1 the letter 'a' is assigned to race and the letter 'b' to gender. Their combined effects on oppression may be represented as:

Equation 1:   oppression = a + b + (ab)
        [i.e., oppression = race + gender + (race × gender)]

Thus, a black woman will experience the oppressive effects of patriarchy, a term that refers to the system of social structures and practices that subordinate women, as will a white woman. However, patriarchy is not a simple concept whereby all men dominate all women equally. Women will experience patriarchy differently based on their class, race, sexuality, age, and so on (Collins 1990; Emberley 1993; Maracle 1996; Moane 1999). In other words, a black woman will experience patriarchy differently from a white woman because it will be mediated (affected, influenced) by her racial identification or skin colour. All other things being equal, a black woman will likely experience a more complicated and potent form of oppression emanating from sexism and patriarchy than will a white woman. Just attempting to sort out whether particular incidents of abuse or certain obstacles to development and progress that a black woman experiences are the result of her gender or her race or both is a question and struggle that the white woman does not experience. This additional and complex effect of oppression is reflected in the interaction component in Equation 1. The interaction of race and gender is not a part of the gender component of oppression or the race component. As in the example of common table salt, it is a separate factor in itself and contains oppressive effects separate from either gender or race.

Just as a black woman experiences sexism differently from a white woman, so too does she experience racism differently from a black male. Both experience racism, but only the black woman also experiences patriarchy as a form of oppression, and patriarchy will mediate how she experiences racism. This exacerbates the level and severity of the racial oppression she experiences and thus makes the black woman's racial oppression more complex or multi-dimensional than racial oppression experienced by a black male (all other things being equal). The black woman, as mentioned above, may face a constant dilemma of wondering whether it is her race or her gender that accounts for some of her negative experiences and therefore what her target for remedying the treatment ought to be.

The above scenario of an interaction between two forms or sources of oppression is relatively simple (conceptually at least) compared to situations in which more than two forms of oppression interact with each other. Let us look at an example of multiple

What Is It about Me?

Nancy, a black woman, is a member of the Department of Social Work at a university. Six months ago, she was appointed head of the department. One of her new duties was to attend meetings of the Academic Senate, the senior academic committee in the university, comprised of deans, department heads, and other senior academics. Most of the members of Senate were white men who had been at the university for years. During the first few meetings that Nancy attended, she noticed that whenever she spoke, she received polite attention but then the discussions would proceed as if she had not said anything. As time went on, the polite attention disappeared. Other Senate members would interrupt her and act as though she were invisible. In discussions with some of her female colleagues about what was happening, she was told that it was a gender issue and that she should raise it at a Senate meeting. In conversations with some of her family and black friends, she was told it was a race issue and that she should raise it at a Senate meeting. This is probably a situation in which Nancy is experiencing sexism and racism simultaneously. Obviously, it is a delicate issue for Nancy. How should she approach the Senate?

oppression involving three forms or sources of oppression (e.g., race, gender, and class). As with Equation 1, let us assign letters to each of these forms of oppression: a = race, b = gender, and c = class. The following equation reflects their combined effects on oppression:

Equation 2:   oppression = a + b + c + (ab) + (ac) + (bc) + (abc)
[i.e., oppression = race + gender + class + (race $\times$ gender) + (race $\times$ class) + (gender $\times$ class) + (race $\times$ gender $\times$ class)]

In this example, the black woman, who experiences a more complex form of racial oppression than a black male because of her gender and who also experiences a more complex form of gender oppression than a white woman because of her colour, has these two forms of oppression mediated by her class position. If she is poor, she is oppressed by class, which in turn exacerbates her experiences with the other two forms of oppression with which she may be struggling. And in turn, her class oppression may become more intense, severe, and pervasive because of her gender and race oppressions. Equation 2 shows four interactive effects associated with three forms of oppression compared to one interactive effect associated with two forms of oppression only. Obviously, the interactive effects of multiple oppression increase exponentially with the addition of more forms of oppression.

The above equations illustrate the complexity of multiple oppressions. As different forms of oppression are added to an already oppressive situation, the interactions increase exponentially, which in turn increase the complexity (and perhaps the severity) of oppression on a person. The equations do not reveal anything about the nature of an interaction or how much an interaction contributes to oppression, but it is unrealistic to attempt to measure interactions, since they will vary in different contexts at different times with different individuals. The point of the above exercise is to show what an interaction or intersection is, to demonstrate how they contribute to the complexity of oppression, and to highlight the interactional nature and effects of oppression.

Multiple oppression becomes even more complex when forms of domination or privilege are factored into the situation. It was suggested earlier that the identities of most people contain both dominant and subordinate characteristics. Just as different forms of oppression interact with one another, so too different forms of domination interact with other forms of domination as well as with different forms of oppression. If the black woman in the examples above is affluent instead of poor, her experiences with oppression would be affected in the following ways. First, she obviously would not be oppressed as she would be if she were an exploited worker or poor. Second, her other forms of oppression (race and gender) would not be made worse by her class position. Finally, her class position would mediate or alleviate some of the negative effects of being black and a woman. For example, she would be able to purchase such services as superior health care, live in a comfortable house in a relatively crime-free neighbourhood, send her children to decent, well-equipped schools, and pay for legal services to fight instances of gender or race discrimination. The black woman's privileged class position would not eliminate her experiences with gender and race oppression, but unlike her black sisters living in poverty, this position would mediate or alleviate some of the severity, harshness, and pervasiveness of the oppression she did experience.

A caution should be noted here. The above analysis does not mean that a hierarchy of oppressions can be created simply by summing the number of different forms of oppression a person may be experiencing and subtracting the number of different forms of domination one occupies from the sum total. Oppression is irreducibly a qualitative and not a quantitative experience (Wineman 1984). The above exercise illustrating how interactions form and contribute to oppression over and above the simple summing of two or more sources or forms of oppression was not meant to represent the totality of the oppressive experience. What is lacking is the qualitative measure of each interaction with respect to its impact on oppression. Yes, we can identify sources of oppression and ascertain their interactions, but we cannot quantify the impact or effect of oppression. It varies too much from individual to individual and from situation to situation. One form of oppression may be experienced as more severe than a combination of two other forms of oppression because there is enormous individual variation within any particular oppressed group (to be discussed below).

For example, a white working-class older woman (oppressed by class, gender, and age) is not necessarily more oppressed than a black working-class male (oppressed by class and race). Nor is it true that every black woman is more oppressed than every black male, since she may have material and/or personal resources that he does not.

The intersectional nature of oppression holds significant implications for an anti-oppressive social work practice. It helps the social worker to see that oppression seldom comes in a single form. It also helps us to understand that it is not simply a case of identifying and summing the different oppressions that an oppressed person may be experiencing in an effort to obtain an appreciation of his or her total situation. Social workers should also be aware of the ways that different forms of oppression intersect with each other and how these intersections contain oppressive effects themselves. They will then recognize that not all members of a particular oppressed group experience oppression in the same way or with the same severity or intensity. Just as there is heterogeneity between groups of oppressed people, there is also heterogeneity within each oppressed group, as suggested in the above discussion of the mediating effects of different forms of oppression and domination. We now need to examine the concept of heterogeneity in more detail.

Heterogeneity within Oppressed Groups

When we consider different forms and sources of oppression and different groups of oppressed people, there is a danger that we might view and treat everyone within a particular group as the same. As suggested in the discussion on intersecting oppressions and as Lyotard (1988) argues, any homogenization of people oversimplifies the complexities and varieties of social reality because it does not acknowledge the incredible diversity inherent within people's various gender, class, race, age, sexuality, and other social dimensions. So, for example, although all people of colour may be oppressed as non-white people, there is great diversity among people of colour that will result in more or less oppression.

Wineman argues that our contemporary socio-economic-political system has an inherent capacity for creating and maintaining deep divisions both among oppressed groups and within each oppressed group. These divisions among oppressed groups serve the interests of the dominant group in that the competition among subordinate groups for some resources and recognition is a major obstacle to their recognizing common interests and issues and organizing and mobilizing around them. Making matters even worse for subordinate groups is the fact that the fragmentation and segmentation of oppression occur not only among oppressed groups but within each oppressed group as well. There are gradations or hierarchies of privilege and advantage within each oppressed group. In a society marked by oppression, inequality, and competition, these gradations tend to motivate people who hold relative advantages to defend their positions and to support the status quo. This often causes resentment on the part of those who are relatively disadvantaged towards those who rank immediately above them (Wineman 1984). And just as deep divisions among different oppressed groups inhibit notions and actions of solidarity among them, so divisions within oppressed groups inhibit solidarity on the part of members of each group.

Various forms and sources of oppression, along with divisions or hierarchies within each oppressed group, are presented below. The purpose is not to offer a complete or well-developed overview of each form of oppression addressed—other social work texts do this (e.g., Thompson 1997). Rather, the intention is to present a succinct version of the nature of several selected forms of oppression and to highlight the divisions that exist within each oppressed group. Although I focus on several forms of oppression individually in order to show the heterogeneity within each, it should be remembered that oppression tends to be a multiple phenomenon. I isolate different forms in this section for analytical purposes only.

Classism

In Canada and the US, there is much less awareness of class than there is in most other Anglo democracies. If you ask students (and others) what class they think they are part of, most will reply 'middle class' even if their income is much less or much more than those in this particular class. In reality, we all live in very separate economic worlds. Class is a very powerful force in most societies, although it is not as well recognized as many other forms of oppression. And people like me lament the fact that it has all but disappeared from the social work literature, even though it was the basis upon which social work was established and our social welfare state and social work practice is still largely class-based, albeit with influences from other social groupings. For example, class is racialized in Canada and even more so in the US.

Today, class is not the simple concept that it might have been when Karl Marx was writing in the mid-nineteenth century about the exploitation of workers by capitalists. Marx divided society into two major classes: the bourgeoisie or capitalist class, who own the means of production (factories, equipment), and the proletariat or working class, who have to sell their labour to the capitalists to survive. Marx devoted his entire intellectual life to writing about the evils of capitalism, which included the exploitation and oppression of workers by the economically and politically powerful capitalist or ruling class. Thus, classism has come to mean the form of exploitation and oppression emanating from the social divisions of class. Of course, society (including social class) has changed significantly since Marx's time to the extent that his original analysis is no longer applicable to the current form of capitalism. However, many developments in Marxist thought attempt to update the basic tenets of his analysis and apply them to today's situation (e.g., Agger 1998; Giddens 1995; Habermas 1975).

Class today is a complex phenomenon comprising different social, economic, and political theoretical conceptualizations (Thompson 1998). The working class today is not the relatively homogeneous social group with common interests that Marx wrote about. Rather, it is a highly stratified and multi-layered hierarchy of people characterized almost as much by conflicting interests as by common interests.

A typical representation of the stratified class divisions may be seen in Figure 7.4. Gilbert (2002) has devised a similar model of class for the US in which he includes income and attained educational levels for each stratum. People do not choose their social class. Members of the poor and working class are limited by the opportunities available or not available to them in our capitalist economic and social system. Political leaders, the corporate elite, the mass media, and the educational system often portray Canadian (and American) society as a meritocracy in which rewards are allocated on the basis of individual merit alone. However, the uneven playing field of social class gives crucial advantages to those from privileged backgrounds (Marsiglia and Kulis 2009).

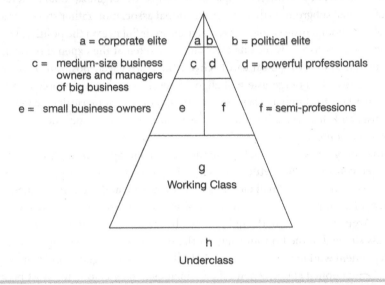

a = corporate elite

c = medium-size business owners and managers of big business

e = small business owners

b = political elite

d = powerful professionals

f = semi-professions

g
Working Class

h
Underclass

Figure 7.4

The dominant groups at the top of the hierarchy consist of two subgroups: (1) people who exert corporate power and domination through their ownership and/or control of major industrial, commercial, and financial firms and (2) persons who exert state power through their positions as elected leaders and cabinet ministers within national and state governments.[3] The former subgroup controls the means of production and historically has been known (by Marxists) as the capitalist class.

In most Western democracies, elected leaders have a much closer relationship with the corporate elite than they do with the job-dependent working class. Marxists have referred to political leaders as 'business class allies,' and many elected leaders come from or aspire to the corporate sector while the job-dependent working class is grossly under-represented in government. Given the corporate sector's economic power and its influence over and close relationship with the political sector, it should be no surprise that government decisions, on the whole, tend to favour capital accumulation at the expense of the working class (e.g., favourable tax provisions for corporations, anti-union legislation).

The two groups just below the corporate and political leaders in Figure 7.4 consist of (1) the owners of medium-sized businesses and key managers in the corporate sector and (2) self-employed members of powerful professional groups, such as law, medicine, engineering, and academe. These people probably have more in common with those above them than they do with the job-dependent working class or the underclass. In fact, they are often referred to (in Marxist terms) as the 'bourgeoisie.' Even though the bourgeoisie must work for a living, this group is the aristocracy of the working class—members enjoy certain privileges, such as high social status, prestige, and high incomes relative to other occupational groups. The organizational preference of the professional subgroup is that of a professional association rather than a union. Collectively, the bourgeoisie is able to exert significant influence on the political sector and frequently does so to advance its own interests, often at the expense of workers (e.g., the privatization of medical care). Given their privileged position in society, it is not likely that the bourgeoisie will align themselves with poor people and job-dependent workers to eliminate classism. The bourgeoisie is numerically greater than the capitalists and their allies but not as powerful. However, by any measurement, members of the bourgeoisie are part of the dominant class.

Below the bourgeoisie is another layer in the class hierarchy comprising two groups that together constitute the petite (or petty) bourgeoisie. One group consists of small business owners (e.g., small factories or workshops), and the other is made up of members of semi-professions, such as social workers, nurses, schoolteachers, and journalists. Arguably, they form the bulk of the middle class, with other sectors of the middle class situated in the bottom rungs of the bourgeoisie and the upper rungs of the job-dependent working class. The term 'middle class' is ambiguous and somewhat mythical. As mentioned above, when asked which class they belong to, most people are likely to say 'middle class,' especially if they do not possess a class analysis. In any event, both groups in this social positioning aspire to climb up the socio-economic ladder, with small-business owners dreaming of becoming owners of large businesses and the semi-professions copying and/or adopting the cultures and organizational frameworks of the established professions. Given their lack of economic and political power, as well as their upwardly mobile aspirations, they are a relatively malleable group that often carries out the bidding of the dominant group. They do this by providing employment (small businesses account for most jobs) and by caring for and controlling the job-dependent working class and the poverty-stricken underclass. Most people in this class division are able to obtain a decent or at least adequate level of living and may not see or believe in the need for fundamental social change as key to addressing the social problems and conditions experienced by those in class rungs beneath them.

The vast majority (two-thirds to three-quarters) of people in advanced capitalist societies belong to the working class or proletariat. This group consists of industrial, construction, farm, clerical, distributive, and service workers; skilled, semi-skilled, and unskilled workers; young and old workers; male and female workers; blue-collar labourers and pink-collar workers; migrants, the unemployed, and underemployed workers; full-time, casual, part-time, and seasonal workers. In other words, the working class consists of all the people whose main (and usually only) source of income is the sale of their labour power and/or transfer payments from the state. Recessions hit this group harder than any other group, and unemployment is higher within it than within any other group except the underclass. This group makes less money, owns less, owes more, and has less education, less access to societal goods, fewer opportunities, less respect or status, and less political power than any other group in society except the underclass. It carries out most of the necessary but menial and dangerous jobs for the dominant groups and purchases the same products that they themselves make, with a profit going to the capitalists or bourgeoisie. They depend on and pay for the services of professionals. They pay their taxes and have fewer tax breaks than the groups above them, which effectively means that they subsidize the incomes and operating costs of the people above them on the hierarchy. Those occupying a higher tier on the class scale oppress the working class at every level and in multiple ways.

The underclass is the final group on the class hierarchy. It represents a growing group of people who have no attachment to the labour market. Members of this group are permanently trapped outside the traditional divisions of class because such divisions are based on the type of work that one does. This group is different from the working poor or the temporarily unemployed, since members have either never worked in the past or will never work again. They comprise homeless persons, mentally ill people, long-term unemployed individuals, and sick and disabled persons. In the United States, members of the underclass are typically black, Hispanic, or marginalized and excluded poor white people. In Australia and Canada, they are typically Aboriginal or people of colour (often refugees) or marginalized and excluded poor white people. They have little in the way of social services, and their poverty and their acts of survival (i.e., their attempts to obtain food, clothing, and shelter) are often criminalized. It is left to the police to control and manage them by what Wachholz and Mullaly (1993) call covering up and mopping up after the shortcomings of society and its welfare state. In the absence of adequate social, economic, and psychiatric supports, the police use criminal statutes to charge members of the underclass with such crimes as vagrancy, panhandling, prostitution, sleeping (and urinating) in a public place, and petty theft if a person tries to maintain some level of subsistence. Instead of the conditions of homelessness and poverty being criminalized, the acts of survival of the underclass are what is criminalized (Wachholz and Mullaly 1993). The underclass is despised, feared, pitied, and rejected by members of all other class divisions. They are society's disposable or throwaway population. They are at the bottom of the bottom of our class system and have little hope of ever leaving it.

This brief overview of class illustrates its divisions and some of the conflicts of interest that exist among these divisions. Workers or the working class are by no means a homogeneous group of people. Not only do conflicting interests, mistrust, suspicion, and resentment exist among categories or divisions of class, they also exist within each class division. For example, there is significant resentment and animosity on the part of the working poor towards the non-working poor. The former have inculcated many of the myths and stereotypes about people on welfare. They see themselves working hard to eke out a basic living and perceive people in receipt of welfare to be living the 'life of Riley' while laughing up their sleeves at those who work. Both groups may be poor, but society has driven a deep wedge between them that militates against any notion of or attempt at solidarity. It is not uncommon for political leaders to play these two groups off against each other. Thus, when poor people and their allies criticize welfare rates as too low, politicians often respond that an increase in welfare benefits would give recipients more money than the working poor receive in wages and would have to be paid for by the working poor. The outrage from the working poor, who are struggling on a daily basis to make ends meet, is almost immediate.

In sum, class is a complex sociological, political, economic, and cultural concept that has significant implications with respect to social inequality and life chances. Members of particular class divisions are oppressed not only by those in higher positions on the class hierarchy but also by persons occupying the same class division. The same can be said about race.

A Despicable Political Response

A number of years ago in the Canadian province of New Brunswick, a campaign by anti-poverty groups and their allies sought to increase welfare rates, especially for children's school supplies and for winter fuel. The minister of social services finally responded to this request. She rhetorically but publicly said that she wondered how the 'working poor' would feel about such an increase, since it would be paid for by the working poor and probably put welfare rates on par with or even above their hard-earned income (which it would not). There was an immediate expression of outrage from the working poor (letters, calls to radio phone-in shows, and the like) against such an increase, and the movement for higher rates died.

Racism

Racism is the belief that human abilities are determined by race, that one race is inherently superior to all others and therefore has the right to dominate all other races. Underpinning racism is the assumption that racial classification is based on biological evidence. Skin colour, for example, is thought to be associated with other biological characteristics such as intelligence. Essentialism is also part of racism in that there is a belief that everybody classified as belonging to a particular racial group possesses the same characteristics (Thompson 1997). There is no biological validation for many of the popular ideas concerning racial classification (Banton and Harwood 1975, cited in Thompson 1998). Rather, racial classifications are social constructs or ways to make sense of the social world rather than biological types. In spite of the absence of scientific validation, racial categorization remains a fixed concept because it carries out certain ideological and political functions for the racially (white) dominant group. The categories of race are not value-neutral but constitute a hierarchy of racial groups in which white groups are dominant because of their socially constructed superiority (Ahmad 1990). And as Thompson (1998) argues, this socially constructed superiority lies at the basis of racism. Racism operates at three levels—at the personal level as a personal ideology and/or as individual beliefs and actions, at the cultural level in the form of a system of cultural messages, and at the structural or institutional level in the form of institutional policies and social practices.

Although race as a biological category is questionable,[4] racism is not. Even though race scholars have understood for decades that race is a social construction, racial classification based on physical traits is so engrained in Eurocentric societies that getting people to think otherwise is a major challenge (Sisneros et al. 2008). 'It is society's belief that race exists that provides its significance' (Marger 1997, cited in Sisneros et al. 2008, 35). Through the assumption of racial superiority, racism has had profound negative effects on people of colour within most Eurocentric societies and the countries they colonized. As discussed in previous chapters, people of colour are subject to disparaging stereotypes and are oppressed and discriminated against at the personal, cultural, and structural levels of society. All non-white people are subject to racism, but they do not constitute a homogeneous group, since there are colour and cultural differences among non-white people. In fact, these differences constitute a hierarchy of racism experienced by people of colour that is constructed and imposed by the dominant white group. Wineman's (1984, 172) description of the racial hierarchy in the United States is similar to that of most other Eurocentric nations: 'social distinctions are made, more or less subtly, between Latino/as [Hispanics], Asians, Native Americans, and Blacks (and between lighter and darker skinned Blacks)—as well as between people of colour who adopt white speech patterns and cultural trappings, and those who don't; as a rule, the lighter you are, physically and culturally, the "better". However, success on white terms usually requires people of colour both to recant their culture and to accept with grace a permanent position of marginal inferiority (Wineman 1984).

The system of stratification imposed on people of colour by the white society, based on shadings of skin colour and conformity to the dominant culture on its terms, is often internalized by people of colour. This reinforces the stratified divisions imposed by the dominant group both among the various groups of non-white people and within each group. Stratification based on shades of skin colour evokes a profound internalization of racist oppression, which may result in people of colour adopting racist attitudes and behaviours towards each other. Divisions are created and sustained among black persons, Aboriginal people, Asian groups, and Hispanic people.

Just as stratification creates and sustains divisions among various groups of people of colour, it also nurtures divisions within each group based on skin colour, class, and lifestyle (Wineman 1984). People of colour are not only divided along class, gender, sexual orientation, age, and other lines of social division but in terms of their relationship with the dominant white group as well. Individuals who are 'whiter' (physically and culturally) often dissociate themselves for a variety of psychological and sociological reasons from others in their identity group who are not as 'white.' Conversely, those at lower levels on their respective racial hierarchies often resent those above them and view them as traitors to their own 'race.' For example, First Nations people in North America who appear to other First Nations people to have been co-opted by white society are often referred to in a derogatory manner as 'apples'—red on the outside but white on the inside. Similarly, Australian Aborigines may refer to those among them who appear to have adopted white lifestyles and culture as 'coconuts'—brown on the outside but white on the inside. The term 'Uncle Tom' has long been used by many African-Americans to refer to other African-Americans who have ingratiated themselves to white people in attempts to assimilate into white middle-class culture.

In sum, race is a complex social construction that has significant implications for people with respect to equality and life chances. However, the social and psychological degradations attached to racism go well beyond employment, income, housing, or welfare. Wineman says it best: 'Racism attacks the core of people's sense of their own value, and it ultimately attacks their right to exist. . . . When you are taught from birth that you are inherently inferior, you are taught in the same breath that you are inherently powerless' (1984, 128). The divisions within each category of people of colour guarantee this powerlessness.

Sexism

The emotional, sexual, and psychological stereotyping of females begins when the doctor says: 'It's a girl.'
    — Shirley Chisholm, first black woman to be elected to the US Congress (1968), first black woman to run for president of the United States (1972)

Although defined in different ways in the feminist literature (e.g., biological, materialist, social constructionist[5]), 'patriarchy' (literally interpreted as the law of the father) refers to a system of social structures and practices that subordinate women to men. A closely related term is 'sexism,' which refers to a set of social, economic, political, and cultural beliefs, attitudes, and practices that oppress women (Bishop 1994). Patriarchy and sexism reinforce each other. Together they produce a situation in which women earn less, face greater obstacles to advancement, and are harassed more in the workplace than men; carry out a much greater load of domestic labour and are subject to the 'double shift' more than men; experience domestic and sexual violence more than men; suffer from social, economic, and political inequalities more than men (Thompson 1997; 1998). An extreme form of oppression based on sexism is 'misogyny,' which refers to the hatred, fear, and mistreatment of women by individual men (Bishop 1994).

Sexism is similar to racism in that they are both based on notions of biological determinism and essentialism. Whereas racism involves associating a biological difference (i.e., non-white) with such socially constructed characteristics (differences) as inferior intelligence, fear of working, untrustworthiness, and undependability, sexism involves associating a biological difference (i.e., female) with such socially constructed characteristics (differences) as passivity, emotionality, natural caregiving, irrationality, and weakness. Racism and sexism also comprise essentialist beliefs in that all people of colour are considered to have the above socially constructed characteristics associated with people of colour and all women the above socially constructed characteristics associated with women. And, of course, these negative essentialist characteristics are used by the dominant groups to rationalize the subordination of people of colour and women.

Women, like all oppressed groups, do not constitute a homogeneous group with regard to their oppression. Although all women are oppressed by patriarchy, not all women are oppressed to the same degree or experience oppression in the same way. As noted above, a woman's oppression will be mediated by her class, race, and other social characteristics. In addition to differences that emanate from various combinations of intersecting forms of oppression, women are also differentiated along other lines that affect the level or extent of oppression they experience. For example, women are often ranked by both men and women according to the social status of their husbands or male partners. For the most part, if the social status of a particular woman's male partner is high, she is accorded a higher degree of status, respect, treatment, and privilege than the female partner of a man who does not have high social status. This causes resentment in some women, who often perceive the higher social status as undeserved and the female recipient as a manipulative opportunist. Conversely, the woman who attains high status by her association with a privileged male has more in common with other women (and men) in her social class than with those who do not. Usually, this means that she will have less commitment to changing the system that has facilitated her relatively privileged position. Wineman (1984) identifies another group of women accorded some degree of status by many men and some women in that they are ranked according to conventional standards of beauty or appearance and sexuality. The closer a woman is to these ideals of beauty and sexuality, the more respect, admiration, opportunities, and privileges are available to her. Conversely, the further women are from these beauty standards, the less status they are likely to be accorded (by men and women). Sex objectification is part of sexism and, like social status, is a source of division among women.

Another source of division among women as an oppressed group is the internalization of their oppression on the part of some women. Thus, some women believe that gender equality is not only unattainable but also undesirable. They believe in the traditional family unit (headed by a man), traditional family values (woman is the domestic worker in the family), and biological determinism (because the woman gives birth, she is therefore the natural caregiver). They also subscribe to the idealized notion that a woman will be protected, provided for, and put on a pedestal by her man if she properly looks after him, his home, and his children. Such women resent 'feminists' who criticize this type of arrangement and in turn are resented by many women who believe that such notions and actions of servitude to men only reinforce the subordination of women.

Heterosexism

We are taught that sex and gender are synonymous and that only one of two options is assigned at birth. Socialization into gender roles occurs based on this assignment and includes the belief that male is superior to female and that we are all supposed to be heterosexual. Although gender and sex are often assumed as synonymous, in fact they are not. Gender is the social construct related to the roles, behaviours, and attitudes we expect from people based on their assignment as either male or female, while sex refers to the biological designation of male and female, based primarily on reproductive organs (Sisneros et al. 2008). And although gender identity was once assumed to be a dichotomous choice—masculine or feminine—we now understand gender as a continuum rather than as a dichotomy. A person may identify as male, female, bisexual, transgender, or intersexual (Boston Women's Health Book Collective 1998, cited in Sisneros et al. 2008). The abbreviation GBLT is currently used to refer to the entire gay or non-heterosexual community. Transgender is a label currently in transition. The important point for our focus on oppression here is that there are negative consequences for individuals who exhibit gender behaviour that falls outside that which has traditionally been identified as either masculine or feminine.

Heterosexism is a form of oppression whereby heterosexuality is considered to be the only acceptable and viable life option (Blumenfeld and Raymond 1988). It is considered natural by society, and all other alternatives are considered unnatural. Heterosexism oppresses gay, lesbian, bisexual, and transgender people. Some writers (e.g., Bishop 1994) argue that it also oppresses anyone who exhibits gender behaviour that does not fit the traditional one-man, one-woman monogamous marriage or union with children. 'Homophobia' is an irrational fear or hatred of or discomfort with homosexual people or homosexuality that is often manifest in individual violence or structural discrimination. Unlike most crimes of violence in general, violence prompted by homophobia tends to be perpetrated by strangers rather than by acquaintances. Only recently has homosexuality been removed as a psychiatric disorder from the DSM-III manual (*Diagnostic and Statistical Manual of Mental Disorders*, 3rd edition) in the United States. And until relatively recently, it was illegal in Britain. There continue to be anti-gay campaigns to deny lesbian, gay, bisexual, and transgender (LGBT) persons certain basic rights, such as same-sex pension benefits, and many churches (particularly fundamentalist churches) continue to teach that homosexuality is an abominable sin. And as mentioned in Chapter 2, in the most recent general election (4 November 2008) in the US, California placed a proposition on its ballot aimed at changing the state constitution to restrict the definition of marriage to opposite-sex couples only. The voters of California passed the proposition, thus eliminating the right of same-sex couples to marry.

One of the unique aspects of oppression towards homosexuality is its lack of visibility. Unless one states that one is gay or lesbian or bisexual or transgender, there is usually nothing to indicate that one is. This invisibility is an impediment to organizing as a group, since no one knows how big the group is and members do not know who most other members are. It is also an impediment to receiving support from other homosexual or non-heterosexual persons (Bishop 1994). And as with people of colour and women, divisions within the gay, lesbian, and bisexual community maintain its fragmentation and lack of solidarity and inhibit organizing efforts against heterosexism. Obviously, the term gay, lesbian, bisexual and transgender (GBLT) denotes different categories of persons within the homosexual or non-heterosexual community. Wineman (1984) presents some examples of other divisions—there are people who are 'closeted' and those who are 'out,' along with a range of individuals who are out in some situations and closeted in others. And even among those who are out, there are divisions between those who appear more or less straight and those who flaunt their difference. There are divisions between 'good gays and lesbians' (with relatively conventional lifestyles) and 'bad gays and lesbians' (with so-called outrageous lifestyles). The former often resent the latter because in their eyes, outrageous behaviour such as 'gay pride' parades play into some of the negative stereotypes that the heterosexual community has of homosexual people. Conversely, the 'bad gays and lesbians' resent the 'good gays and lesbians' because the latter do not appreciate or approve of the 'in-your-face' political statements that the outrageous behaviour symbolizes. And, of course, oppression experienced by the GBLT community intersects with other forms and sources of oppression based on class, race, age, ability, and so on. As with other oppressed groups, gay, lesbian, bisexual, and transgender persons may form an oppressed community, but it is a diverse and divided community as well. It is a prominent part of the web of oppression.

Ageism

Thompson (1997) makes the point that age is not just a matter of biological maturation. It is also a social division or a dimension of the social structure wherein power, privilege, and opportunities are allocated to some and powerlessness, social exclusion, lack of respect, and alienation are allocated to others. The basis of such allocation is age, and the two groups affected mainly in a negative way are children and older people, although most of the literature on ageism focuses on the latter group.

Bishop (1994) assigns children to a separate form or category of oppression that she terms 'adultism.' Generally, the term 'ageism' refers to oppression (at all levels) of a group of people solely on the basis of their age.

At one time, older members of many societies were accorded great respect because of their endurance in the face of death and the knowledge, experiences, and wisdom they had accumulated throughout their lives. Even today, there are societies in which the elderly are highly regarded and venerated. In Aboriginal communities in Australia and North America, for example, tribal elders officiate at many community ceremonies and play an active leadership role in most decision-making bodies. For the most part, however, whereas older citizens were once revered for their endurance and wisdom, they are now often associated with degeneracy, death, senility, incontinence, frailty, and madness (Cole 1986). Furthermore, because of their exclusion (voluntary or enforced) from the labour market, many perceive them as no longer making a contribution to the economy. And in a capitalist system in which one's merit or worth is measured primarily not by one's qualities as a person but by the position one occupies in the economy, both the young and the old tend to be devalued because they have no value on the altar of capitalism. The elderly in particular are seen as useless and even a drain on the resources of society. Young people escape these judgments because of their potential for contributing to the economy in the future, but the elderly are often regarded as having outlived their usefulness. Our language often reflects the demeaning way in which society views older people, as evidenced in phrases such as 'over the hill' and 'old fuddy-duddy.' Thompson (1997) outlines a number of other assumptions and stereotypes about elderly people that reflect and reinforce ageism. They are often considered and treated as childlike, ill (including hard of hearing), lonely, asexual, poor, unintelligent (and unaware of current events), and inhuman. This list could be extended to include other assumptions, such as forgetful, meddling, and needy.

As suggested by the above assumptions attached to old age, this group of oppressed people (as with all other oppressed groups) tends to be perceived as homogeneous. Elderly persons, however, are divided along lines of class, gender, race, and other social dimensions. As well, they are divided along lines of age (the young-old—60 to 64, the middle-old—65 to 74, and the old-old—75 and older), wellness (healthy, active, frail, ambulatory), independence (living independently in one's own home, living in a care facility), political involvement, and so on. As with other oppressions, the stereotypes of ageism can be internalized by older people (Marshall 1990), resulting in negative self-images, low morale, lack of confidence, and higher morbidity. It can also lead to older persons avoiding other older persons because they do not want to be associated with or be around a group of senile, incontinent, and morbid old people. Thus, there is a 'we-they' dynamic whereby some members of an oppressed group will dissociate themselves from it on the basis of stereotypes imposed on the group and some older persons will denigrate other older persons by using ageist stereotypes. And as with all other forms of oppression, ageism intersects with all other sources and forms of oppression. Poverty is often associated with old age, as is disability, race, gender, and so on. Most people will experience old age at some point and therefore will experience ageism as well. We should talk openly about ageism and aging issues; otherwise, if they remain hidden, society will continue, unwittingly or not, to believe that ageism is acceptable. We should also be aware of the heterogeneity of older (and younger) citizens and know that there are many competent, articulate, and creative older people who contradict the prevailing stereotype.

Ableism

Everyone is vulnerable to experiencing a disability either directly as a result of injury, illness, or simple aging or indirectly by having a family member, friend, or co-worker experience a disability. Some disabilities are visible, others are not; some are present at birth, others are not; and some strike suddenly, while others progress slowly (Sisneros et al. 2008). Society's views of disability reflect a social and cultural construction whereby persons labelled as disabled are often those who do not conform to the prevailing cultural definition of normality. Many of the problems experienced by persons labelled as mentally or physically disabled arise primarily from an ideology of ableism that stigmatizes them and discriminates against them. This process of labelling results in the disability becoming the person's master status (Marsiglia and Kulis 2009).

Ableism, sometimes referred to as 'disableism' (e.g., Thompson 1997; 1998), is the systematic oppression of a group of people with disabilities. This form of oppression is manifest in the combination of personal prejudices, cultural expressions and values, and social forces that marginalize people with disabilities and portray them in a negative light, thus oppressing them. The disability, which can be either physical or mental (or both), is such that it prevents a person from carrying out particular activities (e.g., walking, caring for oneself, working, learning, participating in community activities). It may be temporary, indefinite, or permanent (Barker 1987). Bishop (1994) refers to people with disabilities as 'physically or mentally challenged persons' and cautions against using the label 'disabled people' because it suggests that 'people with disabilities' (the term preferred by persons oppressed by ableism) are not complete as people.

Traditionally, the attention has been on the medical aspects of disability—treating and compensating for the impairment and attempting to make the disabled person more comfortable. The medical model locates the problem within the person with a disability. It views this person as abnormal with respect to the normal standards of mobility and ability and how the body or mind should work. The body or mind is considered at fault and is treated with medical interventions (Sisneros et al. 2008). This narrow view overlooks disability as a social construction (Black 1995) and as a social division. A whole group of people are separated and systematically excluded from full participation in the mainstream of society because of the existence of a disability. Their barriers to participation are ideological as well as physical or mental (Thompson 1997). The disability itself has been socially constructed as a form of dependency in that disabled persons have been portrayed as helpless, dependent, needy, asexual, and not able to contribute to society. As well, disabled persons suffer the same treatment as elderly people in a capitalist society—if you have no value in the economy, you have no value as a person.

Within recent years, a powerful 'disabled people's movement' has challenged the medicalization and individualization of people with disabilities and the view of them as tragic (pitiable) victims. It has also emphasized a social model of health and promoted the 'rights' of people with disabilities and denounced the view of them as 'charity cases.' The social model locates the problem of disability within the context of the environment, social structures, values, and supports (Sisneros et al. 2008). Because this model recognizes the oppressive nature of negative social views, which stigmatize and stereotype disabled individuals, it is the model most relevant to anti-oppressive social work. Many jurisdictions now have legislation that prevents discrimination on the basis of disability in such areas as employment, housing, and access to public buildings and transportation. However, people with disabilities continue to be oppressed on the personal level (revulsion, discomfort, seeing them as charity cases), cultural level (cruel jokes and stereotypes, omitting them from advertising and popular culture), and structural level (discrimination, exclusion, and inequality).

Although people with different physical and mental difficulties all share the powerful bond of disability, they are still among the most divided and fragmented of all oppressed groups. Not only are there divisions among persons with disabilities based on class, gender, race, and age, which exist within all other oppressed groups, but many different types of disability serve to divide this group of oppressed persons. Persons with mental disabilities face different forms of discrimination from those experienced by persons with physical disabilities do. Those who move with the aid of wheelchairs or those who are deaf face different challenges from those of people who suffer chronic pain or have incurred serious head injuries or are blind. And as with all other sources or forms of oppression, the experience of people who are oppressed by ableism is affected by intersections of other oppressions and/or privileges.

In sum, this section on the heterogeneity of oppression within oppressed groups has provided an overview of six different forms or sources of oppression. From this review, it is clear that heterogeneity is characteristic of each. There are, of course, other forms of oppression (e.g., religion, geographical region, language). However, it is believed that the major forms of oppression with which social work is currently involved are classism, racism, sexism, heterosexism, ageism, and ableism. A danger in reading about different forms of oppression is to assume that any particular oppressed group is united and that every member shares the same experiences and is affected in the same way. The divisions within any oppressed group present an obstacle for members in organizing and mobilizing against their oppression.

Conclusion

In this chapter, I have focused on the concepts of multiple oppression, intersectionality, and intra-group heterogeneity. To date, social work has often treated oppression as though it comprised a number or collection of singular forms or sources of oppression. Some writers have paid lip service to the fact that oppression seldom occurs in a simple, singular form but have not gone much beyond this recognition. As well, there is a tendency to totalize each oppressed group, overlooking the considerable variation and heterogeneity within each oppressed group.

A major purpose of this chapter was to contribute to an understanding of multiple oppression. Wineman's (1984) rudimentary intersectional model of oppression illustrates how the various oppressions within the individual identity interact beyond a simple additive or cumulative notion (such as the single-strand or parallel models). This intersectional model, along with the recognition that intersecting oppressions are both complex and potentially volatile, provides social workers with more informed insights into the complex lived realities of the people with whom they work. A greater understanding of the intersectional nature of oppression is contained in the concept or metaphor of a web, developed by Sisneros et al. (2008). The web model of intersectionality helps us to locate a person along the continuum of various forms of oppression and to see where the various intersections of oppression occur for any individual (including ourselves). However, in spite of these advances in the conceptualization of multiple oppression and its intersections, much more theoretical development is needed in this area. A host of challenging and unresolved conceptual issues remains. Such concepts and dynamics as multiple identities, the fluidity of group membership, contextual variables (e.g., specific sites of political engagement), individual or psychological variables (e.g., self-esteem), status within an oppressed group, and individual variations in experiences of oppression obviously affect relationships of domination and subordination. Although they are part of the phenomenon of multiple and intersecting oppressions, no model shows how they reinforce, complicate, contest, or modify either each other individually or oppression in general. It seems that the best we can do at this point as anti-oppressive social workers is to be aware that oppression is a multiple and intersecting social phenomenon and that these concepts and dynamics are essential parts of how oppression operates (Baines 2000).

This chapter also discussed the incredible diversity (i.e., heterogeneity) that exists within all forms of oppression. Oppression not only occurs between the dominant group and subordinate groups but between and among various subordinate groups as well as within each group. Every so-called identity group contains a hierarchy of privilege that serves to fragment group solidarity and often results in those holding higher status or privilege oppressing others in the group in order to retain their privileged position. The heterogeneity that exists within subordinate groups also adds to the complexity of intersecting oppressions. For example, two black people living in poverty may have different qualitative experiences of oppression if one is much lighter in colour than the other. Again, much more conceptual and empirical work is needed in this area. In the meantime, the material in this chapter should help social workers to resist overly simplistic or reductionist explanations of oppression and to inform their anti-oppressive practice. The latter will be addressed in the next chapter.

Critical Questions for Discussion

1. Can poverty be understood and explained by only considering class? Why or why not? What groups are most susceptible to poverty in Canada? Why?

2. Why do most people consider Canada a classless or a middle-class society? Why do most people answer 'middle class' when asked what their social class is?

3. Using the web of oppression in Figure 7.3, situate yourself in each section of the web according to your current situation. Create a web of yourself by drawing a line to connect your positions across the wedges. Examine the intersections between dimensions of oppression. Now imagine the barriers that are created when one occupies multiple positions far from the centre of the web.

4. Despite many legal advances, violence against women is still a significant social problem. Why do you think this is? Can laws change social behaviour such as violence?

5. How is heterosexism socially constructed, and what is the current construction? What role does the media play in this social construction?

6. Some provinces still have mandatory (age 65) retirement policies even though they also have human rights legislation that says it is unlawful to discriminate on the basis of age. Do you think mandatory retirement is discriminatory? Why or why not?

7. What factors contribute to the social and economic conditions in which many Aboriginal people in Canada live? In what ways does colonization still affect them today?

Further Readings

hooks, bell (1981). *Ain't I a Woman: Black Women and Feminism*. Boston: South End Press. In this classic study, cultural critic bell hooks examines how black women, from the seventeenth century to the present day, were and are oppressed by both white men and black men and by white women. Illustrating her *intersectional* analysis with moving personal accounts in *Ain't I a Woman*, hooks is deeply critical of the racism inherent in the thought of many middle-class white feminists who have failed to address issues of race and class. While acknowledging that the conflict of loyalty to race or sex is still a dilemma, hooks challenges the view that race and gender are two separate phenomena, insisting that the struggles to end racism and sexism are inextricably intertwined.

McMullin, Julie (2004). *Understanding Social Inequality: Intersections of Class, Age, Gender, Ethnicity, and Race in Canada*. Don Mills, ON: Oxford University Press. This book explores the complex issues surrounding social inequality using an intersectional framework developed by the author. Structures of inequality are examined with respect to how they are organized along lines of class, age, gender, race, and ethnicity. These structures show that power, ideology, and the distribution of material, cultural, and social resources are important aspects of inequality.

Sisneros, Jose, et al. (2008). *Critical Multicultural Social Work*. Chicago: Lyceum Books. This book explores multicultural social work from a critical perspective. The text examines oppression and diversity across multiple dimensions, such as race and ethnicity, gender, sex, sexual orientation, and ability/disability. Tools and techniques are provided that enable the reader to recognize their own perspectives and find meaning and importance in what they learn. The history and a basic framework for evaluating issues of diversity are presented, and the authors guide practitioners through enlightened self-reflection to encourage awareness and sensitivity as they work with service users.

Wineman, Steven (1984). *The Politics of Human Services*. Montreal: Black Rose Books. Though written 25 years ago, this book remains one of the best for its identification and treatment of heterogeneity within and among oppressed groups, for its analysis of and model-building efforts with respect to intersecting oppressions, and for using this analysis in forming alliances and coalitions of oppressed groups in their struggle for liberation.

Chapter 8

Anti-Oppressive Social Work Practice at the Personal and Cultural Levels

For the oppressors, 'human beings' refers only to themselves; other people are 'things.'
—Paulo Freire

Introduction

A major aim of this book has been to present oppression as the explanatory cause of most social problems. This view contrasts with that whereby social problems are attributed to some presumed weakness or deficiency on the part of the individual (the conservative view) or to a few limited imperfections of an otherwise equitable and just society (the liberal view). Sometimes students and practitioners (and some instructors) will criticize books such as mine and other social justice–oriented social work books for not having enough practice material and for not presenting a how-to-do-it approach to anti-oppressive practice. I understand the need for wanting a clearer sense of how to carry out anti-oppressive practice or any other progressive form of social work practice. Unfortunately, anti-oppressive practice, which attempts to change the world as we now know it, does not lend itself to a recipe book format or to a how-to-do-it procedural manual. Social problems, social inequality, and oppression are highly complex phenomena that cannot be reduced to the level of carrying out an interview or implementing a family therapy approach or operationalizing a step-by-step treatment plan or following a 12-step program. Dominelli (2002) reminds us that social workers of all political stripes are constantly negotiating within a context of ambiguity and uncertainty. For example, our context comprises not just the immediate practice situation but also the employing organization, the government and its policies, the professional association and its values and practice standards, society and its values and expectations, and so on. As Baines (2007, 29) says,

> Anti-oppressive practices, like other forms of social justice oriented practice, are lenses for viewing the world, ways of asking questions and techniques for reaffirming social justice oriented social workers' commitment to resist, expand resources to the oppressed, redistribute power and resist again in the new spaces and opportunities that open up as a result of that resistance.

We should also remember that by looking for anti-oppressive practice prescriptions and formulae to follow, there is a danger of using social categories in a reductionist way that denies individual differences (Millar 1998/99). It is overly deterministic to assume that oppression has the same effects on all people within a particular social group such as poor people or persons with disabilities or people of colour and so on. Pugh (1997) cautions us against oversimplified anti-oppressive approaches that imply that individual responses to life in a sexist or racist society can be predicted, when in reality all that can be predicted is a range of particular responses across a social group. I agree with Thompson (1997) when he argues that we must go beyond the personal level in order to tackle oppression and discrimination, but I also agree with Millar (1998/99) that we must not move so far beyond the personal level that the complexity of individual lives is obscured. How-to-do-it practice recipes do not help the social worker to engage with complexity and individuality (i.e., the diversity that exists among those who are oppressed) or to conceptualize the connection between individual psychology and structural oppression in a non-deterministic way.

All this is not to say that there is no existing anti-oppressive practice content in the current social work literature. It is hoped that this book will expose the reader to current anti-oppressive social work practice literature, which is currently substantial and growing exponentially. The information and analyses presented in the preceding chapters are, in my view, useful for developing an informed understanding of oppression, which is necessary for carrying out emancipatory or liberatory strategies that confront, resist, challenge, and undermine oppression in all its forms and wherever it exists.

Most writers in the area of anti-oppression (e.g., Bulhan 1985; Gil 1998; Leonard 1997; Moane 1999; Thompson 1998, 2002) agree that anti-oppressive interventions are limited when they focus on only the individual level or the structural level. Bulhan outlines the pitfalls of using either approach to the exclusion of the other. The former, which focuses on the immediate and private problems of individuals, loses sight of their shared victimization and the need for social transformation. 'The result is usually either a minimalist view of change or, worse, a conservative outlook that blames the victim' (Bulhan 1985, 269). The latter, which works towards community and social transformation, overlooks the fact that people are the subjects of history and tends to disengage the very persons on whose behalf the change is ostensibly sought. 'The result is at best an imposition of change from the "top," a paternalistic attitude toward the oppressed and a veiled tyranny in practice' (Bulhan 1985, 269). Both approaches fail to adopt a dialectical perspective whereby interventions at both the individual and community or societal levels are carried out simultaneously, with each informing and influencing the other.

The above caution of not adopting a binary either/or approach to anti-oppressive interventions is a reflection of the 'personal is political' feminist principle or dialectic that has been incorporated into much of contemporary social work theory and practice. It is also a reflection of the need to avoid emphasizing either 'human agency' only or 'social structures' only in anti-oppressive practice and to accept that the two constitute a dialectic.[1] This dialectical view of the individual/agency and the political/structural tends to include 'culture' as a part of the political or structural level. However, as explained previously (especially in Chapters 2 and 4), my approach is to treat 'culture' as separate from (although related to) the political or structural realm. This three-pronged conceptualization of oppression occurring at the personal, cultural, and structural levels is consistent with the conceptual frameworks of such recent writers as Dominelli (1997), Galtung (1990), Sisneros et al. (2008), and Thompson (1997; 1998; 2002).

As argued throughout this book, oppressive conditions, processes, and practices exist at the personal, cultural, and structural levels. Challenges to bringing about change in oppressive situations are created by the psychological and interpersonal diffi-culties associated with oppression, by the mystification and hegemony of the dominant culture, and by the material and political conditions of oppression. An anti-oppressive social work practice is further challenged by the fact that much of the oppression and domination at all three levels is internalized both by oppressor and oppressed groups as well as by the multiple or intersecting nature of oppression and domination.

This chapter offers an overview of anti-oppressive social work practice informed by and based on the conceptualization and analysis of oppression and domination carried out in the previous chapters. Specifically, the chapter considers some perspectives, priorities, and issues involved in anti-oppressive social work practice at the personal and cultural levels. Also included is a section on 'challenging the organization' in terms of any oppressive features that may be part of the culture and expectations of an organization that employs social workers. Anti-oppressive social work practice at the structural level—along with some of the themes, principles, and prerequisites of anti-oppressive social work practice—is presented in the next chapter.

Anti-Oppressive Practice at the Personal Level

Having just made the argument that anti-oppressive social work must avoid non-dialectical approaches in which the social worker would focus on the individual or the cultural or social context to the exclusion of the others, I may appear to be contradicting myself by dividing anti-oppressive social work practice into categorical forms or levels of personal, cultural, and structural practice. I may be creating the impression that these levels are mutually exclusive and that social workers ought to attend to one or another level only. This certainly is not my intention. Anti-oppressive social work practice requires modes of interventions that bridge the separation between existential freedom and socio-political liberty. It is true that much anti-oppressive social work practice will involve activities of social care in which the victims of unemployment, inadequate housing, and lack of opportunities are consoled or partially compensated to make their situation a little more palatable. These activities, however, should be carried out in such a way that links are made: (1) between personal problems and their structural causes; (2) between therapeutic insights and conscious deeds that enable oppressed persons to change the view they might have of themselves as inferior beings; and (3) between the frustration of being denied basic individual rights and the collective action needed to attain these rights. Anti-oppressive work at any level in any area is dialectical work.

The personal level of anti-oppressive social work practice includes intrapsychic and interpersonal processes. Both of these processes involve interaction with other individuals, are interrelated with each other, and involve changes at the personal or individual level. Social work in the intrapsychic area involves counteracting the damaging psychological effects of oppression discussed in Chapter 3 and building personal intrapsychic strengths to take action against oppression. Social work in the interpersonal area involves building relationships with others on a one-to-one or group basis to analyze oppressive conditions, to reclaim group identity, and to change social and psychological patterns associated with oppression. An overview of anti-oppressive social work in each of these two personal areas is presented below.

Intrapsychic Area

Dominelli (2002, 85) asserts that mainstream social workers or 'proponents of the maintenance school of social work have (always) worked with individuals in the hopes of getting them to adopt accepted social norms, and pathologizing them when their endeavours fail.' Anti-oppressive social workers, on the other hand, focus on the specifics of a particular situation in a holistic way and mediate between the personal and structural components. The role of the anti-oppressive worker in a therapeutic setting, according to Dominelli (2002) and White (1993), is to open up discursive spaces in which individuals can develop their own interpretations of their own experiences and to see how dominant discourses operate to suppress their stories.

In Chapter 3, we saw that studies reviewed by Moane (1999) revealed that oppression leads to a loss of personal identity, a sense of inferiority or low self-esteem, fear, powerlessness, suppression of anger, alienation, isolation, and guilt or ambivalence. The main aims of anti-oppressive social work at the intrapsychic level are to counteract the personal intrapsychic damages associated with oppression and to build strengths in the individual for developing solidarity and community with others and for taking action (individual and collective) against oppression. Individual work, group work, or community work may be used separately or in some combination to achieve these aims.

Sometimes a person may require some individual counselling before she or he is emotionally ready to participate in a group. This can take the form of introspective counselling or behavioural therapy or any other type of individual work that will help to stabilize a victim of oppression, relieve some pain and torment, change symptoms and behaviours, and build some strengths. Physical challenges can be used as a starting point for the reconstruction of self (Herman 1992), and spirituality in its broadest sense is recommended by several writers (hooks 1993; Maracle 1996; Starhawk 1987) to aid in undoing the damage caused by oppression. The important point for anti-oppressive practice is that regardless of what individual approach is used, it should not decontextualize human activity or treat it in a desocialized or ahistorical way (Bulhan 1985). Otherwise, personal changes may actually be concessions to the prevailing social order in that the person has been helped to adjust to it rather than change it. The source and situation of oppression must be central in any individual work. As well, individual work is not an end in itself but the means to connecting or reconnecting with other persons similarly oppressed so that they might together reflect on their situation and engage in collective actions to change it.

Identity issues were discussed in Chapter 3 in which it was noted that dominant groups will impose on subordinate groups socially constructed identities that portray members of subordinate groups as different and inferior. These imposed identities, which are then reinforced in the dominant culture through dominant discourses and negative stereotypes and through the media, social institutions, the education system, literature, and so on, are presented as natural and immutable. Effects of such imposed identities on members of subordinate groups can be devastating because there appears to be no escape from them. If the oppressed person does nothing about them and suffers in silence, it reinforces the stereotype and negative image in the minds of the dominant group. If the oppressed person protests an imposed negative identity, he or she can be labelled as a troublemaker or accused of being too sensitive. It is a no-win situation for many oppressed persons. Exploring the identity issues outlined in Chapter 3 with a service user is an important aspect of working with individuals because they are integral to a person's sense of self. Massaquoi (2007) argues that identity is a central component of resistance (to oppression) in that affirming identities gives energy for resistance whereas negative messages about identity can deplete an individual's capacity for resistance. Dominelli (2002, 107) articulates the importance of identity formation work for both the service user and the social worker:

> Identity attributes underpin individuals' understandings of themselves and the world they live in. . . . At the same time, social workers have to develop an awareness of their own identity and sense of who they are, for these affect their sense of the world, their place within it and their relationships with others including professional ones.

There is a need early in the process for building strengths to acknowledge and express the many negative feelings associated with oppression, such as shame, guilt, anger, self-hatred, fear, and frustration. Often, these emotions, especially anger (Daly 1984), are suppressed, causing psychological or physical harm to the one suppressing them, or misdirected (Thompson 1998; Wilson 1993) at family members, loved ones, and others who are similarly oppressed (i.e., horizontal hostility). These feelings are frequently difficult to identify, let alone express, because their causes or sources are mystified through the explanations provided by the dominant group in the form of victim-blaming myths, stereotypes, and ideologies. Feminist writers, including Daly (1984) and Herman (1992), argue that the oppressed person must understand her oppression and be able to name the agents of oppression before repressed or unexpressed feelings can be acknowledged, understood, and expressed. Critical analysis and the development of awareness or consciousness-raising regarding oppression are seen by most writers as key in the process of building strengths (e.g., Dominelli 1997; Freire 1994 [1970]; Gil 1998; Marsiglia and Kulis 2009; Moane 1999; Mullaly 2007; Thompson 1997, 1998; Young 1990). As awareness of injustice and oppression grows, oppressed people are more able to identify the social causes of their oppressed situation and less likely to blame themselves (Longres 1986; Midgely 1982). Moane (1999) found that developing awareness of the structural causes of one's oppression and building strengths reinforce each other. As awareness of injustice and oppression grows, oppressed people are less likely to blame themselves for their oppression and are more able to identify the social causes of their negative emotions and experiences. These insights in turn help them to develop their analyses of their oppression as well as to build confidence and the capacity for seeking social changes.

Although a certain amount of consciousness-raising may occur in one-to-one counselling sessions (e.g., providing the oppressed individual with statistics or factual information on some aspect of his or her oppression, exploring with individuals their life histories or stories), the most effective mode of consciousness-raising occurs in groups of individuals who share the same oppressive situation (Longres and McLeod 1980; Marsiglia and Kulis 2009; Mullaly 2007; Young 1990). However, as suggested above, a common experience of oppressed persons upon joining a group is to feel overwhelmed and lack the confidence to speak out. Many people feel the need for some kind of personal development to build up self-esteem and confidence before participating in a group. Personal development can occur through individual counselling or by taking a personal development course, such as assertiveness training or leadership development. Mulvey (1994, cited in Moane 1999) found that such courses do increase people's confidence and assertiveness. However, she also found that without a social analysis, such courses may reinforce and perpetuate a 'blame the victim' ideology in that they overemphasize human agency by cultivating the belief that problems in living can be solved through personal change only (Kitzinger and Perkins 1993; Mulvey 1994). Thus, although it would seem that personal development is often a necessary first step in an ongoing process of change and empowerment, personal development programs and courses should be framed within a social or critical analysis of oppression and social injustice.

Exploring individual life stories or histories is important for the social worker to get an understanding of the personal meaning of oppression (Millar 1998/99; Milner and

O'Byrne 2002). Social workers should not be hesitant in asking service users about how race or gender or sexual orientation factors are affecting their situation (Milner and O'Byrne 2002). Not only can such stories illuminate how histories of families and other relationships may have acted as conduits of oppression but also how they may have been supportive (Millar 1998/99). Milner and O'Byrne (2002) urge social workers to respectfully ask service users to share their stories of struggle and survival in the face of structural inequality, not only asking about their wounds or their lack of a sense of justice but also about their capacity for self-nurturance and the strengths they received from their membership in a particular identity or community group. To facilitate this exploration, social workers can share similarities and differences with respect to their own experiences with both power and oppression. The focus should remain, however, on the task of restoring or repairing the intrapsychic strengths of the service user. Milner and O'Byrne (2002, 47) present a checklist of questions that the anti-oppressive social worker should ask himself or herself as a way of learning more about the service user's perceptions, experiences, and resulting psychological consequences and as a way of closing the 'difference gap' between worker and service user:

- Has the person been able or invited to tell their story of injustice?
- How can their experiences be validated?
- What awareness do they have of the impact of oppression?
- What beliefs do they have about their capabilities and about the possibility of escape from their plight?
- Do they blame themselves or blame social inequity?
- How can they be empowered to take action?
- With whom could they collaborate—could a support network be mobilized?
- What resources do they have access to, and what other resources could be located?
- What would improve their sense of control over their life?
- How could they be engaged in a change process?
- How could services be more sensitive to their special needs?
- How could their potential and strength be released so that they can challenge unfairness and meet their needs?

Other topics that may be brought into the process of undoing damage and restoring intrapsychic strengths are the importance of creating a sense of self by self-defining one's identity as a response to the definitions (including stereotypes) imposed by the dominant group; reconceptualizing power and self-determination to advance oneself and to limit or destroy the power of others (Miller 1986); 'recovering historical memory' (Martin-Baro 1994) as a means of fostering identity and a sense of culture and community; and endorsing the individual's agency and validating their own knowledge base as a way of ensuring that 'difference' is discussed and not ignored in the interaction between social worker and service user (Dominelli 2002). These liberating processes are discussed below in the context of social work practice in the interpersonal or intra-group area. Although they may be carried out on a one-to-one basis with a social worker, they are part of the larger processes of recovery, normalization, and reconnecting with others and therefore are most effective in a group context (Herman 1992; Longres and McLeod 1980; Mullaly 2007).

Before looking at anti-oppressive social work practice at the interpersonal level, a few words must be said about the potentially oppressive 'social worker–service user' relationship, which, although it is inherent in any kind of social work at any level, is most relevant at the one-to-one intrapsychic level. Bulhan (1985, 271) best states the dilemma of therapeutic intervention: '[F]or how can an intervention liberate the patient from the social oppression when the "therapist-patient" relationship itself is suffused with the inequities, nonreciprocity, elitism, and sado-masochism of the oppressive social order?' Bulhan is referring to the 'culture of professionalism' discussed in Chapter 3, which involves such inequities as the power of the professional and the perceived or felt powerlessness of the oppressed service user, the comfort of the professional's office (often alien to the service user), the professional's values (often foreign to the service user), and the discourse of the professional that differentiates helper from helpee, expert from layperson, and professional from client. Given this power imbalance, Bulhan (1985, 271) asks,

> By what conjurer's tricks could one effect fundamental changes in the personality, relation with others, and social conditions of the oppressed when presumably the 'healing' relation itself is a microcosm of the status quo of oppression? Is it therefore surprising that the oppressed have not come in droves to seek help from mental health professionals and, if a few of them turn to 'therapy' as a last resort, that they soon drop out and return to their old travails?

To avoid reproducing oppressive patterns and relations while working with oppressed persons, three vital themes of anti-oppressive practice must be kept in mind at all times. The first is the assumption that oppressed persons must be the agents of their own change, whether it is individual, cultural, or social change. Moane (1999, 183) emphasizes the importance of this control when she says,

> Change is a process which individuals undergo in their own social context and through their own processes. It is fundamental that this process of change is experienced by individuals as one in which they are in control, rather than as a re-enactment of patterns of domination. . . . Developing agency is itself a central part of the liberation process.

The second theme or principle is to manage power in a way that promotes empowerment (Dominelli 2002). Preston-Shoot (1995, 23) says that at an intrapersonal level, empowerment entails a readiness to scrutinize personal bias, use of power, and the potential to oppress; to explore the implications for, and effect on practice of personal experience of and involvement in sources of inequality. It involves a willingness to question personal assumptions and values, how these might reproduce oppression, and to perceive alternative perspectives.

The third theme or principle that should help in avoiding the reproduction of oppression while attempting to carry out anti-oppressive social work practice is to ensure that one's practice is critically reflective. Thompson (1998) states that reflective practice, which has its roots in the work of Donald Schon (1983; 1987), integrates theory and practice through a process of 'reflection-in-action.' It takes the form of the practitioner engaging in a reflective conversation with the situation and, as Thompson (1998, 204) argues, 'can be used to promote an ethos in which equality issues [including the relationship between the social worker and the service user] are openly and explicitly on the agenda.' Thompson further argues that the reflection must be critical in the sense of not taking existing social arrangements for granted. Otherwise, the reflection becomes another routine, uncritical form of practice that may legitimate existing relations of inequality and oppression. Critical self-reflection is discussed in more detail in the next chapter.

Interpersonal Area

Preston-Shoot (1995) says that anti-oppressive practice at the interpersonal level involves a willingness on the part of the social worker to build upon people's strengths, experiences, and perspectives and to recognize the diversity in experiences of power and inequality and of the interactions of multiple oppressions. 'It entails a willingness to embrace other people's perspectives, and to understand the connections between people's experiences, context, and their behaviour' (1995, 23).

Just as there is a good deal of agreement in the literature that consciousness-raising is a critical element in the process of liberation, there is also widespread agreement that becoming part of a group process with other persons who are similarly oppressed is the most effective way for oppressed persons to (1) develop political awareness, (2) self-define a more genuine identity than the one imposed on them by their oppressors, (3) develop the confidence to 'come out' and assert their more authentic identity, and (4) establish solidarity in order to take action against their oppression (Adam 1978; Bishop 2002; Dominelli 2002; Freire 1994 [1970]; Herman 1992; hooks 1993; Leonard 1984; Mullaly 2007; Pharr 1988; Withorn 1984). However, as mentioned above, some persons will need individual counselling before they are ready for a group experience.

Adam (1978) argues that as members of particular oppressed groups enter into communication with other members, they become acquainted with their identity as defined by their own group. As oppressed persons share their experiences of frustration, unhappiness, anxiety, hurt, and blocked opportunities, they find common patterns of oppression structuring these personal stories. Dominelli (2002) argues that identity issues provide a powerful foundation for individuals to use in the creation of groups or collective organizations. Black people, white women, gay and lesbian persons, and disabled people have all organized around their identities for the purpose of mutual support, social analysis, and taking action to change their situations. Young notes that what were originally experienced as private, personal problems are now seen in terms of their political dimensions. She writes of this consciousness-raising process:

> Aspects of social life that appear as given and natural come into question and appear as social constructions and therefore as changeable. The process by which an oppressed group comes to define and articulate the social conditions of its oppression, and to politicize culture by confronting the cultural imperialism that has denigrated or silenced its specific group experience, is a necessary and crucial step in confronting and reducing oppression [Young 1990, 153–154].

Marsiglia and Kulis (2009) believe strongly that group work with oppressed populations is an integral part of their 'culturally grounded social work' approach. They point out that some of the difficulties that oppressed communities experience in their quest for social, economic, and spiritual development emerge from misunderstandings about their cultural status, social inequality, lack of support systems, and stereotypical media portrayals. These and other factors reinforce a negative master status of who the groups are.

> By employing a mutual aid approach, group work provides an effective counterforce to the devaluation of cultural identities that occurs when cultural minorities are cast as the 'other'. In groups, individuals can deconstruct and challenge stereotypical messages from the majority culture and can become aware of their own internalized oppression. The group helps them normalize their feelings and perceptions [Marsiglia and Kulis 2009, 206].

Marsiglia and Kulis argue that this kind of group work connects individuals with their cultural roots, explores what they have in common with respect to their past, present, and hopes for the future, and maximizes the potential of their narrative life stories. This culturally grounded group experience helps members become aware of their identity in the context of their cultural background and its connection to their experiences of oppression. Dominelli (2002, 112) maintains that identity groups are effective organizations for self-definition and affirmation activities. 'Moreover, by constructing alternative discourses around their identity attributes, oppressed groups have been able to tackle the internalisation of oppressive relations amongst their own members who have accepted the naming of their traits as inferior by the dominant group.' Examples are the redefining of 'black' as a trait to be proud of ('black is beautiful') by the American civil rights and black power movements. Similarly, the 'gay and lesbian pride' movement has developed a discourse around the concept of 'pride' whereby the message is that gay, lesbian, bisexual, and transgender persons should be proud of their sexual orientation and not ashamed of it.

Gay Pride

Very few establishments welcomed openly gay and lesbian persons in North America in the 1950s and 1960s. Those that did were often bars, and police raids on gay bars occurred routinely in the 1960s. The Stonewall Inn, which was located in the Greenwich Village neighbourhood of New York City, catered to the gay community. On 28 June 1969, police raided the Stonewall Inn but quickly lost control of the situation when a few patrons struck back at the officers and attracted a large crowd that was incited to riot. Tensions between the police and gay residents of Greenwich Village erupted into more protests the next night and several nights later. Within weeks, gay Village residents organized into social action groups with the goal of establishing places for gay and lesbian persons to be open about their sexuality without fear of being arrested. Within a few years, gay and lesbian rights organizations were founded across the world. The first gay pride parade marches took place on 28 June 1970 in New York and Los Angeles. Today, gay pride events are held annually throughout the world near the end of June to commemorate the Stonewall Riots—the birth of the modern GLBT pride movement. The word 'pride' is used as an affirmation of one's self and the GLBT community as a whole. The movement has furthered the cause of gay rights by lobbying politicians and increasing visibility with respect to educating the general population about issues that are of concern to the GLBT community. The movement has three main premises: that people should be proud of their sexual orientation and gender identity, that diversity is a gift and should be celebrated, and that sexual orientation and gender identity are inherent and cannot be intentionally altered. It should be noted that on 28 August 1969, soon after the Stonewall riots, Pierre Trudeau, then Canada's justice minister, decriminalized homosexual acts for consenting adults over the age of 21 and uttered his famous statement, 'The state has no place in the bedrooms of the nation.'

Paulo Freire also talks about the importance in the liberation process of oppressed people coming together and engaging in dialogue in order to self-define their identity. Freire calls this process of dialogue and consciousness-raising 'conscientizacao,' or 'conscientization.' It lies behind his pedagogy or political education of oppressed persons. He contends that once oppressed people begin to engage in dialogue, perceptions of themselves, their oppressors, and social conditions often change and they begin to remove the blinkers of their 'banking education' (i.e., the traditional one-way mode of education in which, instead of dialogue, a teacher issues communiqués and makes deposits that a students receives, memorizes, and repeats). Through dialogue, contradictions are discovered, which leads to more dialogue and an exploration of previously unseen possibilities with respect to non-oppressive conditions and actions for liberation. 'It is only when the oppressed find the oppressor out and become involved in the organized struggle for their liberation that they begin to believe in themselves' (Freire 1994 [1970], 47).

One activity that can assist an oppressed group in becoming more aware of all aspects of its oppression and in self-defining its identity is to carry out what liberation theologist Martin-Baro (1994, 30) calls 'the recovery of historical memory.' This activity undermines and challenges the ahistorical propaganda that the situation of oppression is a natural reality and fosters a sense of solidarity and identity among oppressed persons (Moane 1999). Martin-Baro (1994, 218) says of the recovery of historical memory:

> Only insofar as people and groups become aware of their historical roots, especially those events and conditions which have shaped their situation, can they gain the perspective they need to take the measure of their own identity. Knowing who you are means knowing where you came from and on whom you depend. There is no true self-knowledge that is not acknowledgement of one's origins, one's community identity, and one's history.

Lee Maracle (1996, 40), the Aboriginal and feminist activist, also emphasizes the importance of knowing one's history for asserting the reality of oppression and the wish for self-determination:

> Before I can understand what independence is, I must break the chains that imprison me in the present, impede my understanding of the past, and blind me to the future. Without a firm understanding of what our history was before the settlers came to this land, I cannot understand how we are to regain our birthright as caretakers of the land and continue our history into the future.

Developing a sense of history has been an area of considerable activity with a number of oppressed groups, particularly within the women's movement, black liberation movements, decolonization movements, and Aboriginal or First Nations movements for self-government and self-determination. The loss of culture of these groups involved the erasure of subordinate groups from historical writings and records and/or distortions of their role and place in history. This leaves subordinate groups with 'a lack of awareness of their own lives, their contribution to culture and society, and their accomplishments and achievements. A sense of identity and of pride is thus undermined, and the oppressed are deprived of a sense of their own situation as historically constructed and as changing over time' (Moane 1999, 130). Anyone who has been involved in teaching the history of a particular oppressed group to members of that group or in learning one's history as an oppressed person will be aware of the profound changes in consciousness that students experience.

Adam (1978) argues that when members of an oppressed group come together to discuss their oppressive situation, a dialectical movement towards integration occurs whereby group members discover each other and in the process discover themselves. He points out that for this to occur, a certain withdrawal on the part of the subordinate group from an inhospitable social environment controlled by the dominant group is necessary. However, he cautions that this social withdrawal could lead to a ghetto-type situation, which may provide a safe haven from the dominant group on the one hand but is stifling and confining for the oppressed individual on the other. Thompson (1998) also argues that some degree of withdrawal or separation is to be expected, because greater progress can often be made if members of the dominant group are not present or involved in subordinate groups' meetings and planning. He gives as examples some women's groups and some groups of black people who deliberately exclude men and white persons, respectively, from meetings. He echoes Adam's concern with ghettoization, which some women's groups (e.g., radical feminists) and some groups of black persons advocate, stating that separatism can become an end rather than a means to an end. Other writers, such as Peter Leonard, have also noted that 'some' degree of segregation is a necessary element for emancipation and symbolic community identity. Leonard points out that some groups have developed their own social services, which are more relevant than mainstream services to their needs, but they still participate in the wider social services network. Speaking specifically of cultural, racial, and ethnic minority groups, he notes that 'they want or accept the maintenance of difference but without the hierarchy which is rooted in colonialism' (Leonard 1997, 70).

The importance of segregated groups in the liberation process should not be interpreted to mean that social workers should not have any involvement with groups of oppressed persons. The significance of the above discussion for social workers is twofold. First, social workers who have had some prior involvement with some group members should not feel rejected if they are not invited to or are excluded from such groups. Letting members of the group know that you are available to them on an individual or group basis may be all that you can do at this time. Second, knowing the importance of the liberating functions performed by segregated groups, the anti-oppressive social worker should encourage the formation of such groups and support them in every way possible. There will still be plenty of opportunities to work with oppressed persons on a group basis, as evidenced in the discussion that follows.

Groups of or for oppressed persons can have a number of purposes and functions. They can be therapy groups in which the members attempt to acknowledge and express negative emotions, find a voice for self-expression, identify personal strengths, and alter destructive relationship patterns (Moane 1999). They can be consciousness-raising groups in which members engage in social analysis in attempts to relinquish their victim or survivor[2] identity and to develop a sense of commonality against the shared difficulties of oppressive conditions and dynamics. They can be social or political action groups in which members strategize and plan campaigns to take action that will bring about social changes to counteract oppressive conditions, processes, and practices. They can be self-affirming groups in which members re-author dominant discourses in ways that challenge stereotypes as well as the view that it is not possible for oppressed people to change their situation. They can also be used for building confidence by placing affirming role models in the public domain, promoting positive images of the group, and endorsing self-directed courses of action (Dominelli 2002). Groups may focus on emotional or cognitive content. They may be highly structured or informal. They may be long-term or short-term. Membership may be open or closed. Members may share feelings or emphasize tasks. Groups are usually dynamic, change over time, and may shift from one focus or purpose to another. For example, Freire argues that oppressed groups seeking liberation must engage in critical reflection on their common situation of oppression in order to understand it. However, this exercise cannot be only an intellectual process, since action will be required to change the situation of oppression. But such action must also be reflected on. In this way, action will lead to increased awareness, which in turn will lead to more action—'only then will it be a praxis (i.e., reflection on reality and action to change reality)' (Freire 1994 [1970], 47). Given the obvious importance and necessity of the group experience for oppressed individuals, the anti-oppressive social worker must be familiar with group work theory, structures, processes, and dynamics.

Don't Take It Personally

I have been struck by the number of times some of my progressive social work colleagues have expressed hurt or anger or a sense of unfairness or lack of appreciation when they have been rejected or rebuked by members of subordinate groups—especially when they (my colleagues) have actually defended, supported, and fought for the interests of these groups. Such experiences show how difficult anti-oppressive practice really is and how necessary it is to understand the dynamics of liberation, which includes periods of segregation on the part of subordinate groups and the release and expression of suppressed anger when confronting members of the oppressor group (even sympathetic members). I remember the days when early second-wave feminism entered the university sector and how hurtful it was to be treated like some kind of enemy by many of my female colleagues when in my view, I was on their side. I often felt like saying, 'Jeez, how are you going to make any progress or win anything if you treat your allies like this?' I also remember some of my Aboriginal students in the early phases of

Don't Take It Personally (*continued*)

our relationships lumping me in with the colonizer group, including white racists. I often felt like saying, 'Can't you see all the things I've done to give you a voice in this university and the number of times I've taken crap from white people because I've tried to defend your interests?' As well, there have been a good number of times when I have worked with anti-poverty groups and been treated in a hostile manner because I had a 'cushy' job and didn't have to wonder how I was going to feed my family. My initial impulse was to launch into some kind of diatribe about my background not exactly being a privileged one and that they should be happy they had someone like me as an ally. We are all human, which means that we all feel some hurt when something is said to or about us that we believe is unfair. However, to react in the ways suggested above would be counterproductive in working with oppressed groups. Knowing the dynamics of liberation and knowing that members of oppressed groups will often see a member of the dominant group as representative of the whole group should help us to avoid personalizing rejection when we carry out anti-oppressive practice.

Okay, Take It Personally If You Want, but I'm Moving On!

In an interesting article entitled 'A resettlement story of unsettlement: Transformative practices of *taking it personally*' (emphasis added), Martha Kuwee Kumsa in Baines (2007) objected to my advice in the above box that anti-oppressive social workers not take it personally when they are rejected or rebuked by subordinate group members even when the worker has actually defended, supported, and fought for their interests. I think that Martha misunderstood what I was saying. The basis of her objection was that she had been hurt one time by members of a subordinate group with whom she was working (she was a member of the group herself) *for something she did in the group* and she could not help but take this hurt personally. My advice was that workers not take it personally when they are the targets of hostility on the part of members of a subordinate group not for anything they may have done but for who they are—that is, because of the social category to which they belong and over which they have no control.

Martha also said that I could not understand the experiences of someone inside her group because I was an 'outsider' and that an insider's knowledge has more validity than an outsider's. I do not disagree with any

Okay, Take It Personally If You Want (*continued*)

of this, although I think the fact that I (and most other people) have been an 'insider' with respect to an oppressed group means that I can empathize with if not fully understand her experiences. I also think that she has a valid point when she makes the distinction between an outsider and an insider, although the nature of privilege and oppression means that most people have experienced both in their lives. It is not a simple 'we-they' dynamic. In any event, I thought carefully about this issue and have concluded that my advice is sound. I wish to share my reasoning for this conclusion, because at some point criticism and hostility will likely be directed at other anti-oppressive workers who attempt to become allies to oppressed groups.

First, I do not believe that anyone can shield themselves totally or not feel hurt when they are rejected, rebuked, or blamed for being a member of an oppressor group. What I was trying to do was to reduce these feelings so that social workers would not wallow in them, or feel excessive misplaced guilt, or perhaps even abandon their efforts to carry out anti-oppressive social work practice. I was not urging members of privileged groups to become tough, as Martha suggested I was.

Second, how can I take it personally when the persons who reject me and my efforts to be an ally do not know me personally? They only know me as a member of a privileged group, a group that has done them harm, but not everyone in a group is the same or behaves in the same way. I think that the hostility and rejection directed at me is really directed at the social category to which I belong—an accident of birth over which I had no control. Knowing that it is not personal helps me to cope with such rejection or hostility and to carry on with my efforts at anti-oppressive social work.

Third, not only is there a danger of burning out as a result of feeling excessive guilt if I take these things personally, I think it is also a coward's way out because it means that I can avoid the political and moral questions associated with oppression and privilege and not have to do anything about my privilege or the harm that it causes other groups.

Fourth, I agree with Robert Jensen (1999) when he says that guilt is appropriate only when one has wronged another. I have felt guilt for sexist or racist or heterosexist things I have said or done in my life, even when they were carried out unconsciously. But that is because I did something wrong, not because I am an 'outsider' by virtue of the colour of my skin or my sex or my class.

Fifth, focusing on individual feelings of guilt is counterproductive because it makes us look at the issue from a psychological point of view rather than from a political or moral standpoint.

Okay, Take It Personally If You Want (*continued*)

Finally, I will not and should not feel guilty for (or proud of) being a privileged member of society, because I had no control over this situation, just as oppressed persons had no control over whether they were born (for the most part) into various oppressed groups. However, as a privileged member of society, I would feel guilty if I did nothing about my privilege, because even though I may not *perpetrate* acts of oppression, I will still *perpetuate* oppression if I do nothing. I have an obligation to study and understand my privilege and work towards a society from which privilege and oppression have been eliminated. I refuse to let feelings of guilt interfere with carrying out this obligation.

For all these reasons, I will, as suggested by Anne Bishop (2002, 110) 'take responsibility for helping to solve the problems of historical injustice without taking on individual guilt.' So others may take it personally if they feel so inclined, but as for me, I'm moving on!

Thank you, Martha, for providing me with the opportunity to think about this important issue.

Because 'empowerment' is a key concept of anti-oppressive social work practice, I was surprised and puzzled by a claim made in a recent edited Canadian textbook on anti-oppressive social work practice. One of the authors stated that the term empowerment is now used rarely and only very cautiously in social justice–oriented social work, given its remake as an individualistic, entrepreneurial set of feel-good behaviours. I find this claim troubling for a number of reasons. First, it is dead wrong, as any cursory review of recent progressive social work literature from any English-speaking country will attest.[3] Second, it shows a lack of understanding of what the concept of 'discourse' is all about[4] (even though I know this is not true on the part of the author). And third, on a practical level, surely the author is not suggesting that social justice–oriented social workers drop all terms from their vocabulary that right-wing or entrepreneurial groups take up and use in a different sense. What about the term 'human rights,' which is now being used by the West to intervene in developing countries (McLaughlin 2005)? What about the terms 'social justice' and 'fairness' that are used by conservatives to promote social Darwinian solutions to social problems and as a rationalization for eliminating progressive equity and affirmative action policies? Are we to tell our students and others that they should not read classic social justice pieces by such celebrated writers as bell hooks and Paulo Freire just because the term empowerment, which is central to their writings, is used? I think we would have an extremely limited social justice vocabulary and a limited literature base if we were to eliminate all such borrowed or appropriated or 'refashioned' concepts or terms.

In any event, 'empowerment' is a term used by many progressive social workers all over the world today to refer to a process through which oppressed people reduce their alienation and sense of powerlessness and gain greater control over all aspects of their lives and their social environment. There is by now a substantial literature testifying to the empowering effects that the above-mentioned consciousness-raising activities engender among oppressed people (e.g., Adam 1978; Bishop 1994; Butler and Wintram 1991; Freire 1994 [1970]; Herman 1992; hooks 1993; Pharr 1988). By becoming aware of existing oppressive social patterns and non-exploitative and egalitarian alternatives, by self-defining their own identity, by recovering their history, and by establishing solidarity with each other, members of oppressed groups gain a sense of confidence that enables or empowers them to attempt to overcome their situation of oppression.

Anti-oppressive social work practice necessitates a reconceptualization of power[5] and self-determination. Whereas power was traditionally viewed as something that the dominant group possessed and subordinate groups lacked, postmodern thought (see Foucault 1988, for example) has helped us to see that power is not an absolute entity concentrated among a powerful few. This latter view was a tenet of structural Marxists such as Althusser (1969), who rejected human agency as a factor in social theory. Foucault (1988) argued that power is a much broader and complex phenomenon in that it is not an absolute possession of the ruling class but a result of the interactions between individuals, groups, organizations, and institutions. As anti-oppressive social workers, we cannot give power to individuals. They must claim it for themselves. 'Empowerment is the realization of that claim' (Dominelli 2002, 118). However, we can facilitate such claims. Power is ubiquitous to all social relations, a factor that is fluid and open to influence and change. Everyone is able to exercise power, albeit some can exercise more than others, because every decision and every action is an act of power. It is both enabling and confining (Rojek, Peacock, and Collins 1988). It allows one individual or group to dominate others through discursive practices—the powerful ideas and assumptions of particular discourses—but power is also manifest in 'resistance'—the ability of an individual or group to struggle against oppression (Thompson 1998). The notion of resistance provides oppressed people and anti-oppressive social workers with a powerful tool of empowerment for confronting and challenging oppression. Resistance is discussed more fully in the next section of this chapter.

Much has already been said in this chapter about consciousness-raising and its importance to anti-oppressive practice. Elsewhere (Mullaly 2007), I have discussed several elements of progressive social work practice that separate it from conventional practice. Four of these elements—'the personal is political,' normalization, reframing, and dialogical communication—also have relevance for carrying out anti-oppressive social work practice in groups (or at other levels of intervention) and are especially integral to consciousness-raising. A brief and updated overview of each element is presented below. It must be noted that although I present these elements separately, in reality they cannot be separated that easily, for they are all interrelated, functionally intertwined, and mutually reinforcing.

One element in anti-oppressive social work at any level of practice is linking the personal with the political. This is a method of analysis developed and refined by feminists for 'gleaning political insights from an analysis of personal experience—in particular, female experience' (Collins 1986, 215). The 'personal is political' analysis forces the social worker beyond carrying out mere psychosocial manipulations, which in effect pathologize people. This type of analysis has relevance and utility for understanding all forms and sources of oppression in our society. It can be used to better understand the nature and extent of racism in our society and how it contributes to the oppression of visible minority groups. It can be used to better understand the nature of colonialism and how it contributes to the oppression of Aboriginal persons in our society and to the oppression of developing countries by the developed societies. It can be used as well to better understand oppression based on classism, ageism, physical disability, mental disability, heterosexism, and so on. What conventional social workers treat as private problems belonging to isolated individuals, anti-oppressive social workers would treat as public problems belonging to a society characterized by oppression along such lines as classism, sexism, ageism, heterosexism, and racism. The 'personal is political' analysis is a recognition that the social environment is critical in shaping who we are in terms of our personality and intrapsychic formation and what we are in terms of our personal situation (Mullaly and Keating 1991). In every case, the anti-oppressive social worker would link the individual's personal situation to larger social dynamics such as class, race, and gender. For example, the worker would not define a resource-poor person (or let the person define himself or herself) as simply someone living in poverty but instead would define the person as someone who is oppressed by class. The first definition has the potential to blame the person, whereas the second clearly places the blame on social oppression. This type of analysis, of course, puts the onus on the social worker to have some knowledge about classism, sexism, patriarchy, racism, and other forms of oppression. It does not preclude intervention at the individual or family level, for example, but instead of dealing with each level by itself, makes the connection between private troubles and the structural source of these troubles in every case.

A second element that assists the consciousness-raising process is 'normalization.' The purpose of normalization[6] is to dispel any notion that any particular difficulty an oppressed individual may be experiencing is unique and idiosyncratic to that person only when in fact the difficulty is a logical outcome of oppression being experienced by many members of that subordinate group. As discussed in Chapter 6, many oppressed persons will internalize guilt, shame, and blame for their oppressive living conditions because they have accepted the dominant messages that they are responsible for causing the social problems they are experiencing. The anti-oppressive social worker can assist in the normalization process in one of two ways: (1) by giving factual information to the individual or individuals who blame themselves for their oppressed condition (e.g., an unemployed person blaming himself or herself for being unemployed in a context where the unemployment rate is high) or (2) by encouraging members of a subordinate group to share the problems they have experienced and by assisting them to critically analyze their experiences in terms of the larger social dynamic of oppression. The emphasis is not on the uniqueness or individuality of a person's situation but on the sameness and common ground of the oppressed persons. Normalization moves away from the traditional 'personal inadequacy' mindset that ascribes all social problems to personality defects or dysfunctional families or inferior cultures by locating them in their proper social context.

Redefining or reframing is a consciousness-raising activity in which personal troubles are redefined in social or political terms, thus providing an alternative explanation. The troubles may be experienced at the personal level, but they come from a particular social and historical context. Redefining social problems identifies this context. Rose and Black (1985) argue that the traditional 'personalist' definition of social problems has several oppressive effects on persons who use social services. First, it invalidates the service user by validating the larger system. Second, it decontextualizes the service user by separating his or her subjectivity from the materialist context that frames and influences all social life. Third, it shapes people's behaviour to correspond to the given social reality, and the more one deviates from this 'proper and appropriate' behaviour, the more severe is society's treatment. Fourth, it saturates service users with a new language, a language of pathology and deviance that contains such concepts as diagnosis, treatment, symptoms, acting-out behaviour, resistance, and so on. Finally, it forces service users to accept the problem definition imposed on them—in other words, to accept an alien reality. If one were seeking an operational definition of oppression, these five effects of the prevailing definition of problems on service users would be a good starting point. Redefining involves the social worker and oppressed persons in a process of deconstruction and reconstruction. In every instance, self-blaming explanations for problems are challenged, deconstructed, and examined in terms of the oppressed individual's specific situation and reconstructed or redefined in terms of their connection with the larger socioeconomic-political system. Rather than working on personal change and accommodation to society, the task is to engage people as producers and participants in comprehending and acting on their contextual environment.

The recovery of historical memory, the personal is political, normalization, and redefining techniques are some of the means of carrying out consciousness-raising. The medium within which these activities are carried out is dialogue, between the social worker and oppressed persons and among oppressed persons.

Dialogue is the vehicle for uncovering people's subjective reality and opening it to critical reflection.

Dialogue cannot be professional interviewing, application of therapeutic technology, instructions for improved functioning or casual conversation. It is purposive in both process and focus. It directs itself to validation of the oppressed as persons, attempting to demonstrate their capacity to inform you, and it struggles to direct the content towards depiction and analysis of the objective situation. . . . To unveil oppressive reality is to be willing to enter it more fully, to encourage the elaboration of expression, to support the expression of experiences, to initiate the early steps in critical reflection [Rose and Black 1985, 45].

To be able to engage in meaningful dialogue, the anti-oppressive social worker must develop a dialogical relationship with service users—a relationship based on horizontal exchange rather than vertical imposition (Freire 1994 [1970]). A dialogical relationship is one in which all participants in the dialogue are equals, each learning from the other and each teaching the other. Of course, the social worker will have some skills and insights that the service user does not, but the service user has experiences and insights that the worker lacks. The anti-oppressive social worker must make conscious efforts to dispel any myths of expert technical solutions to fundamental political problems. Wisdom, experience, and expertise are accepted and validated 'from below' as well as 'from above' (Ife 1997). The worker may 'problem-pose' but not 'problem-solve,' since the latter activity must be shared by the worker and oppressed individuals or groups. Both work together so that they can ask the questions as well as think about the answers. As a result, both will come to a better understanding of the issue, both will learn, and both will act (Ife 1997). Criticism of conventional social work practice has often centred on its elitist, impersonal, and overly technical approach. As anti-oppressive social workers, we do not want to reproduce the kinds of social relations that have oppressed people in the first place. 'In essence, a dialogical relationship is exchanging, comparing and communicating, rather than indoctrinating, proselytizing and generally issuing a "communiqué"' (Moreau 1979, 89).

One very important component of working with oppressed persons is the *process* of liberation. Most process models of change or development comprise a number of stages or sequential steps that an individual, group, or community passes through. When considering process, however, one must be cautious about using developmental stages to understand human behaviour and social change, because they invite linear and reductionist ways of thinking. Process models of liberation can often be interpreted as going from a situation of oppression through a series of discrete and linear stages that, if each is carried out successfully, will lead to the next stage in the forward path to liberation. Social change and human behaviour do not usually operate in this kind of linear fashion. They are more fluid and complex. A danger in assuming a linear or stages of progress model of change is that the oppressed person or the anti-oppressive social worker may become disillusioned or frustrated because the stages are not occurring as prescribed or expected and give up on the process. Instead of stages of progress towards liberation, Bishop (1994, 83) argues that the liberation process is more like a spiral. She claims that this 'spiral of human liberation' has been well documented and outlines its path:

> It begins with breaking the silence [about one's oppression], ending the shame, and sharing our concerns and feelings. Story-telling leads to analysis where we figure out together what is happening to us and why, and who benefits. Analysis leads to strategy, when we decide what to do about it. Strategy leads to action, together, to change the injustices we suffer. Action leads to another round: reflection, analysis, strategy, action. This is the process of liberation [1994, 83].

Even the notion of the spiral is problematic in that it may suggest to some that progress occurs in an onward and upward direction. However, the spiral concept is an improvement over most developmental models because it does not suggest that social change and changes in human behaviour are linear processes. It accommodates the postmodern insight that people often shift back and forth from one role or identity to another (consistent with the notion of multiple identities) rather than dropping a particular role or identity altogether (e.g., victim role or identity), as is implied in a linear process model. Also, the idea of liberation as a spiral does not suggest that social change will never be blocked or even reversed at various times throughout the liberation process, as do most linear, developmental process models. This is not to say that developmental models are useless. They may provide a general direction for liberation and may alert us to certain shifts in roles or identities that, along with other changes, could occur in the process. A major contribution of postmodern thinking has been making us aware that changes in social conditions and/or human behaviour do not occur in identifiable, discrete, linear stages of progress.

When working with groups of oppressed people and using linear developmental models of change, it is important to keep the above limitations of such models in mind. For example, Sean Ruth (1988) presents a model consisting of three stages that he believes reflect the process of liberation. Although there can be no ideal type or universal model of liberation, Ruth's model appears to follow the general direction of anti-oppression or liberation that writers such as Bishop (1994) and Freire (1994 [1970]) suggest. Although it is beyond this book to outline Ruth's model, it is enough to say that it, and others like it, should be used as a rough guide rather than a definitive map with respect to the process of liberation.

Obviously, much more could be said about anti-oppressive social work practice at the personal level. The intention here is to outline the major components of such practice. It is assumed that social work practitioners and students possess the core conventional micro skills of social work practice, such as relationship-building, active listening, assessment, interviewing, engagement, and so on, that are necessary for any kind of social work practice. As well, much of anti-oppressive social work practice at the cultural and structural levels is related to and overlaps with anti-oppressive practice at the personal level. Anti-oppressive social workers may carry out the bulk of their practice at one level or another, but they will also be involved at the other levels as well. This will become clearer as we move into a discussion of anti-oppressive social work practice at the cultural and structural levels.

Anti-Oppressive Practice at the Cultural Level

In Chapter 4, we examined the concept and some of the makeup of the dominant culture and discussed how the dominant group maintains and reproduces its hegemony. You will recall from that earlier discussion that the dominant culture oppresses subordinate groups through such means as the mass media, the use of stereotypes, and dominant discourses and that professions such as social work sometimes contribute to cultural oppression. Here we consider some anti-oppressive practices that social workers and/or groups of oppressed persons might employ in attempts to undermine cultural imperialism and other oppressive actions and processes at the cultural level. Specifically, we will look at the following: counter or alternative cultures, acts of resistance, confronting stereotypes, language and counter-discourses, using the media, and minimizing the oppressive effects of professionalism.

In Chapter 4, we saw how culture is a major site of domination. However, as Agger (1992; 1998), Hall (1988), Hall et al. (1978), and Leonard (1997) argue, culture can also be a site of resistance to domination. In contrast to the notion of a 'cultural essentialism' whereby the dominant culture is presented as homogeneous and authentic, postmodern critique suggests that culture is always partial, contested, and changing (Leonard 1997). Hobsbawm and Ranger (1993) argue that culture is not static but is continually being socially constructed and is always in a state of flux. Therefore, culture is always open to the development of new practices. Seidman likens culture to a text in that both are made up of words or signs that contain meanings. However, meanings are not free-floating but are attached to social interests, power relations, and material life—'they are created by real living, struggling individuals whose lives are enmeshed in social institutions and unequal social relations' (Seidman 1998, 202). Members of the Birmingham School of Cultural Studies contend that only by relating cultural meanings to social conditions can we understand their ideological role in, for example, promoting or challenging social privilege. Agger (1998, 8) argues that 'culture can be remade, even where it is controlled at the epicenter of global capitalism's global village.' He points out that culture is not simply laid on people from above but is a transaction between producers or distributors of culture and consumers of culture. Consumers participate in the constitution of cultural meanings, and the meanings they make of the cultural messages may be different from what the producers intended. This insight is potentially empowering for consumers (including oppressed persons) of culture.

In *Cultural Studies As Critical Theory*, Agger (1992) presents the notion of 'cultural politics' as an important complement to traditional 'class politics.' He points out that although there may be a single dominant culture, many other cultures often intersect with one another—cultures of class, gender, race, and nation, among others. Culture does not serve to integrate society but is instead a realm of conflict over meanings. Mainstream (dominant) culture tends to ignore cultural meanings and alternatives that fall outside its dominant discourse, practices, and hegemony. Agger calls for a decentring and decanonizing of culture, which he views as a political act that will contribute significantly to the decentring of wealth and power. The decentring of the dominant culture is a fundamental challenge to the dominant order. One major way of achieving this is to engage in cultural conflict and politics by denouncing all forms of cultural oppression, along with supporting, developing, bringing to light, and celebrating alternative cultures that have been suppressed by the dominant culture.

Ethics and Culture (Not All Cultural Practices Are Inherently Good)

A caution that one must exercise when involved in social work with diverse groups and/or different cultures is not to adopt a view of culture and cultural practices as a form of 'anything goes.' It is one thing when a group has cultural practices that fall outside those of mainstream society but are not hurtful to anyone, but it is quite another thing when cultural practices result in physical or emotional injury. Marsiglia and Kulis (2009) remind us that social workers may experience situations in which the cultural norms and practices of a group are in conflict with the profession's code of ethics and/or the law of the land. The question members of subordinate cultural groups might ask is: 'Who has the right to decide which cultural practices are acceptable or unacceptable? Don't all cultural groups have a right to self-determination?'

Marsiglia and Kulis present two examples of culture conflict. The first is the disciplinary norm of spanking and other harsh methods of punishment on the part of an immigrant group that may bring them into contact with child welfare authorities. The second is an instance of oppressive behaviour with cultural roots—female circumcision, which is grounded in notions of ethnic culture and religion held by various African immigrant communities on the one hand and is viewed as genital mutilation in North American and European mainstream society. What is the role of the anti-oppressive social worker, and what are the guidelines (legal and professional) in each situation?

Alternative Cultures

Many groups have politicized culture by using alternative culture as the basis of a social movement. Young (1990) differentiates a libertarian insistence that people be allowed to do their own thing, no matter how unconventional, from cultural politics. Although cultural politics may often celebrate suppressed practices and novel expressions when they arise from and speak for oppressed groups, its critical function allows it to identify the aspects of culture that contribute to domination and to call for their collective transformation. The feminist movement carried out (and continues to carry out, albeit with reduced solidarity and overall commitment) one of the most far-reaching movements of cultural politics. Guided by its 'personal is political' slogan, it reflected on, criticized, and offered alternatives to all aspects of everyday male culture—gender-exclusive language, stereotypical jokes, sexist advertising, literature, dating practices, norms of child-rearing, workplace practices, codes of dress, public policy and the manner it was made, and countless other supposedly trivial and frivolous elements of behaviour. There may be disagreement on the merits of the changes, the way they were brought about, and how much has changed, but there can be no disagreement that the feminist movement has significantly decentred the dominant male culture that existed in the 1950s and 1960s and before.

People of colour have also critiqued aspects of the dominant white culture and promoted their own cultures. African North Americans, in particular, have managed to carry out a cultural revolution by confronting the stereotypes and norms imposed on them by the dominant culture and by exerting their own dress, music, jewellery, speech, politics, hairstyles, foods, literature, and history. Many of these cultural products and expressions, previously suppressed, devalued, and even ridiculed by white society, are now sought out and enjoyed by members of all racial and ethnic groups.

Other subordinate groups who have been defined as the Other, the different, and the deviant have also politicized culture. Groups such as old people, First Nations persons, and disabled individuals have organized and asserted the positive aspects of their specific experiences and culture. Suzanne Pharr (1988, 66), for example, writes about the experience of lesbians surviving in the face of oppression by building community and celebrating lesbian culture:

> Despite the harsh damaging effects of homophobia, we have created a magnificent lesbian culture of books and music and crafts and film and paintings and newspapers and periodicals. We have created social communities in cities, lesbian land communities in rural areas, and retirement communities for older lesbians. With little support except from other lesbians, we have created lesbian counselling centers, support groups for chemically dependent lesbians, coffee houses, lesbian retreats and art festivals and music festivals, healing centers, outdoor clubs, support groups for lesbian survivors of battering, rape and incest, rituals for our passages, and our spirituality support groups for lesbian mothers, lesbians of color, differently abled lesbians, Jewish lesbians. The list goes on and on.

Members of subordinate groups need to experience consciousness-raising in order to develop, promote, and celebrate alternative cultures or countercultures. Group members must, of course, first reclaim their own authentic identity before they can promote the culture associated with it. As Young (1990, 124) says, 'The dissolution of cultural imperialism . . . requires a cultural revolution which also entails a revolution of subjectivity.'

Resistance

Resistance to subordination, exploitation, and alienation has been alluded to throughout this book. For Foucault (1990), resistance is an aspect of relations of power that takes on local forms. Political and economic power tends to be concentrated among the dominant group, particularly among the elite of the dominant group. This type of power may be used to constrain or oppress subordinate group members in various ways, as outlined in previous chapters. Early radical social work tended to focus almost exclusively on the major apparatuses of power and domination—the abstractions of the state, capitalism, mass culture, and even the welfare state—searching for cracks and contradictions from which to mobilize collective resistance. Leonard (1997) argues that we must shift our attention from an exclusive focus on these macro systems and examine the micro processes of power relations. In other words, we must identify the diverse everyday experiences of heterogeneous subjects as they struggle with the relationships among determining social structures, the internalization of dominant discourses, and what remains of their own autonomy. Resistance is also a form of power, which may be manifest in the everyday ways that oppressed groups and individuals struggle against domination. Foucault (1990, 95) asserts that 'where there is power, there is resistance.'

Akua Benjamin (2007, 196) defines resistance from an anti-oppressive perspective as 'all those acts or actions in which an individual or individuals take a stand in opposition to a belief, an idea, an ideology, a climate, a practice or an action that is oppressive and damaging to an individual and social well-being.' She argues that social transformation work means that we must resist and struggle against social injustice in all its manifestations, as well as the unjust social relations that produce them. She also points out the importance of being strategic with respect to acts of resistance and that we should ask ourselves such questions as: Who are our allies? What is to be gained and lost, and can we afford the trade-off? We need critical analysis and critical reflection in building strategies of resistance and transformation at all stages of the process, not just at the beginning. Finally, Benjamin cautions us that resistance involves risk to the social worker, so the best way to carry out acts of resistance is to join with others and use shared analyses, strategies, and tactics.

Resistance can occur on an individual or collective basis, and it can take the form of micro or macro processes. A service user disrupting the order of a social agency by not keeping or being late for appointments may be an example of an individual exercising resistance to the power and control that the agency has over that person. A social worker protesting an oppressive policy of the agency where he or she is employed is an example of resistance at the organizational level (see the section Challenging the

Organization below). A social movement is an example of resistance at the macro level where large-scale change is sought. Everyone has the ability and agency to exercise personal or micro resistance to domination. Its target often views this type of resistance as sabotage, but it is a protest by the individual against exploitative or discriminatory or unfair treatment (i.e., oppressive treatment). An industrial example might help to clarify the matter. In the large automobile manufacturing plants in Detroit in the 1970s, people worked on assembly lines and had to carry out small, routine, mundane, boring, and repetitive tasks. The work provided no job satisfaction and was associated with high absenteeism as well as alcohol and drug abuse. One of many acts of resistance to this situation was that workers would place empty soda pop bottles inside the door panels of expensive cars before the cars rolled off the assembly line. Of course, the bottles would roll around inside the panels, making a terrible noise as soon as the car was driven. This action, labelled 'industrial sabotage' by the automobile manufacturers, was not a planned social action strategy on the part of the workers. It is an example of the micro resistance of everyday life, one that in this case eventually forced the manufacturers to make changes to the assembly line, reducing its mind-numbing and soul-destroying aspects.

One aspect of micro resistance is that it is usually an individual act whereby individuals engaging in it are often unaware that others are doing likewise. If the anti-oppressive social worker becomes aware of behaviour that may be a form of micro resistance, he or she should not write it off as irresponsible behaviour. Rather, it should be explored with the individual and other similarly oppressed individuals to assess its full meaning. It is also incumbent on the anti-oppressive social worker to encourage and promote wider and more organized forms of collective resistance based on alternative ideologies and knowledge claims that confront, challenge, and attempt to change dominant discourses. Thompson (1998, 54) states, 'As power operates primarily through discourse (ideas, assumptions, knowledge, frameworks of understanding), such dominance can be challenged through acts of resistance, through the use of countervailing power to undermine dominant discursive practices.' Pease (1999) argues that for subordinate groups to resist dominant discourses and their places within them, it is helpful if they have alternative discourses available to them. However, even if alternative discourses are not in circulation, it is still possible to resist dominant discourses by working on their internal contradictions (Weedon 1987, cited in Pease 1999) and using them as a basis for developing new discourses.

Alternative Discourses

Dominant discourses contradict and submerge the interests of subordinate groups, as was discussed in Chapter 4. A crucial anti-oppressive practice, then, is to challenge and confront oppressive discourses. Consciousness-raising helps subordinate groups become aware of the oppressive features of dominant discourses. One way of resisting, confronting, and attempting to change dominant discourses is to develop and/ or promote alternative or counter-discourses that in themselves provide powerful critiques of dominant discourses. If, as Peter Leonard (1997) asks, the object of collective resistance is to challenge dominant discourse, against what targets might such resistance be mounted? The simple answer is that resistance should be mounted against any discourse that oppresses, directly or indirectly, any social group of people.

Although more than a discourse, feminism (all schools) is regarded as an alternative discourse that resists and challenges the hegemony of male domination, and it has significantly modified the dominant discourse of patriarchy. Similarly, the dominant discourse of white supremacy has been challenged by black nationalists, black liberation philosophers and theologians, black academics, and black activists. Eurocentric discourses have been challenged by Afrocentricity,[7] Orientalism,[8] and post-colonial discourses. The dominant discourse of heterosexuality has been confronted by the discourses of the gay, lesbian, and bisexual movement. Capitalism, as the dominant economic discourse, has been challenged by a number of alternative economic discourses, including those of different schools of socialism and Marxism. Almost all (if not all) major discourses that are dominant and oppressive have been challenged in varying degrees by alternative or counter-discourses.

Freeloaders

In the face of a backlash against welfare recipients in Australia in the late 1990s by neo-conservative politicians (most of whom were bourgeois white males) and the mainstream media (controlled by bourgeois white males), Anthony O'Donnell (1999, 133) gave a wonderful alternative discourse to both welfare dependency and sexism when he said:

> the fact that many men are unable to cook, wash or iron clothes, or generally carry out household chores makes them dependent on women, and if we are concerned about scroungers, perhaps it is this group of freeloaders to whom we should be directing our attention.

He then went on to make the point that 'interdependency' is an inescapable fact of the human condition and that how we organize this interdependency requires more thought and discussion. It cannot be willed away by neo-conservative tough talk of 'moral rearmament.'

Even discourses within larger discourses have been confronted by alternative discourses. For example, the discourse of 'welfare dependency' that forms part of the larger discourse of welfare and capitalism has been challenged by a discourse of 'interdependency' (Bulhan 1985; Leonard 1997). Traditional discourses of work and the family and the current discourse on the inevitability and economic determinism of global capitalism, all of which are parts of the larger discourse on capitalism and the welfare state, have also been challenged by counter-discourses (Leonard 1997). As noted in Chapter 4, the oppressive aspects of professional or expert discourses have been exposed and confronted by many writers, such as Margolin (1997) and Leonard (1997), and those of social agency discourses have been challenged by many writers as well, including Mullaly (2007), Rose and Black (1985), and Thompson (1998).

In resisting and challenging dominant discourses, it is helpful to have knowledge of more than one discourse and to recognize that meaning is plural (Pease 1999). A major role and task of the anti-oppressive worker is to be knowledgeable about existing alternative discourses and skilled in analyzing and deconstructing oppressive discourses as well as in developing (or assisting with the development of) alternative discourses. An important component of alternative discourse work is confronting stereotypes that form parts of the dominant discourse. It is to this task that I now turn.

Confronting Stereotypes

Every subordinate group has certain stereotypes imposed on it by the dominant group, which function to justify the oppression experienced by subordinate groups. One of the goals of consciousness-raising, as noted above, is to enable members of subordinate groups to self-define their own identity, and for this to occur, stereotypes must be exposed, challenged, and rendered unacceptable. Subordinate groups and those who work with them may confront and attempt to counteract negative stereotypes in various ways.

One approach to challenging and overcoming stereotypes is to develop a positive image among members of subordinate groups. 'Black is beautiful,' a slogan of African-Americans in the 1960s, not only contributed to a cultural revolution among the black population of North America but also unsettled the dominant white body aesthetic, which previously (stereo)typed black bodies as ugly and inferior. Similarly, Afro hairstyles replaced hairstyles requiring various straighteners among black North Americans and were actually adopted by a number of white North Americans. The African-American feminist bell hooks (1993) argues that developing a positive black-centred body image is necessary for black persons to confront the many ways that socialization has instilled self-hatred, alienation from black culture and spirituality, unrealistic standards, negative emotional patterns, and racist stereotypes.

A positive image can be developed through the identification of strong role models among the subordinate population. For example, several years ago, the First Nations people in Canada waged a war against the use of drugs by their children by having prominent and high-profile First Nations adults, such as athletes, artists, politicians, and academics, speak out against drug and alcohol abuse. The women's movement has had many prominent women to draw upon as role models. For example, Geraldine Moane (1999) talks about how the former president of Ireland, Mary Robinson, was a very important source of encouragement and inspiration for women. It was not so much her achievements that made Mary Robinson such a positive role model but her personal integrity and her courage in speaking out for women as a feminist. Can there be any doubt about the positive impact Barack Obama has had (and continues to have) on black people, not just in the US but in North America in general, in Kenya (his father's country of origin) and other parts of Africa, and in other parts of the world with black populations? Fictional persons can also be used as role models to promote a positive image, as evidenced by black feminist writers who frequently cite characters in the writings of Toni Morrison and Alice Walker, characters who often embody strength, compassion, and agency (hooks 1993, cited in Moane 1999).

A sense of history is helpful in highlighting the culture and achievements of the subordinate group. This history in turn helps to break down the inferior stereotypes of the oppressed group. The novel *Roots* (Haley 1977) reflects the history of black North Americans from the time they were enslaved and brought from Africa. The book and the subsequent television series based on it became a source of pride for North American black people because it was a story of resistance to oppression, of the struggle for survival of a people who had suffered immensely under slavery and oppression. (The later controversy over the revelation that Alex Haley had 'invented' significant parts of his panoramic saga rather than basing it entirely on documentary and genealogical research perhaps said more about the need for the dominant white discourse to devalue the book's tremendous impact than it did about the 'authenticity' of the *Roots* saga.) Many oppressed groups such as women, First Nations people, and gay and lesbian persons have drawn pride, support, and inspiration from histories of resistance, from the knowledge that every oppressed group has always resisted its oppression, and from the perseverance and ingenuity that are intrinsic to stories of resistance. However, we should not assume that historical reclaiming or remembering is an easy task for oppressed persons. Homi Bhabha (1994, 63), a post-colonial writer, cautions us against adopting a cavalier attitude towards the process of intense discovery and disorientation that is involved with 're-membering.' Building on Fanon's work of linking the psychological with the political in developing (re-membering) an authentic cultural identity among colonized peoples, he says, 'Re-membering is never a quiet act of introspection or retrospection. It is a painful re-membering, a putting together of the dismembered past to make sense of the trauma of the present.'

Another way of countering negative stereotypes is to develop or draw upon positive or affirmative stereotypes associated with the subordinate group. Leela Gandhi (1998) cites scholarship that argues that anti-colonial nationalist movements regularly draw upon affirmative Orientalist stereotypes to define an authentic cultural identity in opposition to that imposed by Western civilization. For example, the resistance led by the revolutionary Mahatma Gandhi against Britain depended on a cultural image of India as corporate, spiritual, and consensual. Consequently, enthusiastic Indian nationalists responded to pejorative stereotyped images of East Indians as caste-dominated, despotic, and patriarchal with reformist zeal and energy (Fox 1992, cited in Gandhi 1998). The affirmative stereotypes were instrumental in India becoming a utopian alternative to the aggressive capitalism and territorialism of the West, visited by countless scholars, spiritualists, writers, and travellers.

Gandhi and a Very Good Idea

Journalistic legend has it that on one occasion when Mahatma Gandhi was visiting England, he was asked by an earnest young reporter, 'Mr. Gandhi, you have been in England now for several days. What do you think about modern civilization?' In some versions of this story, Gandhi laughed, and in others he became pensive before answering, 'I think it would be a very good idea' (Gandhi 1998, 22).

The First Nations people of North America and Australian Aborigines have also drawn upon and developed affirmative or positive stereotypes that are more in accordance with their authentic identities than those imposed on them by Eurocentric groups. Aboriginal people have developed a positive image of living in harmony with nature and of practising a spirituality that has certain mystical properties. Many white people today are attracted (often to the point of cultural appropriation) to these aspects of Aboriginal culture, viewing them as alternatives or solutions to such problems as environmental devastation, alienation, existential meaninglessness, cynicism towards government and organized religions, individual and corporate greed, and cutthroat competition. Affirmative stereotypes such as these would seem to have the potential to act as a countervailing force to negative stereotypes.

Negative stereotypes also can be confronted by a reversal technique whereby the characteristics that form a negative stereotype of a particular group are turned around and applied to the dominant group. A group of poor people in Vancouver calling itself End Legislated Poverty has used such a technique. Tired of being stereotyped as lazy, dependent, chronically unemployed welfare bums, the group developed a discourse about rich people that included the same negative concepts. In other words, End Legislated Poverty applied the same negative stereotype to wealthy people that they had imposed upon them. Some examples are:

- Wouldn't the wealthy feel better about themselves if they worked for their money rather than inheriting it?
- Wealthy people are too dependent on the tax system. How can we change it to make them more independent?
- Would counselling help break the culture or cycle of wealth?
- Is greed intergenerational? And if so, would closing tax loopholes help break intergenerational wealth?
- Are wealthy people too dependent on wealth?
- If tax loopholes were closed, would the wealthy lose the incentive to work?

Another example of an oppressed group (GLBT) applying the same negative stereo-type to the dominant group that they had imposed on them is contained in the following box.

Heterosexual Questionnaire

Please answer the following questions as honestly as possible.
1. What do you think caused your heterosexuality?
2. When and how did you first decide you were heterosexual?
3. Is it possible that your heterosexuality is just a phase you may grow out of?
4. Is it possible that your heterosexuality stems from a fear of others of the same sex?
5. If you have never slept with a member of your own sex, is it possible that you might be gay if you tried it?
6. If heterosexuality is normal, why are so many mental patients heterosexual?
7. Why do you heterosexual people try to seduce others into your lifestyle?
8. Why do you flaunt your heterosexuality? Can't you just be who you are and keep it quiet?
9. The great majority of child molesters are heterosexual. Do you consider it safe to expose your children to heterosexual teachers?
10. With all the societal support that marriage receives, the divorce rate is spiralling. Why are there so few stable relationships among heterosexual people?
11. Why are heterosexual people so promiscuous?
12. Would you want your children to be heterosexual, knowing the problems they would face, such as heartbreak, disease, and divorce?

Created by Martin Rochlin, PhD, January 1977, and reprinted from *Creating Safe Space for GLBTQ Youth: A Toolkit*, 2005 (Washington: Advocates for Youth).

Young argues that when oppressed groups assert the value and specificity of their own cultures, the dominant culture becomes relative or is 'relativized.' In other words, it becomes more difficult for the dominant group to present its norms, values, and patterns of thinking as neutral and universal. When women, gay and lesbian persons, people of colour, and other oppressed groups assert the validity, positive values, self-development, and traditions of their particular cultures, the dominant culture is forced to see itself as one specific culture (i.e., Anglo, white, straight, Christian, masculine) among many. Young (1990, 166) elaborates on this point: 'By puncturing the universalist claim to unity that expels some groups and turns them into the Other, the assertion of positive group specificity introduces the possibility of understanding the relation between groups as merely difference, instead of exclusion, opposition, or dominance.'

Challenging the Organization

Most social workers work in agencies, whether public or private. Most agencies were established within a conservative or liberal paradigm and therefore tend to reflect such fundamental beliefs and values as: (1) capitalism is not perfect but is the best system there is, and therefore social work should attempt to help people hurt by the system cope with it and fit into it; (2) social agencies should have no political agenda; and (3) workers should accept agency rules and procedures. Challenging the agency's conservative assumptions and its explanations and remedies for social problems is part of the social justice movement in social work, which dates back at least to the 1890s with the establishment of the settlement house movement (Benjamin 2007), although the modern version of progressive social work began around 1975 (Mullaly 2007). Progressive-minded social workers have always challenged the organization, and this challenge has never been easy or risk-free. We owe much to progressive writers and practitioners of earlier times who put their jobs, careers, and reputations on the line because they were committed to social justice. It was they who gave us an analysis of capitalism, an analysis of how social work was an unwitting agent of capitalism, an analysis of how the agency carried out functions of social control, and an early understanding of oppression. It was they who developed strategies and tactics of resistance, along with guidelines and methods for protecting ourselves from reprisals from the agency. Challenging the organization or one's employer has always been risky, difficult, and stressful. Every time period has its challenges, and the present period is no exception, as evidenced by the regressive changes brought about by globalization that are outlined below. These changes have had a negative impact on the workplace such that new analyses and strategies of resistance are needed. At the same time, we should not reject all earlier work in this area, as has been suggested by a couple of authors in a recent book on anti-oppressive practice. Today's workplace may represent a 'new field of struggle,' but we should not cast away the earlier work of a dedicated group of progressive social workers who gave us a tradition of challenging the agency and who developed many of the analyses and understandings of oppression in the agency that we continue to use as the basis for confronting social injustice in our very own workplaces.

The new work conditions and changed goals in the workplace that accompanied globalization have by now been well documented in the literature (see Baines 2004, 2007; Dominelli 2002, 2004; Ferguson 2008; Ife 1997; Mullaly 2007). The 'new managerialism' that lies at the core of these changes is based on a belief that all that is needed to make organizations, including social services organizations, more effective and efficient is a generic set of business and entrepreneurial skills. This philosophy has resulted in:

- the standardization of work practices and skills based on technical (versus professional) considerations;
- standardized assessment forms (e.g., risk assessments) that protect the organization;
- people with no background in social work assuming managerial responsibilities;
- managers with social work backgrounds identifying themselves more as professional managers than as professional social workers and de-emphasizing such social work values as human well-being, equity, and human rights in favour of managerial values of efficiency, effectiveness, and cost containment;
- many social work positions now defined as 'case managers,' with top-down control and authority replacing notions of self-determination, empowerment, and democracy;
- a loss of autonomy with respect to creative, innovative, and empowering social work practice;
- a belief that social problems can be solved by technical means rather than seeing them as moral, political, and structural problems that are not amenable to managerial solutions;
- a dramatic increase in the amount of paperwork required by social workers (compiling statistics, completing computer-based assessments, preparing legal documents, updating case recordings, and so on);
- increased regulation and carrying out a 'best practices' model (i.e., deskilling);
- reduced resources and tighter (more restrictive) laws;
- a flexible labour force (part-time, contract, casual social work positions).

Preston-Shoot (1995) has emphasized the importance of having supervisors or managers with an anti-oppressive orientation with respect to workers having the ability to challenge anything oppressive in the new work setting. Among his conditions for such challenging are: (1) managers who make it safe for workers to challenge policies and behaviour and who endorse anti-oppressive practice principles; (2) those with power specifying the basis or reasons for decisions and empowering others to question both the decisions and the grounds for making them; (3) those with power clarifying what power can and cannot be shared or transferred and why, with opportunities to challenge these decisions; (4) people performing tasks in open and negotiable ways; and (5) people specifying clear and realistic standards for practice.

Based on a study exploring different methods used by feminist practitioners to make anti-oppressive principles 'come alive' in the everyday workings of women's services and feminist agencies, Barnoff and Coleman (2007) present five strategies for carrying out anti-oppressive practice at the direct service level that could apply to any agency: assisting service users to navigate systems; empowerment and capacity-building; educating other service providers; educating service users; and engaging authentically.

The first strategy—assisting service users to navigate systems—is recognition that the various systems (legal, medical, social service, immigration) perpetuate oppression for many people. Activities on the part of the anti-oppressive social worker include facilitating an understanding of choices and providing information about the systems and the means to utilize it, sharing information on how the systems actually work, interacting with those who work in the system and advocating on behalf of service users, and ensuring that service users have as much control as possible over the agenda. The second strategy—promoting empowerment—is a long-term goal that focuses on helping people develop the strength and skills needed to advocate and negotiate systems for themselves. It includes activities such as social analysis of personal situations, role-modelling, encouraging service users to find and use their own voices in their own interests, demonstrating respect for the views of service users, working in a collaborative way with service users, and facilitating meaningful and equitable participation of service users in the services they utilize. The third strategy—educating other service providers—is aimed at the long-term goal of transforming the system by carrying out subtle kinds of education (about the nature of the problem and where the service users are coming from with regard to their experiences and so on) and advocacy each time the anti-oppressive social worker interacts with other service providers. The fourth strategy—educating service users—involves consciousness-raising or critical education (in the Paulo Freire sense) that occurs slowly over time in an informal (dialogical) way. It uses critical questions, deconstructing people's myths about how the world works, analyzing oppressive discourses, and offering rather than imposing alternative ways of understanding for consideration. The fifth strategy—engaging authentically—means creating safe spaces for service users in which the worker is present, fair, warm and welcoming, real, non-judgmental, honest with respect to who he or she is, and open to all service users and demonstrates honest caring and concern for service users.

In *The New Structural Social Work* (2007), I presented a section on challenging agencies that might hold some of the same oppressive thought and ideological structures that are present in the larger society. I think it is worth reproducing here an outline of some ways to challenge or resist oppression in the agency as well as an outline of some ways to protect ourselves from any possible serious reprisals from the agency.

Ways of Challenging or Resisting Oppression in the Agency

- Push for definitions of problems and solutions that are grounded in people's lived realities, and do not blame victims (also ensure that case recordings reflect these realities).
- Every staff meeting or supervisory session is an opportunity to raise questions about traditional assumptions and conventional approaches.

Ways of Challenging or Resisting Oppression (*continued*)

- Circulate articles that contain structural analyses of problems dealt with by your agency.
- Bring in anti-oppressive speakers who have different analyses than the agency does.
- Work through your union or professional association to raise concerns about work requirements that force workers to hurt service users.
- Develop brochures and other forms of information outlining the rights and entitlements of service users, and distribute them routinely.
- As a regular and routine part of your practice, refer all service users to existing alternative groups and organizations (to be discussed in the next chapter).
- Push for more peer and group supervision and decision-making.
- Seek out and network with sympathetic co-workers. Develop collective approaches and support others.
- Confront any behaviour or comments that defame/demean service users or reflect negative stereotypes.
- Have realistic expectations; accept that change takes time but is nonetheless worth pursuing.

In calling for social workers to become 'Organizational Operators' (i.e., someone who seeks to have a positive influence on the organization), Thompson (1998) would add the following to the above list:

- Promote practice that is critically reflective.
- Make the value base of equality and the affirmation of difference open and explicit.

Protecting Ourselves from Reprisals

- Form a caucus or support group of like-minded people and use it for peer support and collective action.
- Know your agency—legislation affecting it, agency policies, formal and informal power relations, points of vulnerability, who can and cannot be trusted—and use this knowledge strategically to promote anti-oppression.

Protecting Ourselves from Reprisals (*continued*)

- Become valuable to the agency by doing your work in a competent manner.
- Avoid adventurism and martyrdom.
- Work through your union or professional association to promote anti-oppression.
- Avoid militant confrontations. Searching questions are usually more effective than accusations or attacks.

Thompson (1998) presents a number of guidelines for 'elegant challenging' by social workers. If challenging the punitive, moralistic, and/or oppressive actions or attitudes of others in the workplace is to be effective, one needs to:

- be tactful and constructive rather than launching a personal attack;
- avoid 'cornering people' and allow them to save face;
- choose an appropriate time and place for the challenge rather than presenting an immediate challenge;
- not be punitive—the aim is to promote equality and anti-oppression, not to create unnecessary tensions and hostilities;
- acknowledge explicitly or implicitly the vulnerability of all of us with respect to oppressive practices;
- undertake the challenge in a spirit of compassion and social justice rather than taking the moral high ground.

Conclusion

This chapter presented an overview of anti-oppressive social work practice at the personal and cultural levels and in the organization. The primary tasks of anti-oppressive social work practice at the individual level are to repair or counteract the intrapsychic damages associated with oppression and to build strengths in the individual for developing solidarity with others in order to take action against their oppression. Critical analysis and consciousness-raising are the major means for carrying out these tasks. Consciousness-raising is also an integral part of anti-oppressive social work at the interpersonal level, as are a number of other liberating practice elements that were presented. Just as culture is a site of oppression, so too can it be a site of challenge and conflict. Promoting alternative cultures, developing strategies of resistance, challenging dominant discourses with alternative discourses, and confronting negative stereotypes are some of the anti-oppressive social work practices at the cultural level. Finally, one of the most contentious aspects of anti-oppressive social work was addressed—how it can be carried out in a mainstream agency without the worker receiving some kind of reprisal, including the loss of his or her job. There are risks involved in challenging a culture of oppression, especially in today's work environment, yet a number of ways exist to minimize risk and protect ourselves. Risk minimization is restricted only by the limits of our creativity and imagination. The greater risk is to do nothing.

Critical Questions for Discussion

1. In this chapter and others, I have sometimes used the phrase 'victims of oppression.' Some social work academics and practitioners object to the use of the word 'victim' because, they claim, it denotes a state of helplessness on the part of the person. In other words, they can do nothing about their situation. I do not see it that way—that because someone is victimized, they therefore have no agency. I think I have been victimized many times in my life, but I do not think it necessarily rendered me helpless. What do you think? Can you recall times when you were victimized? If so, how did it happen? Were you always completely helpless to do anything about your victimization?

2. A structural analysis of social problems usually points to some kind of structural explanation or cause for the problem. What place does 'personal responsibility' or 'agency' play in social problems? Does a structural explanation for a social problem (e.g., child abuse) necessarily mean a person's bad behaviour is excused?

3. One of the insights of postmodernism is that 'power' is not concentrated among a powerful few but is ubiquitous to all social relations. What power might a social assistance recipient have with respect to his or her social worker and the agency? What acts of resistance might be available to the recipient? What power might social work students have relative to their instructors and their school?

4. Where and how do people acquire a sense of social justice or a social conscience? Where did yours come from? When? How did it develop? What was the experience of some of your classmates or colleagues with respect to the development of their social conscience?

5. What are some of the stereotypes and discourses attached to poor people, women, black persons, gay or lesbian people, persons with disabilities, and non-Christians? How would you as an anti-oppressive social worker bring up the subject of stereotypes with a service user, and what might a counter-discourse for each of these groups be?

Further Readings

Allan, June, Bob Pease, and Linda Briskman, eds. (2003). *Critical Social Work: An Introduction to Theories and Practices*. St Leonards, Australia: Allen and Unwin. This book offers a systematic overview of core theories and practice issues in challenging domination and oppression. Using a critical theoretical approach that incorporates postmodern, feminist, structural, and post-colonial perspectives, it explores the link between personal and social change. The causes of people's marginalization are examined in relation to class, race, ethnicity, gender, and other forms of oppression. Case study chapters explore theory and practice issues in working with immigrants, indigenous people, women, men, families, people with psychiatric disabilities, and those experiencing loss and grief.

Gandhi, Leela (1998). *Postcolonial Theory: A Critical Introduction*. St Leonards, Australia: Allen and Unwin. This ground-breaking critical introduction to the burgeoning field of post-colonial studies is an excellent starting point for readers new to the field. It is the first book that maps out the field in terms of its wider philosophical and intellectual context, drawing important connections between post-colonial theory and post-structuralism, Marxism, and feminism. The author assesses the contributions of major post-colonial figures such as Edward Said, Gayatri Spivak, and Homi Bhabha and also points to post-colonialism's relationship with earlier thinkers such as Frantz Fanon and Mahatma Gandhi.

Thompson, Neil (1998). *Promoting Equality: Challenging Discrimination and Oppression in the Human Services*. London: MacMillan. This book provides a theoretical framework for understanding discrimination, oppression, and related issues. It addresses questions relating to power, health, the organizational context of social work, and strategies that can be employed to promote equality in the human services. Written by one of the foremost figures in anti-discriminatory/anti-oppressive social work, the book focuses on the implications for practice.

White, Michael, and David Epston (1990). *Narrative Means to Therapeutic Ends*. New York: W.W. Norton. Although this book was published almost 20 years ago, it is still the first book one should read when learning about narrative counselling. This is the book that started the current focus on narrative therapy. It contains just four chapters, and each explains a significant part of narrative counselling, including the story or narrative and its relationship to knowledge and power, how the process of 'externalizing' the problem works, a storied therapy or how writing letters and making documents for clients can be an effective therapy tool, and making counter-documents. Narrative therapy is an effective form of anti-oppressive social work at the personal level of practice.

Chapter 9

Anti-Oppressive Social Work at the Structural Level and Selected Principles of Anti-Oppressive Social Work

'Sometimes you've gotta put your principles aside and do the right thing.'
—St Louis cab driver to J. Fletcher

Introduction

This chapter looks at anti-oppressive social work practice at the structural level. It focuses on both confronting and changing the social institutions, policies, laws, and economic and political systems that operate in a way that benefits the dominant group at the expense of subordinate groups. As well, the chapter presents several principles of anti-oppressive social work practice that are relevant at all levels of practice and to all social workers who have committed themselves to anti-oppression in both their professional and their personal lives. Finally, I present what I consider one of the most important elements in challenging oppression in any form, in any area, at any level, and with any group or individual—the constructive use of anger.

Anti-Oppressive Practice at the Structural Level

Anti-oppressive social work practice at the structural level attempts to change the institutional arrangements, social processes, and social practices that work together to benefit the dominant group at the expense of subordinate groups. Size, reasonableness, and militancy are not the criteria for structural change. Rather, it is the nature of the change that determines whether or not it is structural—that is, whether or not it contributes to a fundamental change in or transformation of the social or economic or political system. Social reform is not a part of social transformation unless it represents one step in a long-range strategy for more fundamental change. For example, an unemployment insurance scheme may be put in place to assist unemployed workers on a personal level, but it does nothing to eliminate the structural factors that caused the unemployment in the first place. Another example is that a policy of affirmative action may be enacted to assist women or people of colour or persons with a disability in obtaining employment, but the policy does nothing to eliminate sexism, racism, or ableism. Although such measures may ameliorate problems, they also tend to cover over issues of oppression by making a sexist, racist, and ableist society appear to be humane.

I emphasize here that the distinction between structural and cultural is somewhat arbitrary. Rather than a clear boundary between them, there is some degree of overlap. For example, although the discourses on capitalism and the welfare state were mentioned in the previous chapter, obviously they are discourses about structures as well. Thus, they could just as easily have been placed in this chapter. Given the overviews and analyses of social, economic, and political structures presented in Chapter 5, this section focuses on a number of forms, strategies, and processes of anti-oppressive social work aimed at transforming these structures. Specifically, it looks at alternative services and organizations, new social movement theory and coalition-building, critical social policy practice, and revitalization of the political sector.

Alternative Services and Organizations

One way for anti-oppressive social workers to contribute to social transformation is to create, develop, and/or support alternative social service organizations that serve and are operated by members of particular oppressed groups. Just as anti-oppressive workers support and, if appropriate, work with consciousness-raising groups of oppressed people, so too they support and work with alternative or group-specific services and organizations. These alternative services and organizations are usually established because traditional, mainstream social services have been set up by the dominant group and tend to operate in accordance with dominant norms, values, and expectations. In other words, mainstream services and organizations are culturally specific (i.e., to the dominant culture) and sometimes will unintentionally contribute to the oppression of subordinate groups.

> If a cohesive radical movement is to emerge, focus on an alternative human services policy and program could serve an important integrating function. Because the recipients of human services are overwhelmingly poor and/or female and/or people of colour and/or young or old, it is an issue which creates bridges between the 'narrow' interests of pivotal oppressed groups. Because human services implicate economic and political and social issues, radical alternatives could create a 'cutting edge' in efforts to achieve comprehensive change [Wineman 1984, 20].

In other words, alternative services and programs are counter-systems to mainstream social agencies and can be used ultimately to establish 'a base from which larger social changes can be eventually effected' (Moreau 1979, 87).

Alternative services and organizations are founded on different principles, values, and ideals from those of our traditional services and organizations. Attempts are made to institutionalize more egalitarian forms of social relationships by incorporating community control, mutual support, and shared decision-making as key features. Alternative services usually spring from the work of a specific oppressed community or movement, such as people living in poverty; women; First Nations people; gay, lesbian, bisexual, and transgender people; and social service users. Examples of alternative services are welfare rights groups, tenants associations, rape crisis centres, transition homes for battered women and their children, off-reserve Native friendship centres, gay and lesbian associations, groups of former psychiatric patients, Alcoholics Anonymous, and prisoners' societies.

Anti-oppressive social workers understand that alternative services represent attempts by oppressed people to connect the personal with the political and to gain control over their own destiny. Workers may support alternative services in a variety of ways: by becoming involved with them to the extent that they can without endangering their employment in mainstream agencies; by providing material resources, since alternative organizations are usually strapped for funds (e.g., money, stationery, photocopying); by providing inside information from one's own organization (e.g., notice of a pending policy that will negatively affect the alternative organization so that it can prepare to rebut or fight it); by referring users of a mainstream service to an alternative service (e.g., most persons applying for public assistance would benefit from membership within a welfare rights group); and by encouraging the formation of such services or organizations where none exist.

Anti-oppressive social workers must be careful not to romanticize alternative organizations. Anyone who has ever been associated with such an organization knows how difficult it is to work collectively and co-operatively and to share all decision-making when we in the West have been socialized into working and living in social institutions in which hierarchy, specialization, and an over-reliance on rules prevail. Withorn (1984) cautions us that old habits die hard, our expectations for alternative services are often too grand, and we may not always be clear on what an anti-capitalist, anti-racist, feminist practice is. In addition, Carniol (2000) warns workers who have developed a critical awareness and are involved with alternative services against becoming arrogant and self-righteous and forgetting the importance of listening to and learning from the very groups we see as most oppressed. Most writers on the subject of alternative services point out the problem of funding these services because of a strong push towards co-optation on the part of establishment funding agencies such as United Way and government departments.

Peter Leonard views alternative organizations as a prefigurative form of postmodern organization. He asserts that an alternative service is a minority, unstable, and often transitory form of organization but one that has continued to survive as a vehicle for identity politics. It engages in a 'struggle to achieve, for specific populations of the Other—women, cultural and racial minorities, gays and lesbians, people living in

Whose Ethics?

I once worked with a welfare and tenants rights group (an alternative organization) that operated in the neighbourhood in which I grew up. I had known most of the members of this group all my life. Although most lived on the edge of the law, they were deeply concerned about the living conditions in the neighbourhood and were able to employ their considerable 'street smarts' in using the organization to obtain services and benefits for neighbourhood residents and to defend their rights. Some of the tactics and strategies, although ingenious and effective, will never be found in standard community organization textbooks (unfortunately). I remember one occasion when the executive of the organization was to present a brief on housing to city council (this neighbourhood had some of the worst slum housing in Canada—dirt floors, holes in roofs, burst water pipes in the winter, no lights in dark stairwells, rats as big cats, and so on). It was not so much the brief that the executive was counting on but the fact that the stationery room at city hall was located around the corner from the council chambers. When the group went into the council chambers to present their brief, a few members stayed back. One man, whom I will call Big John (he was about 6' 6" tall) and who always wore a full-length coat with many pockets sewn inside it (you can guess the reason why), went into the stationery room while two others kept guard outside. Big John took a stack of stationery (and maybe a few supplies) with the city letterhead (Office of the Mayor) on it and stuffed everything he took inside the pockets of his long coat. After the council meeting, the group went back to its neighbourhood office and used the stationery with the city letterhead to type letters to slum landlords who owned many of the buildings in the neighbourhood. The content of the letters was to the effect that the landlords had 30 days to fix up their buildings and if they didn't, they would be prosecuted to the full extent of the law. Before the scam was discovered, the group estimated that about 30 houses were repaired and that approximately 100 families had close to adequate housing for the first time in a long, long while. I remember one of my bourgeois colleagues asking me whether I thought the tactic was ethical. My initial reaction was to suggest that the person pose that question to the families who lived in the firetraps. However, my response was to ask the person: Would it have been ethical not to do it?

poverty—justice, equality and welfare' (Leonard 1997, 111). However, Leonard points to an inherent political problem with alternative organizations. Although their aim is usually to challenge the state and its dominant discourses to recognize and respond to difference, they themselves tend to be relatively homogeneous. Members tend to share a common set of beliefs and experiences on the basis of a shared culture, race, gender, or other social characteristic. Although these organizations may be committed to the value of diversity, their membership is often homogeneous. The political problem is how such organizations can form long-term alliances with other organizations and build solidarity that transcends difference. I attempt to answer this question below.

Situational Ethics (or 'Sometimes You've Gotta Put Your Principles Aside and Do the Right Thing')

I have told the story of Big John in the box above many times to show that situations are not always as simple as people might at first think. That is, actions are not always right or wrong; it depends, in my view, on the situation. I remember telling this story to a social work class several years ago when I was giving a guest lecture. One student, who I later learned was a 'man of the cloth' (i.e., an ordained minister) became irate and yelled at me, 'What you did and what you are doing is terrible. You are condoning theft, impersonation of an elected official, deception, and God knows what else.' I tried to engage him in a discussion and asked, 'Are rules and principles always the same thing as doing what is right? Are you arguing that rules and principles are more important than people?' At this point, he got up from his seat, shook his head, glared at me, and left the room. This, of course, was not the first time that someone (usually a mainstream, politically conservative person with many privileges) rose and left during one of my lectures, so I was able to continue and have a discussion with the rest of the class about 'situational ethics.' The following is a brief explanation of situational ethics, taken mainly from Titus, Smith, and Nolan (1994) and Fletcher (1966).

Although situational ethics is not new, it became a topic of interest among many philosophers and theologians in the 1960s and especially after the 1966 publication of Joseph Fletcher's controversial book *Situation Ethics: The New Morality*. It was Joseph Fletcher who quoted a St Louis cab driver, 'Sometimes you've gotta put your principles aside and do the right thing.' Proponents of situational ethics view it as a middle ground between two extreme approaches: legalism or formalism, whereby one is to go by the book and follow the letter of the law (e.g., the minister above), and antinomian relativism, in which there are no absolutes or rules at all (e.g., some nihilistic or 'anything goes' forms of postmodernism—what Geertz calls 'witless relativism'). The Canadian Association of Social Work's 2005 Code of Ethics is an example of legalism or formalism decreeing that one should not break any of its 'professional' standards of conduct. Some ethical theories suggest that legalistic rules or principles must never be broken. Critics of this position argue that it is wrong because it makes rules more important than people. Some antinomians reject rules entirely. Critics of their position argue that it would lead to complete chaos and give people no guidance on choosing between two alternative courses of action. In contrast, the situationist respects laws and may often follow them but is free to make the right choice according to the situation.

Situational ethics does have an absolute norm or standard, but it is to be applied in a non-legalistic and flexible manner in accordance with the situation. The goal of situational ethics is to apply this 'absolute' to the extent possible in a particular situation rather than applying a law that is intended for different circumstances. What is this norm or absolute that forms the basis of situational ethics? For most situationists, it is love or a concern for the best interests of others. Christians would call this 'agape love.' Buddhists would call it 'karuna' or compassion. 'This is not only the desire to ease the pain of another person, but the ability to do so' (Hanh 2004, 3).[1] We act out of love or compassion for others, trying to do our best to serve their interests rather than acting out of concern for some abstract rule (e.g., thou shalt not steal). A lie is not intrinsically wrong; it is only wrong if it harms people but may sometimes be right. If love means stealing food to feed the poor or stealing city hall stationery to obtain better housing for the poor, you steal. Love and justice are the same. There can be no love without justice. Consider any example of an injustice—a child living in poverty, a person arrested without charges, oppressed persons experiencing social terrorism or structural violence, the oppression of persons because of the social group of which they are members. These are all examples of a lack of love. It is important to understand, however, that when we think we are acting in the best interests of others, our actions should be motivated by compassion and empathy, not by sympathy or pity.

Clearly, situational ethics has much relevance for social work, especially for anti-oppressive social work that has social justice as its focus. In the box above, the community group was acting out of love for persons living in poverty in the neighbourhood where I grew up. The clergyperson in the social work class where I shared this story may condemn me to eternal damnation, but I and my mates acted out of love and concern for the people living in horrible conditions of poverty. Our professional association would probably condemn me as well for not following its rules or principles (Canadian Association of Social Workers 2005)—that is, for not acting in a *professional* manner. Frankly, I was and am more concerned for the people in whose interests we acted than I was or am about some conservative code of ethics that only pays lip service to social justice and from which most of the progressive elements contained in the 1994 version were removed (see Mullaly 2006; 2007 for a critique of the 2005 code). I would like to see situational ethics become part of the social work curriculum, keeping in mind that most situationists do respect and follow laws and rules and are informed by tradition. However, I believe that anti-oppressive social workers should be free to make the right choice according to the situation and have an ethical theory for guidance. Ironically enough, the only program I am aware of that has situational ethics in its curriculum is the police course at Charles Sturt University in Wagga Wagga, New South Wales, Australia.

New Social Movement Theory and Coalition-Building

Social movements before the onset of global capitalism tended to be initiated by the working class to counter the worst excesses of industrial capitalism. Unions were organized around class issues and promoted social democracy as the countervailing ideology to capitalism. Both unions and social democracy played a crucial role in the development of the Keynesian welfare state. Leaders of these working-class movements tended to be disaffected bourgeois intellectuals (Leonard 1997). The major political goal was to gain state power, which would then be used in the interests of subordinate populations.

Fisher and Kling (1994) have identified two inherent weaknesses of these early social movements involved in resisting capitalism. First, those in power within the movements developed an increasingly parochial and self-serving agenda as prosperity weakened identification with the working class. Second, these movements may have achieved power as the voice of disadvantaged workers, but they also silenced the voices of women, minorities, and young people just entering the workforce. As well, the global economy without national regulation and control has undermined the old-style social movements. New social movements concerned with such issues as gender, race, sexuality, the environment, and human rights have replaced the old class- and workplace-based movements as forms of collective resistance to developments in late (i.e., global) capitalism (Fisher and Karger 1997; Leonard 1997).

Five characteristics differentiate new from old social movements (Fisher and Karger 1997). First, they are organized around geography or communities of interest and much less often at the workplace. Second, they are organized around cultural identities, such as people of colour, gay men, lesbian women, students, and ecologists, so that labour becomes one constituency among many. Third, the predominant ideology is that of a neo-populist view of democracy that rejects hierarchy, communism, or nationalism. Fourth, the struggle over culture and social identity plays a greater role in community movements than it did in the work-based movements of the past. Fifth, new social movement strategies focus on empowerment and community autonomy, thus seeking independence from the state rather than state power. 'Identity, community and culture become the contexts through which people come to construct and understand political life' (Fisher and Kling 1994, 9). Most important, the new social movements give voice to those who were previously silenced in the old social movements.

As noted earlier, a political problem arises from the formation of multiple identity groups and their associated social movements. How do they form alliances and build solidarity that transcends (rather than subjugates) their differences? An important part of social transformation work is to develop and/or participate in social movements. However, social movements usually require alliances or coalitions of different groups, especially if large-scale fundamental social change is the goal. A major obstacle to building coalitions is that many groups with potentially shared political interests will focus solely on their respective single issues. This tendency has some obvious problems, which Biklen (1983) delineates in his discussion of self-help groups: (1) social issues are defined in a narrow parochial fashion; (2) single-issue groups often fail to make alliances with other groups whose interests they share because there is no awareness of the common causes of the oppression that each group experiences; (3) when single-issue groups focus on single issues, they may even compete with each other for resources, attention, acceptance, and political dominance; and (4) even when a single-issue group effects change in a particular area, it is not likely to bring about broad social change.

Wineman (1984, 159) contends that the biggest obstacle to coalition-building is the ability of the current socio-economic-political system 'to create and sustain deep divisions among oppressed people.' This segmentation of oppression has historically been manifest in perceived conflicts of interest running along lines of class, gender, race, age, sexual orientation, and so on. With this segmentation, each group is prone to analyzing society along parochial lines whereby a single but different basic source of oppression is identified by each group. For example, conventional Marxist analysis places economic organization and class oppression as the fundamental societal problem; black persons, Aboriginal people, and other people of colour may identify racism as the fundamental source of oppression; women's organizations may identify patriarchy as the fundamental source of oppression.

As Wineman points out, the problem with each oppressed group identifying a single source of oppression is 'that it at once fails to create a basis for unity which respects the dignity and felt experience of all the oppressed . . . who are supposed to become unified, and it fails to generate a practical strategy . . . [to] challenge all forms of oppression' (1984, 163). Without unity, a competition emerges among oppressed groups for resources and attention. And in any competition, there are winners and losers. Overcoming the imposed divisiveness among oppressed groups and other barriers to coalition-building requires a number of actions and strategies. Four such actions and/or strategies originally developed by Wineman are presented below.

First, an essential element of successful coalition-building is to create a 'mutual expression of solidarity' (Wineman 1984, 182). This does not mean that one oppressed group must submerge its perceived interests in the name of unity. Rather, members of groups oppressed in one way will identify with members of groups who are oppressed in other ways, regardless of the severity (but not pretending that all oppressions are equally severe). This kind of mutual identification is necessary to overcoming competing claims regarding who is more oppressed and to bringing about the unity required for successful creation of a broader-based movement.

Second, it is important to understand that mutual identification of one another's oppression, by itself, may only lead to sympathetic understanding unless it is recognized that all forms of oppression are related. 'Different oppressions intersect at innumerable points in everyday life and are mutually reinforcing, creating a total system of oppression in which one [category of oppression] . . . cannot be addressed in isolation from all the others' (Wineman 1984, 169). It may be true that sexism is at the base of gender inequality, that racism is at the base of racial inequality, and that classism is at the base of economic inequality, but it is also true that inequality is a value and an established practice in our present society. It makes no political sense for workers to demand economic equality but ignore gender inequality as someone else's problem or for women to demand gender equality but ignore racial inequality. Although each oppressed group may fight oppression on its own front, the recognition that we live in a society that requires inequality for its very survival will help to cultivate coalitions among groups by providing them with a common goal— the transformation of our present society based on inequality to one based on true equality, not just equal opportunity.

Third, related to a goal of social transformation is a shared political analysis as a prerequisite for coalition-building. Whatever the original causes of various forms of oppression, the fact is that they have become culturally ingrained into our society and have themselves become mutually reinforcing. Coalition-building for purposes of broad structural change becomes more crucial but more realistic when oppressed people understand that the same political and economic elite that allows the devastation of our environment for profits is also responsible for the immoral and gross inequalities of living conditions between rich and poor; that the same political and economic elite that promotes imperialist policies abroad for economic gain is also responsible for policies at home that discriminate against the poor, women, people of colour, gay and lesbian persons, and so on; and that the same political and economic elite that promotes militarism for political and economic domination is also responsible for consumerism whereby people measure their own and others' worth and social standing in terms of what they own. This kind of awareness makes it imperative for anti-oppressive social workers to join with the women's movement, the peace movement, the environmental movement, the human rights movement, and any other movement seeking a transformation of society in order to end oppression of any kind.

Fourth, an important dynamic of oppression that should facilitate coalition-building is that 'no category of oppression, however distinct, creates an irreducible group which is only oppressed in one way' (Wineman 1984, 167). Chapter 7 asserted that oppression does not occur in a single-strand fashion; rather, oppression is a multiple social phenomenon in which various forms of oppression intersect each other (see Figure 7.2). Racism does affect people of colour, but people of colour include the working class, women, gays and lesbians, the young and old, and the disabled. In turn, classism affects the working class, but the working class consists of women, people of colour, gay and lesbian people, young and old persons, and disabled persons. Most oppressed people are multiply oppressed. This dynamic should help oppressed groups overcome any tendency towards single-constituency movements and assist in developing within a subordinate group what Wineman calls 'a flowering of internal caucuses based on sex, race, class, sexual orientation, age, disability, and various combinations of these characteristics' (1984, 220). An internal caucus is a recognition of the fact that people bring their gender, race, class, sexual orientation, and other characteristics with them into various struggles. A caucus of women within an anti-poverty group's struggle against economic exploitation becomes a link between women's organizations and poor people's organizations. An Aboriginal women's caucus within an anti-poverty group becomes a link between First Nations, women's, and anti-poverty organizations. These internal caucuses not only manifest overlapping oppressions among single-constituency organizations but become the points of contact between various oppressed organizations and spearhead common goals and joint actions.

Social work could develop internal caucuses within its own professional associations or union branches. There are members of all subordinate groups within social work. A caucus of gay, lesbian, and bisexual social workers could be established within a professional association or union of social workers, along with caucuses of social workers of colour, social workers with disabilities, unemployed social workers, older social workers, female social workers, resource-poor (currently or in the past) social workers, those of non-English-speaking background, and so on. These internal caucuses would serve two functions: (1) to keep the membership of the social work union or association sensitive to and informed about issues of oppression from their own colleagues and (2) to communicate and interact with various outside organizations and groups of subordinate persons, which effectively ensures that social work is linked to the network of oppressed groups.

Critical Social Policy Practice

David Gil (1998) outlines from an anti-oppressive perspective a number of limitations of conventional social policy analysis, development, and advocacy. First, conventional policy practice tends to focus on single issues such as homelessness, hunger, domestic violence, and crime. This approach is based on the mistaken assumption that these single issues are separate problems rather than different symptoms of underlying common causes (i.e., domination, exploitation, oppression, and injustice), but unless these causes are addressed, the problems are not likely to be overcome. Second, major aspects of the prevailing cultural and institutional realities tend to be treated as fixed realities or constants rather than as dynamic, contested, and changing variables. Thus, conventional social policy tends to maintain the status quo. Third, conventional policy frequently lacks causal or explanatory theories for the problems targeted for intervention, which results in policies being formulated on the basis of symptoms rather than causes (e.g., build more jails and hire more police to deal with crime). And fourth, policies are often formulated and pursued on the basis of their political feasibility, even when the policy practitioners know that these policies are not likely to deal effectively with the targeted problems.

Gil (1998; 1992) outlines an alternative approach to social policy analysis, development, and advocacy, which seems to be more in accordance with an anti-oppressive approach. He bases his approach on a number of assumptions that are different from those underpinning conventional social policy. Gil argues that radical or anti-oppressive social policy must use a holistic approach that views social problems as interacting and related symptoms of a larger system characterized by oppression and that real changes will require transformations of entire policy systems rather than marginal adjustments to specific policies. He also contends that anti-oppressive social policy must understand that the institutional and cultural contexts of human societies are the transient results of interactions among people throughout history rather than a consequence of fixed or unchangeable situations. This means that these transient conditions are subject to change by the interactions of people living now and in the future. The conceptual foundation of Gil's theory of social policy lies in 'the essential operating and outcome variables of social life and of policy formulation.'

What Gil means by operating and outcome variables of social life are 'resources, work, rights, governance, and reproduction; and the circumstances and power of people and social classes, the quality of their relations, and the basic overall quality of life. The ability of people to meet their basic needs depends always on the way these variables are shaped by their societies' (1998, 120). Gil believes that the attention given to these operating and outcome variables will give social policy a radical or anti-oppressive edge. The implications of any policy for the structure of society need to be discerned in terms of expected and actual changes to these operating and outcome variables of social life—that is, changes in the relative circumstances and power of individuals and social groups and in the relations among them.

The Revitalization of Political Life

In the first edition of *Structural Social Work* (1993), I called for social work to become involved in electoral politics, and I repeated this call in the 1997 edition and in the 2007 edition. I took to task all social workers who perceived involvement in party politics as either a personal (not a professional) choice or as unprofessional and proposed that the proper role of social work with respect to politics was to lobby governments for particular social policies. I argued then that social work was not politically neutral and that if it removed itself from the political arena as a force for change, it was in effect supporting the status quo. In view of the fact that governments ultimately decide on the nature, shape, size, and quality of social programs, it hardly makes sense for social work not to involve itself in attempting to elect the political party most sympathetic to progressive social policy and social change. If political decisions determine the fate of the welfare state and, in a major way, the nature of social relationships, anti-oppressive social workers must involve themselves in the political arena. They must align themselves with oppressed groups and other groups and organizations that share similar emancipatory goals. This includes supporting political parties committed to social, economic, and political justice for all and not just for a privileged minority. It makes no sense for anti-oppressive social workers not to resist bourgeois political parties or, worse yet, to support them. To support them would be similar to supporting an arsonist's bid for the job of fire chief.

The above call for involvement in electoral politics reflects one of the strategies of the old social movements mentioned above—to win state power and to use that power to transform society. The limitations of the old social movements have already been presented in terms of silencing the voices of many of the subordinate groups that were part of them (e.g., women, people of colour). As well, postmodernists and others have expressed a legitimate concern with any proposal that the state provide the leadership, structure, and resources to meet the common needs of people. The modern nation-state, which was originally established as the collective expression of the ideals of universal reason and order, resulted in structures of domination, control, exclusion, homogenization, and discipline (Leonard 1997).

Given these criticisms of old social movements and any attempt to gain state power, why would I suggest this strategy? It is because I agree with several contemporary writers (e.g., Fisher and Karger 1997; Fisher and Kling 1994; Leonard 1997) who have argued that at some point we must turn our attention to the state and attempt to re-legitimize it. Contrary to neo-conservative dogma, the demands of the global economy require more rather than less government involvement in social, economic, and human affairs. The resources, structure, and legislation needed to ensure that the common needs are met can only be provided, at this point in our history, by the state. Despite its relative weakening in the face of global capitalism, no other institution has the capacity or the resources necessary to rebuild our neglected social and public infrastructure. The promised benefits of a global economy have not been delivered. 'Without a legitimate public sector there are no public citizens, only private consumers' (Fisher and Karger 1997, 177). Government policies of privatization have undermined government legitimacy and responsibility, which has resulted in fewer public services and loss of access to a potentially accountable and responsible public sector.

If the issue of state power is revitalized, two questions must be addressed: (1) who would be involved in attempting to win state power as part of the collective resistance to the developments of global capitalism that adversely affect the wellbeing of large numbers of people? and (2) would the winning of state power by a progressive political party (supported by oppressed groups) necessarily be a step towards the emancipation of these groups? With respect to the first question, it would seem that the old social movements based on the identities of class, trade unions, and the ideals of socialism have lost the will and resources to mount an effective resistance to the New Right and global capitalism (Leonard 1997). Are the new social movements in any better position to mount this resistance? Peter Leonard points out a number of political limitations of new social movements that would interfere with a project of resistance. First, they tend to focus on the different, the local community, and the specific need of a particular social group rather than on some universal claim to rectify large-scale injustices. Second, given the focus on diversity, group identity, and the specific needs of particular groups, there is little opportunity to establish solidarity among the new social movements. Third, because they tend to be community-based and because the workplace can rarely be thought of as a community, the new social movements lack the traditional trade-union movement conflict with capital and its owners. Finally, the strategies of new social movements have focused on empowerment and community autonomy and thus have sought autonomy from the state rather than state power.

What could help new social movements overcome these limitations and become an effective political force for change? The response of several writers (e.g., P. Leonard 1997; S. Leonard 1990; Mullaly 2007; Young 1990) is to suggest that new social movement groups incorporate a 'politics of difference' with a 'politics of solidarity' to overcome the limitations of identity politics. The former would help to ensure that diversity was respected, and the latter would help to ensure that the commonality of oppression, along with a common interest in developing policies that benefited all the diverse groups (i.e., women, people of colour, workers, and so on), was at the fore. The elements of coalition-building discussed above should facilitate this process. Leonard (1997, 176) argues that 'this organized solidarity would need to aim for the winning of state power through the electoral process,' which might or might not require the formation of a new political party, depending on specific circumstances.

The aim of winning state power brings us to the second question posed above: would the winning of state power by a progressive political party (supported by oppressed groups) necessarily be a step towards the emancipation of these groups? The experience to date with respect to social change and social policy outcomes from left-wing governments in the Western world has been less than satisfactory. Instead of attempting to transform capitalism into some form of socialism, most socialist or social democratic or labour governments have brokered deals with big business and labour, which included the development of the welfare state as an attempt to humanize capitalism. During the recessions of the 1980s and early 1990s, they adopted the same retrenchment policies as their bourgeois political counterparts (e.g., cutting back on social spending rather than reforming the tax system). Contemporary national leftist political parties such as Labour in the UK and Australia and the New Democratic Party in Canada, as well as the liberal Democratic party in the US, have all adopted 'Third-Way' policies, which are essentially bourgeois policies couched in progressive rhetoric. State and provincial political parties on the left have not adopted any policies different from those of their national counterparts. Although there is widespread popular cynicism towards the political system today (Fisher and Kling 1994), people concerned with issues of social justice are especially disillusioned by the behaviour and dismal performance of governments and political parties supposedly on the left with respect to these issues. Why then would we expect any more from governments and political parties formed by or supported by coalitions of new social movements? To help answer this question, I again turn to Peter Leonard, one of the most respected writers on progressive social work and social welfare in the English-speaking world.

Leonard (1997, 176–177) avoids the term 'coalition' because it implies to him a political organization too unstable and transitory to serve the purpose of winning state power in the interests of oppressed groups. He prefers instead the term 'a confederation of diversities' in which member organizations would join together to express (rather than subjugate) their separate identities in solidarity with each other. To make this confederation work for all members, it would be based on dialogical communication at every level between those who experience different forms of domination and exploitation. It would also be committed to an internal culture that resisted the urge to homogenize, encouraged discourses of difference, and sought to reclaim previously hidden narratives of subordination and exclusion, all the while continuing to build solidarities. Leonard asserts that a political organization cannot emerge spontaneously but must be constituted from certain already existing economic and political conditions. Three such conditions outlined by Leonard are: (1) shifts in economic circumstances that impinge on the consciousness of subordinate groups, such as dramatic increases in disparities between rich and poor, increased unemployment and underemployment, and increased exploitation of labour; (2) the realization that state power cannot be won on the basis of working-class movements themselves; and (3) a recognition that identity politics, although necessary, is not sufficient to meet the demands of human welfare—a confederation of solidarity is also needed.

We know that contradictions within global capitalism continue to grow—increasing disparities of wealth, concentration of political power, persistent high levels of unemployment and underemployment, the Asian and Russian economic crises of the previous decade and the current (2009) worldwide recession, falling currency values, and in most Western nations, budget surpluses through much the 1990s, now succeeded by recession-related soaring deficits. Leonard (1997) argues that pressure is increasing to explore new forms of politics as the existing ones become discredited. Although there is no guarantee that the current critical situation will lead to a formation of political parties committed to solidarity in defence of diversity, social justice, and equality, he reminds us that the future is determined by acts of human will. Quoting Marx, Leonard says that 'human subjects act, "but not in circumstances of their own choosing."'(1997, 178). It is worth noting that the current world situation came about through the actions of the corporate elite, not because of some law of economic determinism or principle of social evolution. What was made by a small elite group of people can be unmade or remade.

Selected Principles of Anti-Oppressive Social Work Practice

By now, it should be clear what an anti-oppressive social worker is all about. Providing criticisms of and alternatives to traditional mainstream social work, anti-oppressive social workers have had a long-standing interest in the emancipation of oppressed populations as well as an interest in the ways that oppressed persons are able to exercise their agency or personal power (Leonard 1997). For some in (and outside of) social work, this approach has not been popular, not only because it is political and collectivist in orientation but also because it suggests that tinkering with the system or trying to humanize global capitalism is not the answer (Fraser 2008). Anti-oppressive social workers are well aware that the vast majority of social service users are members of oppressed groups who, not coincidentally, enjoy few privileges and are unable to exercise power to the same extent as those who are not oppressed on the basis of their class, gender, race, ethnicity, religion, age, sexuality, or ability (Allan, Pease, and Briskman 2003; Ife 1997; Taylor 1990, cited in Fraser 2008).

Anti-oppressive social workers are committed to a model of practice that is based on rights, not gratitude, and we are not prepared to minimize the pain of hard living conditions by suggesting that over time oppressed people will get used to it. Nor do we accept that oppression is too big to address and change (Hays and Chang 2003). We do not accept the proposition that if people just tried harder and worked harder and mixed more (or less) with family, friends, and neighbours, their social circumstances would radically change (Baskin 2003; Taylor 1990). We do not accept the neo-conservative mantra that poverty can be ameliorated, if not eradicated, by economic growth alone (Ife 2001). We do not accept that inequality is an inherent and intractable part of human nature (Gil 1998; Mullaly 2007), but instead we seek allies for support as we analyze the patterns of injustice that we witness (Brown and Strega 2005).

This final section of Chapter 9 presents a number of principles to help guide the anti-oppressive social worker in his or her practice. I have chosen the principles outlined here because some of them helped me to clarify my teaching of and my writing on progressive forms of social work practice and have informed my social activism over the past 20 years. Other principles have recently been added to my inventory through the course of my work in reading, thinking, and writing in the area of oppression, privilege, and anti-oppression. These principles are not presented in any order of importance or priority.

A Goal of Social Transformation

Gil (1998, 68–85) outlines the following conceptually distinct but overlapping dimensions of social work practice:

- Amelioration: alleviating suffering resulting from systemic oppression and injustice by providing some material goods in a paternalistic (charitable) manner.
- Control: controlling, regulating, and monitoring members of subordinate groups and enforcing change in their behaviours because they are considered immoral and responsible for their own problematic situation due to supposedly personal defects and inadequacies.
- Adaptation: counselling and treatment of oppressed persons to help them adjust to, cope with, and fit into the 'realities' of unjust and oppressive societies.
- Reform: advocating for, initiating, and implementing 'top-down' minor changes in the system (system-tinkering) to reduce the severity of injustice and oppression but not eliminating their root causes.
- Structural transformation: involvement in consciousness-raising concerning the realities of oppression and joining with other social workers, members of oppressed groups, and their allies in acts of resistance and social movements to overcome the fundamental causes of injustice and oppression.

Anti-oppressive social workers will, for the most part, work within the dimension of structural or social transformation. This is not to say that anti-oppressive social workers will never engage in any of the other dimensions but that amelioration, adaptation, reform, and control are not ends or goals in themselves but part of a larger strategy of social transformation. An attempt should be made to link everyday practice at whatever level at which one is working to the goal of social transformation. One of the purposes of this book has been to show how anti-oppressive social work practice can (and must) occur at the personal, group, cultural, and structural levels.

Keeping Up-to-Date with Current Ideas, Literature, Practices, and Developments

Keeping up with new developments, ideas, theories, and practices is part of what it is to be a professional social worker. It is a professional obligation that we owe to the people we serve, to society as a whole, to our profession, and to ourselves. However, experience tells us that many social workers stop reading after they graduate from social work programs. The reasons for this may vary, but a common explanation is that practitioners and managers can become so busy that they do not feel that they have time to read new books or journal articles that may contain new ideas and they lose the plot—or as Thompson (2002) describes it, they 'drift' in their jobs. That is, they lose the focus of their work in that they no longer have a clear vision of what they are trying to achieve (e.g., a just society free of oppression) or how they are going to achieve it. This can result in the means or methods of practice becoming the ends, with workers attempting to become more proficient as counsellors or as family therapists or as group or community workers. Thus, the technical aspects of social work take precedence over the moral and political aspects.

Two consequences of the inability of many social workers to keep up with current literature and developments are: (1) a resistance to progressive approaches such as anti-oppressive social work occurs (ask almost any student about their experiences in their field practicum whether they bring up the subject of structural or anti-oppressive social work) and (2) older ideas and theories such as systems and ecological approaches still tend to dominate thinking and practice in many agencies, even though these approaches are almost 40 years old with a critique almost as old. And, of course, as Thompson (1998) points out, much of the theory underpinning contemporary social work was developed during a time when awareness of issues of oppression was at a much lower level than it is today. 'Consequently, much of the knowledge base on which day-to-day practice draws pays little or no attention to inequality, and can often be seen to condone or exacerbate discrimination' (Thompson 1998, 221).

Thompson makes a very good point when he says that the bulk of traditional social work theory should not be rejected or dismissed out of hand, since this would lead to the loss of a substantial knowledge base and many valuable insights from that base. The challenge he identifies is to rework and revitalize existing theories so that they might be rendered compatible with anti-oppressive social work. However, it must be kept in mind that some theories or parts of theories may have to be rejected because oppressive assumptions may be so ingrained in them that they fall apart without them. An example would be a theory that contains a gender or cultural bias. One way for practitioners to avoid becoming victims of drift and not keeping up with recent literature is for them to become field instructors. I do not know how many times I have heard practitioners who supervise students in a field placement say that they learn as much from the students as the students learn from them. They are referring, of course, to the recent literature and developments in social work that are brought to their attention by the students. It is true that some insecure field instructors will criticize ideas and theories that are unfamiliar to them and denigrate theory in general, but most of the field instructors I know willingly discuss with their students what is new in the curriculum and how it might apply in their particular agencies or services. Another way of fulfilling one's obligation to stay current with recent literature and developments is to discuss them with colleagues in an open manner so that learning can be shared and a collective approach to anti-oppressive development can be adopted (Thompson 1998).

Realistic Expectations

There are no quick and easy strategies for eliminating oppression. Some social workers equate social transformation with overnight revolution and believe that the absence of militant or cataclysmic or large-scale changes is proof that fundamental social change is unrealistic and that progressive forms of social work are ineffective. Gil (1998) reminds us that oppressive institutions have evolved over many centuries and therefore are often perceived as natural, normal, legitimate, and inevitable. Dominant groups will often defend established structures and relationships because they believe that they are fair and/or compatible with their interests. As well, as we have seen, almost everyone occupies at least one position of dominance and therefore benefits in some way (in spite of one's overall position) from the present system. 'In other words, nearly all people are now part of the problem, regardless of personal philosophy, and would have to change their ways of life to become part of the solution' (Gil 1998, 130). Consistent with this assertion is the argument I have made in previous chapters that personal or self-transformation is part of the larger task of social transformation.

Life in general and social work in particular might be a whole lot easier if we anti-oppressive social workers just accepted the way things are and all became mainstream social work practitioners or academics. Certainly, our relationships in our workplaces, at least, would be much more pleasant. However, I think that mainstream social workers are much more susceptible to burnout than anti-oppressive social workers. Their analysis and explanations of social problems do not explain the persistence of problems, nor does their analysis explain why their interventions and practices seem so ineffectual. Over time, with few limited, short-term successful outcomes and many failures from their interventions, they will naturally begin to question themselves and their competencies. Anti-oppressive social workers at least have an analysis that explains why mainstream interventions and traditional approaches to social problems do not work. Poor people did not invent poverty. People of colour did not create racism. Women did not ask to be treated in sexist ways. These are structural problems that can only be satisfactorily resolved by structural change (recognizing that some personal change may be associated with structural interventions). Problems of dominant–subordinate relationships will not be resolved by attempting to have oppressed individuals change their ways. The struggle against oppression can be painful and discouraging at times, but anyone who has ever participated in it knows that it also brings great comradeship, which is deeply rewarding. If we do nothing about oppression, we lose our basic humanity, and, I suggest, we will have at least as much difficulty living with ourselves as mainstream social workers do.

The social transformation of a society characterized by oppression will require a lengthy and difficult process, one that could take decades or centuries. This does not mean that we have to tolerate the status quo. It merely means that we have to be realistic about the outcomes of anti-oppressive social work. The question is not 'how can I start the revolution to end oppression?' Rather, it is 'how can I can contribute to undermining and resisting oppression in my everyday practice and in my everyday personal life?' Our task is to contribute to social transformation in any way we can—in our professional practices and in our personal lives. Although complete social transformation may not occur in the lifetimes of most of us, we will see some fundamental changes. Changes resulting from the women's movement are evidence that this can happen. One of the changes coming from the movement is the common usage of gender-inclusive language today as opposed to the male-dominated language of a few decades ago. This change, of course, is much greater than a simple vocabulary alteration. It has both symbolic and real effects. Language is part of culture. It reflects and contributes to dominant–subordinate relationships. One way of helping to change the culture (such as patriarchy) is to change the language.

Everyone in her or his day-to-day living experiences can contribute to language changes. For example, instead of using the term 'client,' which denotes a relationship of inequality between the social worker (the helper) and the 'helpee,' many social workers today use the term 'service user.' Another area in which an anti-oppressive social worker can make a contribution to undermining some of the oppressive aspects of social work practice lies in case recordings and agency files. Traditionally, case record-ings were written in a diagnostic discourse that tended to pathologize the service user by attributing problems to deficiencies of the individual, family, subculture, and so on. These recordings were guarded like Fort Knox and could be seen only by selected agency personnel. The anti-oppressive social worker could help to de-pathologize the experiences of service users by attributing the problems to racism, sexism, classism, or other forms of oppression rather than resorting to a victim-blaming explanation. Service users could also have access to their files and be given the opportunity to disagree with what has been written and to offer their own narratives. Some agencies have a policy of allowing co-authorship of a joint narrative about problems, needs, and claims (Leonard 1997). This practice recognizes that narratives are open to interpretation and that the service user's knowledge is just as valuable as a piece of universal expert knowledge, which on its own has a tendency to homogenize people within a professional narrative.

Critical Self-Reflection

Critical self-reflection is an element of the critical social theory tradition, which Leonard (1997) argues provides a connection to postmodern critique. Because we all internalize parts of the dominant ideology to varying degrees, it is important to develop reflexive knowledge of the dominant ideology to see how it constrains us and limits our freedom. Most anti-oppressive social writers today advocate critical reflection or critical consciousness-raising (e.g., Baines 2007; Dominelli 2002; Fraser and McMaster 2008; Sisneros et al. 2008; van Wormer 2004). Reflexive knowledge, derived mainly through critical self-reflection, is knowledge about ourselves. It helps us to understand how our identities are largely determined by the dominant ideology. Reflexive knowledge is knowledge about our location within the social order—that is, the forms and sources of our positions of both domination and oppression—and how we may exercise power in our professional and personal lives to either reproduce or resist social features that limit others' agency. It is also knowledge about the source and substance of our social beliefs, attitudes, and values. Such understanding may help us to free ourselves from self-imposed constraints that are derived from the massive legitimating power of the dominant ideology. An ideology is embedded within a particular discourse. Schon (1983, 163) has developed a social work practice (i.e., reflective practice) wherein the practitioner carries out a 'reflective conversation with the situation.' This technique can be used to identify oppressive traces of the dominant ideology or discourse that may be present in our narratives of domination and subordination or in our social work practices. Critical self-reflection is a form of 'internal criticism,' a never-ending questioning of our social, economic, political, and cultural beliefs, assumptions, and actions. It is also a political practice (Leonard 1997) that allows scope for greater sensitivity to issues relating to power, injustice, and oppression and avoids dogma and orthodoxy (Thompson 1998), including stereotypes.

Peter Leonard (1997) discusses an aspect of critical self-reflection that is highly relevant to those of us, including anti-oppressive social workers, concerned with social justice. He argues that without critical self-reflection, there is a danger that we will not discover the parts of oppressive discourses embedded in our consciousness. However, he also points out that critical self-reflection is no guarantee of discovering those oppressive aspects of ourselves. For example, as a white person, I have benefited and continue to benefit from institutional or structural racism. Thus, I can never claim to be non-racist. I can claim, however, that I am anti-racist, which means that I am committed not only to fighting external forms of racism but also to struggling, through critical self-reflection, against the racism that I have internalized. Similarly, I cannot

Critical Self-Reflection Needed Here!

John is a member of the Mi'kmaq First Nation, which is scattered along the east coast of Canada. He is a first-year MSW student in a social work program that publicizes and prides itself as possessing an anti-oppressive curriculum. One day the class was discussing the concepts of 'essentialism' and 'homogeneity.' Many comments and questions were offered regarding how ridiculous it was to assume that a group of people would be the same in every respect or to think that they would all have an essential human nature. Variations on the theme that 'of course people are different, even if they belong to a certain social category' were expressed by several class members. Then John spoke. He asked, 'So, is essentialism or homogeneity like when people (staff and students) in this program always ask me "what do Aboriginals think about this?" or "what is the Native position on that?" Do you really think that First Nations people are so similar that I or any other Aboriginal person can speak for all of them?'

sexism. I can, however, claim to be pro-feminist as long as I fight against external forms of sexism and struggle through critical self-reflection against the elements of the dominant discourse on gender that I have internalized.

The other example that Leonard presents highlighting the importance of critical social reflection is the meaning of democracy. We may think of democracy as an element of emancipation, but deeply embedded in the dominant discourse of democracy are bourgeois and patriarchal assumptions about leadership, representation, majority rule, dissent, and diversity.

Gil (1998) provides us with a beginning list of areas for critical self-reflection:

- the images of social reality that we currently hold;
- the ideas, beliefs, and assumptions that we now take for granted about people, society, and the relationship between the two;
- the perceptions we hold of individual and collective needs and wants, which underpin the actions, thoughts, and social relations of most people;
- our values and ideologies, which derive from our perceptions of needs and interests and affect our choices, actions, thoughts, and social relations.

Burke and Harrison (2002) also emphasize the importance of 'reflexivity' or critical self-reflection in anti-oppressive social work. They argue that it demands that workers continually consider the ways in which their own social identity and values affect (1) the information they gather from service users and (2) the impact it is likely to have on their involvement with any particular service user. Critical reflection, they say, can be carried out with oneself (i.e., Schon's idea of a conversation with the situation), in supervision, in team or unit discussions, and with service users.

In their recent book *Critical Multicultural Social Work* (2008, 22–23), Sisneros et al. argue that because no one can escape societal influences, even those who have anti-oppressive convictions, attitudes, and behaviours are not excluded from perpetuating social inequality—either through overt actions or through inactions. What we do not know about ourselves can have unintended consequences for members of subordinate groups. They urge social workers to assess how we perceive and interact with people who are different from ourselves to identify unconscious biases and present the following set of questions to assist in the critical reflection process.

1. What do I do on a daily basis that might contribute to inequality?
2. What have I learned about how to perceive or how to relate to members of my own group or other groups, and what is the source of that learning?
3. What do I know about how to relate to and interpret the behaviour of others who occupy social locations (i.e., class, gender, race/ethnicity, sexual orientation, ability, religion) that are similar to, as well as different from, my own?
4. What have I learned about how to interpret the behaviour of people whose race/ethnicity, sexual orientation, ability, or religion is different from my own? What if I add class and gender/sex to the equation?
5. What do I know about my conscious intentions when I interact with clients who are African-American, Latino/Latina, Native American, Asian-American, biracial or multiracial, or European-American; refugees or other immigrants; gay, lesbian, bisexual, transgender, or intersex; or people with disabilities?
6. Why do the consequences or outcomes of my actions not fit with or match my good intentions? (Kondrat 1999)

Fraser and McMaster (2008) discuss ways of enhancing critical reflection in their book's chapter on the politics of gender and sexuality. They present a technique they call 'talking across the lines.' This refers to a process in which people are invited to communicate with others different from themselves. When people talk across the lines, they are trying to find common ground with people who think, dress, and act differently from themselves. They look beyond the surface of appearance, status, education, home address, and work role to understand how others are experiencing the world, and in so doing, they get glimpses of other people's worlds so that they can join with them on working against relationships of social inequality and oppression. Talking across the lines, of course, involves self-awareness, and to help enhance this quality, Fraser and McMaster suggest that anti-oppressive social workers carry out audits on themselves, or what they call 'self-audits' of oppression and privilege. They refer their readers to the website www.implicit.Harvard.edu and urge them to undertake the Implicit Association Tests (IAT), which are designed to examine hidden biases and to learn more about attitudes and stereotypes across a number of social dimensions. As well, the authors present a self-audit on gender and sexuality that they developed and which is a useful starting point to assess one's biases, comfortability, and so on with respect to issues of gender and sexuality.

Anne Bishop discusses the importance for anyone who wishes to become an ally of oppressed groups to reflect on his or her own experiences as a member of an oppressed group and as a member of an oppressor group. She asserts that learning about one's own oppression is quite different from learning about oneself as an oppressor because the process of becoming an oppressor is hidden from the person. That is, the oppressor role is equated with normalcy, universal standards and values, and political and cultural neutrality. Nothing adverse is perpetrated on the oppressor to make him or her aware of the role of oppressor: 'Becoming a member of an oppressor group is to be cut off from the ability to identify with the experience of the oppressed. . . . When the oppression is not part of your own experience, you can only understand it through hearing others' experiences, along with a process of analysis and parallels' (Bishop 1994, 95). Bishop argues that oppressed persons always know a great deal more about the oppressor group than the oppressor group knows about oppressed groups. Understanding one's position as an oppressor requires an understanding that one is a member of a particular social group or collective reality and not just an individual member of society. Bishop asserts that it is more difficult to reflect on one's own role as oppressor than it is on one's role as oppressed because the former involves a sense of guilt while the latter involves a sense of anger. It is more difficult to confront guilt than anger because the latter may actually assist in the process of liberation from oppression by releasing energy and propelling the process forward. Guilt, on the other hand, is more likely to inhibit the process of liberating oneself from the position of oppressor. Anti-oppressive social workers should engage in ongoing critical self-reflection of their roles as oppressor and oppressed in both their personal lives and their social work practice.

Self-Care

Anti-oppressive social work is one form of struggle against oppression and in pursuit of equality and social justice. This struggle can be painful and discouraging at times, and what makes it even more painful and discouraging is that progressive social work is often marginalized within our own profession. Mainstream social workers and traditional instructors often write us off as interesting but 'out-of-touch and unrealistic radicals.' In addition, as discussed in previous chapters, social work today is fraught with pressures that can lead to incredible stress, particularly when staff are not adequately supported in meeting the complex and demanding challenges of social problems and societal dysfunction. The stress that is part of the social work experience these days can become so overwhelming that we function below the level of our competence to the point where our practice becomes dangerous work (Thompson 1998). Prolonged exposure to stress can lead to burnout—a psychological condition in which the worker 'functions "on automatic pilot"—that is, in an unthinking, unfeeling way, cut off from the sensitive issues involved in his or her work' (Thompson 1998, 226). Consequently, strategies to promote self-care and staff care are crucial.

Thompson (1998) outlines a few policies and practices geared toward supporting staff:

- preventing pressures from becoming excessive to the point where they lead to burnout;
- being responsive to staff when they experience high levels of stress;
- dealing constructively with the aftermath of stress, for example through debriefing.

Gil (1998, 123) articulates a risk that all progressive social workers face because their perspectives and practices derive from a critique of our current social institutions and dominant culture as interfering with the needs satisfaction and development of subordinate group members and a belief that the real solutions to social problems lie in the transformation of these institutions and culture. 'Many social workers and administrators of social services reject this critique and consider the perspectives of radical [including anti-oppressive] social workers, and their approach to practice, unprofessional, unrealistic, and utopian.' As a result of these negative attitudes towards them, anti-oppressive social workers may experience isolation, persecution, and ridicule in their workplace unless opportunities for mutual support and co-operation are available. Anyone who has lived or worked on the edge or outside the mainstream knows all about marginalization, isolation, ridicule, and defamation on a personal level. This is one strategy that mainstream workers may adopt to deal with the insecurities that arise from the critique of traditional social work and the oppressive conditions in many workplace organizations. It is a form of shooting the messenger so that one does not have to hear the message. Ironically, it is a perverse method of self-care on the part of mainstream social workers. One of the ways of promoting self-care along with 'self-preservation' in the workplace is to establish support groups, which is the subject of the next section.

Support and Study Groups

It has already been emphasized that mutual support and co-operation among social justice–oriented social workers is crucial if we are to avoid being co-opted by the system or agency or if we are to cope with the negative attitudes and behaviours that supervisors and mainstream colleagues may possess and exhibit. There is consensus in the literature and with people's experience of progressive social work that the most important element in carrying out acts of resistance and in protecting oneself from the risks inherent in anti-oppressive practice is to establish and work with caucuses or support groups of like-minded colleagues. Gil (1998) outlines several functions that such groups carry out for their members with respect to support and care. First, they can serve as settings for non-hierarchical, co-operative, mutually caring relationships among anti-oppressive social workers who feel isolated and alienated because their views, values, beliefs, theory, and practice differ from those of their co-workers. Second, they can confirm the realism and sanity of structural social workers, which are sometimes questioned by co-workers and administrators. Third, they can serve as settings for co-operative and critical study of the anti-oppressive practice and activism of members. Finally, members of such study and support groups can recruit new members, initiate the establishment of new groups, and organize networks of such groups.

Studies on the experiences of many graduates from progressive social work programs in Canada show that practices and strategies of resistance are useful in challenging the dominant discourse that blames individuals for all their problems (Lecomte 1990; Moreau and Leonard 1989). There is consensus in the progressive and anti-oppressive social work literature (Baines 1997; Carniol 2000; Galper 1980; Gil 1998; Mullaly 2007) and among progressive social work practitioners that the most important element in successfully carrying out acts of resistance and in protecting oneself from the risks that are an inherent part of such practice is to establish and work with caucuses or support groups of like-minded colleagues (see Mullaly 2007; Thompson 1998 for discussions of ways for progressive social workers to protect themselves).

An example of a study and support group is provided by one progressive social worker in a public hospital in a culturally diverse, impoverished US inner-city community, who was part of such a group:

> Jokingly referring to ourselves as 'the conspiracy,' we shared stories and our outrage over lunch. Without the support of these colleagues, I would have found it difficult to resist the dominant discourse that blames individuals for all their problems. Instead, we continually reframed our problems and our clients' problems to be the result of structural and systemic forces and sought solutions that went beyond those just for individual cases [Baines 1997, 314].

The Constructive Use of Anger

Obviously, anti-oppressive social work practice is not easy. It requires an examination and deconstruction of social work's most cherished assumptions so that we can learn and become part of the resurgence of social critique in the newer forms of political movements that challenge the dominant order in the name of equality and diversity (Leonard 1997). It requires a view of the reality of oppression, not as a closed world from which there is no exit but as a limited situation that can be transformed (Freire 1994 [1970], cited in Rees 1991). It also requires an understanding of the nature and causes of the new social, economic, and political conditions of globalization and the current worldwide reactionary political climate. We cannot theorize and analyze from a distance, however, because most of all, anti-oppressive social work requires a personal and collective commitment to social justice. It is not enough to know that we should involve ourselves in struggle or even to want to become involved in social struggle.

But what is it that would drive a person to take on such an onerous commitment to literally change the world as we now know it? The answer, I think, is to capitalize on a feeling that most social workers concerned about social injustice (at least the ones I know) possess—anger at the degrading material and social conditions experienced on a daily basis by millions of people in the less developed countries and in capitalist countries; anger at governments that cater to the wishes of the wealthy at the expense of women, children, visible minorities, and other marginalized groups; anger at a social welfare system that homogenizes, controls, and monitors people who are forced to go to it for assistance and that has proletarianized its workers; and anger at the discrimination, exploitation, and blocked opportunities that so many people experience today, not because of anything they might have done or who they are as individuals but simply because they belong to particular social groups, which for the most part they did not choose.

Two old community development principles state that (1) the most effective way to overcome apathy and passivity in organizing and mobilizing groups is to identify the major sources of discontent within a community, analyze and stimulate that discontent, and turn it into anger so that community members want to do something about their situation and (2) channel the anger onto the source of the discontent and develop long- and short-term strategies to change the situation. Surely, progressive social workers have no shortage of discontent and anger today.

Traditionally, theoretical understandings of anger have been dominated by psychological perspectives. It was considered in intrapsychic terms, with intrapsychic solutions (Allan 2005). From a Western perspective, bottling up anger was considered potentially harmful to the individual (and/or to the source of anger) and therefore should be recognized, defused, and contained (McKissock and McKissock 1998). Social workers would often help the person experiencing anger to talk about their anger, have someone hear and acknowledge it, understand its source, and show that they are 'on side' with the individual. The task was to contain the anger and not let it get out of control, since it was perceived as a potentially dangerous thing. Allan (2005) points out, however, that anger is neither an inherently positive nor an inherently negative emotion and that just as it may be destructive, it can also be constructive. It depends on how we deal with anger and how we use it. For example, Anne Bishop claims that anger is a source of power and is one of the major reasons that she wrote her celebrated book *Becoming an Ally* (1994; 2002). Dominelli (2002) argues that anger at the injustice of a service user's predicament will often move a practitioner to action and provide the basis for critiquing a social order that creates social injustice in the first place. For the social worker, this may become a defining moment in which he or she begins to appreciate the importance of contextualized practice. Allan (2005) presents a number of examples from her own and others' practices in the area of grief and bereavement in which anger assisted the practitioner in challenging the traditional bias in counselling of 'talking it through' and in carrying out a variety of advocacy and social action activities in work undertaken with bereaved people. Her major message is 'do not disenfranchise anger' but use it constructively.

Feminists have used the construction of anger as a catalyst to attack sexism and patriarchy. According to feminist therapy, women need to get in touch with their anger and turn it outward rather than inward (Goldhor-Lerner 1985), since the latter results in depression, despair, and anxiety, which in turn reproduce women's traditional roles of passivity and submission under patriarchy (Baines 1997). A similar dynamic is operative for social workers who internalize their anger caused by social and workplace injustice.

Peter Leonard argues that a sense of moral outrage at the structures of domination and oppression manufactured and reproduced within the current set of oppressive social arrangements provides the basis for progressive discourses and practices. 'Not intellectual detachment but anger is the human attribute which has the most possibility of generating the kind of individual and collective resistance which is a necessary precondition of emancipation' (Leonard 1997, 162). Thompson (1998) issues an important caution about anger, however. He asserts that anger can be a positive force for change if it is channelled constructively, but if it gets out of control or is misdirected or used as a blanket approach to struggles for liberation, it can be used ideologically by the dominant group to pathologize and stigmatize subordinate group members and their anti-oppressive allies.

I believe that anger reflects a deep moral sense of fairness and, as argued by Bishop above, a source of power for the anti-oppressive social worker. Anger is a gift (Lim 1996, cited in Leonard 1997). It has been the driving force behind all great social movements. It can move oppressed people and their allies from feelings of 'helpless fury' to 'righteous indignation' (Herman 1992, 189). Leonard (1997, 162) argues that anger can be mobilized from internalization as anxiety and depression into externalization as collective resistance: 'Collectively, anger emerges as a moral protest at injustice.' Bishop (1994, 84) identifies anger as a source of power if it is used as 'an expression of our will directed against injustice.'

Anger is what will enable those of us who are committed to anti-oppressive social work to translate our social justice ideals into practice and to continue the struggle for liberation. This struggle can be painful and discouraging at times, but anyone who has participated in it knows that it also brings great comradeship, which is deeply reward-ing. If we do nothing about oppression, we lose our basic humanity. If in our personal lives and in our social work practice, we assist in making oppression acceptable by helping people to cope with it or adjust to it, we not only fail them, we fail ourselves, and we become part of the problem. Social workers who are committed to social justice must join the struggle against oppression in all its forms and at all levels at which it occurs. There is no choice.

Conclusion

Maintain the rage (but use it wisely).

Critical Questions for Discussion

1. Social workers talk a lot about democracy, equality, and participation in decision-making, but most mainstream social service organizations are hierarchical, with decisions made from a top-to-bottom model. What would a flat or horizontal organization look like in which everyone was considered equal in the organization with respect to decision-making? Who would speak for the organization and represent it to other organizations?

2. A criticism of situational ethics is that it provides people with an excuse to commit sins (e.g., lie, steal, commit adultery). How would you respond to this criticism? Can you think of situations in which situational ethics might advance anti-oppressive social work practice with service users or in challenging the oppressive aspects of a mainstream agency?

3. Has your provincial professional association or your local chapter been active in political campaigns, especially at election time (e.g., organizing public meetings with candidates and asking them questions on issues that affect social work and service users)? Has it established coalitions or alliances with organizations representing various oppressed groups? What do you think could be done in these areas?

4. What are some of the ways that you deal with stress and/or look after yourself? Are there some collective ways that you think might supplement your individual self-care activities?

5. How do you handle any anger you experience in your life or in your workplace? Do you have any rules (e.g., I wait for a day now before responding to an irritating e-mail or message)? Can you think of times that it got you in trouble? What kind of trouble? In reflection, what could you have done differently?

Further Readings

Brown, Leslie, and Susan Strega, eds. (2005). *Research as Resistance: Critical, Indigenous and Anti-oppressive Approaches*. Toronto: Canadian Scholars Press. This book is a collection of original pieces by practitioners and researchers from diverse and marginalized locations who place social justice at the very centre of research processes and outcomes. The editors and 13 contributors from research and teaching backgrounds at Canadian universities and within their communities bring their activism, feminism, and scholarship to an understanding of various ways of knowing, being, and doing. The book highlights the relationships between researcher and researched and impinges on the academy by making and taking space within it for marginalized researchers and ideas.

Ferguson, Iain (2008). *Reclaiming Social Work: Challenging Neo-liberalism and Promoting Social Justice.* London: Sage. This book examines how social work's commitment to social justice has been deepened and enriched by its contact with wider social movements such as the women's movement, the trade union movement, the peace movement, the environmental movement, and the disabled persons movement. The book explores the tensions between social work values and a market-driven agenda and locates new resources of hope for the social work profession in developing resistance to managerialism or the pro-business ideology. The author is critical of progressive social work for embracing post-modernism as a framework and for its retreat from class oppression, its de-emphasis of structural/capitalist variables, and its adoption of risk assessments. The book provides an insightful critique of many ideas thought to be progressive in social work and ends on an optimistic note.

Fletcher, Joseph F. (1997). *Situation Ethics: The New Morality.* 2nd edition. Louisville, KY: Westminster John Knox Press. Igniting a firestorm of controversy since its publication in 1966, this book was hailed by many as a much-needed reformulation of morality and as an invitation to anarchy by others. Proposing an ethic of 'loving concern,' the author suggests that certain acts such as lying, stealing, and adultery may be all right depending on the circumstances. The provocative thesis of the book remains a powerful force in contemporary discussions of morality. For social workers who deal with complex life situations and value issues every day, this book should be mandatory reading.

Ife, Jim (2001). *Human Rights and Social Work: Towards Rights-Based Practice.* Cambridge: Cambridge University Press. This book examines current human rights issues and shows how a broader understanding can be used to ground a form of practice that is central to social work, community development, and broader human services. The author extends the idea of human rights beyond the realm of theoretical analysis and into the arena of professional practice and social action, using a critical theory perspective. Drawing on current debates about globalization, this book adds a vital new perspective to the promotion of international human rights.

van Wormer, Katherine (2004). *Confronting Oppression, Restoring Justice: From Policy Analysis to Social Action.* Alexandria, VA: Council on Social Work Education. Katherine van Wormer's *Confronting Oppression, Restoring Justice* examines the twin forces of oppression and injustice and how social policies, cultural institutions, and prevailing ideologies promote or sustain them. Using an internationally informed perspective, she unpacks concepts such as internalization of oppression, injustice, restorative justice, social exclusion, empowerment, and critical consciousness. Readers will find extensive discussion of the skills of critical analysis needed to confront oppression and injustice, backed up by examples of human services programs that successfully deploy strategies of empowerment.

Chapter 10

Unpacking Our Knapsacks of Invisible Privilege

Privilege is not something I take and which I therefore have the option of not taking.
It is something that society gives me, and unless I change the institutions which give it
to me, they will continue to give it, and I will continue to have it, however noble and
egalitarian my intentions.

—Harry Brod, *Men's Lives*

Introduction

The flip side of the coin of oppression is privilege. However, compared to oppression in general and anti-oppressive social work in particular, not much has been written on privilege in the social work literature. This is most unfortunate, because the main reason we have oppression is because we have privilege. It is similar to the relationship between poverty and wealth—we have poverty because we have wealth. If we want to truly understand poverty, we must understand wealth. If we want to do something serious about poverty, we must do something serious about wealth. And if we want to truly understand oppression, we must understand privilege. Oppression and privilege go hand in hand. Just as privilege opens doors of opportunity, oppression slams them shut (Johnson 2006). Just as poverty will always be with us until we do something about wealth, we will always have oppression until we do something about privilege. As articulated by Harry Brod in the quote above, privilege is not something we take; it is given to us by society if we possess the characteristics that society values, such as being male, white, heterosexual, affluent, and non-disabled.

Ferber (2003) offers two major reasons why we have tended to ignore the issue of privilege. First, it implicates those with power, and second, it is far easier to explore the problems faced by oppressed groups than it is to explore our own roles in perpetuating inequality. This is unfortunate, because we are all implicated in systems of oppression. 'Although as individuals we may not believe that we are oppressive people, we still participate in relations of oppression and gain various privileges from that relationship' (Ferber 2003, 320). No matter how much I write or how many classes I teach about inequality, oppression, racism, and sexism, I continue to reap the privileges of being a white male. And although I do not feel ashamed of or guilty about my race or my gender (after all, I have no control over them), I struggle with the knowledge that I am given certain privileges by society because I was born with particular characteristics that society values. I do not have privilege because of who I am as a person or because of what I have done. Rather, I have privilege because of the social categories that, for the most part, I was born into. As stated by Alison Bailey (2004, 307), 'privilege is *granted* and birth is the easiest way of being granted privilege.'

If we focus only on oppression, the structured invisibility of privilege is reinforced. I agree with Alison Bailey (2004, 302) when she says that 'any understanding of oppression is incomplete without recognition of the role privilege plays in maintaining systems of domination.' This chapter will explore the concept and the structural nature of privilege, some of its major characteristics (including its invisibility to privileged persons), the dynamics of privilege or how systems of privilege work, reasons why privileged persons become defensive and uncomfortable in talking about it, and why dominant groups do not see privilege as a problem. We will also discuss the myth of meritocracy, and some of the specific privileges that are attached to various positions of domination will be outlined. Finally, we will explore what all this has to do with us as individuals and as social workers, along with what we can do about privilege to make a difference.

The Nature of Privilege

In Chapter 2, it was mentioned that all of us suffer from some kind of frustration, hurt, and restriction at some point in our lives, but this does not mean that we are oppressed. What determines oppression is when a person is blocked from opportunities to self-development or is excluded from full participation in society or is assigned a second-class citizenship not because of a lack of individual talent or merit but because of his or her membership in a particular group or category of people. Similarly, what determines privilege is not any particular advantages a person might have but whether these advantages were earned or conferred systematically by society on the basis of his or her membership in a particular social group (Heldke and O'Connor 2004; McIntosh 2003). Just as all oppression counts as harm but not all harms count as oppression, all privilege is advantageous, but not all advantages count as privilege (e.g., having a driver's licence, holding political office, becoming a naturalized citizen, which are all *earned* advantages). What determines oppression and privilege is the systematically conferred nature of harms in the former and (*unearned*) advantages in the latter (Bailey 2004). In her classic article on oppression, Marilyn Frye (1983) argues that if we want to determine whether a particular harm or restriction qualifies as oppression, we have to look at that harm in context to see whether or not it plays a role in maintaining a structure that is oppressive. Similarly, Bailey (2004) argues that if we want to determine whether or not a particular advantage qualifies as a privilege, we need to look at the advantage in context to see whether or not it plays a role in keeping complex systems of privilege in place. Sisneros et al. (2008) point out that privileged people may experience hardship but unless these hardships are grounded in structural barriers that affect people in vital and limiting ways, they cannot be considered as forms of oppression.

Thus, there are two kinds of advantages—earned and unearned—and those that are unearned are considered to be privileges. The corollary is that advantages that are earned (e.g., a quality education, skills, a good reputation) are not considered privileges (although one could argue that some advantages or assets are more easily earned if they are accompanied by class, race, gender, or other privileges). Bailey (2004) argues that failure to recognize the differences between earned and unearned assets allows privileged groups to equate all privilege with earned advantages. She gives a wonderful example of a failure to make this distinction, quoting a remark by Ann Richards (a political foe of George W. Bush) that 'Bush was born on third base, but to this day believes he hit a triple.' If one were looking for a definition of privilege in accordance with the above, Marsiglia and Kulis (2009, 17) offer the following: 'Privilege is the unearned advantages of special group membership.' Privileges make people more powerful and profitable because they have more opportunities, advantages, access, and status attached to them (Hays, Chang, and Dean 2004). That is why white, able-bodied, heterosexual, married males continue to own most of the wealth in Anglo-American societies, occupy the most prestigious positions, and control the media and other forms of popular communication (Mullaly 2007).

As suggested above, privilege is often explained in terms of natural abilities or given traits of the individual. Persons with privilege often appeal to these traits or personal characteristics as justification for having privilege in the first place (Heldke and O'Connor 2004). However, privilege is not an individual phenomenon. Oppression will not go away even if we change the attitudes, personalities, and behaviours of all privileged people, because such changes will not end the dominance that has been conferred on members of privileged groups (McIntosh 2003). It is the nature of society and of social systems that must change. 'Individualistic thinking also makes us blind to the very existence of privilege, because privilege, by definition, has nothing to do with individuals, only with social categories we wind up in' (Johnson 2006, 77).

Another explanation for privilege by those with privilege is that it is an outcome of human nature in that it is only natural for different groups to compete with each other for power, dominance, and privilege. In this competition, there will be winners and losers, with those groups who are smarter, stronger, more able and capable coming out on top and getting more than anyone else. Other variations of the human nature argument as presented by Johnson (2006) are that people cannot help but fear the unfamiliar and therefore must be able to keep other groups in their place, or that existing social groups such as men and women are so dissimilar that it is as though they came from different planets (Mars and Venus?) and it is a wonder that we can get along as well as we do, or that there is only one natural orientation (e.g., sexual, religious) and all the rest are unacceptable and bound to cause conflict whenever they become obvious. Although such arguments about human nature may be popular or persuasive among some, Johnson (2006, 3) makes the point that 'the only way to hold on to them is to ignore most of what history, psychology, anthropology, sociology, biology, and, if people look closely, their own experience reveal about human beings and how they live.'

If privilege does not exist because of individual traits or characteristics or because of human nature, then why does it exist? The answer to this question can be found in the relationship between oppression and privilege. As discussed in Chapter 2, oppression occurs because it benefits the dominant group in that it protects a kind of citizenship that is superior to that of oppressed groups. Privilege occurs for the same reason. Similarly, oppression and privilege conjointly protect the privileged group's access to a wider range of better-paying and higher-status work as well as preferential access to and treatment from our social institutions. A correlate to the invisible nature of privilege is that privileged persons believe that having more is an inalienable right that accompanies hard work, vigilance, the courage to take risks, and superior intelligence and capabilities. That oppressed persons do not have more is proof that privilege is earned and not given. Supporting these beliefs about privilege are the same myths that support oppression, as outlined in Chapter 2—namely, the myths of scarcity, of objective information, of might is right or the belief in majority rule even if it tyrannizes the minority, of supremacy or the belief in a superior culture, of class, of equal opportunity or meritocracy, of stereotyping or the belief that all members of a group are the same, of blaming the victim or the belief that individuals are responsible for their own oppression, and of competition and hierarchy. Johnson (2006) adds two more myths supporting the existence of privilege (and oppression) to this list. As with the other myths, the two additions ignore history. First is the myth or belief that things have always been the way they are and will not change. Second is the myth of 'no effect,' which is based on the belief that nothing we do can change the system because it is just too big and powerful. These myths are part of a larger ideology that rationalizes privilege and oppression as necessary for the preservation of society. In examining these myths, it is instructive to keep in mind the definition of a myth—a popular belief or idea that is fictitious or imaginary and does not reflect reality.

In Chapter 7, we looked at the intersectional model of oppression developed by Steven Wineman (1984) and at the 'web of oppression' model developed by Sisneros et al. (2008) as helpful mechanisms for conceptualizing the intersectional nature of oppression and domination. Patricia Hill Collins (2000) refers to these systems as a 'matrix of domination,' and Estelle Disch (2002) calls them a 'matrix of privilege.' Johnson (2006) asserts that if one looks at privilege or oppression as intersectional or as a web or a matrix of either domination or privilege, it simplifies and clarifies the nature of privilege. He states that by understanding that each form of privilege is related to all the others, we can dispense with the useless exercise of trying to determine which is the least or most privileged or least or most oppressive. It also helps us to avoid the trap of thinking that privilege falls along binary lines in that you are either privileged or you are not, because in reality you are usually both. In other words, we can belong (and usually do) in both privileged and oppressive categories. The intersectional models also reveal how different dimensions of privilege are connected to one another and that if we are to work for change, we need to focus on privilege in all the forms it takes (Johnson 2006). 'We won't get rid of racism, in other words, without doing something about sexism and classism, because the system that produces the one also produces the others and connects them' (Johnson 2006, 53). Obviously then, part of the nature of privilege is that all its various forms are connected and interact with one another.

Another major feature of privilege is the fact that it is ubiquitous at the same time that it is invisible to privileged persons (Kimmel and Ferber 2003).[1] Everywhere we look, privileged people are the standard against which everyone else is measured. Most of our political leaders, most of our corporate leaders, most people in the mainstream media and in advertising, most spokespersons, most professional people tend to be white, non-disabled, middle- and upper-class males. Privilege is all around us, and for many of us, it is us. However, privilege also tends to be invisible to those who are privileged. We are not schooled to recognize our privileges in the same way that we are schooled to recognize and be wary of people who are members of subordinate groups. People will tell us that they went to see a 'female doctor,' or they will say they went to see 'the doctor.' Very few will say that they went to see the 'male doctor.' People will tell us they have a 'gay friend,' or they will tell us about a 'friend.' Very few will tell us about having a 'heterosexual friend.' If I, as a white person, talk about a colleague at work, people will assume I am talking about a 'white colleague.' By identifying the race, gender, or sexual orientation of subordinate persons, we draw attention to the markers that explain why these persons are not privileged. By not identifying the markers that are associated with privileged persons, we help to keep privilege invisible. When I look in the mirror, I do not see my privileges, but when oppressed persons look in the mirror, they see their gender or their race or their disability because these characteristics are visible to them every day as the reasons why they are not privileged. When we look at the wage difference between men and women, we always express the difference in terms of what the woman earns compared to the man (which makes the man's wage the standard); for example, women on average earn about 70 cents for every dollar a man earns. This statistic makes the discrimination against women visible. If we were to express the difference in terms of men's wages as a function of women's wages, we would say that for every dollar a woman earns, a man earns about $1.43. That way, it would not be the discrimination that is made visible but the privilege. Just by being a male, a worker receives an extra 43 cents, which represents what Connell (2001) calls the 'masculine or patriarchal dividend'—the unearned benefit accruing to a male just for being male.

Allan Johnson (2006, 7) makes the case that to do something about privilege is not only a moral imperative but a matter of survival:

> The trouble we're in privileges some groups at the expense of others. It creates a yawning divide in levels of income, wealth, dignity, safety, health, and quality of life.

It promotes fear, suspicion, discrimination, harassment, and violence. It sets people against one another. It builds walls topped with broken glass and barbed wire. It weaves the insidious and corroding effects of oppression into the daily lives of tens of millions of women, men, and children. It has the potential to ruin entire generations and, in the long run, to take just about everyone down with it.

Dynamics of Privilege

Johnson (2006) contends that the ease of not being aware of privilege is an aspect of privilege itself, or what he refers to as 'the luxury of obliviousness.' The fact that oppressed groups must be fully attentive to the privileged groups without the latter having to give attention in return is a key aspect of privilege. Because privileged people tend to control the political system, the police, jobs, the education system, and most resources, oppressed groups have to get to know them well in order not to displease them. Privileged persons, on the other hand, have little reason to pay attention to subordinate groups or to how privilege affects them. To be privileged is not having to think about it. 'So strong is the sense of entitlement behind this luxury that males, whites, and others can feel put upon in the face of even the mildest invitation to pay attention to issues of privilege' (Johnson 2006, 22). Sisneros et al. (2008) point out that one of the hidden characteristics of membership in a privileged group is the assumption that the privileged status is the norm whereas the status of the oppressed group is not. As an example, the authors note that the assumption that growing up in a multiracial family or a family with gay or lesbian parents (or a single-parent family) can harm children is not based on any data. The consequences of accepting myths such as these can be disastrous in social workers' work with children and their families.

According to Johnson (2006), one of the reasons why privileged persons pay little attention to the issue or reality of privilege or do not see it as a problem is that they tend to compare themselves with other privileged persons and not with members of oppressed groups. This is so because people make comparisons on the basis of what is valued in society. White people, for example, will compare themselves with other white people because being white is seen as a valued characteristic. Similarly, men will compare themselves with other men and not with women. The effect of this dynamic is that white people do not feel privileged by their race because their comparison group is also white. Likewise, men do not feel privileged by their gender because their comparison group is other men. The paradoxical situation of being privileged without knowing it reinforces the invisible nature of privilege. And, of course, there are consequences to this invisibility. Two major consequences identified by Kimmel and Ferber (2003) are: (1) it is difficult to create or develop a politics of inclusion from invisibility and (2) the invisibility of privilege means that many privileged persons become defensive and irritated when they are confronted with the statistical realities and human consequences of privileges based on racism, sexism, and so on. Anyone who has ever attempted to have a classroom or other discussion on privilege knows that many privileged persons feel like victims themselves. I certainly agree with Kimmel and Ferber (2003) that a major task for anyone concerned with social justice and anti-oppression is to make visible the privilege that masks that invisibility. One way of doing this, which will be discussed below, is to dump out the contents of what Peggy McIntosh (2003) calls our invisible knapsacks of privilege.

As suggested in the preceding paragraph, one reason that privilege is not dealt with constructively or at all by privileged people is that the thought of benefiting from racism, sexism, classism, and so on or behaving in ways that are racist, sexist, classist, and so on can cause a broad range of unpleasant emotions, such as anger, shame, guilt, fault, and frustration (Schmitz, Stakeman, and Sisneros 2001, cited in Sisneros et al. 2008). Or they may not get it at all (Johnson 2006). Even people who see themselves as non-prejudiced can be guilty of holding prejudices (Tatum 1994). The uncomfortable feelings resulting from confronting one's prejudices can create barriers to self-examination or social analysis or other types of learning. And, of course, if we fail to examine our belief systems, world views, and ways of knowing, we will not be adequately prepared for engaging in healthy (i.e., respectful, egalitarian) relationships in a multicultural environment.

> We enter this world lacking assumptions. Through socialization by family, friends, and other people we respect and trust, we learn stereotypes, misinformation, myths, and partial histories that glorify some, vilify others, and erase people and events by making no mention of them at all. Misinformation acquired through early learning is reinforced by institutional and cultural structures such as the media, schools, religion, and governmental and legal systems, as well as traditions and customs [Sisneros et al. 2008, 25].

These myths and misinformation shape how we see ourselves and others and can either bolster or deflate our self-identity depending on our social position. If we do acquire new learnings that puncture the old assumptions we were taught, we are presented with a choice. We can decide to pass on the old misinformation and behave in ways that continue to marginalize people, or we can break the cycle and become allies with oppressed groups in confronting and challenging both privilege and oppression. How to break the cycle will be discussed in the last section of this chapter.

As with oppression, one of the features of privilege is that various privileges intersect and interact with other privileges and with different forms of oppression at the same time. Categories that define privilege exist simultaneously and in relation to one another. In other words, a person can belong to more than one category of privilege (e.g., a white, bourgeois male). Categories that define privilege also exist in relation to categories that define oppression. For example, a person can belong to a category (or categories) of privilege and to a category (or categories) of oppression (e.g., a black male) at the same time. Usually, the more categories of privilege to which one belongs, the more privileged one is apt to be, although not necessarily. For example, a white, unemployed male belongs to two categories of privilege but may not feel any privilege because of his unemployed status. His inability to earn a living may get in the way of his enjoying the unearned benefits that go with being a white male. As Johnson (2006) points out, each of us is a package deal. People never see me, for example, only in terms of my race, or sex, or class but as a white, middle-class, non-disabled, heterosexual, and so on professor. It is tempting to attempt to calculate some kind of cost-benefit analysis of one's privilege by counting the number of privileged categories one falls within, subtracting the number of oppressive categories one belongs to, and arriving at a 'privilege score.' Unfortunately, privilege (and life) is not that simple. The dynamics of multiple privilege or multiple oppression are so bound up with each other that it is impossible to tell where one ends and the next begins. If we are looking at gender and race, for example, how much gender or race counts (i.e., contributes to either privilege or oppression) by itself cannot be determined.

In explaining how systems of privilege work, Allan Johnson (2006) argues that privilege and oppression exist through systems such as family, schools, and workplaces and people's participation in them. The systems are organized around three key characteristics: they are (1) dominated by privileged groups (positions of power tend to be occupied by members of privileged groups); (2) identified with privileged groups (privileged groups represent the cultural standard of comparison for all groups); and (3) centred on privileged groups (because systems are identified with privileged groups, the tendency is to focus attention on them, which makes other groups feel invisible). All three characteristics reinforce the notion that privileged groups are superior to all others and therefore deserve their privilege.

In terms of people's participation in the systems of privilege, Johnson identifies three behaviours or activities that prop up and help to maintain these systems. The first is what he calls following the 'paths of least resistance.' In every social situation, we face an almost endless number of choices. For example, in class a student could sing, yell at the instructor, eat lunch, whistle, carry on a loud conversation, and so on. All these choices vary in terms of the level of resistance that is inherent in each choice, as we would soon discover if we chose an inappropriate path. Singing in class would quickly provoke resistance from other students (and the instructor) in the form of condemnation. By comparison, behaving in a way that is expected in a classroom would be the path of least resistance, which is the one we are most likely to take. We usually follow the path of least resistance for a number of possible reasons. It might be the only one we see. Or we may be aware of other paths but are afraid of the consequences if we do not follow the path of least resistance. For example, we may feel uncomfortable when we hear a friend or colleague tell a racist joke, but we are afraid of being ridiculed or ostracized if we object to it, so we take the path of least resistance and smile or laugh or just remain silent. Another example would be a woman taking the path of least resistance by remaining silently attentive to a male colleague taking up air space and expressing opinions on something that he obviously knows little or nothing about (a not uncommon male tendency, which privilege allows). Another path, one that is likely to meet resistance, would be to challenge the man for what he is saying and doing, which in effect would also raise the possibility of alternative paths, such as the man learning about silence and listening, about supporting others, and about sharing space (Johnson 2006). 'Patterns of dominance and the paths of least resistance that sustain them show up in every system of privilege' (Johnson 2006, 94).

Remaining silent is the second behaviour of people participating in systems of privilege that reinforces privilege identified by Johnson. He (2006, 106) refers to silence as 'passive oppression,' which he defines as 'making it possible for oppression to happen simply by doing nothing to stop it.' Oppression depends upon silence in order to continue. When privileged people do not act or say anything about observed or known acts of oppression at the personal, cultural, or structural level, they are perpetuating privilege and oppression by contributing to a social environment that makes it easy for oppression to occur and for so many to stand by and let it happen. Privileged people may privately disapprove of acts of racism or sexism or gay-bashing and may console themselves with the thought that they themselves would never do such things, but by remaining silent, they are in effect reinforcing and condoning oppression. As long as the vast majority of men remain silent on the issue of sexual harassment and domestic violence or as long as issues of racism in the community or the workplace or the classroom are not addressed by white persons, any social justice intentions or anti-oppressive sentiments are irrelevant to the fact and future of sexism and racism as patterns of inequality and the suffering they cause. Silence is just as oppressive as a visible act of oppression. Most privileged people engage in oppression, not by acting out of hostility or ill-will towards a subordinate group but because they acquiesce in the face of a cultural order that continues the work of oppression. This is all that is required of most privileged people for oppression to continue—that they not notice, that they do nothing, and that they remain silent (Johnson 2006). For those concerned with social justice and anti-oppression, an obvious course of action is to 'speak out.' This will be discussed in the final section of this chapter.

'Othering' subordinate groups is the third behaviour noted by Johnson (2006) that is carried out by privileged people in systems of privilege, which reinforces privilege and oppression. The concept of 'other' was presented in previous chapters with respect to oppressed persons being considered outside and different from the dominant group. That is, representative entities outside one's own gender, social group, class, culture, or civilization—are considered to be the Other. The creation of this binary opposite by privileged groups is known as 'othering.' All non-Western cultures are seen as the Other of the West, while within Western society, women, gay and lesbian persons, and immigrants are often seen as the Other (Sardar and Van Loon 2004). 'The most common representation of the Other is as the darker side, the binary opposite of oneself: we are civilized, they are barbaric; the colonists are hard-working, the natives are lazy; heterosexuals are good and moral, homosexuals are immoral and evil' (Sardar and Van Loon 2004, 13). For oppression to exist, two basic ingredients are required—a group that is being oppressed and an oppressor or privileged group that benefits from oppression. Moraga (2004) argues that in the process, the oppressor/privileged groups externalize their fears by projecting them onto the people who seem to best fit the category of the 'other.' Johnson (2006, 96) claims that 'Other is the key word in understanding how systems are identified with privileged groups. The privileged group is the assumed "we" in relation to "them". The "other" is the "you people" whom we regard as problematic, unacceptable, unlikable, or beneath our standards.' For example, in a white-dominated system, white is the assumed race and all *others* are viewed as non-white. This in effect lumps together a considerable diversity of ethno-racial groups into a single category of 'other' in relation to a white standard. To get a sense of the effect of this practice, Johnson (2006) asks us to imagine a society in which white people are referred to as 'non-coloureds.' The process of othering clearly reinforces privilege in society.

Why Dominant Groups Do Not See Privilege as a Problem

Very few people would like to think that they are oppressive or that they are connected to someone else's misery, no matter how remote the connection. If privileged groups were to see and accept oppression and privilege as their issues, they might want to do something about them. If middle-class people saw poverty as their issue, or if white people saw racism as their issue, or if males saw sexism as their issue, or if non-disabled persons saw ableism as their issue, there would be more engagement by privileged groups in confronting and eliminating relationships of domination and oppression. But this is not happening. Privileged groups are not engaged with these issues, and when they are, it is usually for a short time and with little effect. The fact that they have privilege allows them to avoid the responsibility they have for the perpetration and perpetuation of oppression. They avoid this responsibility because there are so many ways they can fool themselves into thinking that they are not part of the problem. Allan Johnson (2006) outlines a number of these ways, which are summarized here.

1. *Deny and minimize.* One of the easiest ways to 'get off the hook' is to deny that a problem of oppression exists (e.g., 'racism and sexism used to be problems, but they aren't anymore because of the laws and programs that address them'; 'there are no people with disabilities at my workplace, so it isn't a problem for me'). Closely associated with denial is the minimization of experiences with oppression (e.g., 'those Aboriginal people should just quit whining about colonization all the time and get over it'). When the reality of oppression is denied, so too is the reality of the privilege that underpins it, which is just what it takes to avoid responsibility. When privileged people practice this kind of denial and minimization, they are in effect acting as though they know better than oppressed persons do about what they are experiencing and up against, which is the kind of presumption that privilege fosters and allows. In other

words, privilege allows them to define other people's experiences for them and to deny the validity of their claims.

2. *Blame the victim*. Blaming the victim means acknowledging that harm has been done but holding the victim responsible. White people might say, for example, that if Aboriginal people would drop their traditional culture, stop drinking, get an education, and go to work, they would not have the number and severity of social problems that they currently experience. Similarly, when a woman says that she was sexually harassed, men can tell themselves that it was her own fault because she should not have dressed provocatively, or she should not have been where she was, or she sent mixed messages, or she asked for it to happen one way or the other. 'The result of such thinking is that oppression is blamed on the people who suffer most from it, while privilege and those who benefit remain invisible and relatively untouched' (Johnson 2006, 111).

3. *Call it something else*. A more subtle way of avoiding responsibility for oppression and privilege is to call them something else. For example, gender inequality is often referred to as 'the battle of the sexes' or as an anthropological curiosity based on the notion that males and females are from different cultures (if not from different planets) even though they may grow up in the same families, attend the same schools, and watch television together. Any problems or misunderstandings are seen as the result of different ways of communicating. And while there are gender differences in styles of talk, they are more significant than the differences, say, between Chinese and Canadian styles of talk because they serve the purpose of ensuring male privilege. For example, every time a man interrupts a woman and she defers by keeping quiet, a pattern of male dominance and male centredness is acted out once again.

4. *It's better this way*. The ideology that surrounds privilege includes all kinds of claims that the status quo is preferred. White people often claim that people of colour prefer to live with their own or that they cannot afford to live among white people. Both claims are incorrect, since research shows that most people of colour prefer to live in integrated neighbourhoods and that it is racism, not income, occupation, or education that gets in the way of integrated living for most people of colour, especially those in the middle class (Massey and Denton 1998, cited in Johnson 2006). Similarly, patriarchal culture conveys all kinds of messages to the effect that women prefer strong men to dominate them and make all the big decisions or that when a woman says 'no,' she really means 'maybe' or 'yes.' The truth does not matter in these situations because the purpose of the ideology of inequality is to reinforce the status quo (of privilege) by making it appear normal and legitimate. Even when oppressed persons call attention to the divisions and inequalities caused by privilege, they are often accused of creating divisions and problems themselves, with the result that talking about privilege rather than privilege itself is defined as the problem.

5. *It doesn't count if you don't mean it*. We have all experienced a member of a privileged group (including ourselves) saying something or doing something that has racial or sexist or classist overtones. Examples include a man who makes repeated

sexual comments to a female colleague, a white professor who only calls on white students in class, a middle-class person who makes a joke about poor people. When confronted (usually by subordinate group members), the privileged person often responds by becoming defensive and saying something like 'I didn't mean anything.' This kind of response is intended to get the person off the hook, the reasoning being that because the person did not mean any offence, then the action did not happen, since the only thing that connects the person to the consequences of what was said or done is conscious (i.e., bad) intent. This reaction fails to acknowledge that regardless of the intent, the woman or the person of colour or the poor person has been harmed and must deal with it on her or his own. In effect, 'I didn't mean it' or 'It was just a joke' comes very close to saying, 'I didn't say it' or 'I didn't do it,' which is not true. Most of the time, the true message should be that 'I said it' or 'I did it' but 'I did not think about it beforehand.' In most social situations, this kind of response does not get one off the hook. If I steal something and tell the judge that I did not mean anything by it, I will still be held responsible for my actions, and I will have an awareness of the consequences of what I do or do not do. But privilege works against such awareness for privileged persons in all kinds of social situations. As Johnson (2006, 117) says, 'the luxury of obliviousness makes a lack of conscious intent a path of least resistance that's easy to follow without knowing it. The sense of entitlement and superiority that underlies most forms of privilege runs so deep and is so entrenched that [privileged] people don't have to think about it in order to act from it.' People who say 'I didn't think about it' are often telling the truth, which makes it so disarming and such an effective way of defending privilege. The fact that people do not have to think about saying or doing hurtful things to subordinate persons is precisely the problem with privilege and the damage it causes.

6. *I'm one of the good ones.* Another way of avoiding responsibility for oppression and privilege is to make a case that because I am not a bad person (only bad people oppress others), the problem could not have anything to do with me. I can argue that I have no problem with gay and lesbian people in my workplace, that I have an 'End Racism' button on my office door, that I never park in handicapped parking places, and that I like women. And part of my being a good person is that I strongly disapprove of all those bad or flawed people who discriminate against others and I sympathize with people who suffer as a result. However, my silence, inaction, and passive acceptance of the everyday privilege that goes along with people like me makes me part of the problem. I am still on the outside looking in as a concerned but passive observer. When social categories work to my advantage, I must consider that these same categories are working against others through no fault of their own, which then becomes *my* business because I am being privileged at their expense. If people are being oppressed because of racism, sexism, and so on, other people are receiving privileged treatment because of racism, sexism, and so on. If privileged people do nothing, they are in effect supporting and perpetuating oppression. There is no such thing as a neutral position, because doing or saying nothing is a choice that has political consequences.

7. *Sick and tired.* When it comes to the problem of oppression and privilege, privileged persons often do not want to hear about it because it upsets the luxury of obliviousness that comes with their privilege. A common response is saying or making facial gestures that imply, 'Here we go again.' If I had a nickel for every time I have seen a student or a member of an audience that I was addressing (almost always privileged) roll his or her eyes when I start talking about social inequality or oppression, I could probably wipe out the entire federal deficit. Privileged people often become annoyed or irritated with the person who raises issues of oppression and privilege, not because they do not believe that these issues are real but because they feel that they are being put upon or bashed or made to feel guilty. They may feel that a great weight has been placed on their shoulders or that open season on privileged persons has just been declared. However, it is one thing to hear about problems associated with social inequality and oppression, but it is quite another to live with them every day. Yes, life is hard these days for almost everyone, and almost everyone may feel exhausted (as I have often heard from persons of privilege in a defensive manner), but white persons who feel exhausted are not exhausted because they are white. Heterosexual persons are not having a tough time because they are heterosexual. Subordinate group members have to do all the things that make privileged group members tired (from raising families to earning a living to growing older, and so on), but on top of that, they have to struggle with the accumulated stress that oppression piles on them simply because, through no fault of their own, they are in the wrong social categories.

In sum, a number of avoidance mechanisms are available to privileged groups that allow them to avoid feeling any guilt, shame, or responsibility for the deleterious effects of oppression. These mechanisms allow them to live in a world of denial and illusion where they are not involved in the life of society. This option 'puts members of privileged groups inside a tight little circle that cuts them off from what it means to be alive' (Johnson 2006, 124). It means that privileged groups have to distance and insulate themselves from much of humanity—men from women, white persons from people of colour, heterosexual persons from gay, lesbian, bisexual, and transgendered persons—because if they were to get too close to these people, they would find it more difficult to maintain the denial and illusion and would have to deal with the troubles that surround privilege and oppression. Given this situation, it would seem more desirable for dominant groups to accept responsibility for privilege and oppression and view it as a challenge and an opportunity rather than as an affliction or a source of guilt and shame.

A Taxonomy of Everyday Examples of Unearned Privilege

In her groundbreaking and celebrated work, Peggy McIntosh (1990) referred to what she calls the 'invisible knapsack.' The invisible knapsack contains all the benefits or privileges that come to us every day simply because we are white, or middle-class, or straight, or male, or non-disabled or are a member of any other privileged group in society. In the boxes below, I outline selected privileges that are associated with being middle- or upper-class, a member of the white race, male, heterosexual, non-disabled, a member of a two-parent family, and of adult age that precedes old age. I limited the number of privileges in each category to around 15 to 20, although some of the lists compiled by others are quite lengthy. McIntosh's original list of 'white privileges,' for example, contains 46 items. These lists do not reflect the privileges of every person who falls into a particular category. They are both under- and over-inclusive. Other social categories will have an impact on each set of privileges. For example, a black male will not have the same number of privileges or the same qualitative extent of privileges that a white male will have. A white male is automatically seen as an authority figure whereas a black man is not. Carbado (2004) tells us that we have to be careful not to universalize any category of privileged persons or present them as a 'cohesive identity' in ways that deny or obscure the fact of multiplicity or heterogeneity *within* categories of privileged persons. At the same time, people who fall into categories of privilege must do more than identify the privileges that have been conferred upon them. They must also realize how they actively re-enact these privileges interpersonally, culturally, and institutionally. In other words, privileged persons must come to recognize their own complicity in the normalization of privilege.

Middle- or Upper-Class Privilege

- I can avoid members of other classes or races and only be with people like me if I choose.
- I do not worry about going hungry or being homeless.
- I can be charitable or not as I please.
- I can live where I choose and move when and where I choose.
- I can enjoy frivolous spending without worrying about end-of-the-month payments.
- I can join clubs and organizations that many cannot.
- I enjoy respect and trust in most situations from most people.
- I am assumed innocent by the criminal justice system at least until proven guilty.
- I do not have to worry about getting adequate or competent legal help.
- I do not have to shop around for the best buy or wait for sales.
- I can be sure that my children will not be mistreated by teachers and staff at school.
- I do not worry about paying for music lessons or sports memberships for my children.

Middle- or Upper-Class Privilege (*continued*)

- I do not worry about how an emergency might affect me financially.
- I can hire people to help me care for my children or do the housework.
- Entertainment or going out is readily available to me.
- I can take expensive vacations when and where I want.
- I can get discounts on major purchases and preferred interest rates on my investments because I am seen as a valuable customer.
- I do not have to worry about how I can afford my retirement.
- I can afford excellent medical and hospital care.
- I am not presumed to be immoral, lazy, evil, unmotivated, stupid, incompetent, work-shy, alcoholic, or promiscuous because of my social class.
- I can leave my children with an inheritance to make things a little easier for them.
- I can assume that I am entitled to these privileges because of the dominant social beliefs.
- I can take advantage of all the income tax breaks that are not available to those with lower incomes.

Thanks to the Women's Theological Center in Boston for several of the above privileges.

White Privilege

- I can, if I wish, arrange to be in the company of people of my own race most of the time.
- If I should need to move, I can be pretty sure of renting or purchasing housing in an area that I can afford and in which I would want to live.
- I can be pretty sure that my neighbours in such a location will be neutral or pleasant to me.
- I can go shopping alone most of the time, pretty well assured that I will not be followed or harassed.
- I can turn on the television or turn to the front page of the newspaper and see people of my race widely represented.
- When I am told about our national heritage or about 'civilization,' I am shown that people of my colour made it what it is.

White Privilege (*continued*)

- I can be sure that my children will be given curricular materials that testify to the existence of their race.
- If I want to, I can be pretty sure of finding a publisher for this piece on white privilege.
- I can go into a music shop and count on finding the music of my race represented, into a supermarket and find the staple foods that fit with my cultural traditions, into a hairdresser's shop and find someone who can deal with my hair.
- Whether I use cheques, credit cards, or cash, I can count on my skin colour not working against the appearance of financial reliability.
- I can arrange to protect my children most of the time from people who might not like them.
- I can swear or dress in second-hand clothes or not answer letters without having people attribute these choices to the bad morals, the poverty, or the illiteracy of my race.
- I can speak in public to a powerful male group without putting my race on trial.
- I can do well in a challenging situation without being called a credit to my race.
- I am never asked to speak for all the people of my racial group.
- I can remain oblivious to the language and customs of persons of colour, who constitute the world's majority, without feeling in my culture any penalty for such oblivion.
- I can criticize our government and talk about how much I fear its policies and behaviour without being seen as a cultural outsider.
- I can be pretty sure that if I ask to talk to 'the person in charge,' I will be facing a person of my race.
- If a traffic cop pulls me over or if my tax return is audited, I can be sure that I haven't been singled out because of my race.
- I can easily buy posters, postcards, picture books, greeting cards, dolls, toys, and children's magazines reflecting people of my race.
- I can go home from most meetings of organizations I belong to feeling somewhat tied in rather than isolated, out-of-place, outnumbered, unheard, held at a distance, or feared.
- I can take a job with an affirmative action employer without having co-workers on the job suspect that I got it because of my race.
- I can choose public accommodation without fearing that people of my race cannot get in or will be mistreated in the places I have chosen.

White Privilege (*continued*)

- I can be sure that if I need legal or medical help, my race will not work against me.
- If my day, week, or year is going badly, I need not question whether each negative episode or situation has racial overtones.
- I can choose blemish cover or bandages in 'flesh' color that more or less matches my skin.

Taken from Peggy McIntosh, *White Privilege: Unpacking the Invisible Knapsack,* 1990.

Male Privilege

- I can dominate a conversation without being seen as dominating.
- I am praised for spending time with my children and for cooking and doing household chores.
- I am not expected to change my name when I get married.
- I can walk alone in public without fear of being harassed or sexually violated.
- I never worry about being paid less than my female counterparts.
- Prospective employers will never ask me whether I plan to have children.
- I am confident that I will never be accused of sleeping my way to the top in my workplace.
- When I get dressed in the morning, I never worry about whether my clothing will invite sexual harassment.
- I don't have to choose between having a career or having a family.
- I can be moody, grouchy, or abrupt without it being attributed to my sex or to menopause or to PMS.
- If I am sexually active, even promiscuous, I can largely count on not being called a slut or a whore. In fact, I will be seen as a stud in some circles and held in high regard.
- I can count on my wife or partner doing most of the housework and childcare even if she has a job outside the home.
- Should I have a medical problem, I can rest assured that more is known about male health problems and how medicines affect male bodies.

Male Privilege (*continued*)

- I can find positive male role models in positions of authority almost everywhere I look.
- Should a woman with whom I had sex unexpectedly become pregnant, I can rest assured that it will be seen as her fault and her responsibility.
- There is no social pressure on me to marry before the age of 30.
- I can express anger or outrage without being seen as irrational, emotional, or too sensitive.

Thanks mainly to Devon Carbado (2004) and also to Steven P. Schacht (2003) for most of the above male privileges.

Heterosexual Privilege

- I can, if I wish, be in the company of other heterosexual persons every day.
- I can be assured that I will not be blamed for creating or spreading the AIDS virus.
- I don't have to worry about people trying to cure me of my heterosexuality.
- My partner and I can display affection in public without fear of ridicule or harassment.
- I can be assured that I will never be denied medical treatment because I am heterosexual.
- My children will never have to explain why they have parents of different genders.
- I am guaranteed that if I marry, it will be legally recognized in every country in the world.
- I can take a job with almost any employer and be assured that my partner will be included in the benefits package.
- I can be assured that I will never be asked to speak for all heterosexual persons.
- I can be assured that my children will be taught in schools (explicitly or implicitly) about the naturalness of heterosexuality.
- My heterosexuality will be affirmed in every religious tradition.
- I do not have to struggle with 'coming out' or worry about being 'outed.'

Heterosexual Privilege (*continued*)

- I can display my partner's photos at work without causing office gossip or hostility.
- I don't have to worry about being bashed after leaving a social event with other heterosexuals.
- I can apply to adopt children without having my motives questioned.
- I can be assured that I will not be refused hospital visitation rights to see my partner because of my heterosexuality.
- My heterosexuality is never mistaken as a lifestyle but is merely one more component of my personal identity.
- As a heterosexual man, I am welcome to become a Big Brother or leader of a Boy Scout's troop.
- My parents do not love me 'in spite of' my heterosexuality, nor do they blame themselves for it.
- I can introduce my partner to my work colleagues without fearing that it may block me from promotion or other workplace opportunities.
- I don't have to be exposed to someone expressing pity or saying 'that's okay' on learning that I am heterosexual.
- I do not have to worry about any negative consequences that my heterosexuality might have personally on my children, especially as it relates to their social life.
- Whether on television or at the movies, heterosexuality is always affirmed as healthy and normal.
- If a child is sexually abused by a heterosexual person, I do not have to worry about being suspected as a pedophile because of my heterosexuality.
- I will never be accused of recruiting others to join my heterosexual orientation.
- Every day is 'Heterosexual Pride Day.'

Thanks to Devon Carbado (2004) for most of the above privileges.

The next set of privileges was originally developed by Peggy McIntosh as examples of heterosexual privilege. It seems to me, however, that these privileges could just as easily be applied to the traditional form of family that is still considered the norm in North America and in other Anglo democracies—that is, a heterosexual couple with children. This type of family is, of course, a form of heterosexism, but it is also a family type that enjoys certain privileges that are not available to other family forms—single-parent and two-(same-sex)-parent families. The fact that a heterosexual 'different-sex' couple lives together under the same roof triggers all kinds of societal assumptions about their individual worth, politics, life, and values and triggers a host of unearned advantages and powers for each of them (McIntosh 2003).

Traditional Family Privilege

- My children do not have to answer questions about why they have two different-sex parents.
- I have no difficulty finding neighbourhoods where people approve of our household.
- I will never be turned down on an application for housing because there are two parents.
- Our children are given texts and classes that implicitly support our kind of family unit and do not turn them against my choice of domestic partnership.
- I can travel alone with my family without expecting embarrassment or hostility from those who deal with us.
- Most people I meet will see my marital arrangements as an asset to my life or as a favourable comment on my likeability, my competence, and my mental health.
- I can talk about the social event of the weekend without fearing most listeners' reactions.
- I will feel welcomed and 'normal' in the usual walks of public life, both institutional and social.
- As a male adult in a traditional family unit, I can be seen as all right if I work in traditional areas of women's work—nursing, hairdressing, and so on—because I do not live with men.

Non-Disability Privilege

- Because I do not have to be concerned about my disability status, I can simply regard myself as a human being.
- I can be assured that most people do not assume I am incapable of a sex life or of having children.
- I am not likely to be singled out at school based on stereotypes that underestimate my abilities and be put in a special education class that doesn't allow me to develop my potential.

Non-Disability Privilege (*continued*)

- I am not likely to be shuttled into some dead-end, menial job, given inadequate job training, paid less than I am worth regardless of my ability, or separated from other workers on the job.
- I can ask for help without worrying that people will assume I need help with everything.
- I don't have to deal with an endless and exhausting stream of attention to a disability status and can simply take my non-disability status for granted.
- I can succeed without people being surprised because they have low expectations of my ability to contribute to society.
- I can pretty well be assured that heroes, role models, and respected people will share my non-disabled status.
- I can be assured that when I express my ideas, they will not be dismissed or ignored but will be taken more seriously than if I were disabled.
- I can have access to polling stations on election day and vote in privacy without the help of others.
- When I go out in public, I can be pretty sure that I will not be stared at or looked at as odd or not belonging and that most buildings will be accessible to me.
- I can be assured that I will usually be taken seriously and not treated like a child.
- I assume that when I need to travel, I will have access to buses, trains, airplanes, and other means of transportation.
- I am assured that wherever I go, most people will not feel awkward or uncomfortable around me.
- I am assured that I can participate actively in mainstream society and will not be segregated into living situations such as nursing homes or into special schools and sports programs.

Thanks to Allan G. Johnson (2006) for the above examples of non-disability privileges.

Young Adult and Middle-Age Privilege

- I do not have to endure people yelling at me because they assume I cannot hear.
- I can be assured that people will not infantilize me by talking 'baby talk' to me.
- I am assured that other people will not try to make decisions for me, often without consultation.
- I am not likely to be viewed as a burden on society and draining the country's resources.
- I do not have to experience people assuming that I am stupid or cannot do anything for myself.
- I do not have to endure receiving endless advertisements in the mail for funeral arrangements, estate planning, pension and insurance schemes, nursing-home care, and specials on incontinence supplies.
- I am not likely to feel useless, lonely, and suicidal because of my age or have people pity me because they assume I am lonely and useless.
- I can be assured that people will not equate my age with illness and infirmity.
- I am assured that people will not consider me as incapable of having a sex life or that if I do, it must be because I am a 'dirty old man.'
- I don't have to endure being called 'dear' or 'love' by people I don't even know.
- I do not have a steady stream of people coming to my door lying to me about what my house needs and trying to rip me off with various questionable products and schemes.
- I can pretty well be assured that characters my age in the movies or on television will not be made fun of because of their age.
- I am not likely to be referred to in derogatory terms such as an 'old fuddy-duddy' or 'dirty old man' or 'you old fart' or told that I am 'over the hill.'
- I do not have to endure colleagues discounting my scholarship without even reading it because they assume it must be out-of-date or just contains old ideas.

Social Work and Privilege

Because everyone in society is affected by oppression and privilege and because everyone grows up within and participates in systems of privilege and oppression, then privilege is an issue for social workers personally and professionally and for social work organizations. Social workers generally are members of privileged groups. This is not to say that many social workers have not experienced oppression or are not members of oppressed groups. Overall, however, they enjoy many of the privileges outlined earlier in this chapter by virtue of their race, job, education, middle class, professional status, economic status, age, non-disability, and so on. In addition, a service user quickly learns that the social worker often has control over the resources that the service user needs and has decision-making power over certain aspects of the service user's life that the service user does not have over the social worker's (Marsiglia and Kulis 2009). Unfortunately, just as privilege is not handled very well by privileged people generally, so too are social workers and social work organizations often oblivious to or in denial of privilege issues in the course of their social work practice.

Dominelli (2002) points out that privileged people (including social workers) have three strategies available to them to deal with their position of dominance over others (including service users): a demarcationist option, an incorporationist option, and an egalitarian option. These three positions can co-exist and overlap each other, and a person may hold more than one of them simultaneously or at different points in time. Only the egalitarian position is not exclusionary. People who subscribe to the demarcationist strategy tend to have a hierarchical view of the world and orient their actions towards keeping power and resources in their own hands. They follow a 'we-them' demarcation between privileged and inferior people. The incorporationist option allows for collaboration between privileged and subordinate groups, with those who are 'othered' being allowed to permeate the ranks of the privileged group, but only if they know their place and maintain a respectful distance. Low-level reform aimed at improving what is deemed to be a basically sound system is the goal of the incorporationists, which they achieve through the selective inclusion of people drawn from the ranks of the 'other.' This group of selected people are those whom the dominant group thinks they can trust to be true to the values and traditions of the dominant group, and they are given honorary status in the dominant group. However, this honorary status can be withdrawn at any time if the behaviour of the person who is designated as inferior displeases the dominant group. Those in the dominant group who reject the current social system because they consider it unfair and unjust follow the egalitarian option. They seek transformation of a society characterized by inequality and oppression to one that is egalitarian and inclusive of difference on equal terms. Anti-oppressive social workers, even though they may be members of privileged groups, would obviously opt for the egalitarian strategy. The parallels between the demarcationist and neo-conservative social work positions, between the incorporationist and liberal-humanist social work positions, and between the egalitarian and critical social work positions should be obvious at this point.

Marsiglia and Kulis (2009) speak to a few problems with respect to the issue of privilege and social work practice. They claim that the social worker's privilege, if left unchecked, can be a barrier to empathy and an obstacle to culturally grounded practice (i.e., anti-oppressive practice). This is so because privilege makes professionals assume certain things about service users, such as having what the worker has (a car or a comfortable home) or sharing similar experiences (being able to eat a hot breakfast before coming to the agency). Service users are usually aware of privileges enjoyed by the social worker even if the social worker is not.

> If left unaddressed, this perceived privilege can become an obstacle to effective communication and rapport building, as clients [sic] may assume that the professionals cannot understand what they are going through due to their lack of experience with certain oppressive situations. Social workers, including those from minority groups, may be in denial about the privileges they enjoy that their clients [sic] do not. Self-awareness about privilege increases social workers' effectiveness and, in the end, enhances their professional and personal growth. Ignoring privilege or minimizing its impact on the client-worker relationship may compromise rapport and trust, leading to ineffective practice [Marsiglia and Kulis 2009, 17].

In a study of how a group of (self-defined) left-of-centre social workers dealt with issues of class, race, and gender in their everyday work, Donna Baines (2002) reported on a number of observations made by the study participants on some negative ways that some social workers and social work supervisors handled issues of privilege. First, one participant noted that many people feared that if they began to talk about giving up their privilege, they would become subordinated, which had the effect of shutting down all discussion on confronting privilege. Another participant observed that there is a tendency not to acknowledge one's own power; rather, everyone wants to be part of an oppressed group. This sentiment, which is called the 'flight to innocence' by Sharene Razack (1998, cited in Baines 2002), is a way for people to avoid the responsibility for changing relationships of dominance-subordination by 'hiding behind some facet of their identity that locates them close to, or within, subordinated groups' (1998, cited in Baines 2002, 192). This is a revealing observation that supports what Johnson asserts about privilege in that it shows that people are more willing to confront their subordinate status than they are their privileged positions. Baines speculates that because many social work models emphasize seeing the world through the eyes of service users and fail to recognize (or at least address) the power and privileges that social workers possess on the basis of their education, class, employment, race, and so on, the need to identify oneself as a member of an oppressed group is the logical extension of such models. I think it is also a way of denying that part of one's identity is associated with the harm others experience because of oppression and it gets people off the hook in terms of taking any responsibility for doing something about it. I agree with Baines (2002, 192) when she says that 'little is achieved by privileged people sharing powerlessness while much can be achieved by redistributing power and building politicized, affirming identities. Learning how to use power and privilege, rather than denying it [sic], is part of the challenge of the anti-racist [and anti-oppressive] project.'

In addition to how it affects people, the trouble that surrounds privilege also affects organizations such as workplaces (including social work agencies) and universities (including social work programs). The prevalence of privilege and oppression in organizations is one of our best kept secrets for those with privilege and one of our worst kept secrets for members of subordinate groups. Most of the time, people act as though there were no issues of privilege and oppression, and the organization either denies that anything is wrong or is oblivious to it—until a crisis occurs and the typical reaction is panicked efforts at damage control to minimize bad publicity or legal exposure (Johnson 2006). If left unattended, privilege makes organizations increasingly dysfunctional and vulnerable. In a society such as ours that is characterized by relationships of privilege and oppression, the assumption cannot be that because no one has complained, therefore there is no problem with oppression in an organization. The workplace and the university are part of the larger society. People in the workplace or in the university have grown up and been socialized in the larger society. To some degree, the organization has to reflect the larger society, which includes the existence of oppression and privilege. Privilege and oppression must become a part of the organization's agenda, and it must be discussed. The silence must be broken. Otherwise, white men, for instance, will see little reason to examine themselves in relation to the racism and sexism that haunt the lives of so many people or to see how living in a racist and sexist society has influenced them with respect to how they see the world or how they regard women, people of colour, persons with disabilities, and so on (Johnson 2006). It is not enough for the boss or the instructor to treat women as they would men or people of colour as they would white people, because sexism and racism go beyond one person's intentions or behaviours. If privilege and subordination are not discussed in the organization, it becomes very difficult or risky for a member of a subordinate group to raise issues of privilege. If subordinate group members become uncomfortable working or studying in an organization because critical issues are not addressed, the organization will become known as a place where they are not fully welcome. Persons who are not white, heterosexual, male, non-disabled, and so on will realize that they can do better elsewhere, 'someplace where you can look at those with power and influence and see people who look like you' (Johnson, 64–65). Overtime, these other places will do better because of their diverse population of students or workers and because they are able to attract and keep talent from a larger pool of individuals.

What Can We Do?[2]

There are no easy answers to the question of what we can do about the problem of privilege and oppression. There is no recipe book or how-to manual or 12-step program. Nor is there any way around or over the problem. We must confront it head-on and go through it if we are to make a difference. The following are some of the tasks that can be carried out in confronting privilege and unsettling systems of privilege.

1. *Reclaim the words.* One of the inherent characteristics of professionalism is that each profession develops a professional discourse or vocabulary. For a long time, social work had a clinical or therapeutic discourse, mainly because it aligned itself with the medical model and adopted counselling or therapy as ways of dealing with social problems and people experiencing social problems. Much of our discourse today, it seems to me, is a consequence of trying to avoid politically charged terms or words so that we do not offend the public, our employers, mainstream social workers, and so on. In an earlier chapter, I made the argument that the term 'social inequality' is one of those bourgeois, technical, polite, and professional terms that tend to reduce the political charge or the imperative of doing something about the violent outcomes of oppression. We should identify social inequality for what it is—socially sanctioned social terrorism and structural violence. Then maybe we will take it more seriously and try to do more about eliminating it.

Similarly, social work has developed a discourse about difference that has little political charge and does not make people feel uncomfortable when they hear the words in the discourse—words like diversity, tolerance, cultural sensitivity, appreciating difference. Contrast these words with the following: racism, sexism, patriarchy, domination, privilege, oppression, subordination, anti-Semitism, classism. The latter group of words actually names problems, and these words tend to be the vocabulary of people hurt by the problems. People from privileged groups are often uncomfortable with such words because they do not want to look at what they point to. White men, for example, tend not to want to look at sexism or racism. Heterosexual persons do not want to look at heterosexism. Privileged persons would rather hear words such as diversity, appreciating difference, tolerance, and cultural sensitivity, because they are good things to talk about and the language is polite (Johnson 2006). The political function of using terms such as these, however, is that they cover over the troubles associated with racism and other forms of oppression and privilege. And if we cannot talk about a trouble, then we cannot do much about it. 'Words like sexism and privilege point to something difficult and painful in our history that continues in everyday life in our society. That means that there is no way to talk about it without difficulty and pain' (Johnson 2006, 10). One thing we can do then as anti-oppressive social workers is to reclaim the words of oppression and privilege and recognize that a word like 'racist' does not mean 'bad white people' or 'sexist' does not mean 'bad men' or 'feminism' does not mean being a lesbian or man-hater. We can use words like oppression and domination and sexism without being oppressive or dominant or sexist. If we are going to be part of the solution with respect to eliminating oppression and all the harm it causes, then we must drop our defensive sensitivity to that difficult discourse and the reality to which it points.

2. *Acknowledge that oppression and privilege exist.* Most systems of privilege maintain oppression by denying or minimizing its existence, by blaming people experiencing oppression, by calling it something else, or by diverting attention away from it. There would be much more opposition to privilege if people with privilege were aware of

how it affects the everyday lives of subordinate groups. Awareness by itself is not enough, however. We must maintain this awareness in the face of a system characterized by paths of least resistance that lead away from critical awareness of how systems of privilege and oppression work. It is fantasy to think that we can end privilege without changing the system that allows a small minority of privileged people to have a monopoly on political power and to own most of the world's wealth and resources, leaving the rest of the population to fight over what is left. It is also fantasy to think that we can end privilege by changing the way individuals think. The crucial task is to apply our understanding of how systems of oppression and privilege work and to change the systems themselves—social, economic, cultural, political, religious, familial, and so on. Maintaining a critical awareness of privilege takes commitment and work, and to hang onto this awareness we must make it part of our everyday lives.

3. *Pay attention.* Developing an understanding of what privilege and oppression are and how they operate and how we participate in them is the first step in working for change. The simplest way to develop an understanding is to make reading about privilege part of our lives. It is easy to have an opinion, but it takes work to know what you are talking about. Some people assume that because privilege and oppression are part of everyday life or because they have experienced oppression, then they know all they have to know. However, one person cannot possibly experience all that is involved in oppression and privilege. As well, our experiences are so deeply shaped by privilege and oppression that often, what we think we know misses the mark. This is why activists talk to one another and read each other's work, because seeing things clearly is tricky business. There is a vast literature on issues of privilege available in any decent library system, although as Johnson (2006) observes, you would never know it, judging from its invisibility in the mass media and mainstream bookstores. The mass media would rather discuss whether or not men and women are from different planets or have different brains than examine the reality of male privilege. Reading is just the beginning, however, because at some point we have to look at ourselves and society and see whether we can identify what we are reading about. For example, once we have included the concept of 'paths of least resistance' into our everyday consciousness, we begin to see them everywhere. If privileged groups are to take their share of responsibility for dealing with issues of privilege, then we must listen, observe, ask, read, and listen again—we must make it our business to find out for ourselves.

Using My Privilege to Advance the Cause

For the past five years, I have been the dean of the Faculty of Social Work at the University of Manitoba. It is one of the largest social work programs in Canada, with three campuses, three degree levels, a large distance-education

Using My Privilege to Advance the Cause (*continued*)

program, close to 1,000 students, and a budget of approximately $6 million. As dean, I was a member of the senior administration in the university, and I had a very busy job. One day I was giving a guest lecture, and a student asked me the following question: 'You have written a lot on structural and anti-oppressive social work, but don't you think it is all talk? I mean, you have a big job here and are part of management—some would say part of the enemy. How can you write all this stuff and not practise it in your big fancy job?'

Fortunately, it was a question that I had frequently asked myself, so I was able to respond to it based on an ongoing critical reflection I have always carried out with respect to my job and my privileges. I told the class that I viewed my job as doing anti-oppressive social work—just in a different position from that of a mainstream social work job. As dean, I was responsible for many aspects of the faculty, which included hiring (faculty and staff), faculty development, supporting equity measures, curriculum, and policies and procedures—not total responsibility for all of them, but I had significant input and influence, not only because of my position but also because of my scholarship. I was able, for example, to write the faculty position descriptions specifying that one of the criteria for applicants was knowledge of anti-oppressive social work or some aspect of it. I was able to hire staff members from subordinate groups if there were such applications, and I was able to seek out such applicants. I do not think it is right (for all kinds of reasons) for a student from a subordinate group (approximately half our students were Aboriginal) to come into our general office and see a 'sea of white faces'—what has been called in the literature on privilege a 'white-out.' I was able to compose the mission statement for the faculty in a way that reflected social justice and anti-oppressive goals and principles. I was able to hire faculty persons from subordinate groups and support them during their initial adjustment period with the faculty. I was able to push the curriculum agenda towards more anti-oppressive content, although this was always a sensitive matter because not all social work faculty members are in favour of anti-oppressive concepts. I was able to support the equity programs at our social work campus in northern Manitoba where Aboriginal persons made up 80 per cent of the student body. In the inner-city program, we gave preference to applicants who were refugees or immigrants, Aboriginal people, disabled persons, persons of colour, and resource-poor persons (all persons admitted had to meet a minimal academic standard). Now, much of the equity measures were in place when I arrived in Manitoba, but I was

Using My Privilege to Advance the Cause (*continued*)

able to support and help to develop them. On the national level, I recall a meeting of the Canadian Association of Deans and Directors of Schools of Social Work during which a small committee from the Canadian Association of Schools of Social Work presented a proposal to us that would require all schools or faculties of social work to have an equity plan for its programs. This would entail establishing goals with respect to ensuring that the school's personnel, curriculum content, policies (e.g., tenure and promotion) and procedures, and so on would reflect the concerns and issues of groups who have historically faced insurmountable objects with respect to getting into university and who are in subordinate and inferior social positions in today's society. A number of the heads of social work programs seemed quite hostile to the notion of equity as well as to the group who was presenting. I was able to intervene, using my position as dean of a large social work program, as someone who had an extensive publication record and was respected by most of the other social work academics present, and as someone who had been around for a long time and could articulate the need for such a policy. The hostility to the committee and its proposal regarding an equity plan as a standard of accreditation evaporated. In other words, I was able to use my privilege to advance the cause of anti-oppression.

The above is not intended to draw positive attention to me but to show that you do not have to be in a frontline social work position to successfully carry out anti-oppressive practice. The need for such practice is all around us, both in our work lives and in our personal lives.

4. *Learn to listen.* Johnson (2006, 141) says it best in the following passage:

Attentive listening is especially difficult for members of dominant groups. If someone confronts you with your own behaviour that supports privilege, step off the path of least resistance that encourages you to defend and deny. Don't tell them they're too sensitive or need a better sense of humor, and don't try to explain away what you did as something else than what they're telling you it was. Don't say you didn't mean it or that you were only kidding. Don't tell them what a champion of justice you are or how hurt you feel because of what they're telling you. Don't make jokes or try to be cute or charming, since only access to privilege can lead someone to believe these are acceptable responses to something as serious as privilege and oppression. Listen to what is being said. Take it seriously. Assume for the time being that it's true, because given the power of paths of least resistance, it probably is. And then take responsibility to do something about it.

5. *Little risks: Do something.* The more we pay attention to privilege and oppression, the more we will see opportunities to do something about them. Opportunities exist everywhere, beginning with ourselves. We can become cognizant of the paths of least resistance that we follow and our relationship to them that makes it so easy to follow them. For myself, it can mean trying to stop hogging air time and interrupting others (especially women) and learning new ways of listening more and talking less. Or it can mean that I stop avoiding looking at or communicating with persons who have noticeable disabilities and learning to get over my feelings of discomfort and awkwardness. There is no limit to the number of paths of least resistance that I can step off. It is not just a matter of changing personal behaviour, however, because the choices I make are connected to the systems in which I participate. By *openly* changing how I participate in a system, I not only change my behaviour but I also contribute to changing how that system operates. Changing the world involves the dynamic relationship between personal and social change. Other ways that we can help to make a difference include the following:

- *Make noise and be seen.* Every system of privilege and oppression depends on silence. Rather than collude in it, we should show up, stand up, speak out, sign petitions, write letters, volunteer.
- *Find little ways of getting off the paths of least resistance.* It can be as simple as not laughing at a racist or sexist or heterosexist joke or stepping it up a notch and saying that you do not find such jokes funny. It can be writing to the editor of your local newspaper to protest any instances of sexism or racism or any other form of oppression that appeared in the paper. In this way, you interfere with the normal flow of business and subvert the assumption that everybody is going along with the status quo by not going along with it.
- *Dare to make people feel uncomfortable, starting with yourself.* One could ask about the profile of employees in one's workplace if, for example, most of the clerical staff are women and most of the managerial staff are men or if there is a sea of white faces in a university admissions or faculty office to greet members of a diverse society with many faces that are not white. Some people would object to making others feel uncomfortable, but there is nothing comfortable about being a member of an oppressed group, and systems of privilege do a lot more than make people feel uncomfortable. Almost any significant social movement (e.g., the suffragette movement, the civil rights movement, the trade union movement) has depended on discomfort and disruption to bring about social change.
- *Openly choose and model alternative paths.* As we identify the paths of least resistance that we tend to follow, we can identify alternative paths and openly follow them so that people can see what we are doing. Paths of least resistance become more visible when people follow alternatives, just as rules become more visible when they are broken. Any university instructor will tell you

that students tend to sit in the same seat every time they attend class and that it is extremely noticeable when the seating pattern is broken on just one occasion.

- *Openly promote change in how systems are organized around privilege.* The possibilities are almost endless, because privilege is everywhere. We could, for example, advocate for equality in the workplace, not support businesses that engage in unfair labour practices or that are inaccessible to people with disabilities (and tell the businesses why we do not support them), support fair trade businesses, join international organizations such as the anti-globalization movement or the peace movement or the environmental movement or Amnesty International, support 'end legislated poverty' organizations. Openly support and compliment people when they take an alternative path to that of the least resistance.

The above activities for confronting and challenging privilege were developed by Allan Johnson (2006) for anyone in society who might be concerned with issues of privilege and oppression. Obviously, they have relevance for social workers who follow a social justice mandate. In the previous chapter, I outlined a number of principles of anti-oppressive social work practice that are equally relevant to confronting and resisting privilege—everything from having a goal of social transformation to the constructive use of anger.

A number of writers advocate that members of privileged groups become 'allies' of subordinate groups and work collectively to overcome relationships of privilege and oppression (e.g., Sisneros et al. 2008; Bishop 2002). In her book *Becoming an Ally: Breaking the Cycle of Oppression*, Anne Bishop presents a portrait of allies as persons who are socially aware, are connected with *all* other people, have a critical analysis of social structures, possess a collective orientation as opposed to one that is individualistic, have an acceptance of struggle and a sense of process, have an understanding of 'power with' as opposed to 'power over,' and have a high degree of self-understanding, a knowledge of history, and an understanding that good intentions do not matter if there is no action against oppression. She makes the point that the same characteristics are typical of people who are well advanced in their own liberation process. Bishop (2002, 110) says of allies:

allies understand that, as part of various oppressor groups (white, male, able-bodied, heterosexual, middle or above in the class structure), they did not individually bring the situation [of oppression] about and they cannot just reach out with goodwill and solve it. They understand that they must act with others [not for others or on behalf of others] to contribute to change. They believe that to do nothing is to reinforce the *status quo*; . . . They take responsibility for helping to solve problems of historical injustice without taking on individual guilt. Most look for what they can do, with others, in a strategic way, and try to accept their limitations beyond that.

Allies would carry out most if not all of the activities outlined above with respect to confronting and trying to change systems of privilege. Bishop presents an extensive list of questions and guidelines that someone considering becoming an ally to oppressed groups should ask himself or herself. The most important guideline for being an ally, in my view, is that the role of the ally is to help or assist oppressed groups in any way one can in their struggle for liberation. Under no circumstances should one assume that one knows better or should be the leader just because one is a member of a privileged group—this is probably the worst thing one could do. Becoming allies and/or doing something else to combat social injustice and inequality in our society is critical. Although not powerless to affect their own living conditions, oppressed groups cannot, by themselves, do away with entrenched systems of privilege. What is needed is for privileged persons to make the problem of privilege *their* problem and to do something about it (Johnson 2006). Becoming an ally is one way of doing this.

The final action to be mentioned here that we can take to undo our privilege is for each of us to take what Peggy McIntosh calls our 'invisible knapsack' and remove all of its contents. This invisible knapsack contains all the benefits that come to us simply because we are white, or male, or straight, or middle-class, or non-disabled. We have to open that knapsack, dump out the contents, and take a look at all the different ways that these ascribed characteristics (those we are born with) have become so obscured and invisible that we have come to believe that the privileges we have in our lives are the result of some kind of achievement on our parts. In other words, we have to dispel the myth of meritocracy. We must use our unearned advantages to weaken hidden systems of privilege and our arbitrarily awarded power to reconstruct power systems on a broader base.

Conclusion

This chapter focused on privilege, which is the flip side of oppression. The relationship between the two is direct and unambiguous. We have oppression because we have privilege. Privilege benefits one group at the expense of many groups. In discussing the nature of privilege, we saw that it is surrounded by a paradox in that those who have privilege tend not to know it or know how privilege happens from one moment to the next. It is invisible to most privileged persons but not to oppressed groups. For the most part, privileged persons believe that the unearned advantages attached to their special group membership are the outcome of their hard work, vigilance, and cultural superiority. This belief is reinforced by a number of myths, such as the myth of meritocracy. Together, oppression and privilege protect the privileged group's access to a wider range of better-paying and higher-status positions as well as preferential access to and treatment from our social institutions. Like oppression, privilege is multi-dimensional and can only be understood if viewed as an intersectional phenomenon.

When we looked at the dynamics of privilege, we saw that it is not considered a problem by the dominant group because of the 'luxury of obliviousness'—that because they own or control most of society's resources, its social institutions, and political power, they do not have to think about how their privilege negatively affects subordinate groups. Dominant group members tend to compare themselves to other dominant group members and not to members of oppressed groups. We looked at the way systems of privilege operate, and we saw how the behaviours of following 'the path of least resistance,' remaining silent, and 'othering' subordinate groups are used to prop up these systems. We examined a number of mechanisms that allow persons with privilege to avoid any responsibility for oppression and its deleterious effects. I presented specific examples of privileges associated with a number of social groups and argued that privilege has not been handled very well by social work to date. Finally, I suggested a number of activities that confront and challenge privilege. In closing, I offer an excerpt from one of my favourite writers on the subject of privilege, Allan Johnson (2006, 107).

> Having privilege doesn't mean that someone is a bad person. But it does mean that there isn't a single member of a dominant group who doesn't have issues of privilege to deal with both internally and externally, in relation to the world around them. It was handed to them when they were children with no sense of what was wise and good to take into themselves and what was not. And, so they accepted it, uncritically, unknowingly, even innocently, but accept it they did. It wasn't their fault. They have no reason to feel guilty about it, because they didn't *do* anything. But now it is there for them to deal with, just as it's there for women, people of color, people with disabilities, lesbians, and gay men who *also* didn't do anything to deserve the oppression that so profoundly shapes their lives.

in solidarity,
bob mullaly

Critical Questions for Discussion

1. How does privilege also hurt privileged persons or groups?

2. I remember observing a situation recently in which a man held a door open for a woman, who reacted by saying, 'I can open the door myself, thank you.' The man said in a surprised tone, 'I was only being polite.' What do you make of this door-opening ceremony? Is there more going on than the man might realize? What cultural messages are being conveyed about men and women? Do you think the same man might be as 'polite' at home, sharing equally in the housework and childcare?

3. Identify any critical incidents in your life that led to your increased awareness of privilege enjoyed by members of your group.

4. Discuss how the 'invisibility of privilege' might be made evident to other social workers or fellow students who are from privileged backgrounds without making them feel guilty or defensive.

5. How would you open people up to the idea of male or gender or heterosexual privilege without turning them off?

6. Does your agency or school have a diversity training program? If not, why not? If so, does it include white privilege? If not, how can you help it to provide a safe forum for the exploration of the realities and challenges of white privilege?

Further Readings

Anderson, Sharon A., and Valerie A. Middleton, eds. (2005). *Explorations in Privilege, Oppression, and Diversity*. Belmont, CA: Thomson, Brooks/Cole. This book is a collection of personal stories by social workers, psychologists, and counsellors who have all confronted oppression, prejudice, and privilege. One of the biggest challenges to being an effective practitioner is recognizing, struggling with, and using one's privilege in the service of oppressed groups. This collection of narratives is designed to help readers understand that privilege has many faces and many statuses and that individuals are subject to it either as agents of oppression, targets of oppression, or both.

Bishop, Anne (2002). *Becoming an Ally: Breaking the Cycle of Oppression*, 2nd edition. Crows Nest, NSW, Australia: Allen and Unwin. This book seeks out the roots of sexism, racism, and all other forms of oppression that divide us. It suggests ways to change, particularly through becoming allies of oppressed peoples when we are in the role of oppressor. It looks for solutions by examining the process through which we came to recognize ourselves, first as people who have experienced oppression, then as members of privileged groups.

Heldke, Lisa, and Peg O'Connor, eds. (2004). *Oppression, Privilege, and Resistance: Theoretical Perspectives on Racism, Sexism, and Heterosexism*. New York: McGraw-Hill. This anthology is grounded in a distinct theoretical framework that provides coherence and cohesion to the readings that the book comprises by presenting the phenomena of racism, sexism, heterosexism, and classism as interlocking systems of oppression. Resting on this model of oppression are two connecting sets of theories: one concerned with privilege—the flip side of oppression—and the other with resistance—the response to oppression.

Johnson, Allan G. (2006). *Privilege, Power, and Difference*, 2nd edition. New York: McGraw-Hill. I have found this book to be the most informative and accessible of all books I have read dealing with privilege. It provides a framework that is conceptual and theoretical on the one hand and grounded in the experience of everyday life on the other. Many examples are provided to enable readers to see the underlying nature and consequences of privilege and how they are connected to it, which is the only thing that gives us the potential to make a difference.

Kimmel, Michael, and Abby Ferber, eds. (2003). *Privilege: A Reader*. Boulder, CO: Westview Press. This book looks at privilege along the dimensions of gender, class, race, and sexual orientation. A wide range of contributors challenge the reader to think more critically about the many inequalities in society and how the dynamics that create inequality for many benefit others. The book uses an intersectional approach to explore the ways that race, class, gender, and sexuality interact in the lives of those who are privileged by one or more of these identities.

Notes

Chapter 1

1. A subsequent analysis by this author of British (Coulshed and Orme 1998) and Australian (O'Connor, Wilson, and Setterlund 1998) introductory social work textbooks revealed the same lack of discussion of social problems as a concept in both books. Each of these books was the only one in its respective country considered to be an introductory text with respect to the criteria used in the American textbook study.

2. Use of the term 'conflict' is problematic, since it is used by different writers to refer not only to a perspective but also to a theory or to a paradigm as well as to other constructs that have a critical element. The term 'perspective' is adopted here because many different conflict theories are based on the conflict perspective, and to call a perspective a theory is to confuse the two. The position adopted here is that a perspective has descriptive and analytical qualities but no prescriptive component. Theory emanates from a perspective but includes a prescription.

3. The conflict theorist recognizes that there are personal difficulties, issues, or problems (e.g., relationship difficulties, marriage breakdown) that are not directly attributable to structural factors. However, a social problem, by definition, affects large numbers of people and usually has a social cause.

4. One of the earliest concepts of critical social theory that was developed to answer the question 'why do people seemingly accept social structures that dominate, exploit, and oppress them?' is 'false consciousness.' Today, this term raises the ire of many (but not all) post-modernists, post-structuralists, and feminists because it suggests that not only is there a false consciousness but there must also be a 'true consciousness,' and who is to say or judge what is true or false for other people? Although I personally think that this dichotomous 'true–false' criticism is a distortion of what critical social theorists mean by the term, I do understand that it does not have the same meaning outside a Marxist discourse that it does within. For this reason, I will use terms such as 'acceptance of' and 'resignation to' to refer to the phenomenon whereby people seemingly support a society that oppresses them and appear to participate willingly in their own oppression.

5. This is not to say that ideologies are totally internally coherent. As Thompson (1998, 21) points out, 'it is not uncommon for ideologies to encompass a range of contradictory or logically incompatible ideas—the need for ideology need not rest on rational argument.' See also Hall 1986.

Chapter 2

1. Thompson (1998) argues convincingly that use of the word 'tolerance' with respect to differences is problematic, because it conveys that something is 'wrong with' or 'negative about' the particular difference. The position taken in this book is that group and cultural differences should be promoted and celebrated, not just accepted or tolerated.

Chapter 3

1. Woman's beauty, narrowly defined by men, was an important category of physical beauty but deviated from the notion of 'ideal beauty' because it was

associated with inferior qualities of weakness, delicateness, emotionality, etc.

2. When I lived in Australia (1995–1996, 1997–2003), it was not unusual to read or hear references to all non-white people, including Asian and Middle-Eastern people, as black.

3. I remember walking one day with a fellow PhD student during noon hour in Yorkville, a trendy part of downtown Toronto, when a copper-coloured Rolls Royce drove by. Everyone within eyesight stared at this truly magnificent car. I said something like, 'Man, what a car!' My fellow student, who lived in the Toronto catchment area, looked at me pensively and with a high level of fabricated empathy said, 'It must have been quite an adjustment for you when you moved from the Maritimes to Toronto.' I replied, 'Why would you say that?' He responded, 'Well, given all the poverty and awful living conditions in the Maritimes, you would have had to get used to all this wealth and sophistication here in Toronto.' I replied, 'The only thing I've had to get used to since I moved here are assholes like you!' Of course, this worldly person had never been to the Maritimes. I also found it interesting that although I worked hard and was a very good student (much better than most), it did not alter the stereotype of Maritimers held by many (but not all) of my instructors and fellow students. They rationalized my positive attributes as being the exception to the rule rather than questioning the stereotype—obviously a coping mechanism in defence and denial of their privileged social position.

Chapter 4

1. For a succinct and insightful discussion of culture in the contexts of modernity and postmodernity, see Leonard 1997, chapter 3. For an overview of the cultural studies movement, see Agger 1992; Grossberg, Nelson, and Treichler 1992; and Sardar and Van Loon 2004.

2. Biklen echoes Gitlin's (1980) contention that members of social action and subordinate groups, among others, tend to be naive in their dealings with the media in that they seem unmindful of the media's tendency to promote dominant social values. To help counter this tendency, Biklen discusses the following strategies in preparing for media exposure: (1) Speak as a representative of a group, since individuals without a group affiliation will generally be perceived as oddballs or deviant (unless they are perceived to be experts). (2) Ensure that the group defines the issue in clear and simple terms (preferably emphasizing one point only). Otherwise, the media will define the issue from the dominant perspective. (3) Plan to control the issue or message by developing 10 different ways to say it. Otherwise, the media are apt to lead the group off-track with questions that do not relate directly to the group's message. (4) Because there is considerable competition for news publicity, make the event or issue newsworthy (i.e., give it entertainment value or present it as an issue that affects a large number of people or that involves a significant injustice or that is supported by [or will receive support from] authoritative groups [experts, intellectuals, formal organizations, influential people, and so on]). (5) Know the opposing view in order to critique it when the media ask for a response to it. (6) Develop a list of media outlets and reporters who are sympathetic to the cause or issue and will treat it fairly.

3. For a complementary view of hegemony, see Laclau and Mouffe (1985), who trace the concept from the late nineteenth-century debates on working-class unity to the contemporary emergence of new antagonisms and forms of emancipatory struggle. This work develops the concept

of hegemony beyond the essentialism and universalism of classical Marxist thought: 'it (the discourse of the universal) has been replaced by a polyphony of voices, each of which constructs its own irreducible discursive identity' (1985, 191).

4. I am not convinced that social work must organize itself along professional lines to achieve these ends, but I accept that others do. For a discussion of this issue, see Mullaly 2007, 340–5).

Chapter 5

1. Social murder is the subject of a book entitled *Social Murder and Other Shortcomings of Conservative Economics* (2007), by Robert Chernomas and Ian Hudson, two colleagues in the Economics Department of the University of Manitoba. It examines the connections between the destructiveness of global capitalism and the professional economists who help keep it that way. I am grateful to them for their contribution to progressive thought in general and to progressive economics in particular. Their work is similar to my own in that over the years, I have attempted to draw the connection between the persistence of social problems and the mainstream social work writers, educators, and practitioners who help keep it that way.

2. Potocky (1998) notes that the dominant theory of multicultural social work in the United States is that of cultural sensitivity (my experience in social work in Canada and Australia has convinced me that the situation is similar in both these countries). The aim of this theory is to increase worker and agency sensitivity to different cultural norms and to decrease (but not eliminate) institutional racism. Cultural sensitivity enables white social workers to better establish a 'helping relationship' with other races and cultures so as to make services more accessible

and to advocate for the enactment of equal rights legislation. Although the cultural sensitivity model represents an advance over the earlier colour-blind and assimilationist (melting pot) approach to issues of race and culture, it can actually, although unintentionally, allow racism to persist but in a more respectable form (Ahmed 1991; Thompson 1997). The cultural sensitivity model ignores the fact that cultures and races are ranked in order of perceived merit, and it ignores the power relations between people of colour and white people in history and in the present (Ahmed 1991; Williams 1989).

3. Multiculturalism as a concept and as a public policy issue dates back to the 1970s in most Western industrialized countries; there have been many progressive activists and supporters of multiculturalism. However, Agger contends that the concept of multiculturalism has been appropriated to some extent by some schools of post-modernism and consequently a change in meaning has occurred. It has also been appropriated by social work, as outlined above in Note 2. Basically, Agger argues that multiculturalism is a recognition and acceptance of cultural pluralism but does nothing to change the situation of there being one dominant culture with all others subordinate to it. The argument of earlier multicultural activists that there not be a hierarchy of cultures is part of the position of the 'politics of difference' approach today.

4. The interpretation of these events, of course, varies (see Mullaly 1997a). Conservatives view welfare capitalism as governments pandering to the working class and other subordinate groups (e.g., minorities, feminists) in exchange for political popularity. Liberals view it as a genuine attempt to humanize capitalism for all groups, both dominant and subordinate. Critical social theorists, including Marxists, feminists, and social

democrats, view welfare capitalism as a social institution that reinforces capitalism by disguising its true oppressive nature and by 'conning' the general public into thinking that the government is acting in their best interests first (O'Connor 1973).

5. For a fuller discussion on the nature of human beings (i.e., whether they are political or apolitical by nature) and its relationship to politics and political theory, see Berry (1986).

6. The book by Sidanius and Pratto is used here because it is relatively recent, it brings together an impressive amount of international empirical evidence, and it focuses on social inequalities as forms of institutional discrimination and structural oppression. There is a vast literature on social inequality, including national and international accounts, studies, and analyses. All nations are characterized by social inequality, although it varies from country to country in terms of how great the discrepancies are between dominant and subordinate persons. For example, among Western democracies, the United States has the greatest discrepancies in levels of living between dominant and subordinate groups, whereas the Scandinavian countries are among those having the least. The purpose here is to show how these inequalities help to maintain and reproduce oppression and how this oppression has violent consequences. The evidence presented in this chapter is meant to be illustrative rather than exhaustive.

7. I am indebted to Rosalie Chappell, *Social Welfare in Canadian Society* (1997), for many of the references in this section documenting the situation of Canadian First Nations people.

point of view, see Moane 1999. It is from her book that I draw much of the material for this section on the psychology of oppression. Also see *Critical Psychology: An Introduction* by Fox and Prilleltensky (1997).

2. Individuals may also shape (within limits) their social environment. They have some choices (e.g., how to interpret particular discourses and mediate their impact and whom to interact with). They can influence their birth family and the families they establish themselves. And they may choose to resist and fight oppression rather than resigning themselves to it.

3. Shulman (1992) notes that the central idea of gaining one's sense of self by exploitation of others can be seen in many different oppressive relationships with which social workers deal—the abusing parent and abused child, the battering husband and his partner, straight society's repression of gay, lesbian, and bisexual persons, discrimination against people of colour by white people, and so on.

4. Agger (1998) describes interpretive social theory as the set of theories that seeks to understand the meanings that people attach to their actions in everyday life. Unlike critical theory, interpretive theories do not attempt to mobilize social action, and unlike positivist theory, they do not attempt to produce social laws.

5. Gil does not condemn all religions. He points out that many religions place primacy on social justice, equality, and liberation from oppression as values (e.g., liberation theology).

6. I am indebted to Hussein Bulhan (1985) for his succinct and insightful explanation of Fanon's theory of a Manichean psychology.

Chapter 6

1. For an overview of the psychology of oppression and liberation from a critical

Chapter 7

1. As Donna Baines (2007) points out, there have been feminist writers

(Marxist and socialist feminists, as well as black feminists) outside of social work who explored overlapping oppressions, starting in the early 1980s.

2. Mutual oppression occurs in the form of different oppressed persons or groups oppressing each other.

3. I am aware that the globalization of the economy has meant the loss of some state government autonomy to the corporate sector. The extent of corporate influence and coercion over national governments is a debatable issue, but certainly most governments all over the world have aligned themselves with the corporate agenda at the expense of the social services sector. In fact, many of the world's elected leaders come from or aspire to become part of the corporate elite.

4. Lena Dominelli (1997), among others who write in the area of race relations, contends that race is a social construction because there is only one race of people—*Homo sapiens*.

5. See Williams (1989) for a discussion of these differences.

Chapter 8

1. For a discussion of the concept and use of dialectic in progressive social work, see Mullaly 2007.

2. Some writers (e.g., Bishop 1994; Butler 1978) speak of liberation as a journey in which one starts out as a victim, moves to becoming a survivor, and ends up as a warrior or activist fighting against oppression. However, it should not be interpreted as a linear, forward-moving, and uninterrupted journey.

3. Recent examples of works in which empowerment is used as a major theme or concept include: (1) from the UK: Adams, Dominelli, and Payne 2002; Dominelli 2002; Ferguson 2008; Payne 2005, 2007; Thompson 1998, 2001; (2) from Canada: Hick 2006; Lundy 2004; Mullaly 2007; preamble in the 2005

CASW *Code of Ethics*; (3) from Australia: Allen 2003; Costello 2003; Maidment and Egan 2004; Martin 2003; (4) from US: Gil 1998; Gutierrez and Lewis 1998; Lee 2001; Marsiglia and Kulis 2009; van Wormer 2004. In addition to these major books, there is a plethora of journal articles over the past decade in which it is common to find empowerment as a focus or major theme. Katherine van Wormer, a progressive American social work writer, points out that the term 'anti-oppressive social work' is not used in the US. Instead, she claims that the empowerment approach is the American equivalent to anti-oppression. There is an entire tradition of empowerment social work coming from the US where the concept of empowerment has been especially important in feminist social work and in work with women of colour. It is also interesting that in the anti-oppressive practice social work textbook edited by Baines, in which she makes her claim that empowerment is not used much these days in social justice social work, the second chapter has empowerment as one of its major themes.

4. Discourse includes not only language but the rules governing the choice and use of language and how the ideas and language will be framed. A discourse is a framework of thought, meaning, and action (Thompson 1998) that does not reflect knowledge, reality, or truth but creates and maintains them. A discourse embodies certain interests and ideological positions, which in turn means that some pieces of knowledge will be given prominence while others may be rendered invisible. A discourse, then, reflects only particular constructions of reality, particular ways of selecting and organizing that vast universe of knowledge. Discourses are linguistic systems of statements through which we speak of ourselves and our social world (Leonard 1997). Each ideology has its

own discourse, which consists of a set of assumptions about the social world. Each academic discipline has a discourse that reflects its view of the social world, and each group in society has a discourse reflecting its world view. The profession of social work has a professional discourse, and the progressive wing of social work has a slightly different discourse reflecting its ideological position(s). Similarly, the business sector has a particular discourse, one that closely approximates that of conservative politicians. The discourse of the progressive wing of social work is quite different from that of the business sector or the conservative politician, given their differing ideologies and world views. Therefore, although all these groups may include a term such as 'empowerment' within their respective discourses, the meanings of this term vary considerably. Thus, I do not understand Baines's concern that because the business establishment includes empowerment in its discourse, we should avoid the term in our social justice discourse. Surely we do not understand the business sector to mean social justice when they use the term empowerment, just as we do not understand social justice–oriented social workers to mean individualistic feel-good activities when they use the term empowerment. The term may be the same, but it is used by two different groups with two different discourses, giving it two different meanings.

5. For an insightful and informative discussion on power, see Thompson 1998.

6. This concept of normalization is very different from Foucault's notion of normalization. The latter refers to standards of acceptable social behaviour and the mechanisms or systems of rewards and punishments put in place to promote adherence to these standards.

7. Afrocentricity is a 'philosophical model predicated on traditional African assumptions that reflect the "original"

cultural values (i.e., interdependency, collectivity, and spirituality) of Africans before the advent of European and Arab influences' (Schiele 1994, 13). Today, Afrocentricity, as a world view, is increasingly being used by black people (one of the largest groups of 'diaspora') all over the world as a counter-discourse to Eurocentricity.

8. Orientalism refers to the processes by which the 'Orient' was, and continues to be, constructed in European thinking and discourse. Popularized by Edward Said (1978), Orientalism is the way in which the West deals with the Orient—making statements about it, authorizing views about it, studying it, describing it, teaching it, settling it, and ruling over it. In short, it is a Western way of dominating, restructuring, and having authority over the Orient (or over any Other). The relationship between the West (or the Occident) and the Orient is one of power, domination, and a complex hegemony (Ashcroft, Griffiths, and Tiffin 1998). Being aware of how Orientalism works is a tremendous step for the people of the Orient to be able to resist it and develop counter-discourses.

Chapter 9

1. Thanks to my colleague, Dr Deborah Stienstra from Disability Studies at the University of Manitoba, for helping me to clarify and extend my thinking in this area.

Chapter 10

1. I am indebted to Michael Kimmel for this analysis contained in his chapter 'Introduction: Toward a pedagogy of the oppressor' found in Kimmel and Ferber, *Privilege: A Reader* (2003).

2. As with many ideas in the chapter, I am indebted to Allan G. Johnson (2006) for much of this section.

References

Adam, Barry D. (1978). *The Survival of Domination: Inferiorization and Everyday Life*. New York: Elsevier.

Adams, Robert, Lena Dominelli, and Malcolm Payne, eds. (2002). *Critical Practice in Social Work*. Basingstoke, UK: Palgrave.

Agel, Jerome, ed. (1971). *The Radical Therapist*. New York: Ballantine Books.

Agger, Ben (1989). *Socio(ontology): A Disciplinary Reading*. Urbana: University of Illinois Press.

—— (1991). 'Critical theory, poststructuralism, postmodernism: Their sociological relevance', *Annual Review of Sociology* 17: 105–131.

—— (1992). *Cultural Studies as Critical Theory*. London: Falmer Press.

—— (1998). *Critical Social Theories: An Introduction*. Boulder, CO: Westview Press.

—— (2006). *Critical Social Theories: An Introduction*, 2nd edition. Boulder, CO: Westview Press.

Ahmad, B. (1990). *Black Perspectives in Social Work*. Birmingham: Venture.

Ahmed, S. (1991). 'Developing anti-racist social work education practice', in CD Project Steering Group, ed., *Setting the Context for Change*. London: CCETSW.

Albert, M., et al. (1986). *Liberating Theory*. Boston: South End Press.

Alexander, David (1987). 'Gendered job traits and women's occupations'. (University of Massachusetts, PhD thesis).

Al-Krenawi, Alean, and John R. Graham, eds. (2003). *Multicultural Social Work in Canada*. Toronto: Oxford University Press.

Allan, June (2003). 'Practising critical social work', in June Allan, Bob Pease, and Linda Briskman, eds., *Critical Social Work: An Introduction to Theories and Practices*. Crows Nest, NSW, Australia: Allan and Unwin.

—— (2005). 'Being angry: Advocacy, social action and the bereaved'. Paper presented at the 7th Annual Conference on Grief and Bereavement in Contemporary Society, King's College, London, UK, 12–14 July.

Allan, June, Bob Pease, and Linda Briskman, eds. (2003). *Critical Social Work: An Introduction to Theories and Practices*. St Leonards, Australia: Allen and Unwin.

Althusser, Louis (1969). *For Marx*. London: Allen Lane.

Anderson, M.L., and P.H. Collins (2004). *Race, Class, and Gender*, 5th edition. Belmont, CA: Thomson Wadsworth.

Anderson, Sharon A., and Valerie A. Middleton, eds. (2005). *Explorations in Privilege, Oppression, and Diversity*. Belmont, CA: Thomson, Brooks/Cole.

Anleu, Sharyn L. Roach (1999). *Deviance, Conformity and Control*. South Melbourne, Australia: Longman.

Anthias, F., and N. Yuval-Davis (1992). *Radicalized Boundaries: Race, Nation, Colour, Class and the Anti-Racist Struggle*. London: Routledge.

Apter, M.J. (1983). 'Negativism and the sense of identity', In Glynis M. Breakwell, ed., *Threatened Identities*, 75–90. Chichester: Wiley.

Arnowitz, Stanley (1992). *The Politics of Identity: Class, Culture, Social Movements*. New York: Routledge.

Ashcroft, Bill, Gareth Griffiths, and Helen Tiffin (1998). *Key Concepts in Post-Colonial Studies*. London: Routledge.

Astbury, Jill (1996). *Crazy for You: The Making of Women's Madness*. Melbourne, Australia: Oxford University Press.

Bachrach, P. (1969). *The Theory of Democratic Elitism*. London: University of London Press.

Bailey, Alison. (2004). 'Privilege.' In Lisa Heldke and Peg O'Connor, eds., *Oppression, Privilege, and Resistance: Theoretical Perspectives on Racism, Sexism, and Heterosexism*, 301–316. New York: McGraw-Hill.

Bailey, Roy, and Mike Brake, eds. (1975). *Radical Social Work*. New York: Pantheon Books.

Baines, Donna (1997). 'Feminist social work in the inner city: The challenges of race, class, and gender', *Afilia* 12, (3): 29–33.

―――― (2000). 'Everyday practices of race, class and gender: Struggles, skills, and radical social work', *Journal of Progressive Human Services* 11, (2): 5–27.

―――― (2001). 'Race, class, and gender in the everyday talk of social workers: The ways we limit the possibilities for radical practice', *Race, Gender, and Class* 9, (1, special issue on social work).

―――― (2002). 'Radical social work, race, class, and gender', *Race, Gender, and Class* 9, (1): 145–167.

―――― (2003). 'Race, class, and gender in the everyday talk of social workers: The ways we limit the possibilities for radical practice', In W. Shera, ed., *Emerging Perspectives on Anti-Oppressive Practice*, 43–64. Toronto: Canadian Scholars Press.

―――― (2004). 'Pro-market, non-market: The dual nature of organizational change in social services delivery', *Critical Social Policy* 24, (1): 5–29.

―――――, ed. (2007) *Doing Anti-Oppressive Practice: Building Transformative Politicized Social Work*. Halifax: Fernwood.

Bannerji, Himani (2000). *The Dark Side of the Nation: Essays on Multiculturalism, Nationalism and Gender*. Toronto: Canadian Scholars Press.

Banton, M., and J. Harwood (1975). *The Race Concept*. Buckingham, UK: Open University Press.

Barbour, Rosaline S. (1984). 'Social work education: Tackling the theory-practice dilemma', *British Journal of Social Work* 14: 557–577.

Barker, Robert L. (1987). *The Social Work Dictionary*. Silver Spring, MD: National Association of Social Workers.

Barnoff, Lisa, and Brienne Coleman (2007). 'Strategies for integrating anti-oppressive principles: Perspectives from feminist agencies', in Donna Baines, ed., *Doing Anti-Oppressive Practice: Building Transformative Politicized Social Work*, 31–49. Halifax: Fernwood.

Bartky, S.L. (1990). *Femininity and Domination: Studies in the Phenomenology of Oppression*. London: Routledge.

Baskin, C. (2003). 'Structural social work as seen from an Aboriginal perspective', in Wes Shera, ed., *Emerging Perspectives on Anti-oppressive Practice*, 65–80. Toronto: Canadian Scholars Press.

Baudrillard, J. (1983). *Simulations*. New York: Semiotext(e).

Baughman, E. Earle (1971). *Black Americans: A Psychological Analysis*. New York: Academic Press.

Bauman, Zygmunt (1992). *Intimations of Postmodernity*. London: Routledge.

―――― (1998). *Work, Consumerism and the New Poor*. Philadelphia: Open University Press.

Beagley, J.M. (1989). 'Gender issues in child abuse: She must have known what was happening', *Child Abuse Review*, 3 (2).

Beauvoir, Simone de (1961). *The Second Sex*. New York: Bantam.

Benjamin, Akua (2007). 'Afterword— Doing anti-oppressive social work: The importance of resistance, history and strategy', in Donna Baines, ed., *Doing Anti-Oppressive Practice: Building Transformative Politicized Social Work*, 191–204. Halifax: Fernwood.

Berger, Peter L., and Thomas Luckmann (1966). *The Social Construction of Reality*. New York: Doubleday.

Berry, Christopher J. (1986). *Human Nature*. Atlantic Highlands, NJ: Humanities Press International.

Best, S., and D. Kellner (1991). *Postmodern Theorizing*. London: Macmillan.

Bhabha, Homi K. (1994). *The Location of Culture*. London: Routledge.

Biklen, Douglas P. (1983). *Community Organizing: Theory and Practice*. Englewood Cliffs, NJ: Prentice-Hall.

Bishop, Anne (1994). *Becoming an Ally: Breaking the Cycle of Oppression*. Halifax: Fernwood.

—— (2002). *Becoming an Ally: Breaking the Cycle of Oppression*, 2nd edition. Crows Nest, NSW, Australia: Allen and Unwin.

Black, Rita Beck (1995). 'Diversity and populations at risk: People with disabilities', in Frederic G. Reamer, ed., *The Foundations of Social Work Knowledge*, 391–416. New York: Columbia University Press.

Blumenfeld, W.J., and D. Raymond (1988). *Looking at Gay and Lesbian Life*. Boston: Beacon Press.

Bonilla-Silva, E. (1997). 'Rethinking racism: Towards a structural interpretation', *American Sociological Review* 62, (3): 465–480.

Boston Women's Health Book Collective (1998). *Our Bodies, Ourselves: For the New Century*. New York: Touchstone.

Brake, M. (1980). *The Sociology of Youth Culture and Youth Subcultures: Sex, Drugs 'n' Rock and Roll*. New York: Routledge.

Breakwell, Glynis M. (1986). *Coping with Threatened Identities*. London: Methuen.

Brittan, Arthur, and Mary Maynard (1984). *Sexism, Racism and Oppression*. Oxford: Blackwell.

Brod, Harry (1989). 'Work clothes and leisure suits: The class basis and bias of the men's movement', in Michael Kimmel and Michael A. Messner, eds., *Men's Lives*, 289. New York: MacMillan.

Brodribb, S. (1992). *Nothing Mat(t)ers: A Feminist Critique of Post-modernism*. New York: New York University Press.

Bromley, D., and C.F. Longino, Jr. (1972). *White Racism and Black Americans*. Cambridge, MA: Schenkman.

Brown, L., and S. Strega, eds. (2005). *Research as Resistance: Critical, Indigenous, and Anti-Oppressive Approaches*. Toronto: Canadian Scholars Press.

Bulhan, Hussein A. (1985). *Frantz Fanon and the Psychology of Oppression*. New York: Plenum Press.

Burke, Beverley, and Philomena Harrison (2002). 'Anti-oppressive practice', in R. Adams, L. Dominelli, and M. Payne, eds., *Critical Practice in Social Work*, 227–236. Basingstoke, UK: Palgrave MacMillan.

Burr, V. (1995). *An Introduction to Social Constructionism*. London: Routledge.

Butler, Sandra (1978). *Conspiracy of Silence: The Trauma of Incest*. San Francisco: Volcano Press.

Butler, Sandra, and C. Wintram (1991). *Feminist Groupwork*. London: Sage.

Canadian Advisory Council on the Status of Women (CACSW) 1990. *Women and Labour Market Poverty*. Ottawa: CACSW.

Canadian Association of Social Workers (CASW) (2005). *Code of Ethics*. Ottawa: CASW.

Carbado, Devon (2004). 'Straight out of the closet: Men, feminism, and male heterosexual privilege', in Lisa Heldke and Peg O'Connor, eds., *Oppression, Privilege, and Resistance: Theoretical Perspectives on Racism, Sexism, and Heterosexism*, 395–419. New York: McGraw-Hill.

Carlen, P., and A. Worral, eds. (1987). *Gender, Crime and Justice*. Milton Keynes, UK: Open University Press.

Carniol, Ben (1979). 'A critical approach in social work', *Canadian Journal of Social Work Education* 5, (1): 95–111.

—— (1992). 'Structural social work: Maurice Moreau's challenge to social work practice', *Journal of Progressive Human Services* 3, (1): 1–20.

—— (2000). *Case Critical*, 4th edition. Toronto: Between the Lines.

Chappell, Rosalie (1997). *Social Welfare in Canadian Society*. Scarborough, ON: Nelson.

Clarke, G. (1990). 'Defending ski-jumpers: a critique of theories of youth subcultures', in S. Frith and A. Goodwin, eds, *On Record*, 81–96. New York: Pantheon.

Clarke, Janet (2003). 'Reconceptualizing empathy for anti-oppressive, culturally competent practice', in Wes Shera, ed.,

Emerging Perspectives on Anti-Oppressive Practice, 247–263. Toronto: Canadian Scholars Press.

Clarke, Michelle (1991). *Fighting Poverty through Programs: Social and Health Programs for Canada's Poor Children and Youth*. Ottawa: Children*Enfants*Jeunesse *Youth (CEJY).

Clough, Patricia Ticineto (1994). *Feminist Thought: Desire, Power, and Academic Discourse*. Cambridge, MA: Blackwell.

Coates, John (1991). 'Putting knowledge for practice into perspective', *Canadian Social Work Review* 8, (1): 82–96.

Cole, Thomas R. (1986). 'Putting off the old: Middle class morality, antebellum Protestantism, and the origins of ageism', in David Van Tassel and Peter N. Stearns, eds, *Old Age in a Bureaucratic Society*. New York: Greenwood.

Collins, Barbara G. (1986). 'Defining feminist social work', *Social Work* 31, (3): 214–219.

Collins, Patricia Hill (1990). *Black Feminist Thought*. London: Unwin Hyman.

——— (1998). *Fighting Words: Black Women and the Search for Justice*. Minneapolis: University of Minnesota Press.

——— (2000). *Black Feminist Thought: Knowledge, Consciousness, and the Politics of Empowerment*, 2nd edition. New York: Routledge.

Comack, Elizabeth (2008). 'Racialized policing', *Winnipeg Free Press* 17 December, A15.

Connell, R.W. (2001). *Gender*. Oxford: Polity Press.

Costello, Susie (2003). 'Families: Reconstructing social work practices', in June Allan, Bob Pease, and Linda Briskman, eds, *Critical Social Work: An Introduction to Theories and Practices*, 139–154. Crows Nest, NSW, Australia: Allen and Unwin.

Coulshed, Veronica, and Joan Orme (1998). *Social Work Practice: An Introduction*. Basingstoke, UK: Macmillan.

Cudd, Ann E. (2006). *Analyzing Oppression*. New York: Oxford University Press.

Curtis, James, et al. (1988). *Social Inequality in Canada: Patterns, Problems, Policies*. Scarborough, ON: Prentice-Hall Canada.

Dahl, Robert (1970). *Modern Political Analysis*, 2nd edition. Englewood Cliffs, NJ: Prentice-Hall.

Dalrymple, Jane, and Beverley Burke (1995). *Anti-Oppressive Practice: Social Care and the Law*. Buckingham, UK: Open University Press.

Daly, Mary (1984). *Pure Lust: Elemental Feminist Philosophy*. Boston: Beacon Press.

Dant, T. (2003). *Critical Social Theory: Culture, Society and Critique*. London: Sage.

Day, Lesley (1992). 'Women and oppression: Race, class and gender', in Mary Langan and Lesley Day, eds, *Women, Oppression and Social Work*, 12–31. London: Routledge.

Day, Richard (2000). *Multiculturalism and the History of Canadian Diversity*. Toronto: University of Toronto Press.

Dekeseredy, Walter S., and Ronald Hinch (1991). *Woman Abuse: Sociological Perspectives*. Toronto: Thompson Educational Publishing.

Denzin, Norman K. (1991). *Images of Postmodern Society: Social Theory and Contemporary Cinema*. London: Sage.

Disch, Estelle (2002). *Reconstructing Gender: A Multicultural Anthology*, 3rd edition. New York: McGraw-Hill.

Dominelli, Lena (1988). *Anti-racist Social Work: A Challenge for White Practitioners and Educators*. Basingstoke, UK: Macmillan.

——— (1997). *Anti-Racist Social Work*, 2nd edition. London: Macmillan.

——— (2002). *Anti-oppressive Social Work Theory and Practice*. Basingstoke, UK: Palgrave MacMillan.

——— (2004). *Social Work Today: Theory and Practice for a Changing Profession*. Cambridge: Polity Press.

Dominelli, Lena, and Eileen McLeod (1989). *Feminist Social Work*. Hampshire, UK: Macmillan Education.

Donald, J., and S. Hall, eds. (1986). *Politics and Ideology*. Milton Keynes, UK: Open University Press.

Donaldson, L. (1999). 'Ten tips for better health.' London Stationery Office. www.archive.officialdocuments.co.uk/document/cm43/4386-tp.htm.

Du Bois, W.E.B. (1969). *The Souls of Black Folk*. New York: New American Library.

Ebony (1986). Special edition on black families, August.

Emberley, J.V. (1993). *Thresholds of Difference*. Toronto: University of Toronto Press.

Engels, F. (1987 [1845]). *The Condition of the Working Class in England in 1844*. London: Penguin.

Eyerman, Ron (1981). *False Consciousness and Ideology in Marxist Theory*. Atlantic Highlands, NJ: Humanities Press.

Eysenck, H.J. (1971). *Race, Intelligence and Education*. London: Temple Smith.

—— (1973). *The Inequality of Man*. London: Temple Smith.

Fanon, Frantz (1967). *Black Skin: White Masks*. New York: Grove Press.

—— (1968). *The Wretched of the Earth*. New York: Grove Press.

—— (1986). *Black Skin: White Masks*. London: Pluto.

—— (1989). *Studies in a Dying Colonialism*. London: Earthscan.

Featherstone, B., and B. Fawsett (1994). 'Oh no! Not more isms: Feminism, postmodernism, poststructuralism and social work education.' Paper presented at the IASSW Congress, Amsterdam.

Featherstone, Mike (1991). *Consumer Culture and Postmodernism*. London: Sage.

Ferber, Abby L. (2003). 'Defending the culture of privilege', in Michael Kimmel and Abby Ferber, eds., *Privilege: A Reader*, 319–330. Boulder, CO: Westview Press.

Ferguson, Iain (2008). *Reclaiming Social Work: Challenging Neo-liberalism and Promoting Social Justice*. London: Sage.

Ferguson, Iain, Michael Lavalette, and Gerry Mooney (2002). *Rethinking Welfare: A Critical Perspective*. London: Sage.

Fisher, Robert, and Howard J. Karger (1997). *Social Work and Community in a Private World: Getting out in Public*. White Plains, NY: Longman.

Fisher, Robert, and Joe Kling (1994). 'Community organization and new social movement theory', *Journal of Progressive Human Services* 5, (2): 5–24.

Fleras, Augie (2001). *Social Problems in Canada: Conditions, Constructions and Challenges*. Toronto: Prentice-Hall.

Fletcher, Joseph (1966). *Situation Ethics: The New Morality*. Philadelphia: Westminster Press.

Foucault, Michel (1963). *The Birth of the Clinic*. London: Tavistock.

—— (1976). *The Archaeology of Knowledge*. New York: Harper and Row.

—— (1977). *Discipline and Punish*. New York: Pantheon.

—— (1978). *The Archaeology of Knowledge*. London: Tavistock.

—— (1980). *Power/Knowledge: Selected Interviews and Other Writings 1972–77* ed. C. Gordon. Brighton: Harvester Press.

—— (1988). *Politics, Culture, Philosophy: Interviews and Other Writings 1977–1984*. New York: Routledge.

—— (1990). *Introduction*, v. 1 of *The History of Sexuality* (1978). Reprint. New York: Random House.

Fox, D.R., and I. Prilleltensky, eds. (1997). *Critical Psychology: An Introduction*. London: Sage.

Fox, R. (1992). 'East of Said', in Michael Sprinker, ed., *Edward Said: A Critical Reader*, 144–156. Oxford: Blackwell.

Fraser, Heather (2008). 'Power, privilege and oppression: From a structural social worker's perspective' (RMIT, Melbourne, Australia, unpublished paper).

Fraser, Heather, and K. McMaster (2008). 'Gender, sex and power', in M.Connolly and L. Harms, eds., *Social Work: Contexts and Practice*. Oxford: Oxford University Press.

Freire, Paulo (1994 [1970]). *Pedagogy of the Oppressed*, 2nd edition. New York: Continuum Publishing.

Fromm, Erich (1966). *The Heart of Man*. New York: Basic Books.

Frye, Marilyn (1983). *The Politics of Reality: Essays in Feminist Theory*. Trumansburg, NY: Crossing Press.

Galper, Jeffry (1975). *The Politics of Social Services*. Englewood Cliffs, NJ: Prentice-Hall.

——— (1980). *Social Work Practice: A Radical Perspective*. Englewood Cliffs, NJ: Prentice-Hall.

Galtung, Johan (1990). 'Cultural violence', *Journal of Peace Research* 27, (3): 291–305.

Gandhi, Leela (1998). *Postcolonial Theory: A Critical Introduction*. St Leonards, Australia: Allen and Unwin.

Garner, Roberta, ed. (2000). *Social Theory: Continuity and Confrontation, a Reader*. Buffalo, NY: Broadview Press.

Garrett, Paul Michael (2002). 'Social work and the just society: Diversity, difference and the sequestration of poverty', *Journal of Social Work* 2, (2): 187–210.

Geertz, C. (1986). 'The uses of diversity', *Michigan Quarterly Review* 25, (1): 105–23.

George, Usha (2000). 'Towards anti-racism in social work in the Canadian context', in Agnes Calliste and George J. Sefa Dei, eds., *Anti-Racist Feminism*, 111–121. Halifax: Fernwood.

George, Usah, and Sarah Ramkissoon (1998). 'Race, gender, and class in the lives of South Asian women in Canada', *Afilia* 13, (1): 102–119.

Giddens, A. (1995). *A Contemporary Critique of Historical Materialism*, 2nd edition. London: Macmillan.

Gil, David G. (1976a). 'Social policies and social development: A humanistic-egalitarian perspective', *Journal of Sociology and Social Welfare* 3, (3): 242–263.

——— (1976b). *The Challenge of Social Equality*. Cambridge, MA: Schenkman.

——— (1992). *Unravelling Social Policy*, 5th edition. Rochester, VT: Schenkman.

——— (1994). 'Confronting injustice and oppression', in Frederic G. Reamer, ed., *The Foundation of Social Work Knowledge*, 231–263. New York: Columbia University Press.

——— (1998). *Confronting Injustice and Oppression: Concepts and Strategies for Social Workers*. New York: Columbia University Press.

——— (2004). 'Foreword', in Katherine van Wormer, *Confronting Oppression, Restoring Justice: From Policy Analysis to Social Action*. Alexandria, VA: Council on Social Work Education.

Gilbert, D. (2002). *The American Class Structure in an Age of Growing Inequality*. Belmont, CA: Wadsworth.

Gitlin, Todd (1979). 'Prime time ideology: The Herpmanic process in television entertainment', *Social Problems* 26, (3): 251–266.

——— (1980). *The Whole World Is Watching*. Berkeley: University of California Press.

Goldhor-Lerner, H. (1985). *The Dance of Anger*. New York: Harper and Row.

Gordon, D. (1999). Message posted 21 July on the Spirit of 1848 Electronic Listserve.

Gould, K. (1987). 'Life model versus conflict model: A feminist perspective', *Social Work* (May/June): 346–351.

Gramsci, Antonio (1971). *Selections from the Prison Notebooks*. London: Lawrence and Wishart.

Greenberg, David (1988). *The Construction of Homosexuality*. Chicago: University of Chicago Press.

Grossberg, Lawrence, Cary Nelson, and Paula Treichler, eds. (1992). *Cultural Studies*. New York: Routledge.

Gutierrez, L., and E. A. Lewis (1998). 'Strengthening communities through groups: A multicultural perspective', in H. Bertcher, I.F. Kurtz, and A. Lamont, eds., *Rebuilding Communities: Challenges for Groupwork*, 5–16. New York: Haworth Press.

Habermas, Jürgen (1975). *Legitimation Crisis*. Boston: Beacon Press.

Haley, Alex (1977). *Roots*. London: Hutchinson.

Hall, S. (1986). 'Variations of liberalism', in J. Donald and S. Hall, eds., *Politics and Ideology*, 36–69. Milton Keynes, UK: Open University Press.

—— (1988). *The Hard Road to Renewal: Thatcherism and the Crisis of the Left*. London: Verso.

Hall, S., et al. (1978). *Policing the Crisis: Muggings, the State and Law and Order*. London: Macmillan.

Haney, Eleanor H. (1989). *Vision and Struggle: Meditations on Feminist Spirituality and Politics*. Portland, ME: Astarte Shell Press.

Hanh, Thich Nhat (1997). *True Love: A Practice for Awakening the Heart*. Boston: Shambala Publications. Translated from the French, *Vivre en pleine concience* (1997).

Hardy, Jean (1981a). *Values in Social Work*. London: Routledge and Kegan Paul.

—— (1981b). *Values in Social Policy: Nine Contradictions*. London: Routledge and Kegan Paul.

Harris, C. (2001). 'Beyond multiculturalism? Difference, recognition and social justice', *Patterns of Prejudice* 35, (1): 11–34.

Harris, V. (1991). 'Values of social work in the context of British society in conflict with anti-racism', in *Setting the Context for Change*, 152. London: CCETSW.

Hartmann, Heidi (1981). 'The unhappy marriage of Marxism and feminism', in Lydia Sargent, ed., *Women and Revolution*, 1–41. Montreal: Black Rose Books.

Harvey, David (1989). *The Condition of Postmodernity: An Enquiry into the Origins of Cultural Change*. Cambridge, MA: Basil Blackwell.

Hays, D.G., and C.Y. Chang (2003). 'White privilege, oppression and racial identity development: Implications for supervision', *Counselor Education and Supervision* 43: 134–145.

Hays, D.G., C.Y. Chang, and J.K. Dean (2004). 'White counselors' conceptualization of privilege and oppression: Implications for counselor training', *Counselor Education and Supervision* 43: 242–257.

Head, S. (1996). 'The new, ruthless economy', *The New York Review* 43, (4, 29 February).

Healey, Joseph F. (1995). *Race, Ethnicity, Gender and Class*. Thousand Oaks, CA: Pine Forge.

Health Canada (1989). *Issues: Drug Use by the Elderly*. Ottawa: Health Protection Branch, 20 September.

—— (1991a). *Health Status of Canadian Indians and Inuit*. Ottawa: Minister of Supply and Services Canada.

—— (1991b). *Services to Elderly Patients with Mental Health Problems in General Hospitals: Guidelines*. Ottawa: Health and Welfare Canada.

—— (1992). *Aboriginal Health in Canada*. Ottawa: Health and Welfare Canada.

—— (1994). *Suicide in Canada: Update on the Report of the Task Force on Suicide in Canada*. Ottawa: Health Canada. Health and Welfare Canada.

—— (1998). 'Taking action on population health: A position paper for health promotion and programs branch staff', Health and Welfare Canada, www.hc-sc.gc/hppb/phdd/pdf/tad_e.pdf.

Healy, Karen, and Peter Leonard (2000). 'Responding to uncertainty: Critical social work education in the postmodern habitat', *Journal of Progressive Human Services* 11, (1): 23–48.

Hebdige, D. (1979). *Subculture: The Meaning of Style*. London: Methuen.

—— (1988). *Hiding in the Light: On Images and Things*. New York: Routledge.

Hegel, G.W.F. (1966 [1807]). *The Phenomenology of Mind*. London: Allen and Unwin.

Heidegger, Martin (1971). 'Building, dwelling, thinking', in Martin Heidegger, *Poetry, Language, Thought*. New York: Harper and Row.

Heldke, Lisa, and Peg O'Connor (2004). *Oppression, Privilege, and Resistance: Theoretical Perspectives on Racism, Sexism, and Heterosexism*. New York: McGraw-Hill.

Heller, Agnes (1987). *Beyond Justice*. New York: Basic Books.

Herman, J.L. (1992). *Trauma and Recovery.* New York: Basic Books.

Herrnstein, R.J. (1971). *IQ in the Meritocracy.* Boston: Little, Brown.

Hick, Steven (2006). *Social Work in Canada: An Introduction,* 2nd edition. Toronto: Thompson.

Hobsbawm, E.J., and T. Ranger, eds. (1993). *The Invention of Tradition.* Cambridge: Cambridge University Press.

Hodges, Andrew, and David Hutter (1974). *With Downcast Gays: Aspects of Homosexual Self-Oppression.* London: Pomegranate.

hooks, bell (1981). *Ain't I a Woman? Black Women and Feminism.* Boston: South End Press.

——— (1990). *Yearning: Race, Gender and Cultural Politics.* Boston: South End Press.

——— (1993). *Sisters of the Yam: Black Women and Self-Recovery.* Boston: South End Press.

Hopton, John (1997). 'Anti-discriminatory practice and anti-oppressive practice', *Critical Social Policy* 17: 47–61.

Horton, John (1966). 'Order and conflict theories of social problems as competing ideologies', *American Journal of Sociology* 72, (May): 701–713.

Howe, David (1987). *An Introduction to Social Work Theory.* Aldershot, UK: Wildwood House.

——— (1994). 'Modernity, postmodernity and social work', *British Journal of Social Work* 24: 513–532.

Hugman, R. (1991). *Power in Caring Professions.* London: MacMillan.

Ife, Jim (1997). *Rethinking Social Work.* Lance Cove, NSW, Australia: Addison-Wesley Longman.

——— (2001). *Human Rights and Social Work: Towards Rights-Based Practice.* Cambridge: Cambridge University Press.

Jamrozik, Adam, and Luisa Nocella (1998). *The Sociology of Social Problems: Theoretical Perspectives and Methods of Intervention.* Cambridge: Cambridge University Press.

Jay, Martin (1973). *The Dialectical Imagination.* Boston: Little, Brown.

Jensen, A.R. (1969). 'How much can we boost IQ and scholastic achievement?' *Harvard Educational Review* 39: 1–23.

Jensen, Robert (1999). 'More thoughts on why system of white privilege is wrong', *Baltimore Sun,* 4 July.

Johnson, Allan G. (2000). *The Blackwell Dictionary of Sociology: A User's Guide to Sociological Language,* 2nd edition. Malden, MA: Blackwell.

——— (2006). *Privilege, Power, and Difference,* 2nd edition. New York: McGraw-Hill.

Jordan, Bill (1991). 'Competencies and values', *Social Work Education* 10, (1): 5–11.

Jordan, B., and C. Jordan (2000). *Social Work and the Third Way.* London: Sage.

Jost, J.T. (1995). 'Negative illusions: Conceptual clarification and psychological evidence concerning false consciousness', *Political Psychology* 16: 13–15.

Kanpol, B. (1997). *Issues and Trends in Critical Pedagogy.* Cresskill, NJ: Hampton Press.

Kanuha, V.K. (1999). 'The social process of "passing" to manage stigma: Acts of internalized oppression or acts of resistance?' *Journal of Sociology and Social Welfare* 26, (4): 27–46.

Karl, M. (1995). *Women and Empowerment, Participation and Decision-Making.* London: Zed Books.

Keller, Evelyn Fox (1986). *Reflections on Gender and Science.* New Haven, CT: Yale University Press.

Kellner, Douglas (1989). *Critical Theory, Marxism, and Modernity.* Baltimore, MD: Johns Hopkins University Press.

——— (1990). *Television and the Crisis of Democracy.* Boulder, CO: Westview Press.

Kimmel, Michael, and Abby Ferber, eds. (2003). *Privilege: A Reader.* Boulder, CO: Westview Press.

Kitzinger, C., and R. Perkins (1993). *Changing Our Minds: Lesbian Feminism and Psychology.* London: Onlywomen.

Kojeve, A. (1969). *Introduction to the Reading of Hegel.* New York: Basic Books.

Kondrat, M.E. (1999). 'Who is the "self" in self-aware: Professional self-awareness from a critical theory perspective', *Social Services Review* 73, (4): 451–477.

Kovel, Joel (1984). *White Racism: A Psycho-history*, 2nd edition. New York: Columbia University Press.

Kuhn, Thomas S. (1970 [1962]). *The Structure of Scientific Revolutions*, 2nd edition. Chicago: University of Chicago Press.

Kumsa, Martha Kuwee (2007). 'A resettlement story of unsettlement: Transformative practices of taking it personally', in Donna Baines, ed., *Doing Anti-Oppressive Social Work: Building Transformative Politicized Social Work*, 111–127. Halifax: Fernwood.

Laclau, E., and C. Mouffe (1985). *Hegemony and Socialist Strategy: Towards a Radical Democratic Politics.* London: Verso.

Langan, Mary, and Lesley Day, eds. (1992). *Women, Oppression and Social Work.* London: Routledge.

Laursen, Kay (1975). 'Professionalism', in Harold Throssell, ed., *Social Work: Radical Essays*, 47–71. St Lucia, Queensland, Australia: University of Queensland Press.

Lecomte, Roland (1990). 'Connecting private troubles and public issues in social work education', in Brian Wharf, ed., *Social Work and Social Change in Canada*, 47–71. Toronto: McClelland and Stewart.

Lee, J.A.B. (2001). *The Empowerment Approach to Social Work Practice*, 2nd edition. New York: Columbia University Press.

Lees, Ray (1972). *Politics and Social Work.* London: Routledge and Kegan Paul.

Leonard, Peter (1984). *Personality and Ideology: Towards a Materialist Understanding of the Individual.* London: Macmillan.

——— (1994). 'Knowledge/power and postmodernism', *Canadian Social Work Review* 11, (1): 11–26.

——— (1995). 'Postmodernism, socialism and social welfare', *Journal of Progressive Human Services* 6, (2): 3–19.

——— (1997). *Postmodern Welfare: Reconstructing an Emancipatory Project.* London: Sage.

——— (2001). 'The future of critical social work in uncertain conditions', *Critical Social Work* 2, (1).

Leonard, Stephen T. (1990). *Critical Theory in Political Practice.* Princeton, NJ: Princeton University Press.

Lerner, G. (1986). *The Creation of Patriarchy.* Oxford: Oxford University Press.

Levitas, R. (2001). 'Against work: A utopian incursion into social policy', *Critical Social Policy* 21, (4): 449–465.

Lewontin, Richard C., Steven Rose, and Leon J. Kamin (1984). *Not in Our Genes: Biology, Ideology, and Human Nature.* New York: Pantheon Books.

Lim, O. (1996). 'Anger is a gift' (McGill University, unpublished research paper).

Lister, R. (1999). 'First steps to a fairer society', *The Guardian*, 9 June.

Littleton, Christine (1987). 'Reconstructing sexual equality', *California Law Review* 75, (July): 1279–1337.

Longres, John (1986). 'Marxian theory and social work practice', *Catalyst* 5, (4): 13–34.

Longres, John, and Eileen McLeod (1980). 'Consciousness raising and social work practice', *Social Casework* 61, (5): 267–276.

Lukács, G. (1971). *History and Class Consciousness.* London: Methuen.

Lundy, Colleen (2004). *Social Work and Social Justice: A Structural Approach to Practice.* Peterborough, ON: Broadview Press.

Lyman, Stanford M., ed. (1995). *Social Movements: Critiques, Concepts, Case-Studies.* New York: New York University Press.

Lyotard, J.F. (1988). *The Differend: Phrases in Dispute.* Minneapolis: University of Minnesota Press.

McCarthy, John, and William Yancey (1971). 'Uncle Tom and Mr. Charlie: Metaphysical pathos in the study of racism and personal disorganization', *American Journal of Sociology* 76, (January): 648–672.

McDaniel, Susan A., and Ben Agger (1984). *Social Problems through Conflict and Order*. Don Mills, ON: Addison-Wesley.

McDonald, Peter, and Mikki Coleman (1999). 'Deconstructing hierarchies of oppression and adopting a 'multiple model' approach to anti-oppressive practice', *Social Work Education* 18, (1): 19–33.

Macey, Marie, and Eileen Moxon (1996). 'An examination of anti-racist and anti-oppressive theory and practice in social work education', *British Journal of Social Work* 26: 297–314.

McFarland, Joan, and Robert Mullaly (1996). 'NB works: Image vs. reality', In J. Pulkingham and G. Ternowetsky, eds, *Remaking Canadian Social Policy: Staking Claims and Forging Changes*, 202–219. Halifax: Fernwood.

McGregor, Craig (1997). *Class in Australia*. Sydney: Penguin.

McIntosh, Peggy (1990). 'White privilege and male privilege: A personal account of coming to see correspondences through work in women's studies'. Reprinted in *Independent School* 49, (2): 31–36.

———— (2003). 'White privilege and male privilege', in Michael Kimmel and Abby Ferber, eds., *Privilege: A Reader*. Boulder, CO: Westview Press.

McKerl, M. (2007). 'Multiculturalism, gender, and violence: Multiculturalism—is it bad for women?' *Culture and Religion* 8, (2): 187–217.

McKissock, D., and M. McKissock (1998). *Bereavement Counselling: Guidelines for Practitioners*. Terrigal, NSW, Australia: The Bereavement C.A.R.E. Centre

McLaughlin, Kenneth (2005). 'From ridicule to institutionalization: Anti-oppression, the state and social work', *Critical Social Policy* 25, (3): 283–305.

McLellan, Betty (1995). *Beyond Psychoppression: A Feminist Alternative*. North Melbourne, Australia: Spinifex.

McRobbie, A. (1981). 'Settling accounts with subcultures: A feminist critique', in T. Bennett et al., eds., *Culture, Ideology and Social Process*, 111–124. London: Batsford.

Maidment, Jane, and Ronnie Egan, eds. (2004). *Practice Skills in Social Work and Welfare: More Than Just Common Sense*. Crows Nest, NSW, Australia: Allen and Unwin.

Mannoni, O. (1962). *Prospero and Caliban: The Psychology of Colonization*. New York: Praeger.

Maracle, Lee (1996). *I Am Woman. A Native Perspective on Sociology and Feminism*, 2nd edition. Vancouver: Press Gang.

Marchak, M. Patricia (1981). *Ideological Perspectives on Canada*, 2nd edition. Toronto: McGraw-Hill Ryerson.

Marger, M.N. (1997). *Race and Ethnic Relations: American and Global Perspectives*. Belmont, CA: Wadsworth.

Margolin, Leslie (1997). *Under the Cover of Kindness: The Invention of Social Work*. Charlottesville: University of Virginia Press.

Marshall, M. (1990). *Social Work with Old People*, 2nd edition. London: Macmillan.

Marsiglia, Flavio Francisco, and Stephen Kulis (2009). *Diversity, Oppression, and Change: Culturally Grounded Social Work*. Chicago: Lyceum Books.

Martin, Jennifer (2003). 'Historical development of critical social work practice', in June Allan, Bob Pease, and Linda Briskman, eds., *Critical Social Work: An Introduction to Theories and Practices*, 17–31. Crows Nest, NSW, Australia: Alllen and Unwin.

Martin-Baro, Ignacio (1994). *Writings for a Liberation Psychology: Essays, 1985–1989* eds. A. Aron and S. Corne. Cambridge, MA: Harvard University Press.

Marx, K., and F. Engels (1967). *The Communist Manifesto*. New York: Pantheon.

———— (1978). *The Marx-Engels Reader*. New York: Norton.

Massaquoi, Natisha (2007). 'Crossing boundaries to radicalize social work practice and education', in Donna Baines, ed., *Doing Anti-Oppressive Practice: Building Transformative Politicized Social Work*, 176–190. Halifax: Fernwood.

Massey, Douglas S, and Nancy A. Denton (1998). *American Apartheid: Segregation and the Making of an Underclass*. Cambridge, MA: Harvard University Press.

Memmi, Albert (1963). *Portrait of a Jew*. London: Eyre and Spottiswoode.

——— (1967). *The Colonizer and the Colonized*. Boston: Beacon Press.

——— (1968). *Dominated Man*. Boston: Beacon Press.

——— (1973). *The Liberation of the Jew*. New York: Viking.

Merchant, Carolyn (1978). *The Death of Nature*. New York: Harper and Row.

Meszaros, I. (1970). *Marx's Theory of Alienation*. New York: Harper and Row.

Midgely, James (1982). *Professional Imperialism: Social Work in the Third World*. London: Heinemann.

Millar, Malcolm (1998/99). 'Psychology and anti-oppressive social work: Understanding the complexity of individual lives', *Social Work and Social Sciences Review* 8, (1): 25–41.

Miller, Alice (1980). *For Your Own Good: Hidden Cruelty in Child-Rearing and the Roots of Violence*. New York: Farrar, Straus and Giroux.

Miller, Jean Baker (1986). *Toward a New Psychology of Women*, 2nd edition. London: Penguin.

Milner, Judith, and Patrick O'Byrne (2002). *Assessment in Social Work*, 2nd edition. Basingstoke, UK: Palgrave MacMillan.

Minow, Martha (1985). 'Learning to live with the dilemma of difference: Bilingual and special education', *Law and Contemporary Problems* 48, (spring): 157–211.

——— (1987). 'Justice engendered', *Harvard Law Review* 101, (November): 11–95.

Moane, Geraldine (1999). *Gender and Colonialism: A Psychological Analysis of Oppression and Liberation*. New York: St Martin's Press.

Moraga, C. (2004). 'La guera', in M.L. Andersen and P.H. Collins, eds., *Race, Class and Gender*, 5th edition, 28–35. Belmont, CA: Wadsworth Press.

Moreau, Maurice J. (1979). 'A structural approach to social work practice', *Canadian Journal of Social Work Education* 5, (1): 78–94.

Moreau, Maurice J., and Lynn Leonard (1989). *Empowerment through a Structural Approach to Social Work*. Ottawa: Health and Welfare Canada.

Mosse, George (1985). *Nationalism and Sexuality*. New York: Fertig.

Mullaly, Robert (1995). 'Workfare: Participation or persecution of the poor?' *Perception* 18, (3–4): 8–13.

——— (1997a). *Structural Social Work: Ideology, Theory, and Practice*, 2nd edition. Toronto: Oxford University Press.

——— (1997b). 'The politics of workfare: NB works', in E. Shragge, ed., *Workfare: Ideology for a New Underclass*, 35–57. Toronto: Garamond Press.

——— (2006). 'Forward to the past: The 2005 CASW Code of Ethics', *Canadian Social Work Review* 23, (1–2): 145–50.

——— (2007). *The New Structural Social Work*, 3rd edition. Toronto: Oxford University Press.

Mullaly, Robert, and Eric Keating (1991). 'Similarities, differences and dialectics of radical social work', *Journal of Progressive Human Services* 2, (2): 49–78.

Mulvey, C. (1994). *Evaluation Report on the Allen Lane Foundation's Funding Programme in Ireland, 1989–1991*. Dublin: Allen Lane Foundation.

Nandy, Ashis (1983). *The Intimate Enemy*. Delhi: Oxford University Press.

National Council of Welfare (1996). *Poverty Profile 1994*. Ottawa: Minister of Supply and Services.

Nelson, C., and D.H. McPherson (2003). 'Cultural diversity in social work practice: Where are we now and what are the challenges in addressing issues of justice and oppression?' in Wes Shera, ed., *Emerging*

Perspectives on Anti-Oppressive Practice, 81–98. Toronto: Canadian Scholars Press.

Ng, R. (1993). 'Racism, sexism, and nation-building in Canada', in C. McCarthy and W. Crichlow, eds., *Race, Identity, and Representation in Education*, 50–59. New York: Routledge.

Nicholson, L.J., ed. (1990). *Feminism/Postmodernism*. London: Routledge.

Nietzsche, F. (1967). *The Birth of Tragedy and the Case of Wagner*. New York: Vintage.

—— (1969). *On the Genealogy of Morals*. New York. Vintage.

Noel, L. (1994). *Intolerance: A General Survey*. Montreal and Kingston: McGill-Queen's University Press.

Oberle, Peter (1993). *The Incidence of Family Poverty on Canadian Indian Reserves*. Ottawa: Indian and Northern Affairs Canada.

O'Connor, Ian, Jill Wilson, and Deborah Setterlund (1998). *Social Work and Welfare Practice*, 3rd edition. South Melbourne, Australia: Longman.

O'Connor, James (1973). *The Fiscal Crisis of the State*. New York: St Martin's Press.

O'Donnell, Anthony (1999). 'Redistribution and risk in the Australian welfare state', in D. Glover and G. Patmore, eds., *New Voices for Social Democracy: Labour Essays*. Annandale, NSW, Australia: Pluto.

Parton, C., and N. Parton (1989). 'Women, the family and child protection', *Critical Social Policy* 24.

Pateman, C. (1970). *Participation and Democratic Theory*. Cambridge: Cambridge University Press.

—— (1989). *The Disorder of Women*. Oxford: Polity Press.

Patterson, O. (1982). *Slavery and Social Death: A Comparative Study*. Cambridge, MA: Harvard University Press.

Payne, Malcolm (2005). *Modern Social Work Theory*, 3rd edition. Chicago: Lyceum Books.

—— (2007). *What Is Professional Social Work?* 2nd edition. Chicago: Lyceum Books.

Pease, Bob (1999). 'Deconstructing masculinity—reconstructing men', in Bob Pease and Jan Fook, eds., *Transforming Social Work Practice: Postmodern Critical Perspectives*, 97–112. London, Routledge.

Pease, Bob, and Jan Fook, eds. (1999). *Transforming Social Work Practice: Postmodern Critical Perspectives*. London: Routledge.

Pharr, Suzanne (1988). *Homophobia: A Weapon of Sexism*. Inverness, CA: Chadron Press.

Pitkin, Hannah (1981). 'Justice: On relating public and private', *Political Theory* 9, (August): 327–352.

Potocky, M. (1998). 'Multicultural social work in the United States: A review and critique', *International Social Work* 40: 315–326.

Powell, Gloria (1973). 'Self-concept in white and black children', in C. Willie, B. Kramer, and R. Brown, eds., *Racism and Mental Health: Essays*. Pittsburgh: University of Pittsburgh Press.

Prescott, J. (2002). 'The heart and soul of the nation', *The Guardian*, 16 January.

Preston-Shoot, Michael (1995). 'Assessing anti-oppressive practice', *Social Work Education* 14, (2): 11–29.

Pritchard, Colin, and Richard Taylor (1978). *Social Work: Reform or Revolution?* London: Routledge and Kegan Paul.

Pugh, R. (1997). 'Considering social difference', in J. Bates, R. Pugh, and N. Thompson, eds., *Protecting Children: Challenges and Change*. Aldershot: Arena.

Radway, J. (1984). *Reading the Romance: Women, Patriarchy and Popular Literature*. Chapel Hill: University of North Carolina Press.

Ramazanoglu, Caroline (1989). *Feminism and the Contradictions of Oppression*. London: Routledge.

Raphael, Dennis, ed. (2004). *Social Determinants of Health: Canadian Perspectives*. Toronto: Canadian Scholars Press.

Razack, Sharene (1998). *Looking White People in the Eye*. Toronto: University of Toronto Press.

Reasons, Charles E., and William D. Perdue (1981). *Ideology of Social Problems*. Scarborough, ON: Nelson Canada.

Rees, S. (1991). *Achieving Power: Practice and Policy in Social Welfare*. North Sydney, Australia: Allen and Unwin.

Reich, Michael (1975). *The Mass Psychology of Fascism* trans. V.R. Carpagno. Harmondsworth, UK: Penguin.

Reynolds, Paul Davidson (1971). *A Primer in Theory Construction*. New York: Bobbs-Merrill.

Riley, Mark (2001). 'Slavery in our times', *The Age* (Melbourne), 4 June, 1, 13.

Rojek, C., G. Peacock, and S. Collins (1988). *Social Work and Received Ideas*. London: Routledge and Kegan Paul.

Rose, Steven, ed. (1982). *Against Biological Determinism: The Dialectics of Biology Group*. New York: Allison and Busby.

——— (1998). *Lifelines: Biology beyond Determinism*. New York: Oxford University Press.

Rose, Stephen M., and Bruce L. Black (1985). *Advocacy and Empowerment: Mental Health Care in the Community*. Boston: Routledge and Kegan Paul.

Rosen, Michael (1996). *On Voluntary Servitude: False Consciousness and the Theory of Ideology*. Cambridge: Polity Press.

Rosenberg, Morris, and Roberta Simmons (1971). *Black and White Self-Esteem: The Urban School Child*. Washington: American Sociological Association.

Round Lake Treatment Centre (1992). *The Next Generation: Native Adolescent Substance Abuse Treatment Model*. Armstrong, BC: Round Lake Treatment Centre.

Rubington, Earl, and S. Martin Weinberg, eds. (1995). *The Study of Social Problems*, 5th edition. New York: Oxford University Press.

Rushton, J. Philippe (1988). 'Race differences in behaviour: A review and evolutionary analysis', *Personality and Individual Differences* 9, (6): 1009–1024.

Ruth, Sean (1988). 'Understanding oppression and liberation', *Studies: An Irish Quarterly Review* (winter): 434–443.

Ryan, W. (1976). *Blaming the Victim*, 2nd edition. New York: Vintage Books.

Said, Edward (1978). *Orientalism*. New York: Pantheon.

Sardar, Ziauddin, and Borin Van Loon (2004). *Introducing Cultural Studies*. Thriplow, Royston, UK: Icon Books.

Saul, John Ralston (2005). *The Collapse of Globalism and the Reinvention of the World*. Toronto: Viking Canada.

Schacht, Steven P. (2003). 'Teaching about being an oppressor', in Michael Kimmel and Abby Ferber, eds., *Privilege: A Reader*, 161–172. Boulder, CO: Westview Press.

Schiele, Jerome (1994). 'Afrocentricity as an alternative world view for equality', *Journal of Progressive Human Services* 5, (1): 5–25.

Schmitz, C.L., C. Stakeman, and J. Sisneros (2001). 'Educating professionals for practice in a multicultural society: Understanding oppression and valuing diversity', *Families in Society* 82, (6): 612–622.

Schon, Donald A. (1983). *The Reflective Practitioner*. London: Temple Smith.

——— (1987). *Educating the Reflective Practitioner*. San Francisco: Jossey-Bass.

Schumpeter, J. (1950). *Capitalism, Socialism and Democracy*. London: Allen and Unwin.

Scott, Joan (1988). 'Deconstructing equality-versus-difference: Or the uses of post-structuralist theory for feminism', *Feminist Studies* 14: 33–50.

Seager, J. (1997). *The State of Women in the World Atlas*. London: Penguin.

Seidman, Steven (1998). *Contested Knowledge: Social Theory in the Postmodern Era*. Malden, MA: Blackwell.

Sennett, Richard, and Jonathan Cobb (1972). *The Hidden Injuries of Class*. New York: Vintage.

Shulman, Lawrence (1992). *The Skills of Helping Individuals and Groups*, 2nd edition. Itasca, IL: Peacock.

Sibeon, R. (1991). 'The construction of a contemporary sociology of social work', in Martin Davies, ed., *The Sociology of Social Work*, 17–67. London: Routledge.

Sidanius, Jim, and Felicia Pratto (1999). *Social Dominance: An Intergroup Theory of Social Hierarchy and Oppression*. Cambridge: Cambridge University Press.

Sills, David, ed. (1968). *International Encyclopaedia of the Social Sciences*, v. 12, Pluralism. New York: Macmillan and the Free Press.

Sin, Rick, and Min Chang Yan (2003). 'Margins as centres: A theory of social inclusion in anti-oppressive social work', in Wes Shera, ed., *Emerging Perspectives on Anti-Oppressive Practice*, 25–41. Toronto: Canadian Scholars Press.

Singh, G. (1996). 'Promoting anti-racist and black perspectives in social work education', *Social Work Education* 15, (2): 35–56.

Sisneros, Jose, et al. (2008). *Critical Multicultural Social Work*. Chicago: Lyceum Books.

Smith, T. (1993). 'Postmodernism: Theory and politics', *The Activist* 3, (7): 31–34.

Spector, M., and J.I. Kitsuse (1987). *Constructing Social Problems*. New York: de Gruyter.

Spender, Dale (1990). *Man Made Language*, 2nd edition. London: Pandora.

Stainton, Tim, and Karen Swift (1996). "Difference" and social work curriculum', *Canadian Social Work Review* 13, (1): 75–87.

Staples, R. (1988). *Black Masculinity: The Black Man's Role in American Society*. San Francisco: Black Scholar Press.

Starhawk (1987). *Truth or Dare*. San Francisco: Harper and Row.

Statistics Canada (1993). *The Violence against Women Survey*. Ottawa: Ministry of Industry, Science and Technology.

Steger, Manfred B. (2003). *Globalization: A Very Short Introduction*. New York: Oxford University Press.

Tajfel, H. (1981). 'Social stereotypes and social groups', in J.C. Turner and H. Giles, eds., *Intergroup Behaviour*, 144–167. Oxford: Blackwell.

Takaki, R. (1993). *A Different Mirror*. Boston: Little, Brown.

Tatum, B.D. (1994). 'Teaching white students about racism: The search for white allies and the restoration of hope', *Teachers College Record* 94, (4): 462–476.

Taylor, Charles (1985). *Philosophy and the Human Sciences*. Cambridge: Cambridge University Press.

Taylor, J. (1990). *Giving Women Voice: Feminism and Community Services*. Melbourne: Brotherhood of St. Laurence.

Taylor, Rupert J. (1991). 'Catalogue of failure', *Canada and the World* (February): 14–19.

Thompson, Neil (1997). *Anti-Discriminatory Practice*, 2nd edition. London: Macmillan.

——— (1998). *Promoting Equality: Challenging Discrimination and Oppression in the Human Services*. London: Macmillan.

——— (2001). *Anti-Discriminatory Practice*, 3rd edition. Basingstroke, UK: Palgrave Macmillan.

——— (2002). 'Developing anti-discriminatory practice', in Dylan Ronald Tomlinson and Winston Trew, eds., *Equalising Opportunities, Minimising Oppression: A Critical Review of Anti-discriminatory Policies in Health and Social Welfare*, 41–55. London: Routledge.

Titus, H., M. Smith, and R. Nolan (1994). *Living Issues in Philosophy*, 9th edition. New York: Oxford University Press.

van Wormer, Katherine (2004). *Confronting Oppression, Restoring Justice: From Policy Analysis to Social Action*. Alexandria, VA: Council on Social Work Education.

Wachholz, Sandra, and Robert Mullaly (1993). 'Policing the deinstitutionalized mentally ill: Toward an understanding of its function', *Crime, Law and Social Change* 19: 281–300.

——— (2000). 'The politics of the textbook: A content analysis of feminist, radical, and anti-racist social work scholarship in American introductory social work textbooks published between 1988 and 1997', *Journal of Progressive Human Services* 11, (2): 51–75.

Waddell, N., and E. Cairns (1986). 'Situational perspectives on social identity in Northern Ireland', *British Journal of Social Psychology* 25, (11): 25–31.

Wagner, David, and Marcia B. Cohen (1978). 'Social workers, class and professionalism', *Catalyst* 1, (1): 25–55.

Walkerdine, V., ed. (1996). 'Social class', special issue of *Feminism and Psychology* 6, (3).

Wasserton, Richard (1980). *Philosophy and Social Issues*. Notre Dame, IN: Notre Dame University Press.

Weedon, Chris (1987). *Feminist Practice and Poststructuralist Theory*. Oxford: Blackwell.

—— (1997). *Feminist Practice and Post-structuralist Theory*, 2nd edition. Oxford: Blackwell.

West, Cornel (1982). *Prophesy Deliverance! An Afro–American Revolutionary Christianity*. Philadelphia: Westminster.

—— (1993). *Race Matters*. Boston: Beacon.

Wharf, Brian, and John Cossom (1987). 'Citizen participation and social policy', in Shankar A. Yelaja, ed., *Canadian Social Policy*, 2nd edition, 266–287. Waterloo, ON: Wilfrid Laurier University Press.

White, M. (1993). 'Deconstruction and therapy', in S. Gilligan and R. Price, eds., *Therapeutic Conversations*. New York: Norton.

Wilkinson, S., ed. (1996). *Feminist Social Psychologies*. Buckingham, UK: Open University Press.

Williams, C. (1999). 'Connecting anti-racist and anti-oppressive theory and practice: Retrenchment or reappraisal?' *British Journal of Social Work* 29: 211–230.

Williams, Fiona (1989). *Social Policy: A Critical Introduction—Issues of Race, Gender and Class*. New York: Basil Blackwell.

Williams, Frank P., and Marilyn D. McShane (1988). *Criminological Theory*. Englewood Cliffs, NJ: Prentice-Hall.

Williams, R. (1981). *Culture*. Cambridge: Fontana.

Willis, P. (1977). *Learning to Labour: How Working Class Kids Get Working Class Jobs*. Aldershot, UK: Gower.

—— (1978). *Profane Culture*. London: Routledge and Kegan Paul.

Wilson, Elizabeth (1993). 'Is transgression transgressive?' in J. Bristow and A.R. Wilson, eds., *Activating Theory: Lesbian, Gay, Bisexual Politics*. London: Lawrence and Wishart.

Wineman, Steven (1984). *The Politics of Human Services*. Montreal: Black Rose Books.

Withorn, Ann (1984). *Serving the People: Social Services and Social Change*. New York: Columbia University Press.

Women's Theological Center (1997). *The Invisibility of Upper Class Privilege*. In 'Class Acts' (a program exploring issues of spirituality, ethics, and theology for women of wealth). Boston, MA.

World Health Organization (1986). 'Ottawa Charter for Health Promotion', World Health Organization, Europe Office, www.hc-sc.gc.ca/hppb/phdd/docs/charter.

Young, Iris Marion (1990). *Justice and the Politics of Difference*. Princeton, NJ: Princeton University Press.

Index